DICTIONARY

OF FOREIGN PHRASES AND ABBREVIATIONS

SECOND EDITION

DICTIONARY

OF FOREIGN PHRASES AND ABBREVIATIONS

Translated and compiled by

KEVIN GUINAGH

Formerly Head
Department of Foreign Languages
Eastern Illinois University

REFERENCE

THE H. W. WILSON COMPANY NEW YORK 1972

DICTIONARY OF FOREIGN PHRASES AND ABBREVIATIONS

Copyright © 1965, 1972

by KEVIN GUINAGH

First Edition 1965
Second Edition 1972

First Printing 1972
Second Printing 1975

Printed in the United States of America

International Standard Book Number 0-8242-0460-3
Library of Congress Catalog Card Number 72-149383

To the memory of Professor Evan T. Sage

EDITOR'S NOTE TO THE SECOND EDITION

The present edition, made possible by the generous reception of the first, has given me the opportunity to increase by more than 750 the number of abbreviations and phrases, to add the sources of numerous expressions, to omit a few and expand others, and to correct some errors, both mine and the printer's. Quotations from Pascal's *Pensées* follow Brunschvicg's text used in *Collection Gallia* published without date by J. M. Dent & Sons, London, those from La Rochefoucauld follow the editing of *La Rochefoucauld: Maximes*, F. C. Green, Cambridge at the University Press, 1946.

The quotations from Publilius Syrus are given different numbers by different editors, who arrange in a loose alphabetical order the material they accept as genuine. For that reason no number is cited.

I am grateful to a number of readers who have given me valuable suggestions.

KEVIN GUINAGH

Temple Terrace, Florida
October 1971

PREFACE

This work has been compiled to aid those who wish to know the meaning of foreign expressions in what they hear or read. The word *phrase* as used in the title is to be understood in the recognized and not uncommon meaning of a pithy, quotable expression, such as a proverb, motto, or maxim. It is not necessarily to be taken in its narrow grammatical use, as, for instance, a preposition followed by an object, though there are many items that could be classified in this way. The entries range from hoary legal principles inherited from the Romans to the wisdom of the common man, *die Weisheit der Gasse (q.v.)*, from terms of philosophy to business expressions. Before the phrases under each letter, there are lists of frequently encountered abbreviations.

People unacquainted with foreign expressions popular in English are often inclined to think that those who scatter such phrases in their writing or conversation are pedantic. There is no doubt that this practice can be overdone, and that at times it may be in bad taste. However, to those who are acquainted with a subject being discussed, the use of such terms is often a short cut to making a meaning clear. In numerous areas, such as law, business, philosophy, medicine, and music, certain foreign phrases have a fixed meaning that is immediately understood by those who are familiar with the subject. Similarly, to people with literary interests certain expressions may brighten a conversation by their aptness or sum up a concept that might otherwise require several sentences for a clear explanation. No matter how theoretically sound attacks by English purists may be, people will continue to employ such phrases, possibly even with greater frequency now that the study of foreign languages is receiving increased emphasis in American education.

The different languages have not been listed separately for the reason that the general reader unacquainted with a foreign expression may not know in what section he should look. In each case the abbreviation for the language is given immediately after the expression. The following abbreviations are used: *Fr*—French; *Ger*—German; *Gk*—Greek; *Heb*—Hebrew; *Ir*—Irish; *It*—Italian; *L*—Latin; *Port*—Portuguese; *Rus*—Russian; *Sp*—Spanish. The language from which most entries have been drawn is Latin. Of the modern languages French predominates, with Italian a distant second.

Quotations in a foreign tongue are often rearranged or adapted from the original. For that reason, if a phrase is not found where the reader searches for it, it may be helpful to look about to find the correct wording. Misquotation is especially frequent in Latin, where the word order is not as uniform as it is in English. Thus one may hear *Errare est humanum, Errare humanum est, Humanum errare est,* or *Humanum est errare.*

When one is certain of the language in which the expression is written but not of the word order or spelling, he may more quickly ascertain both wording and spelling by consulting the list of phrases arranged by languages at the end of the book.

Entries that begin with a definite article are listed under the word following. These articles are as follows: in French, *le, la, les, l';* in German, *der, die, das, des, dem, den;* in Spanish, *el, la, lo, los, las;* in Italian, *il, la, lo, i, gli, le, l';* in Portuguese, *o, a, os, as.* The same principle has been followed in filing items beginning with an indefinite article: in French, *un, une;* in German, *ein, eine;* in Italian and Spanish, *un, una.* This principle does not apply when the meaning is not *a* or *an* but *one* in the numerical sense. Unlike entries in other languages, Greek entries beginning with a definite article are filed under the article. In Latin quotations the letter *j* is used instead of the consonant *i.*

Items longer than a couplet have been omitted since they can hardly be classed as phrases; at the other end of the scale, single words, with a few exceptions, are not included since these are proper material for foreign language dictionaries. Latin and Greek nomenclature used in the biological sciences is not included since this is technical information available in manuals on these subjects.

The translation that follows the identification of the language in which the entry is written is at times literal, though generally it is free. If the entry is a proverb, the corresponding proverb in English may be given. The translation may be followed by a few explanatory words if the meaning of the phrase is not self-evident or if its historical context is of special interest. There may also be a cross reference to a parallel expression found elsewhere in the book.

PREFACE

At the end of many entries the source is given. This consists of the author's name, the work in which the phrase is found, the particular book (if the work is divided into books), the chapter, and the verse or beginning line in the case of poetry. Sometimes a writer is given credit as the author of a quotation even though it is likely that the expression was current long before he lived. For example, many proverbs are found in Cervantes' *Don Quixote*. He is regarded as the author, but no doubt the phrase was old when he wrote it. It may be one of those *Geflügelte Worte (q.v.)* that pass from one language to another. Take the proverb "One swallow does not make a summer." This is heard so frequently that one could be pardoned for thinking that it is original with one of our own writers. However, in Cervantes we read, *Una golondrina sola no hace verano (q.v.)*. The same idea is found in German, *Eine Schwalbe macht keinen Sommer (q.v.)*. In Italian it runs, *Una rondine no fa primavera (q.v.)*. A much earlier version is found in Aristotle, *Mia gar chelidon ear ou poiei (q.v.)*, which was probably an old saw even in his day. In short, a given source does not necessarily indicate the origin of an expression. Often the author who incorporated it in his work receives the credit. The fact that he has adopted the proverb lends it the authority of his genius.

Such a compilation as this is bound to reflect in some measure the tastes and interests of the compiler. Much material, however, must be included because of frequent usage. The problem, then, is one of selection from among thousands of phrases that might be included. For some time I collected expressions that I had heard or remembered. I first went through the sixth American edition (1831) of the once popular *Dictionary of Select and Popular Quotations* published by J. Grigg, Philadelphia, without author statement. The search continued through many English classics, Roget's *Thesaurus*, Brewer's *Dictionary of Phrase and Fable*, *Authors' and Printers' Dictionary* by Collins, Hoyt's *Encyclopedia of Practical Quotations*, Shankle's *Current Abbreviations*, Mawson's *Dictionary of Foreign Terms*, the unabridged dictionaries, and numerous other works. *The Dictionary of Foreign Phrases and Classical Quotations* by H. P. Jones, Bartlett's *Familiar Quotations*, and the *Oxford Dictionary of Quotations* have frequently been consulted with profit. *Classical and*

DICTIONARY OF FOREIGN PHRASES

Foreign Quotations by W. Francis H. King and *Geflügelte Worte und Zitatenschatz* by Georg Büchmann have identified the sources of a number of phrases.

Though the number of entries in such compilations can always be increased, it is hoped that no omission of a frequently used expression or abbreviation will be noted. Suggestions for future inclusion will be welcomed.

I am grateful to Guy R. Lyle, Director of the Emory University Libraries, for suggesting this compilation, and to John Jamieson, Editor of General Publications of The H. W. Wilson Company, for his valuable assistance.

KEVIN GUINAGH

University of Puerto Rico
Mayagüez
November 1964

CONTENTS

ABBREVIATIONS USED IN THIS WORK

cf	compare	*LL*	Late Latin
f	feminine	*m*	masculine
Fr	French	*NL*	New Latin
Ger	German	*OF*	Old French
Gk	Greek	*pl*	plural
Heb	Hebrew	*Port*	Portuguese
Ir	Irish	*q.v.*	which see
It	Italian	*Rus*	Russian
L	Latin	*Sp*	Spanish

DICTIONARY OF FOREIGN PHRASES
AND ABBREVIATIONS

A.A. (Auswärtiges Amt). *Ger*—Foreign Office.

A.A.C. (anno ante Christum). *L*—Year before Christ. Equivalent to B.C., before Christ.

a.a.O. (am angeführten Orte). *Ger*—In the place cited.

A.A.S.S. (Americanae Antiquarianae Societatis Socius). *L*—Fellow of the American Antiquarian Society.

A.B. (Artium Baccalaureus). *L*—Bachelor of Arts.

ab ex. *L*—*See* Ab extra.

abgk. (abgekürzt). *Ger*—Abbreviated.

A.B.I. (Associazione Bibliotecari Italiani). *It*—Association of Italian Librarians.

ab init. *L*—*See* Ab initio.

abs. feb. (absente febre). *L*—While fever is absent. A medical direction.

abs. re. *L*—*See* Absente reo.

A.C. (année courante). *Fr*—The current year.

a.c. (ante cibum). *L*—Before food. A direction on prescriptions indicating that medicine should be taken before meals.

a.c. (argent comptant). *Fr*—Spot cash; ready money. A commercial term.

a.C. (avanti Cristo). *It*—Before Christ; B.C. (*q.v.*).

A.C.L. (assuré contre l'incendie). *Fr*—Insured against fire.

A.D. (anno Domini). *L*—In the year of our Lord. Indicates the number of years from the birth of Christ. In the sixth century, Dionysius Exiguus initiated the system of expressing dates by

1

referring events to the birth of Christ. According to his calculations, Christ was born in 754 A.U.C. (*q.v.*). However, it is generally agreed that Christ was born at least four years before the date set by Dionysius. A.D. is much more frequently used than its equivalent, A.H.S. (*q.v.*).

a.D. (ausser Dienst). *Ger*—Retired.

ad an. (ad annum). *L*—Up to the year ———.

add. (addatur). *L*—Let there be added. Used in pharmacy.

ad 2 vic. (ad duas vices). *L*—For two doses. A medical direction.

ad ex. (ad extremum). *L*—To the extreme or the end.

ad h.l. (**a.h.l.**) (ad hunc locum). *L*—To this place.

ad inf. *L*—*See* Ad infinitum.

ad init. (ad initium). *L*—At the beginning.

ad int. (ad interim). *L*—In the meantime.

ad lib. *L*—*See* Ad libitum.

adr. tél. (adresse télégraphique). *Fr*—Telegraphic address.

adst. feb. (adstante febre). *L*—While fever is present. A medical direction.

ad. val. *L*—*See* Ad valorem.

A.E.F. (Afrique Équatoriale Française). *Fr*—French Equatorial Africa.

aet. (aetas). *L*—Age.

A.G. (Aktiengesellschaft). *Ger*—Joint stock company.

agit. vas. (agitato vase). *L*—Shake well before using. A medical direction.

A.H. (anno Hebraico). *L*—In the Hebrew year. This is calculated by adding 3,760 to the current year of the Christian era.

A.H. (anno hegirae). *L*—In the year of the hegira (year of the

Moslem calendar, dating from the flight of Mohammed from Mecca in 622 A.D.).

A.H.S. (anno humanae salutis). *L*—In the year of man's redemption. Equivalent to A.D. (*q.v.*).

A.L. (anno lucis). *L*—In the year of light. This is computed by adding 4,000 years to A.D. (*q.v.*). Used by Freemasonry.

a.l. (après livraison). *Fr*—After delivery of goods.

a.l. (avant la lettre). *Fr*—Before lettering; proof of an engraving before any inscription has been added.

al. l. (alia lectio). *L*—Another reading; variant of a text.

alt. dieb. (alternis diebus). *L*—Every other day. A medical direction.

alt. hor. (alternis horis). *L*—Every other hour. A medical direction.

a.M. (am Main). *Ger*—On the Main River.

A.M. (anno mundi). *L*—In the year of the world. According to Bishop Ussher's calculations, the world was created in 4004 B.C.

a.m. (ante meridiem). *L*—Before midday. Used to designate the hours between midnight and noon.

A.M. (Artium Magister). *L*—Master of Arts.

amal. (amiral). *Fr*—Admiral.

A.M.D.G. *L*—*See* Ad majorem Dei gloriam.

A.M.M. (Asociación Médica Mexicana). *Sp*—Mexican Medical Association.

A.N.C. (ante nativitatem Christi). *L*—Before the birth of Christ. Equivalent to English B.C., before Christ.

anme (anonyme). *Fr*—Anonymous. Used to indicate limited liability. *See also* Société anonyme.

A.O.F. (Afrique Occidentale Française). *Fr*—French West Africa.

A.O.S.S. (Americanae Orientalis Societatis Socius). *L*—Fellow of the American Oriental Society.

a.p. (anni praesentis). *L*—In the present year.

À.P. (À protester). *Fr*—To be protested later on. A commercial term.

A.P.C.N. (anno post Christum natum). *L*—In the year of our Lord. A variant of A.D. (*q.v.*).

A.P.R.C. (anno post Romam conditam). *L*—In the year after the founding of Rome. The traditional date for the founding of Rome is 753 B.C. Equivalent to A.U.C. (*q.v.*).

ap(r). J.-C. (après Jésus-Christ). *Fr*—After Christ; A.D. (*q.v.*).

aq. (aqua). *L*—Water. This abbreviation is used with a number of adjectives: astr. (astricta), frozen; bull. (bulliens), boiling; com. (communis), common; dest. (destillata), distilled; ferv. (fervens) hot; mar. (marina) sea; pluv. (pluvialis) rain; pur. (pura) pure; tep. (tepida) tepid. Used in medical directions.

A.R.S.S. (Antiquariorum Regiae Societatis Socius). *L*—Fellow of the Royal Society of Antiquaries.

a/s (aux soins de). *Fr*—In care of. Used on postal addresses.

A.S.L.V. (assurance sur la vie). *Fr.*—Life insurance.

A.S.P. (accepté sans protêt). *Fr*—Accepted without protest. A commercial term.

A.T.L. (avant toute lettre). *Fr*—Before all the lettering. *See also* a.l. (avant la lettre).

à.t.p. (à tout prix). *Fr*—At any cost.

A.U.C. (ab urbe condita; anno urbis conditae). *L*—From the founding of the city. The traditional date for the founding of Rome is 753 B.C.

a.u.n. (absque ulla nota). *L*—Without any marking.

av. J.-C. (avant Jésus-Christ). *Fr*—Before Christ. Equivalent to English B.C., before Christ.

Ab abusu ad usum non valet consequentia. *L*—The abuse of a thing is no argument against its proper use. A legal maxim.

À barbe de fou, on apprend à raire. *Fr*—One learns to shave on the chin of a fool. *See also* Alla barba dei pazzi . . . .

À bas. *Fr*—Down with, as in *À bas le traître*, Down with the traitor.

Ab asino lanam. *L*—Wool from an ass; you can't get blood from a stone.

À bâtons rompus. *Fr*—By fits and starts; without method.

À beau jeu, beau retour. *Fr*—One good turn deserves another. It is also used in the opposite sense; a bad turn must expect a bad return.

À beau mentir qui vient de loin. *Fr*—The man who comes from afar can be a great liar.

Abends wird der Faule fleissig. *Ger*—The lazy man becomes industrious in the evening. The implication is that he has loafed all day.

A beneplacito. *It*—At will; at one's pleasure.

Abeunt studia in mores. *L*—Zeal develops into habit.—*Ovid, Heroides, XV, 83.*

Ab extra. *L*—From outside.

Ab extrinseco. *L*—From the outside.

Ab hoc et ab hac et ab illa. *L*—By this man and this woman and that woman; the talk of gossips; such and such a person did or said this or that.

À bientôt. *Fr*—See you soon; so long!

Abiit ad majores. *L*—He has gone to his forefathers; he is dead.

Abiit ad plures. *L*—He has gone to the majority; he is dead.—*Petronius, Satyricon 42, 5.*

Abiit, excessit, evasit, erupit. *L*—He [Catiline] has gone, he has left, he has fled, he has rushed forth.—*Cicero, II Against Catiline, I.*

Ab imo pectore. L—From the bottom of the heart.

Ab incunabulis. L—Literally, from the cradle. Used in connection with books published from the invention of printing to the end of 1500. Such works are called *incunabula*.

Ab initio. L—From the beginning.

Ab initio temporis. L—From the beginning of time.

Ab intestato. L—From or by a person dying intestate, i.e., without a valid will.

Ab intra. L—From within.

Ab invito. L—By an unwilling person.

Ab irato. L—From or by an angry man. The inference is that what was said or done was not really intended but was the result of anger.

À bis ou (et) à blanc. Fr—By fits and starts.

Abnormis sapiens crassaque Minerva. L—Literally, an unusual wise man of rough genius; an unacademic sage with common horse sense. *Horace, Satires, II, 2, 3.*

À bon appétit il ne faut point de sauce. Fr—A good appetite needs no sauce.

À bon chat, bon rat. Fr—For a good cat, a good rat; the parties are well matched.

À bon cheval point d'éperon. Fr—Do not spur the willing horse.

À bon chien il ne vient jamais un bon os. Fr—A good dog does not always get a good bone; merit is not always recognized.

À bon commencement bonne fin. Fr—A good beginning leads to a good end.

À bon compte. Fr—At a bargain.

Abondance de bien(s) ne nuit pas. Fr—It never hurts to be well-off; store is no sore.

À bon droit. Fr—With good reason; rightly.

À bon marché. *Fr*—At a bargain.

À bon vin point d'enseigne. *Fr*—A good wine needs no bush (tavern sign); a good product needs no advertising. *See also* A buon vino . . ., and Vino vendibili . . . .

Ab origine. *L*—From the origin.

A bove majore discit arare minor. *L*—A young ox learns to plow from an older one; the young learn from their elders.

Ab ovo. *L*—From the beginning.

Ab ovo usque ad mala. *L*—From the egg to the apples, i.e., from the beginning to the end of a Roman banquet; from soup to nuts.

À bras ouverts. *Fr*—With open arms.

Abscissio infiniti. *L*—The cutting off of the infinite. In logic the process of rejecting unworkable hypotheses until the correct conclusion is reached.

Absence d'esprit. *Fr*—Absent-mindedness.

Absens haeres non erit. *L*—The man who is absent will not be an heir; out of sight, out of mind.

Absente reo. *L*—The defendant being absent.

Absent le chat, les souris dansent. *Fr*—When the cat's away, the mice will play.

Les absents ont toujours tort. *Fr*—The absent are always in the wrong. The implication is that they are unable to defend themselves.

Absit invidia. *L*—Let there be no envy.

Absit omen. *L*—May there be no ill omen. Omens were prophetic of good or ill and were interpreted by soothsayers, supposed to be skilled in observing signs sent by heaven. When a speaker referred to some evil, he might follow it with this prayer that no harm would follow his mentioning disaster or misfortune. Today, in a similar situation, people may rap on wood, as if this act could ward off evil.

Absque argento

Absque argento omnia vana. *L*—Without money all efforts are in vain.

Absque ulla conditione. *L*—Without any condition.

Absurdum quippe est ut alios regat qui seipsum regere nescit. *L*—It is certainly absurd that a man who cannot rule himself should rule others. A medieval legal axiom.

A buen entendedor, pocas palabras. *Sp*—A few words are enough for a man with understanding.

Ab uno disce omnes. *L*—From one learn all. Aeneas' complete statement reads: Listen now to the trick of the Greeks, and from one crime judge all the Greeks. A maxim for the injudicious.—*Vergil, Aeneid, II, 65.*

A buon vino non bisogna frasca. *It*—See À bon vin . . .; and Vino vendibili . . . .

Abusus non tollit usum. *L*—Abuse does not take away use. *See also* Ab abusu ad usum . . . .

A cader va chi troppo alto sale. *It*—He is set for a fall who climbs too high.

A cane scottato l'acqua fredda pare calda. *It*—To the scalded dog cold water seems hot; the burnt child shuns the fire.

A capite ad calcem. *L*—From head to toe; completely.

A cappella. *It*—In chapel style; unaccompanied choral music.

A cara o cruz. *Sp*—Face or cross (on a coin); heads or tails.

A casar y a ir a guerra no se aconseja. *Sp*—One never advises a person to marry or go to war.

A cavallo donato non si guarda in bocca. *It*—Don't look a gift horse in the mouth. *See also* A cavallo regalado . . . .

A cavallo regalado no hay que mirarle el diente. *Sp*—*See* A cavallo donato . . . .

Accedas ad curiam. *L*—You may appeal the case.

Accelerando. *It*—Speeding up the tempo of the music.

8

Accessit. *L*—He came near; e.g., he nearly won first honors in an academic contest.

Accordez vos flûtes. *Fr*—Tune your flutes; settle the matter among yourselves.

Accusare nemo se debet. *L*—No one is obliged to incriminate himself. A legal maxim.

Acerbarum facetiarum apud praepotentes in longum memoria est. *L*—The mighty remember a cutting witticism for a long time. —*Tacitus, Annals, V, 2.*

Acetum Italum. *L*—*See* Sal Atticum.

À chacun son fardeau pèse. *Fr*—Everyone has his own burden to bear.

À chaque fou plaît sa marotte. *Fr*—Every fool is delighted with his own hobby.

À chaque oiseau son nid est beau. *Fr*—Every bird thinks its nest beautiful; be it ever so humble, there's no place like home. *See also* Ad ogni uccello . . . .

À chaque saint sa chandelle (cierge). *Fr*—To each saint his candle; honor to whom honor is due.

À cheval. *Fr*—On horseback.

A chi consiglia non duole il capo. *It*—The man with ready advice does not have the headache; advice is cheaper than help.

A chi dici il tuo segreto, doni la tua libertà. *It*—You give your liberty to the one to whom you tell your secret.

A chi fa male, mai mancano scuse. *It*—The wrongdoer never lacks excuses.

A chi ha testa, non manca cappello. *It*—A man with a head will not be without a hat.

A chi vuole, non mancano modi. *It*—Where there's a will, there's a way.

À cœur ouvert. *Fr*—With open heart; candidly.

À compte. *Fr*—On account; in part payment.

9

À confesseurs

À confesseurs, médecins, avocats, la verité ne cèle de ton cas. *Fr* —Do not conceal the truth of your situation from your confessor, your doctor, or your lawyer. *See also* Al confessor, medico . . . .

À contre cœur. *Fr*—Reluctantly, unwillingly.

À corps perdu. *Fr*—Headlong; desperately; post haste.

À coups de bâton. *Fr*—With blows from a stick.

À coup sûr. *Fr*—With a sure aim.

À couvert. *Fr*—Under cover.

A cruce salus. *L*—Salvation comes from the cross.

Acta est fabula. *L*—The play is over (words used at the end of a play in ancient Rome). The supposed last words of Augustus. *See also* La farce est jouée.

Acte d'accusation. *Fr*—An indictment.

Acte gratuit. *Fr*—An unwarranted, needless act.

Actum ne agas. *L*—Don't do what has already been done.— *Terence, Phormio, II, iii, 72.*

Actus Dei nemini facit injuriam. *L*—An act of God does wrong to no man. An individual cannot be held responsible for damage beyond his control, caused by lightning, tornado, earthquake, or other natural phenomena.

Actus me invito factus, non est meus actus. *L*—An act I perform unwillingly is not my act.

Actus non facit reum nisi mens est rea. *L*—The act does not make a criminal unless the intention is criminal. Legal maxim.

Actus purus. *L*—Pure act; St. Thomas Aquinas' concept of God, indicating that He is not composed of matter and form.

A cushla agus asthore machree. *Ir*—O pulse and treasure of my heart.

Adagio. *It*—A slow movement in music; in the ballet a slow, graceful movement.

Adagio ma non troppo. *It*—Slowly but not too slowly.

Ad amussim. *L*—Literally, according to a mason's or a carpenter's rule or line; exactly.

Ad arbitrium. *L*—At will.

Ad astra per aspera. *L*—To the stars through difficulties. Motto of Kansas: To the stars through bolts and bars.

Ad captandam benevolentiam. *L*—To win good will. The aim of the orator.

Ad captandum vulgus. *L*—To impress the crowd.

Ad cautelam. *L*—For caution's sake.

Adde parvum parvo, magnus acerbus erit. *L*—Add little to little and you will have a great heap.—Adapted from *Ovid, Amores, I, viii, 90.*

Adel sitzt im Gemüte, nicht im Beblüte. *Ger*—Nobility lies in the heart, not in birth.

À demi. *Fr*—By halves.

A Deo et Rege. *L*—From God and the King.

Adeste, Fideles. *L*—Come, all ye faithful. The music for this Christian hymn was composed by John Reading (1677-1764).

Ad extremum. *L*—To the very end.

Adgnosco veteris vestigia flammae. *L*—I feel the traces of the old flame of love. Through the trickery of Venus the heart of the widowed Dido was distraught for love of Aeneas.—*Vergil, Aeneid, IV, 23.*

Ad gustum. *L*—To one's taste.

Ad hoc. *L*—Created or designed for a particular purpose. The expression is frequently employed to designate a committee formed to investigate a definite subject.

Ad hominem. *L*—*See* Argumentum ad hominem.

11

Adhuc neminem cognovi poetam qui sibi non optimus videretur.
  L—I have yet to meet a poet who did not think himself
  excellent.—*Cicero, Tusculan Disputations, V, 22.*

Adieu, canaux, canards, canaille! *Fr*—Farewell, canals, ducks,
  and rabble! Voltaire's farewell to Holland.

Adieu la voiture, adieu la boutique. *Fr*—Good-bye to the car-
  riage, good-bye to the shop; the affair is all over.

Ad impossibile nemo tenetur. *L*—Nobody is held to the impossible.

Ad infinitum. *L*—Indefinitely into the future.

Ad interim. *L*—Temporarily; in the meantime.

Ad internecionem. *L*—To extermination.

À discrétion. *Fr*—At one's discretion.

Ad judicium. *L*—An appeal to common sense.

Ad Kalendas Graecas. *L*—On the Greek Calends. In the Roman
  calendar the Calends meant the first day of the month. Since
  the Greeks did not have this term, the expression was used by
  the Romans to designate an event that would never occur.

Adler brüten keine Tauben. *Ger*—Eagles do not hatch out doves;
  brave men do not breed cowards.

Ad libitum. *L*—At will; as one wishes. It is used in music where
  the composer leaves interpretation to the performer, or where
  passages may be omitted or varied. In the theater the phrase
  has given rise to the term *ad-libbing*, meaning improvisation.

Ad limina Apostolorum. *L*—A term used to designate a pilgrim-
  age to the basilicas of St. Peter and of St. Paul in Rome.

Ad litem. *L*—For the lawsuit; for litigation. Thus a guardian
  may be appointed *ad litem* to act for an incompetent person.

Ad literam. *L*—Literally.

Ad majorem Dei gloriam. *L*—To the greater glory of God. The
  motto of the Jesuits.

Ad manum. *L*—At hand.

Ad multos annos. *L*—For many years.

Ad nauseam. *L*—*See* Usque ad nauseam.

Ad oculos. *L*—Before one's eyes.

Ad ogni uccello suo nido è bello. *It*—To every bird his own nest is beautiful. *See also* À chaque oiseau . . . .

Ad patres. *L*—Gathered to his fathers; among the dead.

Ad perpetuam rei memoriam. *L*—In perpetual memory of the event.

À droite. *Fr*—To the right. A direction for the traveler.

Ad rem. *L*—Speaking to the point, to the matter in hand.

Adscriptus glebae. *L*—A person bound to the soil; a serf.

Adsum. *L*—I am present. Spoken by students at roll call.

Ad summum. *L*—To the utmost.

Ad un colpo non cade a terra l'albero. *It*—*See* Al primo colpo . . . .

Ad unguem. *L*—To a nicety; accurately.

Ad unum omnes. *L*—To the last man.

Ad usum. *L*—According to custom.

Ad utrumque paratus. *L*—Prepared for either eventuality.

Ad valorem. *L*—According to the value; a tax or duty based on value.

Adversis etenim frangi non esse virorum. *L*—Real men are not vanquished by adversity.—*Silius Italicus, Punica, X, 618.*

L'adversité fait l'homme, et le bonheur les monstres. *Fr*—Adversity makes men but prosperity makes monsters.

Ad vitam aut culpam. *L*—For lifetime or until removed for some fault. A phrase used to indicate length of tenure in an office.

13

Advocatus diaboli. *L*—The devil's advocate. A special official appointed to develop objections to the proposed beatification of a virtuous person.

Advocatus juventutis. *L*—The advocate of youth. An expression patterned after *Advocatus diaboli (q.v.).*

Aegrescit medendo. *L*—He grows sick from the treatment; the remedy is worse than the disease.

Aegrotat daemon, monachus tunc esse volebat:/Daemon convaluit, daemon ut ante fuit. *L*—The devil was sick, the devil a monk would be:/The devil was well, the devil a monk was he. The source of this popular quotation is unknown. It has been stated that it occurs in Rabelais, IV, 24, but this was added by a translator in further explanation of *Passato el periculo . . . (q.v.).*

Aegroto dum anima est, spes esse dicitur. *L*—As long as he is alive, the sick man has hope.—*Cicero, To Atticus, IX, 10.*

Aei gar eu piptousin hoi Dios kyboi. *Gk*—Literally, the dice of Zeus always fall right. Emerson in *Compensation* gives the translation: "The dice of the gods are always loaded."

Aequam memento rebus in arduis servare mentem. *L*—Remember to keep calm in time of trouble.—*Horace, Odes, II, iii, 1.*

Aequo animo. *L*—With a calm mind.

Aerarium sanctius. *L*—A special treasury reserved for emergencies.

Aes triplex. *L*—Triple bronze, characterizing the courage in the heart of man. Title of an essay by Robert Louis Stevenson.—*Horace, Odes, I, iii, 9.*

Aetas parentum, peior avis, tulit/ nos nequiores, mox daturos/ progeniem vitiosiorem. *L*—Our parents, worse than our grandparents, have produced us, more depraved still, and we shall soon give birth to offspring even more corrupt.—*Horace, Odes, III, vi, 46-8.*

14

Aeternum servans sub pectore vulnus. *L*—Forever nursing an offense in one's heart. Originally, a reference to Juno's undying hatred for the Trojans.—*Vergil, Aeneid, I, 36.*

A falta de hombres buenos, le hacen a mi padre alcalde. *Sp*—Because good men were scarce, they made my father mayor.

Affaire d'amour. *Fr*—A love affair.

Affaire d'honneur. *Fr*—An affair of honor, involving a duel with deadly weapons.

Affaire du cœur. *Fr*—A love affair.

Les affaires sont les affaires. *Fr*—Business is business.

Afflavit Deus et dissipantur. *L*—God sent a tempest and they were scattered. An inscription on a medal struck by Queen Elizabeth I after the defeat of the Spanish Armada.

À fond. *Fr*—Thoroughly.

À forfait. *Fr*—By contract.

A fortiori. *L*—For a stronger reason; all the more so.

À fripon fripon et demi. *Fr*—Set a thief to catch a thief.

Agapa ton plesion. *Gk*—Love thy neighbor.—*Thales.*

À gauche. *Fr*—To the left. A direction for a traveler.

À genoux! *Fr*—Down on your knees!

Agenti incumbit probatio. *L*—The burden of proof rests on the accuser.

Agent provocateur. *Fr*—An undercover police or government agent who gains the confidence of suspected criminals or members of an opposing group and encourages them to commit crimes in which they are apprehended.

Age quod agis. *L*—Do what you are doing.

Ager publicus. *L*—Public domain.

Aggregatio mentium. *L*—A meeting of minds.

Agnus Dei. *L*—The lamb of God (words uttered by John the Baptist when he saw Christ coming toward him). This is part of a prayer in the canon of the mass.—*Vulgate, John, I, 29; 36.*

À grands frais. *Fr*—At great expense.

À haute voix. *Fr*—In a loud voice.

À huis clos. *Fr*—Behind closed doors.

Aide-de-camp. *Fr*—A military assistant to a general or other high army officer.

Aide mémoire. *Fr*—An aid to memory; words or notes to assist the memory. In diplomacy, a summary in writing of points to be checked in a possible agreement.

Aide-toi, le ciel t'aidera. *Fr*—Heaven will help you if you help yourself; God helps those who help themselves.

A idos de mi casa, y qué queréis con mi mujer, no hay responder. *Sp*—There is no answer for "Leave my house," and "What do you want with my wife?"—*Cervantes, Don Quixote, II, XLIII.*

Ai mali estremi, estremi rimedi. *It*—For extreme evils, extreme remedies.

Aîné *(m)*, **aînée** *(f)*. *Fr*—Senior.

Ainsi soit-il. *Fr*—So be it; amen.

Aio te, Aeacida, Romanos vincere posse. *L*—I say, Aeacides, that you can defeat the Romans *or* I say, Aeacides, that the Romans can defeat you. An ambiguous reply from the Delphic oracle given Pyrrhus of Epirus, according to tradition.

À la —. *Fr*—In the style or fashion of.

À la belle étoile. *Fr*—In the open air; under the stars.

À la bonne heure. *Fr*—Splendid! well done! right!

À l'abri. *Fr*—Under cover; sheltered.

À la campagne. *Fr*—In the country.

À la carte. *Fr*—According to the menu on which the price of each item of food or drink is listed.

À la dérobée. *Fr*—Furtively, secretly.

À la diable. *Fr*—In a disorderly fashion; highly spiced.

À la française. *Fr*—In the French style or manner.

À la grècque. *Fr*—In the Greek style or manner.

À la lanterne. *Fr*—To the lamppost. The cry of the Paris mob during the Revolution when lampposts served as gallows.

À la lettre. *Fr*—To the letter; literally.

À la mode. *Fr*—According to the fashion.

À la mort. *Fr*—Unto death; forever.

Al bugiardo non si crede la verità. *It*—A liar is not believed even when he tells the truth.

À la napolitaine. *Fr*—Cooked in Neapolitan style.

À la presse vont les fous. *Fr*—Fools follow the crowd.

À la sourdine. *Fr*—Played with a mute; by extension it means slyly, secretly, silently.

Alas sustineo. *L*—I sustain the wings. The motto of ground communications in the Air Force.

A latere. *L*—*See* Legatus a latere.

L'Albion perfide. *Fr*—Perfidious Albion; treacherous England. A French point of view. The English also have slighting phrases for the French, e.g., *taking French leave. See also* La Grande Voleuse.

Al bisogno si conosce un amico. *It*—When in need you learn who your friends are. This is also found in the plural: *Al bisogno si conoscono gli amici.*

Alcinoo poma dare. *L*—To give fruit to Alcinous (king of the Phaeacians who befriended Odysseus. The island that he ruled was known for its fruits); to carry coals to Newcastle.

Al confessor

Al confessor, medico, ed avvocato, non si de' tener il vero celato.
It—One should not hold back the truth from one's confessor,
doctor, or lawyer. *See also* Ao medico . . . .

Al contado. *Sp*—For cash.

Al dente. *It*—A culinary phrase used to describe spaghetti that
is served while it still offers some resistance to the teeth and
has not been cooked so long that it is mushy.

À l'extérieur. *Fr*—On the outside.

Al fine. *It*—To the end. Musical term.

Al fresco. *It*—In open air; painting on fresh plaster.

À l'huile. *Fr*—In olive oil.

Aliena vitia in oculis habemus; a tergo nostra sunt. *L*—Another's
faults are before our eyes; our own are behind us.—*Seneca,
On Anger, II, 28, 6.*

Alieni appetens, sui profusus. *L*—Covetous of the property of
others, wasteful of his own.—*Sallust, Catiline, 5.*

Alieni juris. *L*—Not possessing full legal power. Said of a person
legally dependent upon another, as a slave or a minor.

À l'immortalité. *Fr*—To immortality. The motto of the Forty
Immortals of the French Academy.

À l'improviste. *Fr*—Without a warning; unexpectedly.

Aliquando bonus dormitat Homerus. *L*—*See* Indignor quandoque . . . .

Aliquis in omnibus, nullus in singulis. *L*—Jack of all trades but
master of none.

Alitur vitium vivitque tegendo. *L*—A fault is nourished and
lives by concealment.—*Vergil, Georgics, III, 454.*

Aliud corde premunt, aliud ore promunt. *L*—They hide one
thing in their hearts, but another comes from their mouths.

Alium silere quod voles, primus sile. *L*—If you want another to keep your secret, first keep it yourself.—*Seneca, Hippolytus, 876.*

Al-ki. *Chinookan*—By and by. Motto of the state of Washington in the language of the Chinook Indians.

Alla barba dei pazzi, il barbier impara a radere. *It*—The barber learns to shave on the chin of fools. *See also* À barbe de fou . . . .

Alla cappella. *It*—*See* A cappella.

Allahu akbar. *Arabic*—God is great.

Allá van leyes do quieren reyes. *Sp*—The laws follow the will of kings. Alfonso VI, to determine whether the Gothic or the Roman missal should be used in his kingdom, threw both into the fire, intending to approve the one that survived the flames. When the Gothic did not burn, Alfonso threw it into the fire again and chose the Roman missal. The Spanish proverb grew out of this incident.

Alla vostra salute. *It*—To your health.

L'allegro. *It*—The happy man. Title of a poem by Milton; a companion piece to *Il penseroso (q.v.).*

Allegro moderato. *It*—Brisk in moderate tempo.

Alle Länder gute Menschen tragen. *Ger*—All lands have good men.—*Lessing.*

Aller Anfang ist schwer. *Ger*—Every beginning is difficult. *See also* Arche hemisy pantos.

Aller guten Dinge sind drei. *Ger*—All good things go in threes.

Allez-vous-en! *Fr*—Go away!

Allons, enfants de la patrie! *Fr*—Come, children of the fatherland. The first words of "La Marseillaise," the stirring national anthem of France.

All' ottava. *It*—Notes to be played an octave higher than written.

Alma mater

Alma mater. *L*—Foster mother; one's college or university.

Alma mater studiorum. *L*—Nourishing mother of studies. Linacre's appraisal of Italy's universities in the fifteenth century.

Alma Redemptoris Mater. *L*—Dear Mother of the Redeemer. An antiphon sung at complins on certain Sundays. Mentioned by Chaucer's Prioress in *The Canterbury Tales*.

Al nemico che fugge, fa un ponte d'oro. *It*—Make a bridge of gold for a fleeing enemy, i.e., be happy when an enemy decides to retreat, and speed his flight.

À loisir. *Fr*—At leisure.

Al primo colpo, non cade l'albero. *It*—The tree does not fall at the first blow from an ax; heaven is not reached at a single bound. *See also* Der Baum fällt . . . .

Alta vendetta d'alto silenzio è figlia. *It*—Deep vengeance is the child of deep silence.

Die Alten zum Rat, die Jungen zur Tat. *Ger*—Age for counsel, youth for action.

Alter ego. *L*—Another self; a bosom friend.

Alter idem. *L*—Literally, another the same; a person or thing that is the image of another; another or second self. *See also* Alter ego.

Alter ipse amicus. *L*—A friend is a second self.

Altissima flumina minimo sono labuntur. *L*—The deeper the river the more quietly it flows; still rivers run deep.—Adapted from *Q. Curtius Rufus, Exploits of Alexander, VII, iv, 13*.

Alto rilievo. *It*—High relief. Sculptured figures that project half way or more from a wall.

À main armée. *Fr*—By force of arms.

Ama l'amico tuo col vizio suo. *It*—Love your friend in spite of his faults.

Ama nesciri. *L*—Love to be unknown. The doctrine of self-effacement found in St. Bernard and Thomas à Kempis. *See also* Lathe biosas.

Amantes, amentes. *L*—Lovers are mad. This is derived from *Terence, Andria, I, iii, 13: Inceptio est amentium, haud amantium,* It [a proposed marriage] is the project of mad people, not of lovers.

Amantium irae amoris integratio est. *L*—Lovers' quarrels renew love.—*Terence, Andria, III, 3, 23.*

Amar y saber no puede ser. *Sp*—It is impossible to love and be wise at the same time.

Ama si vis amari. *L*—Love if you wish to be loved.

Amato non sarai, se a te solo penserai. *It*—Nobody will love you if you think of nobody but yourself.

A maximis ad minima. *L*—From the greatest to the smallest.

Ambigendi locus. *L*—Room for doubt.

Âme damnée. *Fr*—Literally a damned soul; a tool, a drudge.

Âme de boue. *Fr*—A low, debased person.

Amende honorable. *Fr*—An acceptable apology.

A mensa et toro (*thoro* is incorrect usage). *L*—A legal separation from bed and board granted a married couple.

Âme perdue. *Fr*—A lost soul.

À merveille. *Fr*—Marvelously well done.

Amico d'ognuno, amico di nessuno. *It*—Everybody's friend, nobody's friend.

Amicus certus in re incerta cernitur. *L*—A sincere friend is discovered in an uncertain issue; a friend in need is a friend indeed.—*Ennius*, quoted by *Cicero, On Friendship, XVII.*

Amicus curiae. *L*—A friend of the court; a person appointed by a judge to assist by giving advice in the handling of a legal case.

Amicus humani generis. *L*—A friend of the human race.

Amicus Plato, sed magis amica veritas. *L*—Plato is dear to me but truth is dearer still. A refusal to abandon one's conclusions when the authority of a great name is invoked.—*Cervantes, Don Quixote, II, LI.* A variation of this saying reads: *Amicus Plato, amicus Socrates, sed major veritas,* Plato is my friend and so is Socrates, but the truth is greater still. Variations of this dictum are based on a passage in Plato's *Phaedo, 40.*

Amicus usque ad aras. *L*—A friend to the very altar; a friend in everything except religion. The expression is ambiguous.

Ami de cour. *Fr*—A friend of the court; a false friend.

Ami du peuple. *Fr*—Friend of the people.

Amigo de todos y de ninguno, todo es uno. *Sp*—Everybody's friend and nobody's friend, it's all the same.

Les amis du vin. *Fr*—Friends of wine, an organization interested in winetasting, fine vintages, and wine tours in Europe.

Amittit merito proprium qui alienum appetit. *L*—He deservedly loses his own property who is greedy for another's.—*Phaedrus, Fables, I, iv, i.*

Amoenitates studiorum. *L*—Refined literary pursuits. This is the source of the title of *Amenities of Literature* by Isaac Disraeli. —*Pliny the Elder, Natural History, preface, sec. 14.*

À moitié. *Fr*—By halves.

À mon avis. *Fr*—In my opinion.

Amor dei intellectualis. *L*—Intellectual love of God.

Amore è cieco. *It*—Love is blind.

Amor fati. *L*—Willing acceptance of whatever fate decrees. According to Nietzsche, greatness lies not only in bearing up under the ills of life but in loving them. In this he approached Spinoza's acceptance of whatever fate had in store for him. The Christian attitude on this is expressed in *Fiat voluntas tua (q.v.).*

Amor gignit amorem. *L*—Love begets love.

Amor nummi. *L*—Love of money.

Amor omnibus idem. *L*—Love is the same for all living creatures.—*Vergil, Georgics, III, 244.*

Amor patriae. *L*—Love for one's native country.

Amor vincit omnia. *L*—Love conquers all.

L'amour courtois. *Fr*—Courtly love of the twelfth and thirteenth century characterized by a gentle, chivalric spirit on the part of poets and knights toward aristocratic ladies.

L'amour, . . . de tous les sentiments le plus égoïste, et, par conséquent, lorsqu'il est blessé, le moins généreux. *Fr*—Love is the most selfish of all the emotions and consequently, when wounded, the least generous.—*Benjamin Constant, Adolphe,* chap. VI.

L'amour et la fumée ne peuvent se cacher. *Fr*—Love and smoke cannot be hidden.

Amour fait beaucoup mais l'argent fait tout. *Fr*—Love can do much but money can do everything.

Amour propre. *Fr*—Self-respect, self-esteem, self-love, or conceit, depending on the context.

L'amour-propre est le plus grande de tous les flatteurs. *Fr*—Self-love is the greatest of all flatterers.—*La Rochefoucauld, Maxims, 2.*

Amt ohne Geld macht Diebe. *Ger*—Offices that carry no pay breed thieves.

A mucho hablar, mucho errar. *Sp*—Much talking, many mistakes.

A muertos y a idos, pocos amigos. *Sp*—The dead and the absent have few friends.

Anagke oude theoi machontai. *Gk*—The gods themselves do not try to fight necessity.—*Simonides of Ceos.*

Anathema sit! *L*—Let him be accursed. An expression used by ecclesiastical authorities when condemning heretics.—*Vulgate, Paul, I Corinthians, XVI, 22.*

Anch' io son' pittore. *It*—I, too, am a painter. Attributed to Correggio on seeing Raphael's painting of Saint Cecilia. This is an exclamation of admiration on the part of Correggio, younger by twenty years than Raphael, for the work of a master. There is also in this expression a feeling of pride at being identified with such a profession.

Ancienne noblesse. *Fr*—The aristocratic class in France prior to the Revolution of 1789.

Ancien régime. *Fr.*—The former regime. Generally used when speaking of conditions in France prior to the French Revolution.

Ancilla theologiae. *L*—The handmaid of theology. Scholastic view of philosophy.

Andante. *It*—Direction that music be played slowly, steadily, and smoothly.

Andra moi ennepe, Mousa, polytropon. *Gk*—Sing to me, O Muse, of the man who wandered afar. The opening words of the epic of the adventures of Odysseus.—*Homer, Odyssey, I, 1.*

Aner ho pheugon kai palin machesetai. *Gk*—He who fights and runs away,/May live to fight another day.—*Menander, Monostichs, 45.*

Angeli, non Angli. *L*—Angels, not Angles. A remark attributed to Gregory, later Pope Gregory the Great. While passing through the Roman forum he inquired about the nationality of certain handsome slaves. On being told they were Angles, he said, "They have the face of angels, and it is fitting that such be co-heirs of heaven with the angels."—*Bede, Ecclesiastical History, II, 1.*

L'Angleterre est une nation de boutiquiers. *Fr*—England is a nation of shopkeepers.—*Napoleon Bonaparte.*

Anguis in herba. *L*—Snake in the grass; a disloyal friend.

Animae dimidium meae. *L*—The half of my soul. A term of endearment applied by Horace to Vergil.—*Horace, Odes, I, iii, 8.*

Anima naturaliter Christiana. *L*—A soul naturally Christian.

Animis opibusque parati. *L*—Prepared in spirit and resources. A motto of South Carolina. *See also* Dum spiro spero.

Animo et fide. *L*—With courage and fidelity.

Animus furandi. *L*—The intention to steal. A legal term.

Animus testandi. *L*—The intention to make a last will.

An nescis longas regibus esse manus? *L*—Don't you know that kings have long arms? The long arm of the law has become proverbial.—*Ovid, Heroides, XVII, 166.*

Anno aetatis suae. *L*—In the year of his age.

Anno ante Christum. *L*—In the year before Christ. Equivalent to B.C.

Anno Domini. *L*—In the year of our Lord. *See* A.D.

Anno humanae salutis. *L*—*See* A.H.S.

Anno mundi. *L*—In the year of the world. *See also* A.M.

Anno urbis conditae. *L*—*See* A.U.C. (Ab urbe condita).

Annuit coeptis. *L*—He (God is meant) has looked with favor upon our beginning. Words on the great seal of the United States adapted from a passage in *Vergil, Aeneid, IX, 625,* in which Ascanius prays to Jupiter for help in slaying an enemy. The words at the bottom of the seal, *Novus ordo seclorum,* mean The new order of the ages, and are based on *Vergil, Eclogues, IV, 5.*

Annus luctus. *L*—A year of mourning. Roman law forbade a widow to remarry within one year of her husband's death. The presumption was that any child born during this period was the offspring of the deceased father. This Roman law was incorporated into subsequent codes of other nations.

Annus magnus *or* **Platonicus.** *L*—The Great Year or the Platonic Year (a period of thousands of years ending when all the stars would be in the same position they were at the beginning of the world). One of these great years would include the four ages, gold, silver, bronze, and iron.

Annus mirabilis. *L*—Astonishing year. Generally refers to 1666 when London experienced a tragic fire and plague.

À nouvelles affaires, nouveaux conseils. *Fr*—For new business, new plans.

Ante bellum. *L*—Before the war; specifically, in the United States, before the Civil War.

Ante lucem. *L*—Before daybreak.

Ante tubam trepidat. *L*—He trembles before hearing the sound of the trumpet, i.e., before the battle begins.

Ante victoriam ne canas triumphum. *L*—Do not celebrate a triumph before victory; don't count your chickens before they are hatched.

Anulatus aut doctus aut fatuus. *L*—The man who wears a ring is either learned or foolish, a bishop or a fop.

Ao medico, ao advogado, e ao abbade fallar verdade. *Port*—Tell the truth to your doctor, your lawyer, and your priest. *See also* Al confessor . . . .

À outrance. *Fr*—To the very end; to the utmost. *À l'outrance* is incorrect.

À pas de géant. *Fr*—With a giant's stride.

A paso de buey. *Sp*—At a snail's pace.

À perte de vue. *Fr*—As far as the eye can reach.

À peu de frais. *Fr*—At little expense.

A piacere. *It*—According to one's wish. *See also* Ad libitum.

À pied. *Fr*—On foot.

À point. *Fr*—Exactly; correctly, rare,when referring to the cooking of meat.

Apologia pro vita sua. *L*—A defense (not an apology in the popular sense) for his life. The title of Cardinal Newman's spiritual autobiography.

26

A posse ad esse. *L*—From possibility to reality.

A posteriori. *L*—In logic a conclusion reached through experience rather than pure reason. Opposed to *a priori (q.v.).*

Apparatus criticus. *L*—Reference works useful in literary studies; a section in a classical author showing variant readings based on the different extant manuscripts of the text.

Apparent rari nantes in gurgite vasto. *L*—Here and there men are seen swimming in the vast abyss. Critics have used this to describe a literary work in which occasional bits of worthwhile material are scattered over a sea of words.—*Vergil, Aeneid, I, 118.*

Appartement meublé. *Fr*—Furnished apartment.

Appetito non vuol salsa. *It*—Hunger is the best sauce. *See also* À bon appétit . . . .

Appetitus rationi oboediant. *L*—Let the appetites obey reason. —*Cicero, Offices, I, xxix, 102.*

L'appétit vient en mangeant. *Fr*—Appetite grows with eating.

Après la mort, le médecin. *Fr*—Calling the doctor when the patient is dead; locking the stable door after the horse is stolen.

Après moi le déluge. *Fr*—After me the deluge. Attributed to Louis XV. *Après nous le déluge,* after us the deluge, is credited to Madame de Pompadour, his favorite. W. Francis H. King in his *Classical and Foreign Quotations* discusses the sources of these phrases at length.

A prima vista. *It*—At first sight.

A primo ad ultimum. *L*—From first to last.

A priori. *L*—In logic a type of reasoning or conclusion derived from self-evident propositions rather than experience. Opposed to *a posteriori (q.v.).*

À propos de bottes. *Fr*—By the way; to change the subject.

À propos de rien. *Fr*—À propos of nothing. Used to describe something that is off the subject.

Aqua fortis

Aqua fortis. *L*—Literally, strong water; nitric acid.

Aqua vitae. *L*—Brandy or any distilled liquor.

Aquila non captat muscas. *L*—An eagle does not hawk at flies; the mighty can afford to scorn the weak.

Aquí se habla español. *Sp*—Spanish is spoken here.

À raconter ses maux souvent on les soulage. *Fr*—We often lighten our troubles by talking about them.—*Corneille, Polyeucte, 1, 3.*

Ara pacis. *L*—Altar of peace.

Arbiter bibendi. *L*—The toastmaster.

Arbiter elegantiae (elegantiarum). *L*—The judge of elegance. Nero conferred this title on his favorite, Petronius, whose word was final in matters of esthetic taste and refined luxury. He was unseated by a rival and took his own life.—*Tacitus, Annals, XVI, 18.*

Arbiter literarum. *L*—A judge or critic of literature.

Arbores serit diligens agricola, quarum adspiciet bacam ipse numquam. *L*—The diligent farmer plants trees the fruit of which he will never see. Adapted from *Cicero, Tusculan Disputations, I, 14.*

Arcades ambo. *L*—Both Arcadians, i.e., gifted in pastoral song; friends of similiar tastes and characteristics. The reference is to Corydon and Thyrsis, shepherds competing in a musical contest.—*Vergil, Eclogues, VII, 4.*

Arcana imperii. *L*—State secrets.

Arcani disciplina. *L*—Discipline of the secret. Policy of Christians in the early centuries of not openly revealing their religion.

Arche hemisy pantos. *Gk*—The beginning is half of everything; well begun is half done.—*Pythagoras.*

Die **Architektur ist die erstarrte Musik.** *Ger*—Architecture is petrified music. This has been attributed to Goethe, but in his *Maxims in Prose, 63,* he credits "a noble philosopher" as the author. Schopenhauer substituted the word *gefrorne* (frozen) for *erstarrte.*

Ardentia verba. *L*—Glowing words; forcible language.

À reculons. *Fr*—Backwards. Used of a backward movement, not necessarily physical.

Argent comptant. *Fr*—Spot cash; ready money. *See also* a.c.

Argumenti gratia. *L*—For the sake of argument.

Argumentum ad crumenam. *L*—An appeal to one's purse; an argument which stresses the profit possible for one's opponent.

Argumentum ad hominem. *L*—An argument that derives its force from its special application to the interests of the individual to whom it is directed. Such an argument may appeal to the prejudices or the private gain of an opponent, to his passion rather than his reason. The same name is given to an argument in which one employs an opponent's words or actions to refute him. It has been said that a popular illustration of the *argumentum ad hominem* is found in the technique of the defense lawyer who, when he is at a loss for arguments, attacks the attorney for the plaintiff, though this is not the current usage of this phrase in the United States.

Argumentum ad ignorantiam. *L*—An argument based on an adversary's ignorance of facts in a controversy.

Argumentum ad invidiam. *L*—An appeal to envy, jealousy, or ill will.

Argumentum ad judicium. *L*—An argument appealing to judgment.

Argumentum ad misericordiam. *L*—An appeal to pity.

Argumentum ad populum. *L*—An argument appealing to the selfish interests of the populace.

Argumentum ad rem

Argumentum ad rem. *L*—An argument to the point under discussion.

Argumentum ad verecundiam. *L*—An appeal to an opponent's sense of decency.

Argumentum baculinum or **ad baculum.** *L*—Argument with a cane; the appeal to force in a debate.

A rivederci (usually spelled **arrivederci**). *It*—Until we meet again.

Arma virumque cano. *L*—I sing of arms and the man.—*Vergil, Aeneid, I, 1.*

A Roma por toda. *Sp*—To Rome for everything.

Arrière-garde. *Fr*—Rear guard.

Arrière pensée. *Fr*—A mental reservation. It does not mean an afterthought.

Arroz con pollo. *Sp*—Rice with chicken.

Ars artium omnium conservatrix. *L*—The art (of printing) that preserves all arts.

Ars (artis) est celare artem. *L*—Art lies in the concealment of art. An axiom among those artists who try to conceal the means by which they produce their effects. It is also a precept among painters who feel that art should reproduce nature.

Ars gratia artis. *L*—Art for art's sake. *See also* L'art pour l'art.

Ars longa, vita brevis. *L*—Art is long, and Time is fleeting, as translated by Longfellow in "A Psalm of Life." *See also* Vita brevis, longa ars.

Ars omnibus communis. *L*—Art belongs to everyone.

Ars Poetica. *L*—The Art of Poetry. Title of a work by the Roman poet Horace.

Ars prima regni est posse invidiam pati. *L*—The first art of a ruler is to be able to bear up under envy.—*Seneca, Hercules Furens, 353.*

L'art de vivre. *Fr*—The art of living; the art of getting the most out of life.

Artes perditae. *L*—Lost arts.

Articolo di fondo. *It*—An editorial or leading article.

L'Art Nouveau. *Fr*—The New Art. Appeared in the nineties and flourished until World War I. Its style, characterized by sinuous, curving lines, greatly affected the decorative crafts, such as jewelry, ceramics, furniture.

L'art pour l'art. *Fr*—Art for art's sake.—*Victor Cousin, Sorbonne Lectures, xxii. See also* Ars gratia artis.

Artz, hilf dir selbst. *Ger*—*See* Medice, cura teipsum.

Asbestos gelos. *Gk*—Unquenchable laughter; hence the proverbial Homeric laughter. Such laughter broke out among the gods when awkwardly limping Hephaestus acted as cupbearer to Zeus in place of the graceful Hebe or Ganymede.—*Homer, Iliad, I, 599.*

Asinus ad lyram. *L*—An ass at the lyre. Said of a person who has no appreciation or talent in matters artistic.

Asinus asino et sus sui pulcher. *L*—An ass is beautiful to an ass and a pig to a pig.

Aspice, viator. *L*—Behold, traveler. Inscription on Roman tombstones.

Gli assenti hanno torto. *It*—The absent are always wrong. *See also* Les absents . . . .

Astraea Redux. *L*—Literally, Astraea returned. She was the goddess of justice, the last of the immortals to leave the earth. Dryden used this as a title for his poem celebrating the return of Charles II after Cromwell's rule.

A-suilish mahuil agus machree! *Ir*—Light of my eyes and my heart.

À tâtons. *Fr*—Gropingly; warily.

Até amanhã. *Port*—Until tomorrow.

Até logo

Até logo. *Port*—Good-bye; till we meet again.

A tergo. *L*—From the rear.

Athanasius contra mundum. *L*—Athanasius against the world. Said of anybody who single-handedly battles heavy opposition. As bishop of Alexandria, he was a vigorous opponent of Arianism and endured exile five times for his support of Christian orthodoxy.

À tort et à travers. *Fr*—At random; without rhyme or reason.

À tort ou à raison. *Fr*—Rightly or wrongly.

À tout prix. *Fr*—At any price; at any cost.

At spes non fracta. *L*—But hope is not yet crushed.

A tuo beneplacito. *It*—At your pleasure.

Au bout de son latin. *Fr*—At the end of his Latin; at his wit's end; in desperation.

Au bout du compte. *Fr*—Literally, at the end of the account; after all; on the whole.

Auch ein Haar hat seinen Schatten. *Ger*—*See* Etiam capillus unus . . . .

Au contraire. *Fr*—On the contrary.

Au courant. *Fr*—In the current of events; well-posted; up to date on current matters.

Audendo magnus tegitur timor. *L*—Great fear is covered up by a display of daring.—*Lucan, Pharsalia, IV, 702.*

Audentes deus ipse juvat. *L*—God helps the brave.—*Ovid, Metamorphoses, X, 586.*

Audentes fortuna juvat. *L*—Fortune is on the side of the brave. —*Vergil, Aeneid, X, 284.*

Aude sapere. *L*—Dare to be wise.

Au désespoir. *Fr*—In despair.

Audi alteram partem. *L*—Hear the other side.

Au fait. *Fr*—Skilled; masterly; well-informed.

Au fond. *Fr*—Basically; at bottom.

Auf Wiedersehen. *Ger*—Until we meet again.

Au grand sérieux. *Fr*—In all seriousness.

Au gratin. *Fr*—Cooked with bread crumbs and grated cheese.

Aujourd'hui roi, demain rien. *Fr*—Today a king, tomorrow nothing; a king today, tomorrow a clown.

Au jus. *Fr*—In the juice; served in its own gravy.

Au lecteur. *Fr*—To the reader.

Au naturel. *Fr*—In the natural style or manner; in the nude.

Aunque la mona se vista de seda, mona se queda. *Sp*—A monkey dressed in silk is still a monkey.

Au pied de la lettre. *Fr*—Literally; exactly.

Au pis aller. *Fr*—If the worst comes to the worst.

Aura popularis. *L*—The whim of the people.

Aurea mediocritas. *L*—The golden mean. This doctrine, popular among the ancient Greeks and Romans, holds that in all activity, e.g., in eating and drinking, gymnastics, and the pursuit of pleasure, the ideal is to avoid excess on the one hand and deficiency on the other.—*Horace, Odes, II, x, 5. See also* In medio stat virtus; Medio tutissimus ibis; Meden agan; Ne quid nimis.

Aurea ne credas quaecunque nitescere cernis. *L*—Don't believe that whatever glistens is gold; all that glitters is not gold.

Aurea prima sata est aetas, quae vindice nullo,/Sponte sua, sine lege fidem rectumque colebat. *L*—The golden age was first; men of that time of their own free will led faithful, upright lives without punishment or laws.—*Ovid, Metamorphoses, I, 89.*

Au reste. *Fr*—Moreover; besides.

Au revoir. *Fr*—Until we meet again.

Auribus teneo lupum. *L*—I hold a wolf by the ears; you face danger if you hold on or let go.—*Terence, Phormio, III, ii, 21.*

Auri sacra fames. *L*—The accursed greed for gold. The complete quotation reads: *Quid non mortalia cogis, auri sacra fames?* To what do you not drive the hearts of men, O cursed greed for gold?—*Vergil, Aeneid, III, 57.*

Aurora borealis. *L*—Literally, the northern dawn; popularly referred to as the northern lights.

Au royaume des aveugles les borgnes sont rois. *Fr*—In the kingdom of the blind the man with one eye is king.

Aurum potabile. *L*—Drinkable gold. In ancient times it was thought that gold in solution was a panacea.

Aus den Augen, aus dem Sinn. *Ger*—Out of sight, out of mind.

Au secours! *Fr*—To the rescue; help!

Au sérieux. *Fr*—In a serious manner.

Aus Kindern werden Leute. *Ger*—Children grow up; the boy is father to the man.

Au soleil. *Fr*—In the sunlight.

Aussitôt dit, ausitôt fait. *Fr*—No sooner said than done.

Aut amat aut odit mulier, nihil est tertium. *L*—A woman either loves or hates; there is no in-between. Typical male generalization.—*Publilius Syrus.*

Autant d'hommes, autant d'avis. *Fr*—So many men, so many opinions.

Aut Caesar aut nullus (aut nihil). *L*—Either Caesar or nothing. Motto of the ambitious.

Aut disce, aut discede: manet sors tertia caedi. *L*—Either learn or leave: a third lot remains, be flogged. Motto of early grammar school of Winchester College, England.

Aut doce aut disce aut discede. *L*—Teach, learn, or leave. Motto of St. Paul's Grammar School, London.

Auto-da-fé. *Port*—Literally, an act of the Faith. A religious demonstration in defense of the doctrines of the Church. This was carried out with dramatic ceremonies at which the heretical views of the unrepentant were recited. The punishments decreed by the Inquisition, sometimes as barbarous as burning at the stake, were executed by the secular power.

Auto de fe. *Sp*—*See* Auto-da-fé.

Autres temps, autres mœurs. *Fr*—Other times, other customs.

Aut vincere aut mori. *L*—Victory or death.

Aux aguets. *Fr*—To be on the lookout; watchful.

Aux armes! *Fr*—To arms!

Avant-coureur. *Fr*—A forerunner.

Avant-garde. *Fr*—Advanced guard; pioneers. Leaders in new art forms not approved by the conservative are usually given this label.

Avant propos. *Fr*—Preface.

Avant que de désirer fortement une chose, il faut examiner quel est le bonheur de celui qui la possède. *Fr*—Before desiring something passionately, one should inquire into the happiness of the man who possesses it.—*La Rochefoucauld, Maxims, 543.*

Avant tout un bon dîner. *Fr*—Before anything else, a good dinner. The reported first words of Napoleon on entering the Tuileries after escaping from Elba.

Avaritiam si tollere vultis, mater eius est tollenda, luxuries. *L*—If you wish to do away with avarice, you must do away with its mother, luxury.—*Cicero, On the Orator, II, xl, 171.*

Ave atque vale. *L*—Hail and farewell. A Roman formula used at funerals when bidding farewell to the dead. The most notable use occurs in *Catullus, CI, 10*, where the poet writes of visiting the grave of his brother.

Ave Maria. *L*—Hail Mary. Greeting of the Angel Gabriel to the Virgin Mary.

A verbis ad verbera. *L*—From words to blows.

Avic machree. *Ir*—Son of my heart.

A vinculo matrimonii. *L*—From the bonds of marriage; a divorce.

À volonté. *Fr*—At will; at pleasure. *See also* Ad libitum.

A vostra salute. *It*—To your health.

À votre santé. *Fr*—To your health.

À vue d'œil. *Fr*—At a glance; clearly.

A vuelta de correo. *Sp*—By return mail.

A vuestra salud. *Sp*—A toast to your good health.

Avvocato del diavolo. *It*—Devil's advocate. *See also* Advocatus diaboli.

Axeite, vinho e amigo, o mais antigo. *Port*—Oil, wine, and friends, the older the better.

¡Ay, bendito! *Sp*—The poor fellow! the poor man! An expression of sorrow or pity. Much used in Puerto Rico.

B

B.A. *See* A.B.

bacc. en dr. (baccalauréat en droit). *Fr*—Baccalaureate in Law.

bacc. ès l. (baccalauréat ès lettres). *Fr*—Baccalaureate in Literature. For the meaning of *ès, see* ès.

bacc. ès sc. (baccalauréat ès sciences). *Fr*—Baccalaureate in Science.

B.A.I. (Baccalaureus in Arte Ingeniaria). *L*—Bachelor of Engineering.

b. à p. (billet à payer). *Fr*—Bill payable.

b. à r. (billet à recevoir). *Fr*—Bill receivable.

B.Ch.D. (Baccalaureus Chirurgiae Dentium). *L*—Bachelor of Dental Surgery.

b.d.s. (bis die sumendum). *L*—To be taken twice a day. A medical direction.

B.E. (brevet élémentaire). *Fr*—A primary school certificate granted a teacher passing French government examinations.

B. ès A. (Bachelier ès Arts). *Fr*—Bachelor of Arts.

B. ès L. (Bachelier ès Lettres). *Fr*—Bachelor of Letters.

B. ès S. (Bachelier ès Sciences). *Fr*—Bachelor of Science.

BGB. (Bürgerliches Gesetzbuch). *Ger*—Civil Code.

b.i.d. (bis in die). *L*—Twice a day. A medical direction.

b.i.7d. (bis in septem diebus). *L*—Twice a week.

B.I.T. (Bureau international du travail). *Fr*—International Labor Office.

B.LL. (Baccalaureus Legum). *L*—Bachelor of Laws.

b.m. (beatae memoriae). *L*—Of blessed memory.

b.m. (bene merenti). *L*—To the well deserving one.

B.P. (Baccalaureus Pharmaciae). *L*—Bachelor of Pharmacy.

B.Q. (Bene quiescat). *L*—May he sleep well.

B.S. (brevet supérieur). *Fr*—An upper elementary school certificate granted a teacher passing French government examinations.

bull. (bulliat). *L*—Let boil. A directive for pharmacists.

b.v. (balneum vaporis). *L*—Vapor bath.

B.V. (Bene vixit). *L*—He lived a good life.

Bacio di bocca spesso cuor non tocca. *It*—A kiss on the lips often does not reach the heart.

Ballon d'essai. *Fr*—A trial balloon released to determine the direction of the wind; a sounding out of public opinion, often in advance of announcement of official policy.

Banco regis. *LL*—On the King's bench.

La barba non fa il filosofo. *It*—The beard does not make the philosopher.

Un barbier rait l'autre. *Fr*—One barber shaves the other.

Bar Mizvah (mitzvah, mitzwah). *Heb*—Son of command; in Hebrew law a boy who has reached the age of responsibility (at the end of his thirteenth year); also the ceremony itself.

Bas bleu. *Fr*—Blue stocking. Often a slighting reference to the preoccupation of women in matters intellectual. The meetings of a London literary club of the eighteenth century were attended by a gentleman who wore blue stockings. His comments so pleased the ladies that the group came to be known as the Blue-Stocking Club.

Basis virtutum constantia. *L*—The foundation of virtue is constancy.

Bas relief. *Fr*—Sculpture in which the subject does not stand out far from the background.

Basso buffo. *It*—A bass singer of comic opera roles.

Basso rilievo. *It*—*See* Bas relief.

Bataille rangée. *Fr*—Pitched battle.

Bâtie en hommes. *Fr*—Built of men. A phrase used to describe the medieval university.

Batti il ferro mentre è caldo. *It*—Strike the iron while it is hot. *See also* Bisogna battere . . . .

Der Baum fällt nicht vom ersten Streiche. *Ger*—The tree does not fall at the first blow. *See also* Al primo colpo . . . .

Beatae memoriae. *L*—Of blessed memory.

Beati pacifici. *L*—Blessed are the peacemakers. One of the eight beatitudes.—*Vulgate, Matthew, V, 9.*

38

Beati possidentes. *L*—Blessed are those who have. In the *Vulgate (Matthew V)* each of the beatitudes begins with the word *Beati*, meaning Blessed. This phrase ironically suggests that there is for the worldly a ninth beatitude.

Beati qui lugent. *L*—Blessed are those who mourn. One of the beatitudes.—*Vulgate, Matthew, V, 5.*

Beatus ille qui procul negotiis. *L*—Happy the man who lives far away from the cares of business. The first line of a poem written in praise of the joys of living in the country.—*Horace, Epodes II, 1.*

Beaucop de bruit, peu de fruit. *Fr*—Much talk, but little to show for it.

Beau garçon. *Fr*—A handsome fellow; a dandy.

Beau geste. *Fr*—A generous or sympathetic gesture.

Beau idéal. *Fr*—The model or ideal of perfection.

Beau monde. *Fr*—The fashionable world.

Beauté du diable. *Fr*—Beauty of the devil; the bloom of youth.

Beaux arts. *Fr*—The fine arts.

Beaux esprits. *Fr*—A brilliant coterie of wits.

Les beaux esprits se rencontrent. *Fr*—Great minds see eye to eye.

Bei Nacht sind alle Katzen grau. *Ger*—At night all cats are gray; by night all witches are fair as day (generally said of women); the darkness covers blemishes.

Bel canto. *It*—Literally, beautiful song; charming, lyrical song, brilliantly performed; a style of singing.

Bel esprit (*pl.* **beaux esprits**). *Fr*—A wit or genius.

Bella matribus detestata. *L*—War detested by mothers.—*Horace, Odes, I, i, 24.*

La belle dame sans merci. *Fr*—The beautiful lady without pity. Title of a poem by Keats.

Belle indifférence

Belle indifférence. *Fr*—An attitude on the part of neurotic persons in which they show indifference to their condition.

Bellende Hunde beissen nicht. *Ger*—Barking dogs don't bite.

Les belles actions cachées sont les plus estimables. *Fr*—Noble deeds that are kept hidden are the most esteemed.

Belles dames du temps jadis. *Fr*—Beautiful women of the days gone by.

Belles lettres. *Fr*—Polite literature, the humanities. *See also* La letteratura amena.

Bellum ita suscipiatur ut nihil aliud nisi pax quaesita videatur. *L*—Let war be undertaken so that nothing else is sought, it would seem, but peace.—*Cicero, On Duties, I, XXIII, 79.*

Bellum omnium contra omnes. *L*—There exists hostility on the part of all men for all men; all men are enemies. Axiom of the egocentric philosophy of Hobbes.

Un bel pezzo di carne. *It*—A beautiful piece of flesh. A description of a pretty girl.

Il bel sesso. *It*—The fair sex.

Benedicite Domino! *L*—Praise the Lord!

Beneficium accipere libertatem est vendere. *L*—To accept a favor is to sell one's freedom.—*Publilius Syrus.*

Beneficium clericale. *L*—Benefit of clergy. During the Middle Ages clerics in England enjoyed exemption from trial by secular authorities.

Beneficium egenti bis dat, qui dat celeriter. *L*—He gives twice who gives quickly to one in need of aid.—*Publilius Syrus.*

Bene qui conjiciet, vatem hunc perhibebo optimum. *L*—I shall always maintain that the best guesser is the best prophet.—*Cicero, On Divination, II, 5.*

Bene qui latuit, bene vixit. *L*—He has lived a good life who has kept himself hidden. Descartes' motto. The expressed ideal of

Francis Bacon, but a maxim he did not follow.—*Ovid, Sorrows, III, iv, 25. See also* Lathe biosas.

Berenicem statim ab urbe dimisit invitus invitam. *L*—Unwillingly he at once sent from the city (of Rome) the unwilling Berenice. From this sentence Racine developed his play *Bérénice.*—*Suetonius, Lives of Twelve Caesars, Titus, vii, 2.*

Berretta in mano non fece mai danno. *It*—Cap in hand never did any man harm; one never loses anything by being polite.

Besser spät als nie. *Ger*—Better late than never.

Das Beste ist gut genug. *Ger*—The best is good enough. In the source this sentence begins with *In der Kunst,* meaning In matters of art.—*Goethe, Italian Journey, at the end of the second letter.*

Bête noire. *Fr*—Black beast; a detested person; one's pet abomination.

Biblia a-biblia. *Gk*—Books that are not books; nonbooks. This implies criticism of irrelevant materials brought together in one volume, simply to make a book.

Biblia pauperum. *L*—Bible of the poor; pictures illustrating Bible stories for the illiterate.

Bibliophile de la vieille roche. *Fr*—A book-collector of the old school whose interests ranged widely and who did not specialize in a narrow area.

Bibliothèque bleue. *Fr*—Popular pamphlets with blue wrappers.

Bien entendu. *Fr*—Of course.

Un bienfait n'est jamais perdu. *Fr*—An act of kindness is never lost.

Bien predica quien bien vive. *Sp*—The man who lives a good life gives the best sermons. *See also* Chi ben vive . . . .

Billet doux. *Fr*—A love letter.

Bis dat qui cito dat. *L*—He gives twice who gives quickly. *See also* Beneficium egenti bis dat . . . .

Bisogna andare quando il diavolo è nelle coda. *It*—You have to move when the devil is at your heels.

Bisogna battere il ferro mentre è caldo. *It*—Strike the iron while it is hot. *See also* Ferrum, dum in igni . . . .

Bis peccare in bello non licet. *L*—There must be no second blunder in war.

Bis pueri senes. *L*—Old men are boys twice; the aged often become childish.

Blagodaryu vas. *Rus*—Thank you.

Blut und Eisen. *Ger*—*See* Eisen und Blut.

B'nai B'rith. *Heb*—Sons of the covenant. The name of a Jewish fraternal and service organization that has spread through the United States and Europe since it was founded in New York in 1843.

Boa noite. *Port*—Good night.

Boca de mel, coração de fel. *Port*—A mouth full of honey and a heart full of gall; sweet lips and a bitter heart.

Bom dia. *Port*—Good morning; good day.

Bona fide. *L*—In good faith.

Bona rerum secundarum optabilia, adversarum mirabilia. *L*—Francis Bacon in his essay *Of Adversity* made this translation: The good things which belong to prosperity are to be wished, but the good things that belong to adversity are to be admired. He expanded a sentence in *Seneca, Letters to Lucilius 66, 28.*

Bona roba (from *buona roba*). *It*—Fine clothes. A name given a prostitute.

Bona vacantia. *L*—Goods of unknown ownership that escheat to the state.

Bon avocat, mauvais voisin. *Fr*—A good lawyer is a bad neighbor.

Bon chien chasse de race. *Fr*—A good dog hunts naturally.

Le bon Dieu est toujours du côté des gros bataillons. *Fr*—God is always on the side of the big armies. Attributed to Napoleon I, but the idea has been variously phrased by several writers.

Le bon genre. *Fr*—Good taste, good style.

Bon goût. *Fr*—Good taste, in both culinary and esthetic meanings.

Bon gré, mal gré. *Fr*—Whether one will or not; willy-nilly.

Boni pastoris est tondere pecus, non deglubere. *L*—It is the duty of a good shepherd to shear, not to skin his flock.—*Suetonius, Tiberius, 34.*

Bonis avibus. *L*—Under good auspices.

Bonis nocet quisquis pepercerit malis. *L*—Whoever spares the wicked harms the good.—*Publilius Syrus.*

Bonjour. *Fr*—Good day; good morning.

Bon mot. *Fr*—A witticism or clever expression.

Bonne année. *Fr*—Happy New Year.

La bonne bouche. *Fr*—Something good saved for the end; a tidbit.

Bonne chance! *Fr*—Good luck!

Bonne foi. *Fr*—Good faith; honest purpose.

Bonne nuit. *Fr*—Good night.

Une bonne race. *Fr*—A good breed.

Bonne renommée vaut mieux que ceinture dorée. *Fr*—A good name is worth more than a golden belt; better a good name than riches.

Bonnet rouge. *Fr*—Red cap worn by French revolutionists.

Les bons comptes font les bons amis. *Fr*—Good accounts make good friends.

Bons dias. *Port*—Good morning.

Bon soir. *Fr*—Good evening.

Le bon temps viendra. *Fr*—There's a good time coming.

Bon ton. *Fr*—Outstanding fashion.

Bonum commune. *L*—The common good.

Bonum ex integra causa, malum ex quocumque defectu. *L*—An action is good when good in every respect; it is wrong when wrong in any respect.

Bon vivant. *Fr*—One to whom the good life is mostly pleasure in eating and drinking; a jolly good fellow.

Bon voyage! *Fr*—Have a good trip!

Borgen macht Sorgen. *Ger*—Borrowing makes for sorrowing.

Böse Beispiele verderben gute Sitten. *Ger*—Bad examples corrupt good customs; evil communications corrupt good manners.

Brevet s.g.d.g. (Sans garantie du gouvernement). *Fr*—A patent without government guarantee as to quality.

Brevi manu. *L*—Literally, with a short hand; off-hand; immediately; in civil law, a term applied to a fictitious transfer.

Brevis esse laboro, obscurus fio. *L*—I strive to be brief, and I become obscure.—*Horace, Art of Poetry, 25.*

Brutum fulmen (*pl.* **bruta fulmina**). *L*—Harmless thunderbolt; vain, senseless threat.—*Pliny, Natural History, II, 43, 113.*

Buena fama hurto encubre. *Sp*—A good reputation may be a mask for theft.

¡Buena suerte! *Sp*—Good luck!

Buenos días. *Sp*—Good morning.

Buey viejo surco derecho. *Sp*—An old ox plows a straight furrow.

Buona notte. *It*—Good night.

Buon capo del anno! *It*—Happy New Year!

Buon giorno. *It*—Good morning.

Buon Natale. *It*—Merry Christmas.

Buon principio, la mitad es hecha. *Sp*—Well begun is half done. *See also* Arche hemisy pantos.

C

c. *See* ca.

C.A. (Centroamérica). *Sp*—Central America.

c/a. (cuenta abierta). *Sp*—Open account.

ca. (circa). *L*—About; approximately.

C.-à-d. *See* C'est-à-dire.

C.A.F. (Coût, assurance, fret). *Fr*—Cost, insurance, freight. In English, C.I.F.

Cantab. (Cantabrigiensis). *L*—Pertaining to Cambridge, usually referring to Cambridge University.

c.a.v. *or* **cur. adv. vult** (curia advisari vult). *L*—The court wishes to take counsel.

c.c. (compte courant). *Fr*—Current account.

c.c. (courant continu). *Fr*—Direct electrical current; d.c. in English.

c/c *or* **c/cte.** (cuenta corriente). *Sp*—Current account.

C. de J. (Compañía de Jesús). *Sp*—Company of Jesus; S.J. in English, initials for *Societatis Jesus*, of the Society of Jesus.

C.d.G. (Compagnia di Gesù). *It*—Society of Jesus; S.J.

C.E.R.N. (Centre européen des recherches nucléaires). *Fr*—European Center for Nuclear Research.

cf. (confer). *L*—Consult.

C.G.I.L. (Confederazione generale italiana del lavoro). *It*—Federation of Italian Trade Unions.

C.G.T. (Confédération générale du travail). *Fr*—General Labor Confederation, the largest labor union in France.

cie. (compagnie). *Fr*—Company.

C.I.G. (Corpus Inscriptionum Graecarum). *L*—A collection of Greek inscriptions.

C.I.L. (Corpus Inscriptionum Latinarum). *L*—A collection of Latin inscriptions.

cir. *See* ca.

C.J.Can. (Corpus Juris Canonici). *L*—The body of canon law.

C.J.Civ. (Corpus Juris Civilis). *L*—The body of civil law.

c.n.s. (cras nocte sumendus). *L*—Medicine to be taken tomorrow night.

Cont. rem. (Continuetur remedium). *L*—Let the remedy be continued.

Coq. in s. a. (Coque in sufficiente aqua). *L*—Boil in sufficient water.

C.P.S. (Custos Privati Sigilli). *L*—Keeper of the Privy Seal.

C.R. *See* Custos Rotulorum.

C.S.C. (Congregatio Sanctae Crucis). *L*—Congregation of the Holy Cross.

C.S.Sp. (Congregatio Sancti Spiritus). *L*—Congregation of the Holy Spirit.

c.v. (cheval-vapeur). *Fr*—Horsepower.

CVP. (Corporación venezolana del petróleo). *Sp*—Venezuelan Petroleum Corporation.

Caballero andante. *Sp*—Knight errant.

Le cabaret est le salon du pauvre. *Fr*—The pub is the poor man's club.—*Gambetta*.

Cacoethes carpendi. *L*—A passion for criticizing.

Cacoethes loquendi. *L*—An uncontrollable desire or mania for talking.

Cacoethes scribendi. *L*—The writer's itch.—*Juvenal, VII, 52*.

Cada cabello faz sua sombra na terra. *Port*—Every hair casts its shadow. *See also* Etiam capillus unus . . . .

Cada cabello hace su sombra en el suelo. *Sp*—Every hair casts its own shadow on the ground. *See also* Etiam capillus unus . . . .

Cada maestro tiene su librito. *Sp*—Every teacher has his own little book, his own special methods.

Cada uno es hijo de sus obras. *Sp*—Every one is the product of his own works.—*Cervantes, Don Quixote, I, IV*.

Cada uno sabe donde le aprieta el zapato. *Sp*—Every man knows where his shoe pinches. *See also* Chacun sent . . . .

Cadit quaestio. *L*—The argument collapses; the argument is ended for want of proof.

Caelum, non animum mutant, qui trans mare currunt. *L*—They change the sky above but not their souls who rush overseas; you can't run away from yourself.—*Horace, Epistles, I, xi, 27*.

Café au lait. *Fr*—Coffee with about the same amount of milk added.

Ça-ira. *Fr*—It will go on. A popular song of the mob during the French Revolution. The burden of the song was that hanging aristocrats from lampposts would go on and on. *See also* À la lanterne.

Calceus major subvertit. *L*—A shoe too large trips the wearer. Often applied to enterprises or projects that fall part because they become too large and unmanageable.

Callida junctura

Callida junctura. *L*—Literally, an artistic joining; a clever literary reference in which an old familiar word is used in a novel setting.—*Horace, Art of Poetry, 47.*

Calvo turpius est nihil comato. *L*—There is nothing more dishonorable than a bald man with a wig.—*Martial, X, lxxxiii, 11.*

Camino real. *Sp*—The royal highway.

Cane scottato ha paura dell'acqua fredda. *It*—The scalded dog has fear of cold water; a burnt child dreads the fire.

Canimus surdis. *L*—We are singing to the deaf; we are preaching to deaf ears. A Roman proverb. It is used in the negative in *Vergil, Eclogues, X, 8.*

Canis in praesepi. *L*—Dog in the manger. A reference found in several literary sources, notably *Aesop 228.* Applied to the attitude of those who, even though they cannot benefit by something themselves, prevent others from enjoying it.

Canis timidus vehementius latrat quam mordet. *L*—A cowardly dog barks more than it bites.—Adapted from *Q. Curtius Rufus, Exploits of Alexander, VII, iv, 13.*

Cantabit vacuus coram latrone viator. *L*—The traveler with empty pockets will sing in the presence of a robber.—*Juvenal, X, 22.*

Cantus planus. *L*—Plain song; Gregorian chant.

Capa y espada. *Sp*—Cape and sword. Type of comedy, by Lope de Vega and Calderón, among others, characterized by involved plots in which love and honor (*see* punto de honor) are the central themes.

Cape et épée. *Fr*—Melodramatic literature in cloak and dagger style.

Capias. *L*—Literally, you may take; a writ ordering an arrest.

Capias ad satisfaciendum. *L*—You may seize to satisfy damages.

Caput gerat lupinum. *L*—Literally, let his be a wolf's head. In Old English law this meant that a man could be hunted down as if he were a wolf.

Caput mortuum. *L*—Literally, dead head; name alchemists gave to worthless material that remained after their experiments; by transfer, a worthless person.

Caput mundi. *L*—The head, the center of the world; a reference to imperial Rome that carried over to the papacy in medieval times.

Cara sposa. *It*—Dear wife.

La caridad bien entendida empieza por sí mismo. *Sp*—Charity, properly understood, begins with oneself; charity begins at home.

A caridade começa por casa. *Port*—Charity begins at home.

Caro sposo. *It*—Dear husband.

Carpe diem, quam minimum credula postero. *L*—Take advantage of today and place no trust in tomorrow.—*Horace, Odes, I, xi, 8.*

Carte blanche. *Fr*—A blank page with one's signature affixed, permitting the holder to write whatever he wishes; an unconditional surrender of one's rights; a blanket authorization.

Carte de visite. *Fr*—Visiting card.

Casa il figlio quando vuoi, e la figlia quando puoi. *It*—Marry your son when you wish, and your daughter when you can.

Cassis tutissima virtus. *L*—Courage is the safest helmet.

Casta est, quam nemo rogavit. *L*—She is chaste whom nobody has asked.—*Ovid, Amores, I, viii, 43.*

Castella in Hispania. *L*—Castles in Spain; castles in the air.

Castello che dà orecchia si vuol rendere. *It*—The castle that listens to proposals has a mind to surrender; the lady who listens is lost.

Castigat ridendo mores. *L*—He corrects morals by ridicule. Originally written as a tribute to a noted actor of comedy, this became the motto of the *Opéra Comique* of Paris.—*Jean de Santeul.*

Castigo te non quod odio habeam, sed quod amem. *L*—I chastise you not because I hate you but because I love you. An ancient preface to a flogging.

Casus belli. *L*—The occasion or pretext for war; the cause of war.

Casus conscientiae. *L*—A case of conscience.

Casus foederis. *L*—A case falling within the stipulations of a treaty.

Casus fortuitus. *L*—A matter of chance.

Catalogue raisonné. *Fr*—A catalogue of books or other articles in which each is described. A statement of value may also be added.

Causa finalis. *L*—Final cause; the purpose for which a thing is made.

Cause célèbre. *Fr*—A celebrated legal trial exciting wide interest.

Cavalier(e) errante. *It*—A knight errant.

Cavalier(e) servente. *It*—A serving cavalier; a married woman's lover; a lady's escort.

Cave ab homine unius libri. *L*—Beware of the man of one book. *See also* Timeo virum unius libri.

Caveat emptor. *L*—Let the buyer beware. This is all that is usually quoted. The full maxim continues, *Quia ignorare non debuit quod jus alienum emit*, meaning Because he should not be ignorant of the property that he is buying.

Caveat venditor. *L*—Let the seller beware.

Cave canem. *L*—Beware of the dog.

Cavendo tutus. *L*—Safe by reason of caution.

Cave quid dicis, quando et cui. *L*—Take care what you say, when, and to whom.

Céad míle fáilte! *Ir*—A hundred thousand welcomes!

Cedant arma togae. *L*—Let arms yield to the toga; let the military yield to the civil power. Motto of Wyoming.—*Cicero, On Duties, I, xxii, 77.*

Cela va sans dire. *Fr*—That goes without saying.

Celsae graviore casu decidunt turres. *L*—Lofty towers fall with a greater crash; the bigger they come, the harder they fall.

Celui qui a trouvé un bon gendre, a gagné un fils; mais celui qui en a rencontré un mauvais a perdu une fille. *Fr*—He who has found a good son-in-law has gained a son, but he who has picked up a bad one has lost a daughter.

Censor deputatus. *L*—A censor charged with the task of examining a book to determine before publication if it contains anything contrary to faith or morals.

Cepi corpus. *L*—Literally, I took the body. The endorsement of a sheriff upon a writ of arrest of a person.

Ce qui fait que les amants et les maîtresses ne s'ennuient point d'être ensemble, c'est qu'ils parlent toujours d'eux-mêmes. *Fr*—Lovers and mistresses keep from being bored when they are together because they always talk of themselves.—*La Rochefoucauld, Maxims, 312.*

Ce qui n'est pas clair, n'est pas français. *Fr*—If it is not clear, it is not French.

Certiorari. *L*—Literally, to be made more certain; a writ ordering a case transferred to a higher court.

C'est à dire. *Fr*—That is to say.

C'est dommage. *Fr*—It's a pity.

C'est double plaisir de tromper le trompeur. *Fr*—It is a double pleasure to deceive a deceiver.—*La Fontaine, Fables, II, 15.*

C'est égal. *Fr*—It's all the same.

C'est la guerre. *Fr*—Blame it on the war.

C'est la profonde ignorance qui inspire le ton dogmatique. *Fr*— The dogmatic manner is the child of profound ignorance.— *La Bruyère, Characters, Of Society, 76 (1), p. 177 in Garapon's edition (Garnier Frères, 1962).*

C'est la vie. *Fr*—That's life for you; that's the way life is.

C'est le dernier pas qui coûte. *Fr*—It is the last step that is difficult. Oliver Wendell Holmes would revise the proverb, *Il n'y a que le premier pas qui coûte (q.v.).*

C'est magnifique, mais ce n'est pas la guerre. *Fr*—It is magnificent but it is not war. A comment of the French general Bosquet on the disastrous charge of the Light Brigade at Balaclava.

C'est presque toujours la faute de celui qui aime de ne pas connaître quand on cesse de l'aimer. *Fr*—It is almost always the fault of the one who loves not to know when he is no longer loved.—*La Rochefoucauld, Maxims, 371.*

Cestui que (qui) trust (*pl.* Cestuis que trustent). *Anglo-Fr*— One who has interest in property legally vested in a trustee.

Cestui que use. *Anglo-Fr*—A person having the use of property held by another.

Cestui que vie. *Anglo-Fr*—A person whose life determines the duration of an estate.

C'est une grande habilité que de savoir cacher son habilité. *Fr* —It takes great skill to know how to conceal one's skill.—*La Rochefoucauld, Maxims, 245.*

C'est une tempête dans un verre d'eau. *Fr*—It is a tempest in a glass of water; a tempest in a teapot. Said of an insurrection in Geneva.—*Paul, Duke of Russia.*

Cetera desunt. *L*—The rest is missing. Found at the end of unfinished literary works or of ancient manuscripts, the endings of which have been lost.

Ceteris paribus. *L*—Other things being equal.

Ceux qui s'appliquent trop aux petites choses deviennent ordinairement incapables des grandes. *Fr*—Those who busy themselves too much with petty things ordinarily become incapable of great ones.—*La Rochefoucauld, Maxims, 41.*

Chacun à sa marotte. *Fr*—Everyone follows his fancy; everyone has some bee in his bonnet.

Chacun à son goût. *Fr*—Every man to his taste; there is no disputing tastes.

Chacun pour soi, et Dieu pour tous. *Fr*—Everybody for himself, and God for everyone.

Chacun selon ses facultés, à chacun selon ses besoins. *Fr*—Everyone should contribute according to his abilities and receive according to his needs. The ideal of a communistic society.—*Morelly, Code de la Nature,* as quoted in *Will Durant's The Story of Civilization, vol. X, p. 81.*

Chacun sent (sait) le mieux où le soulier le blesse. *Fr*—Each person knows best where his shoe hurts. *See also* Cada uno sabe . . . .

Chacun tire de son côté. *Fr*—Everybody pulls for his own side.

Chaire. *Gk*—Welcome; hail; farewell. A greeting either at meeting or parting.

Chaise longue. *Fr*—Literally, a long chair; a chair with an extension for the legs.

Chambres meublées. *Fr*—Furnished rooms.

Champs Elysées. *Fr*—Literally, Elysian Fields; a beautiful avenue in Paris.

Chanson de geste. *Fr*—In French literature an epic poem telling of the exploits of medieval knights. The most famous of these epics is *The Song of Roland.*

Chansons de toile. *Fr*—Songs sung by women as they spun. These medieval stories generally dealt with a maiden's love for a chevalier and the attendant frustrations.

Chant du cygne. *Fr*—Swan song; a final appearance or effort by an artist or public leader, often a farewell to the stage or public service. It is based on the legend that the swan, unmelodious in its life, sings beautifully just before its death.

Chapeaux bas! *Fr*—Hats off!

Chapelle ardente. *Fr*—Literally, a burning chapel, so called because of the great number of candles burning about a body lying in state.

Chaque heure je vous aime de plus en plus. *Fr*—Each hour I love you more and more. Inscription on a popular pendant, advertised as expressing a beautiful sentiment in romantic French. One wonders why the formal *vous* is used instead of the familiar *te*, here *t'*.

Chargé d'affaires. *Fr*—A temporary, duly accredited substitute for a high-ranking diplomat.

Chasseurs à cheval. *Fr*—Light cavalry.

Châteaux en Espagne. *Fr*—Castles in Spain; castles in the air.

Le chat qui dort. *Fr*—*See* Ne réveillez pas . . . .

Chef de cuisine. *Fr*—Head cook.

Chef d'œuvre. *Fr*—Masterpiece.

Cheka (Two initial letters, che and ka, of the words *Chrezvychainaia Kommissiia*). *Rus*—Extraordinary Commission. Soviet secret police replaced by OGPU *(q.v.)* in 1922.

Chercher midi à quatorze heures. *Fr*—To find difficulties where there are none.

Cherchez la femme. *Fr*—Look for the woman in the case.—*Alexandre Dumas, père.*

Chère amie. *Fr*—Literally, a dear friend *(f)*; frequently, a mistress.

Che sarà sarà. *It*—What will be, will be.

Chi fa il conto

Cheval de bataille. *Fr*—A war horse; generally used in the sense of a topic that a person rides to death.

Chevalier d'industrie. *Fr*—A swindler; a man who lives by his wits.

Le cheval volant qui a les narines de feu. *Fr*—The flying horse that breathes fire from its nostrils. A reference to Pegasus, the winged horse.

Chez nous. *Fr*—At our home.

Chi ama, crede. *It*—He who loves, trusts.

Chi ama me, ama il mio cane. *It*—Love me, love my dog.

Chi ascolta alla porta, ode il suo danno. *It*—The man who eavesdrops hears nothing good about himself.

Chiave d'oro apre ogni porta. *It*—A key of gold opens any door.

Chi ben vive, ben predica. *It*—He gives a good sermon who lives a good life. *See also* Bien predica . . . .

Chi compra il magistrato, forza è che venda la giustizia. *It*—He who buys public office is obligated to sell justice.

Chi dice i fatti suoi, mal tacerà quelli d'altrui. *It*—The man who talks about his private affairs will hardly keep the business of others secret.

Chi dorme coi cani, si sveglia colle pulci. *It*—The man who sleeps with dogs wakes up with fleas.

Le chien retourne à son vomissement, et la truie lavée au bourbier. *Fr*—The dog returns to his vomit, and the washed sow to its mire. Said of the fool who repeats his folly.—Translation of *Vulgate, II Peter, II, 22*.

Chiesa libera in libero stato. *It*—A free church in a free state. —*Cavour*.

Chi fa il conto senza l'oste, gli convien farlo (lo fa) due volte. *It*—Those who reckon without their host must reckon twice.

Chi ha denti

Chi ha denti, non ha pane; e chi ha pane, non ha denti. *It*— The man who has teeth has no bread, and he who has bread has no teeth.

Chi la dura la vince. *It*—The man who endures wins; patience overcomes any hardship.

Chi lo sa? *It*—Who knows?

Chimaera bombinans in vacuo. *L*—A monster buzzing in a vacuum. The chimaera was a mythological animal with a lion's head, a goat's body, and a dragon's tail; hence, a fanciful being. The phrase may be used contemptuously of a system or project that is supported by much oratory but is out of touch with the times.

Chi molte cose comincia, poche ne finisce. *It*—The man who begins many things finishes few of them.

Chi niente sa, di niente dubita. *It*—An ignoramus has doubts about nothing.

Chi non ama il vino, la donna, e il canto/Un pazzo egli sarà e mai un santo. *It*—He who does not love wine, woman, and song will be a fool but never a saint. For the German of this conviction, *see* Wer liebt nicht Weib, Wein und Gesang . . . .

Chi non fa, non falla. *It*—The man who does nothing makes no mistakes.

Chi non ha danari in borsa, abbia miel in bocca. *It*—The man who has no money in his purse needs honey in his mouth.

Chi non rompe l'uova, non fa la frittata. *It*—If you want an omelette, you must break some eggs. *See also* On ne saurait faire . . . .

Chi non sa adulare, non sa regnare. *It*—The man who does not know how to flatter, does not know how to rule.

Chi si scusa senz' esser accusato, fa chiaro il suo peccato. *It*— He who excuses himself before being accused confesses his fault.

Chi tace acconsente. *It*—Silence gives consent.

Chi tace confessa. *It*—The man who keeps silent confesses his guilt.

Chi t'ha offeso non ti perdona mai. *It*—The man who has offended you will never forgive you.

Chi troppo abbraccia, poco stringe. *It*—He who tries to seize too much lays hold of little.

Chi va al mulino, s'infarina. *It*—If you go to the mill, you will be covered with flour; he that toucheth pitch shall be defiled therewith.

Chi va piano, va sano e va lontano. *It*—He who travels slowly, goes surely and far.

Chi vuol il lavoro mal fatto, paghi innanzi tratto. *It*—If you wish work badly done, pay in advance.

Chronique scandaleuse. *Fr*—A work revealing scandalous details; shocking gossip.

Ci-devant. *Fr*—Former; formerly. As a noun, it refers to an aristocrat stripped of his rank and prerogatives at the time of the French Revolution.

Ci-gît. *Fr*—Here lies. Beginning of the record written on a tombstone.

Cineri gloria sera venit. *L*—Fame is tardy when it comes to a man's ashes.—*Martial, Epigrams, I, xxv, 8.*

Circuitus verborum. *L*—A circumlocution; a beating about the bush.

Circulus in probando. *L*—Using a conclusion as a premise in an argument; a vicious circle. *See also* Circulus vitiosus.

Circulus vitiosus. *L*—A vicious circle. *See also* Circulus in probando.

Citius venit periculum cum contemnitur. *L*—Danger comes sooner when it is ignored.

Civilitas successit barbarum. *L*—Civilization has replaced the barbarian. Motto of Minnesota when it was a territory.

Civiliter mortuus. *L*—Civilly dead, i.e. legally in a state equivalent to being naturally dead in so far as one's legal rights are concerned.

Civis Romanus sum. *L*—I am a Roman citizen. This boast lost its force when Caracalla gave citizenship to practically all his subjects.—*Cicero, Against Verres, V, LVII.*

Civitas optimo jure. *L*—A community allied to ancient Rome and enjoying full rights.

Civitas sine suffragio. *L*—A community allied to Rome without enjoying voting rights.

Civitates foederatae. *L*—States allied by treaty to ancient Rome.

Civitates liberae et immunes. *L*—Communities free and exempt from taxes in the ancient Roman state.

Civium in moribus rei publicae salus. *L*—The safety of the republic rests on the morals of the citizens. Words on the University of Florida seal.

Clarum et venerabile nomen. *L*—A famous and venerable name. Words originally written about Pompey.—*Lucan, Pharsalia, IX, 199.*

Cloaca maxima. *L*—The largest sewer in ancient Rome.

La codicia rompe el saco. *Sp*—Avarice breaks the sack.—*Cervantes, Don Quixote, I, XX.*

Coeptis ingentibus adsis. *L*—Aid these great beginnings.—*Vergil, Aeneid, X, 461.*

Le cœur a ses raisons que la raison ne connaît pas. *Fr*—The heart has its reasons, of which Reason knows nothing. The first part of this served as the title of a well-known book by the Duchess of Windsor.—*Pascal, Thoughts, IV, 277.*

Cogito, ergo sum. *L*—I think; hence I exist. Advanced by Descartes as *a priori* proof of one's existence.—*Descartes, Discourse on Method, IV.*

Cognovit actionem. *L*—He has acknowledged the action; the defendant confesses that the plaintiff's cause of action is just.

Colleen bawn (English spelling of *Cailín bán*). *Ir*—A fair-haired girl.

Comédie de mœurs. *Fr*—Comedy of manners.

La **Comédie Humaine.** *Fr*—The Human Comedy, the title Balzac gave to his unfinished series of works depicting French society in his day.

La **comédie larmoyante.** *Fr*—Literally, tearful comedy; a tear-jerker. Sentimental domestic theatre of eighteenth century France.

Comes facundus in via pro vehiculo est. *L*—A pleasant, chatty companion on a trip is worth as much as the coach.—*Publilius Syrus.*

Come sopra. *It*—As above.

Como fogo não se brinca. *Port*—One does not play with fire.

Comitas inter gentes. *L*—Comity of nations; courtesy between nations.

Comitia centuriata. *L*—Assembly of the Roman people voting by centuries, of which there were 193 in the early Republic. The century originally numbered a hundred, but later it might number fewer voters.

Comme ci, comme ça. *Fr*—So-so.

Comme deux gouttes d'eau. *Fr*—As much alike as two drops of water; as like as two peas in a pod.

Commedia dell' arte. *It*—Improvised dramatic comedy representing stock characters.

La **commedia è finita.** *It*—The comedy is over; closing line of *I Pagliacci.*

Comme il faut. *Fr*—As it should be; proper.

Comment ça va

Comment ça va? *Fr*—How are you? Popular usage may omit *Comment.*

Comme on fait son lit, on se couche. *Fr*—You must lie on the bed you make.

Comment prétendons-nous qu'un autre garde notre secret, si nous ne pouvons le garder nous-mêmes? *Fr*—How can we require others to keep our secrets, if we cannot keep them ourselves? —*La Rochefoucauld, Maxims, 584.*

Commis voyageur. *Fr*—Commercial traveler.

Communibus annis. *L*—In average years.

Compagnon de voyage. *Fr*—A traveling companion.

Le comparazioni sono tutte odiose. *It*—All comparisons are odious.

Compte rendu. *Fr*—An account rendered; report of proceedings.

Con amore. *It*—With love.

Conatus sese preservandi. *L*—The effort to preserve oneself; the will to live.

Concerto grosso. *It*—A performance of a small group of soloists playing against a much larger group or a full orchestra.

Concordia discors. *L*—Dissonant harmony; a cold war; an armed truce; a feigned friendship.—*Lucan, Pharsalia, I, 98.*

Con diligenza. *It*—With diligence.

La condition humaine. *Fr*—The human situation.

Con dolore. *It*—Mournfully.

Con furia. *It-Sp*—With fury; with mad haste.

Congé d'élire. *Fr*—Permission to elect a bishop granted to a chapter in the Anglican Church. This is generally referred to as a mere formality since the appointments are made by the Crown.

Congregatio de Propaganda Fide. *L*—Congregation for Propagation of the Faith; a division of the Curia of the Roman Catholic Church.

Conjunctis viribus. *L*—With strength united.

Con molta passione. *It*—With much passion. A musical term.

Conseil de famille. *Fr*—Family council.

Conseil d'état. *Fr*—Council of state.

Conseils aux visiteurs étrangers. *Fr*—Advice for foreign visitors.

Consejo a los visitantes extranjeros. *Sp*—Advice to foreign visitors.

Consiglio europeo per le ricerche nucleari. *It*—European Council for Nuclear Research.

Consensus facit legem. *L*—Mutual consent makes the law. When two parties freely agree, the terms, if they do not violate the law, are no longer a matter of legal concern.

Consilio melius vinces (vincas) quam iracundia. *L*—You win more easily by planning than by anger.—*Publilius Syrus.*

Consilium abeundi. *L*—Advice to leave. A suggestion that a scholar cannot make passing grades.

Consuetudo fit altera natura. *L*—Habit becomes second nature.

Consuetudo pro lege servatur. *L*—Custom is to be held as a law, if no specific law exists. Legal maxim.

Consultum ultimum. *L*—*See* Videant consules . . . .

Consummatum est. *L*—It is finished. The last words spoken by Christ from the cross.—*Vulgate, John, XIX, 30.*

Con svantaggio grande si fa la guerra con chi non ha che perdere. *It*—One fights at a great disadvantage with those who have nothing to lose.—*Guicciardini, History of Italy.*

Conti chiari, amici cari. *It*—Good accounts make good friends. For the French equivalent *see* Les bons comptes . . . .

Conticuere omnes, intentique ora tenebant. *L*—All grew silent and waited in eager expectation.—*Vergil, Aeneid, II, 1.*

Contra bonos mores. *L*—Against good morals.

Contra fortuna

Contra fortuna no vale arte ninguna. *Sp*—There is no armor against fate.

Contra mundum. *L*—Against the whole world. Said of anybody who is willing to take on the whole world to bring about conditions in which he believes. Said of the younger Cato, who opposed Caesar, and also of Athanasius, who was exiled five times but kept fighting Arianism.

Copia verborum. *L*—Torrent of words; fluency.

Coram nobis. *L*—In our presence.

Coram non judice. *L*—Before a person not a judge and therefore one having no jurisdiction in the case.

Coram populo. *L*—Before the people; in public. Horace uses the expression in warning the dramatist not to stage murders or other horrors.—*Horace, Art of Poetry, 185.*

Coram publico. *L*—Before the public.

Cordon bleu. *Fr*—Blue ribbon; decoration formerly worn by different orders of knights; a general decoration for distinction in one's field; sometimes, in a light vein, an award for cooking.

Cordon sanitaire. *Fr*—Sanitary cordon; a line of officials charged with preventing the spread of contagion.

Cormach MacCarthy fortis me fieri facit, A.D. 1446. *L*—The brave Cormach MacCarthy caused me to be made, 1446 A.D. The inscription on the Blarney Stone, at Blarney Castle, not far from Cobh, Ireland.

Cor ne edito. *L*—Do not eat your heart; better share your troubles with a friend.—*Pythagoras.*

Corpo di Bacco! *It*— Body of Bacchus. A mild expletive such as Good heavens! *or* What the deuce!

Corps de ballet. *Fr*—Ballet company.

Corps de bâtiment. *Fr*—The main building.

Corps de logis. *Fr*—The main portion of a building.

Corpus Christi. *L*—Literally, the body of Christ; a festival cele-brated in the Roman Catholic Church on the Thursday after Trinity Sunday. In some countries there are processions in the open air in which the priest carries the consecrated host. In the Middle Ages dramas were presented by the trade guilds on this feast.

Corpus delicti. *L*—The basic facts necessary to prove the existence of crime, such as catching a thief with stolen goods, or proof in a murder trial of the actual death of the victim. It does not mean the body of the victim.

Corpus Juris Canonici. *L*—Code of canon law.

Corpus Juris Civilis. *L*—The body of civil law. The collection of Roman laws made under Justinian.

Corpus juris clausum. *L*—A collection of laws to which no new ones may be added.

Corrida de toros. *Sp*—A bull fight.

Corrigenda. *L*—A list of errors to be corrected, inserted in a book after it has been printed. Equivalent to *errata (q.v.)*.

Corrumpunt bonos mores colloquia mala. *L*—Evil communica-tions corrupt good manners.—*Vulgate, Paul, I Corinthians, XV,* 33. This is a translation from *Menander. See* Phtheirousin ethe . . . .

Corruptio optimi pessima. *L*—The corruption of the best man is the worst.

Corruptissima in republica plurimae leges. *L*—The more corrupt the state, the more numerous the laws.—*Tacitus, Annals, III,* 27.

Corva sinistra. *L*—A crow on the left; an evil omen.

Cosa nostra. *It*—Our affair; our business; the name of a secret underworld society, according to testimony presented before a Senate crime investigation committee in 1963.

Cosa rara. *It-Sp*—A rare thing.

Così così

Così così. *It*—So-so.

Così fan tutte. *It*—That's what all women do. Mozart wrote the
music for an *opera buffa* with this title.

Così fan tutti. *It*—That's what all men do.

La Costa Brava. *Sp*—Literally, the wild coast; an area in north-
eastern Spain from the town of Blanes to the French border.

Coup de bourse. *Fr*—A successful deal on the stock exchange.

Coup d'éclat. *Fr*—A shattering blow; a brilliant stroke.

Coup de foudre. *Fr*—Flash of lightning; bolt from the blue.

Coup de grâce. *Fr*—A merciful shot intended to put a wounded
man out of his misery (the classic example is that of the officer
who puts a bullet into the head of a man still living in spite
of shots from a firing squad); a finishing stroke.

Coup de main. *Fr*—A sudden attack or undertaking; a bold stroke.

Coup de maître. *Fr*—A master stroke; a show of skill.

Coup d'épée. *Fr*—A sword thrust.

Coup de pied de l'âne. *Fr*—A kick from the hoof of an ass (a
reference to the story in *Aesop 23* in which the ass kicked a
sick lion). This is applied to kicking a man when he is down.

Coup de plume. *Fr*—A stroke of the pen; by extension this may
be a satire or a fierce attack.

Coup de soleil. *Fr*—A sunstroke.

Coup d'essai. *Fr*—A first attempt.

Coup d'état. *Fr*—A sudden, unexpected overturning of the government of a state usually involving force or the threat of
force.

Coup de tête. *Fr*—Rash or impulsive act.

Coup de théâtre. *Fr*—An unexpected, sensational act or turn of
events.

Coup d'œil. *Fr*—A swift glance.

Le courage est souvent un effet de la peur. *Fr*—Courage is often born of fear.

Courage sans peur. *Fr*—Courage without fear.

Cour des comptes. *Fr*—Audit office.

Coureur de bois. *Fr*—A French trapper working in the Canadian woods who traded with Indians for furs.

Le coût en ôte le goût. *Fr*—The cost spoils the flavor.

Coûte que coûte. *Fr*—No matter the cost.

Crambe repetita. *L*—Warmed-over cabbage; a harping on the same theme.—*Juvenal, VII, 154. See also* Dis krambe . . . .

Cras amet qui numquam amavit, quique amavit cras amet. *L*—Let those love now, who never loved before/ And those who always loved, now love the more.—*The Vigil of Venus* translation of Thomas Parnell.

Crassa negligentia. *L*—Culpable negligence.

Credat Judaeus Apella; non ego. *L*—Let the Jew Apella believe it; I don't. The Romans considered the Jews exceedingly superstitious.—*Horace, Satires, I, v, 100.*

Credat qui vult. *L*—Let whoever wishes believe.

Credebant hoc grande nefas et morte piandum,/ Si juvenis vetulo non assurrexerat. *L*—They used to believe that it was great wickedness, one that should be expiated in death, if a youth did not rise in the presence of the aged.—*Juvenal, XIII, 54.*

Crede experto. *L*—*See* Experto credite.

Crede ut intelligas. *L*—Believe that you may understand.

Credo quia impossibile (absurdum) est. *L*—I believe because it is impossible. An expression frequently cited out of its context where it appears in a series of paradoxes.—*Tertullian, On the Body of Christ, V.*

Credo ut intelligam. *L*—I believe in order that I may understand. A dictum proclaiming the superiority of faith over reason.—*Anselm.*

Credula res amor est. *L*—Love is a credulous thing.—*Ovid, Metamorphoses, VII, 826.*

Crème de la crème. *Fr*—The cream of the cream; the very best; the cream of the crop.

Crescat scientia, vita excolatur. *L*—May knowledge increase and life be ennobled. Motto of the University of Chicago.

Crescit amor nummi, quantum ipsa pecunia crescit. *L*—The love of money increases as the pile grows. The best texts of the original use *crevit*, the perfect tense, instead of *crescit*, the present.—*Juvenal, XIV, 139.*

Crescite et multiplicamini. *L*—Increase and multiply. Motto of Maryland.—*Vulgate, Genesis, I, 28.*

Crescit eundo. *L*—It grows as it goes. Motto of New Mexico.

Creta an carbone notandum? *L*—Is it to be marked with chalk or charcoal? The Romans noted a lucky day with chalk, an unlucky day with charcoal. This is adapted from a passage in which the poet asks if extravagant men should be listed with chalk as sound of mind or with charcoal as mad men.—*Horace, Satires, II, iii 246.*

Cri du cœur. *Fr*—A heartfelt cry of anguish.

La critique est aisée, et l'art est difficile. *Fr*—Criticizing is easy, but art is difficult.—*Destouches, Glorieux, II, 5.*

Croix de guerre. *Fr*—A decoration given for exceptional bravery or service in war.

Crux ansata. *L*—The cross with a hilt. The title of a work by H. G. Wells.

Crux criticorum. *L*—A puzzle for critics.

Crux interpretum. *L*—An especially difficult passage for translators.

Crux mathematicorum. *L*—A puzzle for mathematicians.

Cuando a Roma fueres, haz como vieres. *Sp*—When in Rome, do as the Romans do.—*Cervantes, Don Quixote, II, LIV.*

Cucullus non facit monachum. *L*—The cowl does not make the monk. For a reverse maxim *see* Vestis virum facit.

Cuéntaselo a tu abuela. *Sp*—Tell that to your grandmother.

Cui bono? *L*—For whose good? It is incorrectly used as meaning, What's the use of it? *or* What good end will be served?

¡Cuidado! *Sp*—Watch out; take care.

Cuidado con el tren. *Sp*—Watch out for the train.

Cui malo? *L*—Who will be harmed?

Cui peccare licet, peccat minus. *L*—He who is free to sin, sins less.—*Ovid, Amores, III, iv, 9.*

Cujus est regio, illius est religio. *L*—Whoever governs the region controls the religion. The maxim of countries that have a state religion.

Cujus est solum, ejus est usque ad caelum. *L*—He who owns the ground, owns up to the sky. Legal maxim.

Cul-de-sac. *Fr*—Blind alley; dead end; passage with only one outlet.

Culpa lata. *L*—A fault involving gross negligence.

Culpa levissima. *L*—A very slight fault.

Culpam majorum posteri luunt. *L*—Descendants pay for the shortcomings of their ancestors; children pay for the sins of their fathers.—Adapted from *Q. Curtius Rufus, The Exploits of Alexander, VII, 5, 35.*

Culpam poena premit comes. *L*—Punishment follows at the heels of crime.—*Horace, Odes, IV, v, 24.*

Cum grano salis. *L*—With a grain of salt; to be taken with reservations.

Cum inimico nemo in gratiam tuto redit. *L*—Nobody safely returns into favor with an enemy.—*Publilius Syrus.*

67

Cum laude. *L*—With praise; a phrase appearing on diplomas indicating better than average scholarship. *Magna cum laude*, with great praise is a grade higher, while *summa cum laude* indicates the highest performance.

Cum licet fugere, ne quaere litem. *L*—When you can get off, do not seek a contest with the law.

Cum privilegio ad imprimendum solum. *L*—The privilege of exclusive right to publication.

Cum tacent, clamant. *L*—When they are silent, they shout. Cicero in denouncing Catiline says that the listening senators show their disapproval of their colleague by their silence, whereas if he brought such charges against certain worthy men, the Senate would have laid violent hands upon him. This is an excellent example of the figure of speech called oxymoron.—*Cicero, I Against Catiline, VIII, 21.*

Cunctando restituit rem. *L*—*See* Unus homo nobis cunctando . . . .

Cura animarum. *L*—The care of souls.

Curia advisari vult. *LL*—The court wishes to be advised; the court needs time to deliberate.

Curia regis. *L*—The king's court.

Curiosa felicitas. *L*—A felicity of expression that is the result of careful, studied effort to find the right phrasing. Applied to the style of Horace.—*Petronius, Satyricon, CXVIII, 5.*

Currente calamo. *L*—A free style; a facile pen.

Curriculum vitae. *L*—Biographical data including items of interest to an employer, such as education and experience.

Currus bovem trahit praepostere. *L*—The wagon drags the ox behind it; to put the cart before the horse.

Cursus honorum. *L*—Course of honors; a succession of offices held by the public servant in Rome and separated by the proper intervals.

Cushla machree, mavourneen. *Ir*—Pulse of my heart, my darling.

Custos Brevium. *L*—Keeper of the Briefs; an officer in the old English Court of Common Pleas in charge of documents.

Custos morum. *L*—A censor of morals.

Custos Privati Sigilli. *L*—Keeper of the Privy Seal.

Custos Rotulorum. *L*—Keeper of the Rolls; in England the principal justice of the peace in a county who was charged with the custody of rolls and records.

Custos Sigilli. *L*—Keeper of the Seal.

Cymini (cumini) sectores. *L*—Cutters of cumin seed, which is very small; hence, hairsplitters or quibblers.

D

D.C. *See* Da capo.

D.C. (Democrazia Cristiana). *It*—Party of Christian Democrats.

d/c. (dinero contante). *Sp*—Cash.

d.C. (dopo Cristo). *It.*—A.D. *(q.v.)*.

DD. (dedicavit). *L*—He dedicated.

D.d. (Deo dedit). *L*—He gave to God.

D.D. (Doctor Divinitatis). *L*—Doctor of Divinity.

d.d. (dono dedit). *L*—He gave as a gift.

D.D.D. (Dono dat, dedicat.). *L*—He gives as a gift and dedicates. Sometimes this is understood in the past tense: *Dono dedit, dedicavit.* **D.D.D.** is also interpreted as *Dat, dicat, dedicat:* He gives, devotes and dedicates; also *dat, donat, dicat:* He gives, presents and dedicates.

D. ès L. (Docteur ès Lettres). *Fr*—Doctor of Letters.

D. ès S. (Docteur ès Sciences). *Fr*—Doctor of Sciences.

D.F. *See* Defensor Fidei.

D.F. (distrito federal). *Sp*—Federal District.

D.G. (Dei gratia). *L*—By the grace of God.

dieb. alt. (diebus alternis). *L*—Every other day. A medical direction.

dig. (digeratur). *L*—Let it be digested. A medical direction.

Dipl.-Ing. (Diplom-Ingenieur). *Ger*—Fully accredited engineer.

dir. prop. (directione propria). *L*—With a proper direction.

D. Jur. et Rer. Pol. (Doctor Juris et Rerum Politicarum). *L*—Doctor of Law and Politics.

DM. (Deutsche Mark). *Ger*—German mark.

D.M.P. (Docteur en Médecine de la faculté de Paris). *Fr*—Doctor of Medicine, Paris.

DNB (Deutsches Nachrictenbüro). *Ger*—German News Agency.

D.N.P.P. (Dominus Noster Papa Pontifex). *L*—Our Lord the Supreme Pontiff.

D.O.M. (Deo Optimo Maximo). *L*—To the Supreme Deity.

D.P. (Domus Procerum). *L*—The House of Lords.

DRP (Deutsches Reichspatent). *Ger*—German patent.

Dr. phil. (Doctor philosophiae). *L*—Ph.D., Doctor of philosophy.

D.s.p. *See* Decessit sine prole.

D.V. (Deo volente). *L*—God willing.

Dabit deus his quoque finem. *L*—God will put an end to these troubles, too.—*Vergil, Aeneid, I, 199.*

Da camera. *It*—Referring to music written for a small room; hence, chamber music.

Da capo. *It*—In a musical score, a direction to return to the beginning and repeat a passage.

Da capo al fine. *It*—From the beginning to the end; a direction in a music score.

Da chi mi fido, mi guardi Iddio: da chi non mi fido mi guarderò io. *It*—From those I trust, may God protect me; from those I do not trust, I will protect myself.

Daemon meridianus. *L*—The mid-day devil, who reportedly tempted the monks of the desert when the sun was hottest.

Dail Eireann. *Ir*—House of Representatives in the *Oireachtas*, the Irish Parliament.

Dal detto al fatto vi è un gran tratto. *It*—It's a long haul from words to deeds.

Dalla mano alla bocca si perde la zuppa. *It*—The soup is lost from the hand to the mouth; there's many a slip 'twixt the cup and the lip.

Dalla rapa non si cava sangue. *It*—You cannot get blood out of a turnip.

Da locum melioribus. *L*—Give place to your betters.—*Terence, Phormio, III, 2, 37.*

Dame d'honneur. *Fr*—Maid of honor; lady-in-waiting.

Dames de la halle. *Fr*—Market women.

Damnant quod non intelligunt. *L*—They damn what they do not understand. Adapted from *Quintilian, X, i, 26.*

Damnosa hereditas. *L*—An inheritance damaging because of consequent obligations.

Damnum absque injuria. *L*—Loss without legal wrong; damage done without intended wrong.

Danke schön. *Ger*—Thank you.

Danse macabre. *Fr*—A ghoulish dance, the dance of death. A popular theme starting with a fourteenth century morality play. In subsequent art and verse, Death was often pictured as leading men of various stations of life to the grave. Saint-Saëns has a composition inspired by this theme.

71

Dans l'amour

Dans l'amour il y a toujours celui qui baise et celui qui tend la joue. *Fr*—In love there is always one who gives the kiss and one who extends the cheek. The cynical attitude that in love one person loves and the other suffers himself to be loved.

Dans le doute, abstiens-toi. *Fr*—When in doubt, don't.

Dare pondus idonea fumo. *L*—Useful only to give weight to smoke. An expression used in hostile criticism of a book.— *Persius, V, 20.*

Darne consiglio/Spesso non sa chi vuole,/Spesso non vuol chi sa. *It*—Often those who do not know are ready to give counsel, while those who do know are unwilling.—*Metastasio.*

Das ist mir Wurst oder Wurscht. *Ger*—That's all the same to me; I am indifferent. The North and South German pronunciations of the word for sausage.

Data et accepta. *L*—Expenses and receipts.

Davus sum, non Oedipus. *L*—I am Davus, not Oedipus; I am a simple man, not a problem solver.—*Terence, Andria, II, 24.*

Debitor non praesumitur donare. *L*—The presumption is that a debtor is not making gifts.

De bon augure. *Fr*—Auspicious; an event of good omen.

De bonis propriis. *L*—Out of his own goods; payment made from his own funds.

De bonne grâce. *Fr*—With good grace.

De bons propositos está o inferno cheio. *Port*—Hell is paved with good intentions. *See* Di buona voluntà . . . .

Deceptio visus. *L*—Optical illusion.

Decessit sine prole. *L*—He died without issue.

Decies repetita placebit. *L*—In its original context this means that even though a painting is seen ten times, it is still a pleasing picture; by extension, even though a story has been told ten times, it is still a good one.—*Horace, Art of Poetry, 365.*

Decipimur specie recti. *L*—We are deceived by what appears virtuous; crime often masks as virtue.

Decipit frons prima multos. *L*—The first appearance deceives many; first appearances are often deceiving.—*Phaedrus, IV, ii, 6.*

De Civitate Dei. *L*—*On the City of God*, a work written by Augustine of Hippo in answer to those who claimed that the invasions of the barbarians were punishment by the gods for the neglect of the pagan religion.

De Consolatione Philosophiae. *L*—*The Consolation of Philosophy*, a work by Boethius, who flourished in the first quarter of the sixth century.

Decori decus addit avito. *L*—He adds honor to the honors of his ancestors.

De die in diem. *L*—From day to day.

De droit. *Fr*—By right; rightfully.

De duobus malis semper minus malum est eligendum. *L*—Of two evils one ought always to choose the lesser.—*Thomas à Kempis, Imitation of Christ, III, xii, 2. See also* Minima ex malis.

De facto. *L*—In fact; actually; as a matter of fact, but not necessarily *de jure (q.v.).*

De fait. *Fr*—Truly; in reality. As opposed to *de droit*, in law or by legal right.

Défauts de ses qualités. *Fr*—*See* Il a les défauts . . . .

Défense de —. *Fr*—One is forbidden to —. This is followed by an infinitive, e.g., *Défense d'afficher*, Post no bills; *Défense d'entrer*, Keep out; *Défense de fumer*, No smoking.

Defensor Fidei. *L*—Defender of the Faith. This title on British coins was conferred by Pope Leo X on Henry VIII for his Latin tract on the Seven Sacraments.

De fide. *L*—A matter of faith; said of Catholic dogmas that may not be questioned by the faithful.

De fond

De fond en comble. *Fr*—From top to bottom.

De fontibus non disputandum. *L*—There is no disputing about sources. This is to be understood in areas where science has no definite knowledge, as, for example, the beginning of human speech.

De gaieté de cœur. *Fr*—From cheerfulness of heart; out of sheer gaiety.

D'égal à égal. *Fr*—Equally.

Dégénéré supérieur. *Fr*—A person of superior mental ability with degenerate tendencies.

De gran subida, gran caída. *Sp*—The higher the height, the longer the fall; the bigger they come, the harder they fall.

De gustibus non est disputandum. *L*—There is no disputing about tastes. Different people have different tastes in matters of food and drink; arguing will not change anyone's taste buds. By extension this saying is often applied to matters intellectual and esthetic.

De haute lutte. *Fr*—By force of arms; after a great struggle.

De haut en bas. *Fr*—Downwards; from top to bottom; disdainfully.

Dei gratia. *L*—By the grace of God.

Dei gusti non se ne disputa. *It*—*See* De gustibus non est disputandum.

Dei judicium. *L*—The judgment of God. This was the name given to the ordeal, sometimes of fire or of water; a superstitious method of determining guilt by exposing a person to serious bodily harm or even death. If he survived he was considered innocent.

De integro. *L*—Beginning anew.

De internis non judicat praetor. *L*—The court does not pass judgment on a defendant's intentions. "I didn't mean to do it" is not regarded as an excuse in court.

Dei plena sunt omnia. *L*—All things are filled with divinity.

Déjà vécu. *Fr*—An impression that something has been experienced previously.

Déjà vu. *Fr*—Literally, already seen. Sometimes applied to a mental disorder in which a person imagines he has seen certain scenes or events before. Art critics sometimes dismiss a work with this phrase.

De jure. *L*—Rightfully; legally. It often appears in the same context with *De facto (q.v.)*.

De la mano a la boca se pierde la sopa. *Sp*—*See* Dalla mano alla bocca . . . .

De lana caprina. *L*—The subject concerns goat's wool; a discussion on a matter of no importance.

Delator temporis acti. *L*—An accuser of the past. A pun on *Laudator temporis acti (q.v.)*.

De l'audace, encore de l'audace, toujours de l'audace. *Fr*—Boldness, more boldness, always boldness.—*Danton*.

Del credere. *It*—Of trust. A legal term applied to an agent who, for an extra charge, undertakes to bring about payment for goods which he has sold.

Del dicho al hecho hay gran trecho. *Sp*—There is a big gap between saying and doing.

Delenda est Carthago. *L*—Carthage must be destroyed. The final words of speeches given by Cato the Elder in the Roman senate. Often written: *Ceterum censeo Carthaginem esse delendam,* As for the rest I think Carthage must be destroyed.

Deliberando saepe perit occasio. *L*—Opportunity is often lost by too long debate.—*Publilius Syrus*.

Deliciae epularum. *L*—The delight, the pleasurable items of the banquet.

Deliciae generis humani. *L*—The delight of the human race. Suetonius' tribute to the Emperor Titus, who won general

esteem because of his talent, personality, and good fortune.—
Suetonius, Titus, I.

Deliciae meae puellae. *L*—The delight of my girl. From a poem
to Lesbia's sparrow.—*Catullus, II, 1.*

Delirant reges, plectuntur Achivi. *L*—Kings make mistakes, and
the Greeks (the people) are punished.—*Horace, Epistles, I, ii,
14.*

Delirium tremens. *L*—Mental disorder, characterized by uncontrollable trembling, climaxing excessive consumption of alco-
hol. Often referred to as the d.t.'s.

Delle ingiurie il remedio è lo scordarsi. *It*—The remedy for
wrongs done you is to forget them.

Del senno di poi n'è piena ogni fossa. *It*—Every ditch is full of
the wisdom that came too late. We speak of twenty-twenty
hindsight and Monday morning's quarterback.

De lunatico inquirendo. *L*—A commission appointed by a court
to determine the mental competence of a person.

De luxe. *Fr*—Literally, of luxury; applied to a product that is
elegant or sumptuous. *See* Edition de luxe.

De mal en pis. *Fr*—From bad to worse.

De mémoire de rose, on n'a jamais vu mourir de jardinier. *Fr*—
You have never seen a gardener die of nostalgia for roses.—
Stendhal, Histoire de la Peinture, vol. II, chap. 52. Perhaps a
conscious contradiction of Pope's "Die of a rose in aromatic
pain."—*Essay on Man, I, 200.*

Dementia praecox. *L*—Early insanity; mental disorder beginning in adolescence; now commonly called schizophrenia.

Dementia senilis. *L*—Insanity of the aged.

Le demi-monde. *Fr*—The world of women who live on the
fringes of respectability.

De minimis non curat lex. *L*—The law is not concerned with
trifles.

Demi-tasse. *Fr*—Literally, half a cup; a small cup.

De mortuis nil nisi bonum. *L*—Say nothing but what is good about the dead.

I denari del comune sono come l'acqua benedetta, ognun ne piglia. *It*—Public funds are like holy water, everybody takes some.

Denarius Dei. *L*—God's penny; a small sum of money given by the purchaser to make a contract of sale valid. In French it is known as the *Denier à Dieu*.

De nihilo nihil. *L*—*See* Ex nihilo nihil fit.

De nobis fabula narrabitur. *L*—Of us the tale will be told.

De novo. *L*—Anew.

Deo adjuvante, non timendum. *L*—With God's assistance there is nothing to be feared.

Deo duce, ferro comitante. *L*—With God as our leader and sword in hand.

Deo favente. *L*—With the favor of God.

Deo gratias. *L*—Thanks be to God.

Deo juvante. *L*—With God's assistance.

De omni re scibili et quibusdam aliis rebus. *L*—About everything knowable and certain other items. Sometimes used in criticism of a too ambitious book.

Deo, non fortuna. *L*—From God, not from luck.

Deo volente. *L*—God willing; often abbreviated D.V.

De pied en cap. *Fr*—From head to foot; completely armed. In English *cap-à-pie* is often used, and has the same meaning.

De pilo pendet. *L*—It hangs by a hair. Used to indicate that a matter is in a precarious situation, that the slightest mistake might mean disaster. Dionysius, the tyrant of Syracuse, gave Damocles, one of his flatterers, an opportunity to enjoy the pleasures he thought so delightful. While Damocles was being showered with attention by all the court, the tyrant ordered a sword that was suspended from the ceiling by a horse hair to be lowered. If the hair were to break, the sword would strike the courtier's head. The sword of Damocles has thus come to mean an impending danger. The story may be found in *Cicero, Tusculan Disputations, V, xxi.*

De profundis clamavi ad te, Domine. *L*—Out of the depths have I cried unto Thee, O Lord. A penitential psalm in the office for the dead.—*Vulgate, Psalms, CXXIX, 1.*

De proprio motu. *L*—Of one's own volition.

De race. *Fr*—Pure; thoroughbred.

De rigueur. *Fr*—Compulsory; obligatory in matters of etiquette.

Le dernier cri. *Fr*—The latest fashion; the last word.

Le dernier mot. *Fr*—The last word.

Dernier ressort. *Fr*—*See* En dernier ressort.

De sa façon. *Fr*—Of one's own making.

Le désespoir redouble les forces. *Fr*—Despair redoubles one's energies.

Le dessous des cartes. *Fr*—The underside of the cards.

Desunt inopiae multa, avaritiae omnia. *L*—Poverty wants many things, but avarice wants everything.—*Publilius Syrus.*

De temps en temps. *Fr*—From time to time; occasionally.

Detinet. *L*—He detains; a legal action to regain possession of specific property.

De trop. *Fr*—Too much; too many.

Detur digniori. *L*—Let it be given to one more worthy.

Detur pulchriori. *L*—Let it be given to the more beautiful one. A translation of words written on a golden apple which Paris awarded Aphrodite in a beauty contest with Hera and Pallas Athene.

Deum cole, regem serva. *L*—Worship God and serve the king.

Deus est in pectore nostro. *L*—There is a divinity in our hearts.
—*Ovid, Epistles from the Pontus, III, iv, 93.*

Deus ex machina. *L*—A god from the machine. In Greek dramas
when the resolution of the plot was difficult by natural means,
a god or goddess was lowered on a machine to the stage and
exercised supernatural power in solving the problem. Hence,
by extension, any contrived ending to a play or book.

Deus providebit. *L*—God will provide.

Deus vult. *L*—God wills it. The battle cry of the First Crusade.

Deutsches Reich. *Ger*—The German Empire (1871-1919). This
name continued in use under the Republic.

Deutschland, Deutschland über Alles. *Ger*—Germany over all.
German national anthem, the music for which was taken from
Haydn.

Deux s'amusent, trois s'embêtent. *Fr*—Two enjoy themselves,
three are bored; two is company, three's a crowd.

Devastavit. *L*—Literally, he wasted. A term indicating an administrator's improper management of an estate.

Le **devoir des juges est de rendre justice; leur métier de la
différer.** *Fr*—The duty of judges is to render justice; their
practice is to defer it.—*La Bruyère, Characters, Of Certain
Customs, 43 (1), p. 427 in Garapon's edition (Garnier Frères,
1962).*

Dia duit. *Ir*—God save you.

Dia linn. *Ir*—God with us. An exclamation after sneezing.

Il **diavolo non è così brutto come si dipinge.** *It*—The devil is
not as bad as he is painted.

Di bravura. *It*—With brilliance. Musical term.

Di buona volontà sta pieno l'inferno. *It*—Hell is full of good
will; hell is paved with good intentions. *See also* De bons propositos . . . .

Dicere solebat

Dicere solebat nullum esse librum tam malum ut non aliqua parte prodesset. *L*—[Pliny the Elder] used to say that there was no book so bad that it was not profitable in some particular.—*Pliny the Younger, Letters, III, 5.*

Dicho y hecho. *Sp*—No sooner said than done.

Dicique beatus ante obitum nemo supremaque funera debet. *L*—No man should be accounted happy until after his death.—*Ovid, Metamorphoses, III, 136.*

Dic mihi, si fias ut leo, qualis eris? *L*—Tell me, if you should become a lion, what sort of lion would you be?—*Martial, XII, xcii.*

Dictum meum pactum. *L*—My word is my bond. Motto of the London Stock Exchange.

Dictum (verbum) sapienti sat est. *L*—A word to the wise is sufficient.—*Terence, Phormio, III, iii.*

Diem perdidi. *L*—I have lost a day. Words spoken by Titus one day at supper when he reflected that he had performed no kindness that day.—*Suetonius, Titus, viii.*

Dies ater. *L*—A dark, unfortunate day.

Dies faustus. *L*—A day of good omens; a favorable day.

Dies infaustus. *L*—An unlucky day.

Dies Irae. *L*—Day of wrath. The first words of a thirteenth century hymn attributed to Thomas of Celano, used as the sequence in the Mass for the Dead.

Dies natalis. *L*—Birthday.

Die non. *L*—A day on which the court does not sit.

Dieu avec nous. *Fr*—God with us; God is on our side.

Dieu défend le droit. *Fr*—God defends the right.

Dieu et mon droit. *Fr*—God and my right. Motto on royal arms of Britain.

Dieu le veuille! *Fr*—Please God! God grant it!

Dieu li volt. *OF*—God wills it. The cry that is said to have swept over the crowd attending the Council of Clermont in 1095 when Pope Urban urged warring European knights to undertake a crusade to free the Holy Sepulcher in Jerusalem.

Dieu mesure le vent (froid) à la brebis tondue. *Fr*—God tempers the wind (the cold) to the shorn lamb.

Dieu vous garde. *Fr*—May God keep you.

Les dieux ont soif. *Fr*—*The Gods Are Athirst* (for blood). Title of a novel about the French Revolution by Anatole France.

Di faciant, laudis summa sit ista tuae. *L*—May the gods grant that this will be the peak of your merit. In Shakespeare's *King Henry the Sixth, Part III, I, iii*, these words are uttered by the innocent young Earl of Rutland as he dies at the hand of Lord Clifford.

Difficile est custodire quod multis placet. *L*—It is difficult to guard what is pleasing to many.—*Publilius Syrus.*

Difficile est longum subito deponere amorem. *L*—It is difficult to relinquish in an instant a long-cherished love.—*Catullus, LXXVI, 13.*

Difficile est proprie communia dicere. *L*—It is difficult to give an individual style to common things; it is difficult to avoid clichés when discussing common matters.—*Horace, Art of Poetry, 128.*

Difficile est saturam non scribere. *L*—It is difficult not to write satire. An intelligent man sees so much to censure in society. —*Juvenal, I, 30.*

Difficilia quae pulchra. *L*—Beautiful things are difficult.

Difficilis in otio quies. *L*—It is difficult to find peace of mind in leisure.

Dignus vindice nodus. *L*—A complication worthy of its deliverer. In a play the personal solution by a deity through the *deus ex machina* should not be invoked unless the problem is worthy of such divine interference.—*Horace, Art of Poetry, 191.*

Di grado

Di grado in grado. *It*—From step to step.

Di il vero ed affronterai il diavolo. *It*—Tell the truth and shame the devil.

Di immortales. *L*—The immortal gods.

Di indigetes. *L*—The native gods.

Di inferi. *L*—The gods of the lower world.

Dii penates. *L*—Household gods among the Romans.

Dilexi justitiam et odi iniquitatem; propterea morior in exilio. *L*—I have loved justice and hated iniquity; therefore I die in exile. Last words of Pope Gregory VII, who had fled to Salerno to escape the anger of Emperor Henry IV of the Holy Roman Empire. The first part of this quotation is adapted from *Vulgate, Psalms, XLIV, 7.*

Di manes. *L*—Kindly shades of the deified dead; gods of the lower world.

Dime con quien andas, decirte he quien eres. *Sp*—Tell me who your friends are and I'll tell you what you are.—*Cervantes, Don Quixote, II, XXIII. See also* Dimmi con chi vai . . . .

Dimidium facti qui coepit habet. *L*—The man who makes a start has half the work done.—*Horace, Epistles, I, ii, 40.*

Dimmi con chi vai, e ti dirò chi sei. *It*—Tell me your company, and I'll tell you what you are. *See also* Gleich und gleich . . . and Sage mir, mit wem . . . .

Das **Ding an sich.** *Ger*—The thing in itself, the metaphysical reality. A term in Kantian philosophy.

Dios bendiga nuestro (este) hogar. *Sp*—God bless this home.

Dios le da confites a quien no puede roerlos. *Sp*—God gives candies to those who cannot chew them.—*Alarcón, The Three-Cornered Hat, XXI, last sentence.*

Dio vi benedica. *It*—God bless you.

Dirigo. *L*—I direct. The motto of Maine, the only state holding its elections in September. Politicians keep their eyes on these elections for evidence of a trend. Prior to the New Deal, Republicans claimed, "As Maine goes, so goes the nation."

Dis aliter visum. *L*—The gods decreed otherwise; man proposes and God disposes.—*Vergil, Aeneid, II, 428.*

Di salto. *It*—By leaps.

Disce ut doceas. *L*—Learn in order to teach. Motto of Alcuin, principal of the cathedral school at York and later leader in the revival of learning at the court of Charlemagne.

Disciplina arcani. *L*—Literally, the discipline of the secret. The policy among early Christians of maintaining secrecy about their doctrines and ceremonies.

Disciplina praesidium civitatis. *L*—Training is the safeguard of the state. Motto of the University of Texas.

Di seconda mano. *It*—Secondhand.

Le disgrazie non vengon mai sole. *It*—Misfortunes never come singly. *See also* Ein Unglück kommt . . . .

Disjecti (disjecta) membra poetae. *L*—Scattered members. Horace speaks of the scattered members of the poet, meaning that his work is subjected to garbled quotation.—*Horace, Satires, I, iv, 62.*

Dis krambe thanatos. *Gk*—Warmed-over cabbage is death; repetition is tedious. *See also* Crambe repetita.

Dis manibus. *L*—To the kindly shades of the departed. Used in dedications to persons dead. Dative case of *Di manes (q.v.).*

Dis-moi ce que tu manges, je te dirais ce que tu es. *Fr*—Tell me what you eat and I'll tell you what you are.—*Brillat-Savarin, Physiology of Taste, Aphorism IV.*

Ditat Deus. *L*—God enriches. Motto of Arizona.

Divide et impera. *L*—Divide and conquer. A political maxim. The technique of playing one party against another to gain ascendancy, or of conquering by piecemeal.

Divide ut regnes. *L*—Divide the opposition so that you may rule.

Divina natura dedit agros, ars humana aedificavit urbes. *L*—God made the country and man made the town, as William Cowper might translate it.—*Varro, On Agriculture, III, 1.*

Divina particula aurae. *L*—A particle of the divine in man.

Dobriy den. *Rus*—Good afternoon.

Dobriy vecher. *Rus*—Good evening.

Dobroye utro. *Rus*—Good morning.

Docendo discimus. *L*—We learn by teaching.

Docteur ès lettres. *Fr*—Doctor of Literature.

Doctor Angelicus. *L*—The Angelic Doctor, Thomas Aquinas (1225-1274), the most renowned Scholastic.

Doctor Invincibilis. *L*—The Invincible Doctor, William Of Occam (1280-1347).

Doctor Irrefragabilis. *L*—The Irrefragable Doctor, Alexander of Hales (d.1245).

Doctor Legum. *L*—Doctor of Laws.

Doctor Mirabilis. *L*—The Admirable Doctor, Roger Bacon (1214?-1294).

Doctor Seraphicus. *L*—The Seraphic Doctor, St. Bonaventure (1221-1274).

Doctor Subtilis. *L*—The Subtle Doctor, Joannes Duns Scotus (1271-1308) a Franciscan whose system was critical of the school of Thomas Aquinas.

Doctor Universalis. *L*—The Universal Doctor, Albertus Magnus (1193-1280).

Dolce far niente. *It*—It is sweet to do nothing.

Dolce stil nuovo. *It*—The sweet new style. A style of lyric love poetry that had its origins in the songs of the troubadors and reached its finest expression in Dante.—*Dante, Purgatory, XXIV, 57.*

La **dolce vita.** *It*—The sweet life; life devoted to luxury and pleasure.

Dolendi modus, timendi non item. *L*—There is an end to sorrow, but none to fear.

Doli capax. *L*—Capable of doing wrong; one whose age, sanity, or intelligence argues that he knows right from wrong.

Dolus an virtus quis in hoste requirat? *L*—Who asks whether an enemy won by guile or courage? After slaying some Greeks in a brief encounter, some of the Trojans put on the armor of their victims. It was then that one of the Trojans spoke this sentence, which emphasized the importance of victory without inquiring too carefully into the means by which it was won.— *Vergil, Aeneid, II, 390.*

Domine, dirige nos. *L*—Direct us, O Lord. The motto of the City of London.

Domini canes. *L*—Hounds of the Lord. Medieval pun on the order of the Dominicans, noted for their zeal in pursuing heretics.

Dominus illuminatio mea. *L*—The Lord is my light. Motto of Oxford University.—*Vulgate, Psalms, XXVI, 1.*

Dominus vobiscum. *L*—The Lord be with you.

Domus Procerum. *L*—The House of Lords.

Donatio mortis causa. *L*—A gift made at a time of illness because of the fear of death.

Donde una puerta se cierra, otra se abre. *Sp*—Where one door closes, another opens.—*Cervantes, Don Quixote, I, XXI.*

Donec eris felix, multos numerabis amicos. *L*—While fortune favors you, you'll have many friends.—*Ovid, Sorrows, I, ix, 5.*

Don gratuit. *Fr*—A voluntary donation.

La donna è mobile

La **donna è mobile.** *It*—Woman is fickle. The most popular expression of this idea is in an aria from Verdi's *Rigoletto. See also* Varium et mutabile . . . .

Donner und Blitz! *Ger*—Thunder and lightning! A mild expletive.

Dos-à-dos. *Fr*—Back to back. A term applied to seats on which occupants sit back to back, and to a turn in square dancing; a style of binding in which two books are bound so that they can be opened from opposite sides.

Dos linajes solo hay en el mundo . . . que son el tener y el no tener. *Sp*—There are only two groups in the world: the Haves and the Havenots.—*Cervantes, Don Quixote, II, XX.*

Dos moi pou sto kai kino ten gen. *Gk*—Give me a place to stand and I will move the earth (the world).—*Archimedes.*

Do svidanya! *Rus*—Good-bye; so long.

Double entendre. *Fr*—*See* Double entente.

Double entente. *Fr*—An expression with two meanings, one of which is often risqué.

La **douce France.** *Fr*—Sweet France.

La **douceur de vivre.** *Fr*—The sweetness of living.

Douceur et lumière. *Fr*—Sweetness and light.

Do ut des. *L*—I give so that you may give. In civil law a commutative contract in which equality between giving and receiving is emphasized. This designates an agreement partially fulfilled and therefore binding. In addition to *do ut des*, there are three others: *do ut facias*, I give that you may do; *facio ut des*, I do so that you may give; *facio ut facias*, I do that you may do.

Do ut facias. *L*—*See* Do ut des.

D'outre mer. *Fr*—From overseas.

Dove l'oro parla, ogni lingua tace. *It*—When gold talks, every tongue is silent.

Dove sono molti cuochi, la minestra sarà troppo salata. *It*— When there are many cooks, the soup will be too salty; too many cooks spoil the broth.

Dramatis personae. *L*—A prefatory list of characters in a play; by extension, the term is sometimes used to describe the participants in an actual episode in life.

Drang nach Osten. *Ger*—The push toward the East. The policy of Germany prior to World War I of expanding its influence into Asia.

Droit au travail. *Fr*—The right to labor.

Droit comme un I. *Fr*—Straight as an arrow.

Le droit des gens. *Fr*—International law.

Droit d'impression réservé. *Fr*—Copyright.

Droit du mari. *Fr*—The right of a husband.

Droit du Seigneur. *Fr*—*See* Jus primae noctis.

Droit et avant. *Fr*—Right and forward. Inscription on insignia of the Inspector General of United States Army.

Dubium facti. *L*—Doubt about a fact. *See also* Dubium juris.

Dubium juris. *L*—Doubts as to the application of a law in a particular case, to be distinguished from *Dubium facti*, a doubt about a fact.

Duces tecum. *L*—Literally, you shall lead with you. A writ ordering a person to bring certain evidence into court with him.

Ducit amor patriae. *L*—Love for my country is my guide.

Ducunt volentem fata, nolentem trahunt. *L*—The Fates lead the well disposed; they drag the rebellious.—*Seneca, Letters to Lucilius, cvii.*

Du, du liegst mir im Herzen. *Ger*—You lie close to my heart. A song popular for group singing dating from about 1820; author unknown.

Due teste valgono

Due teste valgono più che una sola. *It*—Two heads are better than one.

Du fort au faible. *Fr*—From the strong to the weak.

Du haut en bas. *Fr*—From top to bottom; disdainfully. *See also* De haut en bas.

Dulce decus meum. *L*—My sweet ornament or glory; my sweet source of fame. Horace's tribute to his literary patron Maecenas.—*Horace, Odes, I, i, 2.*

Dulce est desipere in loco. *L*—It is pleasant to play the fool at times.—*Horace, Odes, IV, xii, 28.*

Dulce et decorum est pro patria mori. *L*—It is sweet and honorable to die for one's country.—*Horace, Odes, III, ii, 13.*

Dum bene se gesserit. *L*—As long as he conducts himself properly.

Dum casta. *L*—As long as she remains chaste. A limitation on a bequest to a widow.

Dum Deus calculat, fit mundus. *L*—While God calculates, the world comes into being. A famous aphorism of Leibnitz.

Dummodo sit dives, barbarus ipse placet. *L*—Even a barbarian pleases, if only he is rich.—*Ovid, Art of Love, II, 276.*

Dum spiro spero. *L*—While I breathe I hope. Motto of South Carolina. For a second motto, *see* Animis opibusque . . . .

Dum vita est, spes est. *L*—While there is life, there is hope.

Dum vivimus, vivamus. *L*—Let us live while we're living.

Duos qui sequitur lepores neutrum capit. *L*—The man who chases two rabbits catches neither one.

Duoviri sacris faciundis. *L*—Two men charged to perform the public sacrifices.

Dura lex sed lex. *L*—The law is harsh, but it is the law.

Durante absentia. *L*—During absence.

Durante minore aetate. *L*—As long as the subject is a minor; until the subject is of age.

Durante viduitate. *L*—As long as the subject remains a widow.

Durante vita. *L*—During life.

Durchgang verboten. *Ger*—Passage through forbidden; no thoroughfare.

Durum et durum non faciunt murum. *L*—Stern measures do not build a protecting wall; harsh repressive measures do not insure security.

Du sublime au ridicule il n'y a qu'un pas. *Fr*—It's only a step from the sublime to the ridiculous. An obvious bit of wisdom that is ancient but generally attributed to Napoleon I, who had the retreat from Moscow in mind.

Dux femina facti. *L*—A woman (Queen Elizabeth) was leader of the exploit. This motto was put on a medal at the time of the defeat of the Spanish Armada.—*Vergil, Aeneid, I, 364.*

E

EE. UU. (Estados Unidos). *Sp*—United States.

e.g. (exempli gratia). *L*—For example.

e.o.o.e. (erreur ou omission exceptée). *Fr*—With the exception of any error or omission.

E.P.D. (En paz descanse). *Sp*—May he rest in peace.

Erzb. (Erzbishof). *Ger*—Archbishop.

escte. (escompte). *Fr*—Discount.

et al. (et alibi). *L*—And elsewhere.

et al. (et alii, aliae). *L*—And others.

etc. *See* Et cetera.

et seq. (et sequentes, sequentia). *L*—And the following.

et ux. (et uxor). *L*—And wife.

E.U. (Estados Unidos). *Sp*—United States.

É.-U. (États-Unis). *Fr*—United States.

E.V. (Eccellenza Vostra). *It*—Your Excellency.

ex off. *See* Ex officio.

Eadem, sed aliter. *L*—The same things but in a different way. Schopenhauer felt this should be the motto of history.

Eau de vie. *Fr*—Water of life; brandy.

È cattivo vento che non è buono per qualcheduno. *It*—It's an ill wind that blows nobody good.

Ecce homo. *L*—Behold the man. An attempt on the part of Pilate to arouse sympathy in the mob for Christ after the scourging and crowning with thorns.—*Vulgate, John, XIX, 5.*

Ecce iterum Crispinus! *L*—Lo, Crispin again; we're back to the same old subject. Said of a person who is constantly putting in an appearance where least expected.—*Juvenal, IV, 1.*

Ecce signum. *L*—Behold the proof.

Ecclesia supplet. *L*—The Church supplies. In cases where a technicality is not observed or a ministrant unwittingly exceeds his powers, the Church regards the action as valid. A term used in theology.

École des beaux-arts. *Fr*—School of fine arts.

École maternelle. *Fr*—School for very young children; preschool and kindergarten in the United States.

E consensu gentium. *L*—An argument based on the general agreement of mankind on a subject.

E contra. *L*—On the other hand.

E contrario. *L*—On the contrary.

E converso. *L*—Conversely.

Écrasez l'infâme! *Fr*—Crush the vile system! The slogan of Voltaire and other precursors of the French Revolution. Voltaire was accused of referring to Christ as *l'infâme*, but the charge seems unwarranted. His hostility was directed against the bigotry and the injustice of the age in which he lived.—*Letter to Jean Le Rond d'Alembert, Nov. 28, 1762.*

Edel ist, der edel tut. *Ger*—Handsome is that handsome does.

Édition à tirage restreint. *Fr*—Limited edition.

Édition de luxe. *Fr*—An expensive edition of a book richly bound, printed on special paper, illustrated artistically.

Editio princeps. *L*—First edition.

Effodiuntur opes, irritamenta malorum. *L*—Wealth is dug from the earth, an incentive to evil.—*Ovid, Metamorphoses, I, 140.*

E flamma petere cibum. *L*—To snatch food from the flames; to attempt a dangerous exploit. The Romans used to throw food on a burning pyre; those who tried to salvage such food were the poorest of the poor.—*Terence, Eunuch, III, 2, 38.*

Egli è povero come un topo di chiesa. *It*—He is as poor as a church mouse.

Ego et Rex meus. *L*—I and my king. Cardinal Wolsey is using proper Latin when he puts himself before King Henry VIII.

Ego sum rex Romanus (imperator Romanorum) et super grammaticam. *L*—I am the king of Rome and above grammar. Words spoken by the Holy Roman Emperor Sigismund at the Council of Constance (1414-18) when a cardinal corrected his Latin.

Eh bien! *Fr*—Well! Well now! Used as a mild interjection.

Eheu fugaces, Postume, Postume, labuntur anni. *L*—Alas, my Postumus, the fleeting years slip by.—*Horace, Odes, II, xiv, 1.*

Ehre, dem Ehre gebührt. Ger—Honor to whom honor is due.

Ehrlich währt am längsten. *Ger*—Honesty is the best policy.

Eile mit Weile. *Ger*—The more hurry, the less speed; make haste slowly.

Eine Hand wäscht die andere. *Ger*—*See* Manus manum lavat.

Ein eigner Herd, ein braves Weib sind Gold und Perlen wert. *Ger*—One's own hearth and an honest wife are worth gold and pearls. Mephistopheles is citing a proverb.—*Goethe, Faust, pt. I, 3155-6.*

Eine Schwalbe macht keinen Sommer. *Ger*—One swallow does not make a summer. *See also* Mia gar chelidon . . . .

Ein Reich, ein Volk, ein Führer. *Ger*—One rule, one people, one leader. The Nazi ideal.

Ein Unglück kommt selten allein. *Ger*—Bad luck seldom comes alone; "When sorrows come, they come not single spies but in battalions," as Shakespeare put it in *Hamlet, IV, 5. See also* Le disgrazie . . . .

Eisen und Blut. *Ger*—Usually heard in English as Blood and iron. Bismarck's philosophy that the great problems of the world can be settled by military force.

Ejusdem generis. *L*—Of the same kind.

Ejus nulla culpa est, cui parere necesse sit. *L*—The man who is forced to obey is not at fault for what he does.

L'élan vital. *Fr*—The life force. The term is central in Bergson's philosophy.

Elapso tempore. *L*—After a certain amount of time has elapsed.

E la sua volontate è nostra pace. *It*—His will is our peace. Matthew Arnold calls this a simple but perfect single line of poetry.—*Dante, Paradiso, III, 85.*

Eli eli, lama sabachthani. *Aramaic*—My God, my God, why hast thou forsaken me?—*Vulgate, Matthew, XXVII, 46.*

Embarras de richesses. *Fr*—The state of having more good things than one knows what to do with; embarrassment caused by a rich variety of possible choices.

Embarras du choix. *Fr*—Difficulty of choice arising from a number of possible selections.

È meglio aver oggi un uovo che domani una gallina. *It*—Better an egg today than a hen tomorrow; a bird in the hand is worth two in the bush.

È meglio domandar che errare. *It*—Better to ask than lose your way.

È meglio esser mendicante che ignorante. *It*—Better be poor than ignorant.

È meglio il cuor felice che la borsa piena. *It*—Better a happy heart than a full purse.

È meglio piegare che rompere. *It*—It is better to bend than break.

È meglio tardi che mai. *It*—Better late than never.

È meglio un uccello in gabbia che cento fuori. *It*—Better a bird in the cage than a hundred outside; a bird in the hand is worth two in the bush.

L'Empire c'est la paix. *Fr*—The Empire is synonymous with peace.

L'empire des lettres. *Fr*—The republic of letters.

Empta dolore docet experientia. *L*—Experience gained in pain is a good teacher; a burnt child shuns the fire.

En ami. *Fr*—As a friend.

En arrière. *Fr*—Behind; in arrears.

En attendant. *Fr*—In the meantime.

En avant. *Fr*—Forward!

En bloc. *Fr*—As one unit, piece, lump, etc.

En boca cerrada no entran moscas. *Sp*—Flies do not enter a shut mouth.

En bonne foi. *Fr*—In good faith.

En clair. *Fr*—In the clear; referring to messages that are not sent in code.

En congé. *Fr*—On leave.

En courant. *Fr*—While on the run; on the side.

En cueros. *Sp*—Naked.

Ende gut, alles gut. *Ger*—All's well that ends well.

En dernier ressort. *Fr*—As a last resort.

En déshabillé. *Fr*—Dressed scantily or carelessly, as in a dressing gown.

En deux mots. *Fr*—Literally, in two words; in short.

En Dieu est ma fiance. *Fr*—My trust is in God.

En Dieu est tout. *Fr*—In God is everything.

En effet. *Fr*—In reality; in fact; quite so.

En évidence. *Fr*—In a conspicuous position.

En famille. *Fr*—In the bosom of one's family; at home.

Enfant de famille. *Fr*—A son or daughter of good breeding. reputable family.

Enfant de son siècle. *Fr*—A child of his age.

Enfant gâté. *Fr*—Spoiled child.

Enfants perdus. *Fr*—Literally, lost children; an abandoned hope. The term is military and is used to designate troops that are in an indefensible position and are considered as good as lost.

Enfant terrible. *Fr*—A child hard to manage; a holy terror.

Enfant trouvé. *Fr*—A foundling.

L'enfer des femmes, c'est la vieillesse. *Fr*—Hell for women is old age.—*La Rochefoucauld, Maxims, 562.*

En grande tenue. *Fr*—In full military dress.

En grande toilette. *Fr*—In full dress.

En Martes ni te cases, ni te embarques, ni de tu casa te apartes. *Sp*—On Tuesday do not marry, go on a voyage, or leave your home. In Spain and Mexico Tuesday is regarded as an unlucky day.

En masse. *Fr*—In a crowd; in a heap.

En mauvaise odeur. *Fr*—In bad odor.

L'ennemi du genre humain. *Fr*—Enemy of the human race.

En nukti boule tois sophois gignetai. *Gk*—In the night counsel comes to the wise; take counsel of your pillow.—*Menander, Monostichs, 150.*

En papillotes. *Fr*—(Hair done up) in paper curlers.

En parenthèse. *Fr*—In parentheses.

En passant. *Fr*—In passing.

En petit comité. *Fr*—In an informal, select group.

En plein air. *Fr*—In the open air.

En plein jour. *Fr*—In the full light of day where all may observe.

En principe. *Fr*—As a rule.

En queue. *Fr*—In a line, as at a box office; behind; in the rear.

En rapport. *Fr*—In harmonious relation; in agreement.

En règle. *Fr*—In order: correct.

En revanche. *Fr*—By way of compensation; to make up for something.

En route! *Fr*—Full speed ahead!

Ense petit placidam sub libertate quietem. *L*—By the sword she seeks placid peace under free government. Motto of Massachusetts.

En somme. *Fr*—In short.

En surtout. *Fr*—Literally, above all. Used in heraldry to indicate position of personal arms, for example, at the top of a shield.

En tapinois. *Fr*—On the sly; stealthily departing.

Entbehre gern was du nicht hast. *Ger*—Gladly do without what you do not have.

Entbehren sollst du! *Ger*—You must refrain, you must renounce pleasure! Faust is complaining that he is too old to devote himself solely to pleasure and too young to crush desire. You must restrain yourself is the only advice he receives.—*Goethe, Faust, pt. I, 1549.*

Entelecheia. *Gk*—In Aristotle's philosophy a form-giving energy in living things directing an organism to the realization of its perfection.

Entente cordiale. *Fr*—A cordial understanding, especially between two governments.

Entente demi-cordiale. *Fr*—A half-cordial understanding; a half-hearted reconciliation.

Entia non sunt multiplicanda sine necessitate. *L*—Beings must not be multiplied without necessity.—*William of Occam.* This is known as Occam's law of parsimony or Occam's razor.

En tout cas. *Fr*—In any case; applied by extension to a combination umbrella and parasol and to an all-weather tennis court.

Entre chien et loup. *Fr*—Literally, between the dog and the wolf; at nightfall.

Entre deux feux. *Fr*—Between two fires.

Entre deux vins. *Fr*—Between two wines; neither drunk nor sober.

Entre nous. *Fr*—Between us; a private understanding.

Entre padres y hermanos no metas tus manos. *Sp*—Don't meddle in the family affairs of others.

En vérité. *Fr*—In truth; indeed.

En voiture! *Fr*—All aboard!

Eo ipso. *L*—By the very fact.

Épater les bourgeois. *Fr*—*See* Pour épater . . . .

Epea pteroenta. *Gk*—Winged words. An expression much used by Homer. *See also* Geflügelte Worte.

E pluribus unum. *L*—One from many. Motto on the great seal of the United States. Adapted from *Vergil, Moretum, 104.*

E pur si muove! *It*—Nevertheless it does move! Fictional remark of Galileo on leaving the trial at which he was forced to renounce his scientific conclusion that the earth moves around the sun.

E (ex) re nata. *L*—Arising from the present circumstances; according to the exigencies of the case.

Erfahrung ist die beste Schule. *Ger*—Experience is the best school. *See also* Usus est optimus magister.

Erin go bragh! *Ir*—Ireland forever!

Eripuit caelo fulmen, mox sceptra tyrannis. *L*—He snatched lightning from heaven and later the scepter from tyrants. Inscription on a bust of Franklin recalling his experiment with the kite and his part in the American Revolution. The words are inspired in part by *Manilius, Astronomica, I, 104.*

Errare humanum est. *L*—To err is human.

Errata (*pl.* of *erratum*). *L*—A list of errors in a book.

Das **Erste und Letzte, was vom Genie gefordert wird, ist Wahrheitsliebe.** *Ger*—The first and last thing that is asked of genius is the love of truth.—*Goethe, Maxims in Prose, 52.*

ès. *OF*—A contraction of *en les,* in the. It is still used, mostly in academic degrees, such as *bacc. ès. l (q.v.).*

Es de vidrio la mujer. *Sp*—Woman is made of glass.

È sempre l'ora. *It*—The right time is always now.

Ese te quiere

Ese te quiere bien que te hace llorar. *Sp*—The man who makes you weep loves you very much.—*Cervantes, Don Quixote, I, XX.*

Es gibt, sagt man, für den Kammerdiener keinen Helden. *Ger*—Literally, there is, they say, no hero for a valet; no man is a hero to his valet.—*Goethe, Maxims in Prose, 164. See also* Il n'y a pas de grand homme . . . .

Es irrt der Mensch, solang er strebt. *Ger*—Man errs as long as he aspires.—*Goethe, Faust, Prologue in Heaven.*

Es ist nicht alles Gold was glänzt. *Ger*—All that glitters is not gold.

Es ist Schade. *Ger*—It is a pity.

Es kann der Frömmste nicht im Frieden bleiben,/Wenn es dem bösen Nachbar nicht gefällt. *Ger*—The gentlest man cannot live in peace, if it does not please his wicked neighbor.—*Schiller, Wilhelm Tell, IV, iii, 124.*

Esprit de corps. *Fr*—The spirit of internal harmony and common purpose that animates an organization.

Esprit de finesse. *Fr*—A witty or shrewd mind.

Esprit des lois. *Fr*—*Spirit of the Laws*, title of a work by Montesquieu.

L'esprit de suite. *Fr*—Team spirit; devotion to the cause.

L'esprit est toujours la dupe du cœur. *Fr*—The mind is always deceived by the heart.—*La Rochefoucauld, Maxims, 102.*

Esprit fort. *Fr*—A person of strong mind or will; a fearless thinker; a skeptic.

Esprit gaulois. *Fr*—The Gallic spirit; a certain freedom of speech characterized by broad, off-color humor. A sharp contrast to the puritanical spirit.

Esse oportet ut vivas, non vivere ut edas. *L*—One should eat to live, not live to eat.—*Cicero, Herennius, IV, xxviii, 39.*

Esse quam videri. *L*—To be rather than to seem to be. The motto of North Carolina. According to Sallust, Cato the Younger preferred to be good rather than to seem good.— *Sallust, Catiline, 54.*

Esse rei est percipi. *L*—The reality of a thing is in its being perceived. Berkeley's theory. The basis of a film called *Film* by Samuel Beckett.

Est ars etiam maledicendi. *L*—There is even an art to slandering.—*Scaliger.*

Est-ce possible? *Fr*—Is it possible? Last words of Paul Doumer, president of France, shot by a Russian Fascist in 1932.

Est modus in rebus. *L*—There is a middle course in everything; there must be moderation in all things.—*Horace, Satires, I, i, 106.*

Esto perpetua. *L*—Live forever. Motto of Idaho.

Esto quod esse videris. *L*—Be what you seem to be.

Est quaedam flere voluptas. *L*—There is a certain pleasure in weeping.—*Ovid, Sorrows, IV, iii, 37.*

Estque pati poenas quam meruisse minus. *L*—It is better to suffer punishment than to deserve it.—*Ovid, Epistles from Pontus, I, i, 62.*

Es wird nichts so schön gemacht/Es kommt einer der's veracht! *Ger*—There is nothing, no matter how beautiful, that is not held in contempt by someone.

Et alibi. *L*—And elsewhere.

Et alii, aliae. *L*—And others.

L'état c'est moi. *Fr*—The state, I am the state. Young Louis XIV's reply to the president of the French *Parlement* when he made some objections in the interest of the state.

L'état major. *Fr*—General staff; staff headquarters.

Et bonum quo antiquius, eo melius. *L*—The more ancient a good, the better.

Et cetera. *L*—And so forth.

Éternel devenir. *Fr*—Eternal becoming.

Et hoc genus omne. *L*—*See* Hoc genus omne.

Etiam capillus unus habet umbram suam. *L*—Even a single hair has its own shadow; in any investigation the smallest bit of evidence can be valuable.—*Publilius Syrus.*

Et id genus omne. *L*—*See* Hoc genus omne.

L'étoile du Nord. *Fr*—Star of the North. Motto of Minnesota.

Et qui nolunt occidere quemquam, posse volunt. *L*—Those who do not wish to kill any man wish they were able.—*Juvenal, X, 96.*

Et semel emissum volat irrevocabile verbum. *L*—The word once uttered cannot be recalled.—*Horace, Epistles, I, xviii, 71.*

Et sequentes *or* **et sequentia.** *L*—And the following.

Et sic de ceteris. *L*—And similarly as to the others.

Et sic de similibus. *L*—And in the same way about similar matters.

Et sic porro. *L*—And so on.

Et spes et ratio studiorum in Caesare tantum. *L*—The future of literature and the inducement to it rest with Caesar alone. Juvenal does not mention which emperor he is addressing; critics feel he may have had Trajan or Hadrian in mind.—*Juvenal, VII, i.*

Et tu, Brute. *L*—And thou, too, Brutus. In Shakespeare the last words spoken by Caesar.—*Shakespeare, Julius Caesar, III, i. Tu quoque, Brute* is a variation of what Caesar is supposed to have said. *See also* Kai su ei ekeinon . . . .

Et uxor. *See* Et ux.

Et verbum caro factum est. *L*—And the Word was made flesh. *Vulgate, John, I, 14.*

Et vir. *L*—And husband.

Eureka! *Gk*—I have found it! The exclamation of Archimedes who, while bathing, discovered how to determine the gold content of a crown made for King Hiero II of Syracuse. This experiment led to the discovery of the law of specific gravity. Motto of California.—*Vitruvius Pollio, On Architecture, IX, iii* and *Plutarch, Pleasure Not Attainable According to Epicurus, 11*.

Das **Ewig-Weibliche/zieht uns hinan.** *Ger*—The eternal feminine/ draws us up and on.—*Goethe, Faust, pt. II, V, closing lines.*

Ex abrupto. *L*—Suddenly.

Ex abundantia cordis os loquitur. *L*—Out of the abundance of the heart the mouth speaketh.—*Vulgate, Matthew, XII, 34.*

Ex aequo. *L*—Of equal merit.

Ex animo. *L*—With spirit; from the heart.

Ex capite. *L*—Literally, from the head; from memory.

Ex cathedra. *L*—Literally, from the chair. Dogmatic utterances of the Pope on matters of faith and morals. The term is sometimes applied to the arrogant, positive expressions of the uninformed.

Excellentia sanandi causa. *L*—Excellence in order to cure. A hospital motto.

Excelsior. *L*—Ever upward. Motto of New York State.

Exceptio probat regulam. *L*—The exception proves the existence of the rule. A Roman legal maxim.

Exceptis excipiendis. *L*—After exceptions have been made.

Ex comitate. *L*—Out of courtesy.

Ex concesso. *L*—From what has already been conceded. An argument based on what has already been granted by an opponent.

Ex curia. *L*—Out of court.

Excusatio non petita fit accusatio manifesta. *L*—An excuse given when unasked betrays clear guilt. *See also* Qui s'excuse . . . .

Excussit subjecto Pelion Ossae. *L*—(Jove) shook off Pelion from underlying Ossa.—*Ovid, Metamorphoses, I, 155. See also* Imponere Pelio Ossam.

Ex debito justitiae. *L*—By reason of a just debt.

Ex desuetudine amittuntur privilegia. *L*—Privileges are lost through disuse. Legal maxim.

Ex dono. *L*—As a gift.

Exeat. *L*—Let him leave. Form used in schools when a student is given permission for temporary absence.

Exegi monumentum aere perennius. *L*—I have built a monument more lasting than bronze.—*Horace, Odes, III, xxx, 1.*

Exemplaire d'auteur. *Fr*—Autographed copy owned by the author.

Exempla sunt odiosa. *L*—Examples are odious.

Exempli gratia. *See* e.g.

Ex ephebis. *L*—Out of the ranks of youths; just arrived at manhood.

Exeunt omnes. *L*—All leave the stage.

Ex gratia. *L*—By special favor, not because of any legal right.

Ex grege. *L*—From the flock; chosen from the others.

Ex hypothesi. *L*—According to the supposition that is the basis of an inquiry.

Ex imo corde. *L*—From the bottom of the heart.

Exitus acta probat. *L*—The result justifies the action. George Washington's family motto.—*Ovid, Heroides, II, 85.*

Ex libris. *L*—A book plate; from the books of — (followed by the name of the owner).

Ex luna scientia. *L*—Knowledge from the moon. The motto of the project Apollo moon flights.

Ex malis moribus bonae leges natae sunt. *L*—Good laws have come about because of bad customs.

Ex mero motu. *L*—Of one's own free will; without compulsion or restraint.

Ex necessitate rei. *L*—Arising from the urgency of the case.

Ex nihilo nihil fit. *L*—From nothing nothing comes. Xenophanes' axiom, basic to his doctrine of the eternity of matter. This Latin proverb is found with slightly different wording in *Lucretius, The Nature of Things, I, 155* and *206*.

Ex officio. *L*—By virtue of holding an office.

Ex opere operantis. *L*—*See* Ex opere operato.

Ex opere operato. *L*—A theological phrase indicating that the efficacy of a spiritual act or a sacrament does not depend upon the state of grace of the ministrant, but upon the proper performance of the rite.

Ex ore infantium. *L*—Out of the mouth of infants.—*Vulgate, Psalms, VIII, 2.*

Ex Oriente lux; ex Occidente frux. *L*—From the East light; from the West fruit. The East has given us philosophy; the West practical, productive industries.

Ex parte. *L*—A statement proceeding from one side only in an argument or investigation and, therefore, likely to be prejudiced.

Ex pede Herculem. *L*—Judge the size of Hercules from his foot; from one part you can estimate the whole.

Experientia docet stultos. *L*—Experience teaches even fools. The sense of this proverb is highly debatable. Even men who have a reputation for wisdom rarely learn the lessons of experience, e.g., that no nation wins a war.

Experimentum crucis. *L*—A crucial test; a decisive experiment.

Experto crede. *L*—*See* Experto credite.

Experto credite. *L*—Believe the experienced. Generally used in the singular, *Experto crede.*—*Vergil, Aeneid, XI, 283.*

Expertus metuit. *L*—The person with experience is fearful; the burnt child dreads the fire. This originally referred to the cultivation of the friendship of the powerful, which seems so pleasant to the inexperienced but in reality is bitter to those who have had the experience.—*Horace, Epistles, I, xviii, 87.*

Explication de texte. *Fr*—The detailed and sometimes painfully slow explanation of a classical text.

Explicit. *L*—Here ends. This word found at the end of Latin manuscripts is followed by the title of the work, often the name of the scribe, and the place and date of the copying or publication; a colophon.

Ex post facto. *L*—After the deed is done; retroactive. Usually applied to legislation.

Expressis verbis. *L*—In express terms; in so many words.

Ex professo. *L*—Professedly; openly; expertly.

Ex relatione. *L*—A phrase on a legal document indicating a relation to a former proceeding, or designating the person on whose behalf action is being taken.

Ex (e) silentio. *L*—From silence; an argument drawn from failure of an opponent to mention a circumstance that might be damaging.

Ex tacito. *L*—Tacitly.

Ex tempore. *L*—Extemporaneously.

Extinctus amabitur idem. *L*—The same man will be loved when dead. Because of envy a man's talent, virtue, and services are often not recognized when he is alive.—*Horace, Epistles, II, i, 14.*

Extra ecclesiam nulla salus. *L*—Outside the church there is no salvation. This dictum attributed to St. Cyprian (210-258) caused much debate among theologians. One explanation that would lessen its rigor is that the Church has a soul and a body; one may be spiritually joined to the Church, but not belong to the visible body of the faithful.

Extra muros. *L*—Beyond the walls.

Extra ordinem. *L*—Outside of its natural order; out of its proper place.

Extra situm. *L*—Away from its natural setting.

Les **extrêmes se touchent.** *Fr*—Extremes meet.—*Mercier, Tableau of Paris, title of chap. 348, vol. IV.*

Ex umbris et imaginibus in veritatem. *L*—From shadows and symbols to reality. Cardinal Newman's epitaph.

Ex ungue leonem. *L*—One can sketch a lion from its claw. *See also* Ex pede Herculem.

Ex vi termini. L—From the force of the term; by definition.

Ex vitio alterius sapiens emendat suum. *L*—A wise man corrects his faults when seeing another's.—*Publilius Syrus.*

Ex voto. *L*—In fulfillment of a vow or promise. When used as an adjective it applies to an offering made to a shrine or to a philanthropic or pious cause.

F

f. (forte). *It*—Loudly. *See also* fff.

f.à.b. (franco à bord). *Fr*—f.o.b. (free on board).

f.a.b. (franco a bordo). *Sp*—f.o.b. (free on board).

f.c. (ferrocarril). *Sp.*—Railroad.

fco (franco). *Fr-It-Sp*—Free of charge; transportation paid.

F.D. *See* Defensor Fidei.

F. de T. (Fulano de Tal). *Sp*—Mr. So-and-So; equivalent of John Doe.

Fec. *See* Fecit.

F.f. (Fortsetzung folgt). *Ger*—To be continued.

FF. (Frères). *Fr*—Brothers. Used mostly in company names, as Bros.

fff. (fortississimo). *It*—As loudly as possible. A super-superlative. *ff* (fortissimo) is the usual superlative.

FF.SS. (Ferrovie dello Stato). *It*—State Railroads.

F.h. (Fiat haustus). *L*—Let a draught be made. A medical direction.

fha. (fecha). *Sp*—Date of a document.

F.I.A.T. (Fabbrica italiana automobili Torino). *It*—Italian Automobile Factory of Turin.

fl. *See* Floruit.

Frl. (Fräulein). *Ger*—Miss.

F.S. (Faire suivre). *Fr*—Please forward. A postal term.

F.L.Q. (Front de libération de Québec). *Fr*—Quebec Liberation Front.

F.u.S.f. (Fortsetzung und Schluss folgen). *Ger*—To be concluded in the next issue.

f.v. (folio verso). *L*—On the reverse side of the page.

Faber quisque fortunae suae. *L*—Every man is the architect of his own fortune. A Roman proverb.

Une **fable convenue.** *Fr*—A fable agreed upon. *See also* L'histoire n'est qu'une fable convenue.

Fabricando fit faber. *L*—One becomes a craftsman by working at his craft.

Fabula palliata. *L*—Roman drama in which the characters wore a Greek garment called the *pallium*. Such Latin plays stressing Greek manners were translated by Plautus and Terence from Greek originals, now extant only in fragments.

Fabula togata. *L*—Roman drama stressing Roman rather than Greek characters and dress. *See also* Fabula palliata.

Facile est inventis addere. *L*—It is easy to add to what has already been invented.

Facile omnes, quom valemus, recta consilia aegrotis damus. *L*—When we are well, we readily give good counsel to the sick.—*Terence, Andria, III, 1, 9.*

Facile princeps. *L*—Easily the leader.

Facilis descensus Averno. *L*—The descent to hell is easy.—*Vergil, Aeneid, VI, 126.*

Facilité de parler, c'est impuissance de se taire. *Fr*—Fluency in speech is an inability to stop talking.

Facio ut des. *L*—*See* Do ut des.

Facio ut facias. *L*—*See* Do ut des.

Facit indignatio versum. *L*—Indignation gives birth to verses. In a similar vein Quintilian wonders why anger makes the unlearned eloquent.—*Juvenal, I, 79.*

Façon de parler. *Fr*—Manner of speaking.

Facta, non verba. *L*—Deeds, not words; action, not talk.

Faenum habet in cornu. *L*—He has hay on his horns; he is dangerous. The figure is based upon the practice in ancient Rome of putting hay on the horns of a dangerous bull.—*Horace, Satires, I, iv, 34.*

Faex populi, faeces *(pl)* **populi.** *L*—The dregs of society: the mob. A disparaging reference to the lowest classes.

Faire d'une mouche un éléphant. *Fr*—To make an elephant out of a fly; to make a mountain out of a molehill.

Faire les yeux doux. *Fr*—To look with love at someone; to make sheep's eyes.

Fait accompli. *Fr*—An accomplished fact; an action which cannot be undone or revoked.

Fait à peindre. *Fr*—Made to be painted; paintable.

Faites votre devoir

Faites votre devoir et laissez faire aux dieux. *Fr*—Do your duty and leave the rest to the gods.—*Corneille, Horace, II, 8, line 710.*

Fait nouveau. *Fr*—A new fact or development.

Falsa lectio. *L*—A false reading; a word erroneously transcribed by an editor or copyist of a manuscript.

Falsus in uno, falsus in omnibus. *L*—Faithless in one thing, faithless in all. The entire testimony of a witness who has lied in one particular may be rejected.

Fama clamosa. *L*—Noisy rumor or scandal.

Fama, malum qua non aliud velocius ullum. *L*—No evil travels faster than scandal.—*Vergil, Aeneid, IV, 174.*

Fama nihil est celerius. *L*—Nothing travels faster than scandal. Adapted from *Fama, malum qua . . . (q.v.).*

Fama semper vivat. *L*—May his fame live forever.

La fame non vuol leggi. *It*—Hunger knows no law.

Fames est optimus coquus. L—Hunger is the best cook.

La farce est jouée. *Fr*—The farce is over. Supposed last words of Rabelais. *See also* Je vais chercher un grand Peut-être! and Acta est fabula.

Far d'una mosca un elefante. *It*—To make an elephant out of a fly; to make a mountain out of a molehill. *See also* Faire d'une mouche un éléphant.

Fas est et ab hoste doceri. *L*—There is nothing wrong in learning a lesson even from the enemy.—*Ovid, Metamorphoses, IV, 428.*

Fata obstant. *L*—The Fates oppose.

Fata viam invenient. *L*—The Fates will find a way.—*Vergil, Aeneid, III, 395.*

Faute de mieux. *Fr*—For lack of something better.

Faux ami. *Fr*—A false friend. Applied to a French word spelled the same as a word in English but having a different meaning, e.g. *sensible, Fr,* which means *sensitive.*

Faux pas. *Fr*—A false step; a blunder, especially in the area of social conventions.

Fax mentis incendium gloriae. *L*—The passion for glory sets a torch to the mind.

Fay ce que vouldras. *OF*—Do what you will; follow your heart's desires. Rule of Gargantua's Abbey of Thélème.—*Rabelais, Gargantua, I, 57.*

Fecit. *L*—He made it. Found inside violins, on paintings, or on statuary with the name of the maker or artist.

Der **Feind steht im eigenen Lager.** *Ger*—The enemy is in one's own camp. *Karl Liebknect,* an opponent of Germany's entry into World War I.

Felice ritorno! *It*—Welcome back!

Felices Pascuas. *Sp*—Literally, Happy Easter; also used to mean Merry Christmas, or Happy holiday.

Felicitas multos habet amicos. *L*—Prosperity has many friends. The implication is that these are not disinterested friends.

Felix quem faciunt aliena pericula cautum. *L*—Fortunate the man who is made cautious by the perils of others.

Felix qui potuit rerum cognoscere causas. *L*—Happy the man who has been able to discover the causes of things.—*Vergil, Georgics, II, 490.*

Feliz Natal. *Port*—Merry Christmas.

Felo de se. *Anglo-L*—A felon upon himself; a person who kills himself.

Femme couverte. *Fr*—A married woman.

Femme de chambre. *Fr*—Chambermaid.

Femme de charge. *Fr*—Housekeeper.

Femme de trente ans. *Fr*—Literally, a woman aged thirty; one who knows the world. Title of a novel by Balzac.

Femme fatale. *Fr*—Siren; a seductive woman.

Une **femme grosse.** *Fr*—A pregnant woman. To avoid misunderstanding, *see* Une grosse femme.

Femme savante. *Fr*—Learned woman. *Les Femmes savantes* (the plural form, here used ironically) is the title of a play by Molière.

Les **femmes peuvent tout, parce qu'elles gouvernent les personnes qui gouvernent tout.** *Fr*—Woman are all-powerful because they govern those who govern everything.

Ferae naturae. *L*—Of a wild, ferocious nature. A legal term applied to undomesticated animals and birds.

Feriunt summos fulgura montes. *L*—Lightning strikes the mountain tops.—*Horace, Odes, II, x, 12.*

Ferme acerrima proximorum odia. *L*—Hatred among close relatives is generally the bitterest.—*Tacitus, Histories, IV, 70.*

Ferme générale. *Fr*—A general farming out of taxes. The object of financiers was to reap a generous profit for collecting what they had advanced the government. This system was abolished in France in 1791.

Fermiers généraux. *Fr*—Farmers general; private financiers who collected taxes for the French government.

Ferrum, dum in igni candet, cudendum est tibi. *L*—Strike the iron when it is hot.—*Publilius Syrus. See also* Man muss das Eisen . . . .

Ferrum ferro acuitur. *L*—Iron is sharpened by iron.

Eine **feste Burg ist unser Gott.** *Ger*—A mighty fortress is our God. The first line of Luther's greatest hymn.

Festina lente. *L*—Hasten slowly.

Fête champêtre. *Fr*—Rural feast with open-air entertainment and rustic sports.

Fête des Fous. *Fr*—A festival of fools. In medieval times, a period of carousing.

Fêtes de nuit. *Fr*—Night festivals.

Feu d'artifice. *Fr*—Fireworks.

Feu de joie. *Fr*—A firing of guns on a joyous occasion; a bonfire.

Feu d'enfer. *Fr*—Hellish fire (from guns).

Feu follet, feux follets *(pl).* *Fr*—*See* Ignis fatuus.

Fianna Fail. *Ir*—Literally, warrior band of the sod; followers of Eamon de Valera, who organized the Nationalist Party in 1927.

Fiat experimentum in corpore vili. *L*—Let experiments be done on a worthless body; experiment on inexpensive materials.

Fiat justitia ruat caelum. *L*—Let justice prevail even though the heavens fall. The original use of this maxim is not so elevating. Seneca tells that a man being hanged for murder was sent by the executioner to Piso when the supposed victim appeared. Piso would not change the sentence of death, but ordered all three hanged: the supposed criminal because the sentence had been passed, the executioner because he had been derelict in his duty, and the supposed victim because he had been the cause of the death of two innocent men.

Fiat lux. *L*—Let there be light.—*Vulgate, Genesis, I, 3.*

Fiat mixtura. *L*—Let a mixture be made. A medical direction.

Fiat voluntas tua. *L*—Thy will be done.—*Vulgate, Matthew, VI, 10.*

Fide et amore. *L*—With faith and love.

Fide et fiducia. *L*—By faith and confidence.

Fide et fortitudine. *L*—By faith and fortitude.

Fidei corticula crux. *L*—The cross is the test or touchstone of faith.

Fidei Defensor. *L*—*See* Defensor Fidei.

Fideli certa merces. *L*—Certain is the reward for the man who is faithful.

Fide, non armis. *L*—By faith, not by arms.

Fide, sed cui vide. *L*—Trust, but take care whom you trust.

Fides et justitia. *L*—Faith and justice.

Fides Punica. *L*—*See* Punica fides.

Fides quaerens intellectum. *L*—Faith seeking understanding.

Fidite ne pedibus. *L*—Place no trust in flight.—*Vergil, Aeneid, X, 372.*

Fidus Achates. *L*—Faithful Achates, loyal friend of Aeneas, often mentioned in the *Aeneid*; by extension, a loyal friend.

Fidus et audax. *L*—Faithful and intrepid.

Fieri facias. *L*—Order to be done. A writ to the sheriff ordering the debtor's property to be reduced to money to cover the amount of the judgment.

Figlie e vetri son sempre in pericolo. *It*—Lasses and glasses are always in danger.

Figurae orationis. *L*—Figures of speech.

Filius nullius. *L*—A son of illegitimate birth.

Filius populi. *L*—Son of the people; a bastard.

Filius terrae. *L*—A son of the earth; a peasant.

Fille de joie. *Fr*—A daughter of pleasure; a prostitute.

Fille d'honneur. *Fr*—Maid of honor.

Fils à papa. *Fr*—Son of an influential father; the fair-haired boy.

Finchè la pianta è tenera, bisogna drizzarla. *It*—Bend the tree while it is young; as the twig is bent, the tree's inclined.

La fin couronne les œuvres. *Fr*—It is the end that crowns the work.

Fin de siècle. *Fr*—End of the century.

Finesse d'esprit. *Fr*—Shrewdness of mind.

Finis coronat opus. *L*—It is the end that crowns the work.

Finis litium. *L*—An end of lawsuits.

Finis origine pendet. *L*—The end depends on the beginning. This motto stresses the importance of getting the right start. Motto of Paul Revere and the seal of Phillips Andover Academy.

Flagellum Dei. *L*—The scourge of God, a name given Attila, the leader of the Huns.

Flagrante bello. *L*—While the war is raging.

Flagrante delicto. *L*—In the very act of committing a crime.

Flak (Fliegerabwehrkanone). *Ger*—Antiaircraft artillery; the exploding shells sent up by these guns.

Flamma fumo est proxima. *L*—Flame is very close to smoke; where there's smoke there's fire.—*Plautus, Curculio, I, i, 53.*

Flecti, non frangi. *L*—To bend, not to break.

Fleur de lys. *Fr*—Literally, flower or blossom of the lily. Heraldic ornament of French royalty.

Floruit. *L*—He flourished. Often used when exact dates are unknown.

Flosculi sententiarum. *L*—Beautiful selections; an anthology of beautiful thoughts.

Flotará sola. *Sp*—It will float alone. A symbol of the independence party in Puerto Rico; seen on decals with the island's flag.

Flux de bouche. *Fr*—Flow of words; talkativeness. *See also* Flux de paroles.

Flux de paroles. *Fr*—Flow of words; garrulity. *See also* Flux de bouche.

Folie de grandeur. *Fr*—Delusions of grandeur.

Fons et origo. *L*—The very fountain and source.

Fons et origo malorum. *L*—The fountain and source of misery.

Force de frappe. *Fr*—A striking force of atomic weapons.

Force majeure. *Fr*—Circumstances beyond one's control. *See also* Vis major.

Forensis strepitus. *L*—The clamor of the forum; the noisy turmoil of the court.

Foris ut moris, intus ut libet. *L*—In public, follow custom; in private, your own sweet will.

Forma bonum fragile. *L*—Beauty is a fragile possession.—*Ovid, Art of Love, II, 113.*

Forma flos, fama flatus. *L*—Beauty is a flower, fame a breath.

Forsan et haec olim meminisse juvabit. *L*—Perhaps it will be pleasant to remember these hardships some day.—*Vergil, Aeneid, I, 203.*

Forte. *It*—Loudly. *See also* fff.

Forte scutum, salus ducum. *L*—A brave shield is the safety of commanders.

Fortes fortuna adjuvat. *L*—Fortune aids the brave.—*Terence, Phormio, II, 2, 25.*

Fortes fortuna juvat. *L*—Fortune helps the brave.—*Pliny the Younger, VI, 16.*

Forti et fideli nihil (nil) difficile. *L*—Nothing is difficult for the brave and loyal.

Fortis cadere, cedere non potest. *L*—The brave man may fall but he cannot yield.

Fortiter et recte. *L*—Bravely and righteously.

Fortiter, fideliter, feliciter. *L*—Bravely, loyally, successfully.

Frangas

Fortiter in re. *L—See* Suaviter in modo . . . .

La **fortuna aiuta i pazzi.** *It*—Fortune helps fools.

Fortuna belli semper ancipiti in loco est. *L*—The fortunes of war are always in doubt.—*Seneca, Phoenician Women, 629.*

Fortunae filius. *L*—A child of fortune.—*Horace, Satires, II, vi, 49.*

Fortuna favet fatuis. *L*—Fortune favors fools.

Fortuna fortibus favet. *L*—Fortune favors the brave.

Fortuna meliores sequitur. *L*—Fortune follows the better man; the better man has all the luck.—*Sallust, History, I, 48, 21.*

Fortuna multis dat nimis, satis nulli. *L*—Fortune gives too much to many, enough to nobody.—*Martial, Epigrams, XII, 10, 2.*

Fortuna nimium quem fovet, stultum facit. *L*—Fortune often makes her darling a fool.—*Publilius Syrus.*

La **Forza del destino.** *It*—The power of destiny. The title of an opera by Verdi.

Fou qui se tait passe pour sage. *Fr*—The silent fool passes for a sage.

Les **fous font les festins et les sages les mangent.** *Fr*—Fools prepare the banquet and the smart ones eat it.

Fra Modesto non fu mai priore. *It*—Brother Modest was never made prior; a modest man does not rise in administration.

Franc-alleu. *Fr*—Land held absolutely free of feudal obligations.

La **France, fille aînée de l'Église.** *Fr*—France, the eldest daughter of the Church.

Franc-tireur. *Fr*—An irregular infantryman in the French army; a sniper.

Frangas, non flectes. *L*—You may break but you cannot bend me. *See also* Flecti, non frangi.

115

Frappé

Frappé au froid. *Fr*—Literally, stamped when cold; blind-tooled. A term used in bookbinding.

Fraus est celare fraudem. *L*—To conceal a fraud is fraud.

Frère de lait. *Fr*—Foster-brother.

Frisch begonnen, halb gewonnen. *Ger*—Well begun is half done. *See also* Arche hemisy pantos.

Fröhliche Weihnachten. *Ger*—Merry Christmas.

Froides mains, chaud amour. *Fr*—A cold hand but a warm heart.

Frontis nulla fides. *L*—Place no trust in appearances; appearances are deceptive.—*Juvenal, II, 8.*

Fructu non foliis arborem aestima. *L*—Judge a tree by its fruit, not its leaves.

Frustra laborat qui omnibus placere studet. *L*—He labors in vain who strives to please everybody.

I **frutti proibiti sono i più dolci.** *It*—Forbidden fruits are sweetest.

¡**Fuera los Yankis!** *Sp*—Out with the Yankees! Yankees, go home. An example of contemporary graffiti.

Fugit irreparabile tempus. *L*—Irrecoverable time flies away.— *Vergil, Georgics, III, 284.*

Fuimus Troes, fuit Ilium. *L*—We were Trojans, and there was a Troy; our glory is past, our day is over.—*Vergil, Aeneid, II, 325.*

Fuit Ilium. *L*—*See* Fuimus Troes . . . .

Functus officio. *L*—Having carried out his duties; no longer in office.

Das **fünfte Rad am Wagen.** *Ger*—The fifth wheel on the wagon; a useless appendage.

Fuori commercio. *It*—Not available commercially.

Fuori i barbari. *It*—Out with the barbarians. The battle cry of Pope Julius II.

Fuori le mura. *It*—Outside the walls (of Rome).

Für Herren. *Ger*—For gentlemen only.

Furia francese. *It*—French fury. Doubtless modeled on *Furor Teutonicus (q.v.).*

Furor arma ministrat. *L*—Rage supplies weapons.—*Vergil, Aeneid, I, 150.*

Furor loquendi. *L*—An uncontrollable desire to talk.

Furor poeticus. *L*—The inspired frenzy of the poet.

Furor scribendi. *L*—Mania for writing.

Furor Teutonicus. *L*—Teuton barbarism. A phrase of Lucan used in the present century to describe German conduct in war.

Der **Fürst ist der erste Diener seines Staats.** *Ger*—The prince is the first servant of his state. An ideal approved by Frederick the Great.

Fuyez les dangers de loisir. *Fr*—Flee the dangers of idleness.

G

gal. (général). *Fr*—Military general.

gaux. (généraux). *Fr*—Military generals.

G.A.Z. *See* Gesamtverzeichnis der ausländischen Zeitschriften.

ges. gesch. (gesetzlich geschützt). *Ger*—Legally protected; patented.

GKW (Gesamtkatalog der Wiegendrucke). *Ger*—Bibliography of incunabula.

G.m.b.H. (Gesellschaft mit beschränkter Haftung. *Ger*—Company with limited liability.

G.P.R. (genio populi Romani). *L*—To the genius of the Roman people.

G.Q.G. (Grand Quartier général). *Fr*—General Headquarters (military).

gral. (general). *Sp*—Military general.

Gage d'amour. *Fr*—A pledge or token of love.

Gaieté de cœur. *Fr*—Light-hearted gaiety.

Galilaie nenikekas. *Gk*—Thou hast conquered O Galilaean! These supposed last words of Julian the Apostate are first found in the work of the Christian historian Theodoret of the fifth century. The Latin translation, *Vicisti, Galilaee,* is more frequently quoted.

Gallia est omnis divisa in partes tres. *L*—All Gaul is divided into three parts.—*Caesar, Gallic War, I, 1.*

Garde à cheval. *Fr*—Mounted guard.

Garde du corps. *Fr*—Body guard.

La **Garde meurt et ne se rend pas.** *Fr*—The guard dies but it does not surrender. Cambronne, commander of the Old Guard at Waterloo, denied making this statement, embarrassing for him since he was taken prisoner at Waterloo. However, the words were engraved on his monument.

Gardez la foi. *Fr*—Keep the faith.

Gardien de la paix. *Fr*—Guardian of the peace; a policeman.

Gaudeamus, igitur, juvenes dum sumus. *L*—Let us rejoice, therefore, while we are young. The first line of a Latin song once popular in college circles.

Gaudet tentamine virtus. *L*—Virtue rejoices in trials.

Gaudium certaminis. *L*—Delight in the struggle; joy in the fight.

Geben Sie acht! *Ger*—Take care; watch out.

Gebranntes Kind scheut das Feuer. *Ger*—The burnt child dreads the fire.

Geflügelte Worte. *Ger*—Winged words. A translation of *Epea pteroenta (q.v.).* It has come to mean an expression that has traveled from one language to another.

Geheime Staatspolizei. *Ger*—Secret State Police under the Nazis. Generally referred to as Gestapo, a combination of the beginning letters of each of the components.

Geld behält das Feld. *Ger*—Money gains the field; money makes the mare go.

La génération spontanée est une chimère. *Fr*—Spontaneous generation is a chimera, a thing of the imagination.—*Pasteur.*

La génie c'est la patience. *Fr*—Genius is patience.

Genius loci. *L*—The protecting spirit or deity of a place.

Gens braccata. *L*—People, such as Gauls and barbarians in general, who wore trousers (breeches), not the toga, as did the Romans.

Gens d'armes. *Fr*—In Middle Ages, men-at-arms; soldiers. The modern term *gendarmes,* policemen, is derived from this phrase.

Gens de condition. *Fr*—People of rank.

Gens d'église. *Fr*—Churchmen; ecclesiastics.

Gens de guerre. *Fr*—The military class.

Gens de la même famille. *Fr*—People of the same ilk. This is not complimentary.

Gens de lettres. *Fr*—The literary world.

Gens de loi. *Fr*—Lawyers.

Gens de peu. *Fr*—Men of the lower orders, of little influence.

Gens de robe. *Fr*—People connected with some phase of the law: lawyers, judges, magistrates, etc.

Gens du monde. *Fr*—People of the world; fashionable people.

119

Les gens qui hésitent

Les gens qui hésitent ne reussissent guère. *Fr*—Those who hesitate rarely succeed.—*Napoléon Bonaparte.*

Gens togata. *L*—The toga-clad nation; the Romans; civilians, in general, as distinguished from the military class.—*Vergil, Aeneid, I, 282.*

Gente baja. *Sp*—The lower classes.

Gente fina. *Sp*—The cultivated, educated class.

Genus homo. *L*—The human race.

Genus irritabile vatum. *L*—The waspish race of poets. This suggests the jealousy that exists among versifiers who each resent the others' pretensions.—*Horace, Epistles, II, ii, 102.*

Genus literarium. *L*—Literary genre.

Georgium sidus. *L*—Former name of the planet Uranus, so named after George III by its discoverer, William Herschel.

Gerebatur. *L*—It was waged. Used with dates to indicate when a war took place.

Gesagt, getan. *Ger*—No sooner said than done.

Gesamtverzeichnis der ausländischen Zeitschriften. *Ger*—Comprehensive Index of Foreign Periodicals; a list of non-German periodicals.

Das **Gesetz nur kann uns Freiheit geben.** *Ger*—Only the law can give us freedom.—*Goethe.*

Gesta Romanorum. *L*—"The Exploits of the Romans," a medieval collection of tales and legends with strong moral lessons.

Gestapo. *Ger*—*See* Geheime Staatspolizei.

Gibier de potence. *Fr*—A gallows bird; jail-bird.

Gigantes autem erant super terram in diebus illis. *L*—There were giants upon the earth in those days.—*Vulgate, Genesis, VI, 4.*

Giovane santo, diavolo vecchio. *It*—A young saint, an old devil.

Glaucopis Athene. *Gk*—Owl-eyed, piercing-eyed Athene. An epithet.—*Homer, Iliad, I, 206* and elsewhere.

Gleich und gleich gesellt sich gern. *Ger*—Birds of a feather flock together.

Glissando. *It*—Notes played in a sliding, slurring, or gliding manner.

Gloria in excelsis Deo. Et in terra pax hominibus bonae voluntatis. *L*—Glory to God in the highest and on earth peace to men of good will. Opening words of the Gloria of the Mass. Adapted from *Vulgate, Luke, II, 14.*

Gloria Patri et Filio et Spiritui Sancto; sicut erat in principio et nunc et semper et in saecula saeculorum. Amen. *L*—Glory be to the Father and to the Son and to the Holy Spirit; as it was in the beginning, is now and ever shall be, world without end. Amen. In Christian churches this is known as the lesser doxology.

Glückliches Neujahr! *Ger*—Happy New Year!

Glück und Glas wie leicht bricht das. *Ger*—Luck and glass, how easily they break; glass and luck, brittle muck.

Gnothi seauton. *Gk*—Know thyself. A maxim on the walls of Apollo's temple at Delphi, attributed to various Greek philosophers.

Gorge de pigeon. *Fr*—Iridescent throat of the dove; used to describe the variegated colors of shot silk.

Gott behüte! *Ger*—God forbid!

Der gottbetrunkene Mensch. *Ger*—The God-intoxicated man. A description of Spinoza by Novalis.

Gott macht gesund, und der Doktor bekommt das Geld. *Ger*—God gives us back our health, and the doctor gets the money.

Gott mit uns. *Ger*—God with us. A popular slogan of the Germans during the First World War.

Gott sei Dank. *Ger*—Thanks be to God.

Gott soll hüten

Gott soll hüten! *Ger*—God forbid!

Goutte à goutte. *Fr*—Drop by drop.

Grâce à Dieu. *Fr*—Thanks be to God.

Gracias a Dios. *Sp*—Thanks be to God.

Gradu diverso, via una. *L*—Following the same route but at a different pace.

Gradus ad Parnassum. *L*—Steps to Parnassus; title of an English textbook on verse-writing in Latin and of musical works by Fux and by Clementi.

Graecia capta ferum victorem cepit. *L*—Captive Greece took its rough victor captive. Though the Romans defeated the Greeks on the battlefield, the conquerors adopted much of the Greek culture.—*Horace, Epistles, II, i, 156.*

Graeculus esuriens. *L*—The starving Greek. Represented by Juvenal as a man who would stoop to any skulduggery to make a living.—*Juvenal, III, 78.*

Grammatici certant et adhuc sub iudice lis est. *L*—The grammarians are still quarreling and the matter is still in dispute. —*Horace, Art of Poetry, 78.*

Grande dame. *Fr*—A woman of queenly bearing; often applied to one who puts on airs.

Grande parure. *Fr*—Full dress.

La **Grande Voleuse.** *Fr*—The great robber; a deprecatory assessment of the British by the French.

Le **Grand Monarque.** *Fr*—The Great Monarch, Louis XIV.

I **gran dolori sono muti.** *It*—Great sorrows have no tongue.

Le **grand prix.** *Fr*—The first prize.

Grand seigneur. *Fr*—A great lord; an aristocrat of the higher ranks.

Les **grands esprits se rencontrent.** *Fr*—Great minds get together; great minds think alike.

Le **grand siècle.** *Fr*—The great century; the age ending with the death of Louis XIV.

Gratia gratiam parit. *L*—Kindness begets kindness.

Gratia placendi. *L*—For the sake of pleasing.

Gratis dictum. *L*—A mere assertion unsupported by evidence.

Graviora quaedam sunt remedia periculis. *L*—Some remedies are worse than the disease.—*Publilius Syrus.*

La **gravité est un mystère du corps inventé pour cacher les défauts de l'esprit.** *Fr*—The grave manner is a mysterious cloak put on by the body to hide the faults of the soul.—*La Rochefoucauld, Maxims, 257.*

Une **grosse femme.** *Fr*—A stout woman.

Der **grosse Heide.** *Ger*—The great pagan, a name given Goethe.

Grosse tête, peu de sens. *Fr*—Big head but little sense.

Guarda innanzi che tu salti. *It*—Look before you leap.

Guarde-vos Deus de amigo reconciliado. *Port*—God preserve you from a former friend with whom you have become reconciled.

Guerra al cuchillo. *Sp*—War to the knife; deadly conflict.

Guerra cominciata, inferno scatenato. *It*—War begun is hell let loose.

Guerre à mort. *Fr*—War to the death.

Guerre à outrance. *Fr*—War to the uttermost; a savage war.

Gute Nacht. *Ger*—Good night.

Guten Morgen. *Ger*—Good morning.

Gute Ware lobt sich selbst. *Ger*—Good merchandise praises itself; good wine needs no bush.

Gutta cavat lapidem, consumitur annulus usu. *L*—Dripping water hollows the rock; the ring is worn away by use.—*Ovid, Epistles from the Pontus, IV, x, 5.* This inspired the line *Gutta*

cavat lapidem, non vi sed saepe cadendo: The drop hollows
the stone not by force but frequent falling. An early use is to
be found in the seventh sermon of Latimer, given before
Edward IV in 1549. *See also* Percussu crebro saxa . . . .

H

h.a. (hoc anno). *L*—In the present year.

hab. fac. poss. (habere facias possessionem). *L*—Cause a certain
person to have possession. A writ of execution in ejectment.

h.c. *See* Honoris causa.

h.d. (hora decubitus). *L*—At bedtime. A medical direction.

H.I., H.J. (Hic iacet *or* jacet). *L*—Here lies.

H.I.S., H.J.S. (Hic iacet—*or* jacet—sepultus—*or* situs). *L*—Here
lies buried.

h.m. (hoc mense). *L*—This month.

H.M.P. (Hoc monumentum posuit). *L*—This monument was
erected by ——.

Hnos. (Hermanos). *Sp*—Brothers.

Hr. (Herr). *Ger*—Mr.

—H.R.I.P. (Hic requiescit in pace). *L*—Here rests in peace —.

h.s. (hora somni). *L*—At bedtime. A medical direction.

H.S.S. (Historiae Societatis Socius). *L*—Fellow of the Historical
Society.

h.t. (hoc tempore). *L*—At this time.

Habeas corpus. *L*—You may have the body; a writ of personal
freedom exercised when a prisoner posts bail and demands a
hearing in court. There are a number of writs that begin with
these two words.

Habemus papam. *L*—We have a pope. Words spoken to the waiting crowd in front of St. Peter's in Rome after the cardinals of the Roman Catholic Church have chosen a new pope.

Habendum et tenendum. *L*—To have and to hold. An expression found in deeds.

Habent sua fata libelli. *L*—*See* Pro captu lectoris . . . .

Habet et musca splenem. *L*—Even a fly will show anger.

L'habitude est une seconde nature. *Fr*—Habit becomes second nature.

Haeret lateri letalis harundo. *L*—The deadly arrow sticks in his side; by transference, deep passion or remorse.—*Vergil, Aeneid IV, 73.*

Hänge nicht alles auf einen Nagel. *Ger*—Don't hang everything on one nail; don't carry all your eggs in one basket.

Hannibal ad portas. *L*—Hannibal is at the gates. A call for action; a cry of alarm. The Carthaginian general was a terror to the Romans during the Second Punic War (218-201).

Hapax legomenon. *Gk*—Said once; a word or an expression used only once. A term used in classical philology.

Hasta la muerte todo es vida. *Sp*—All is life up to death; never say die; where there's life there's hope.—*Cervantes, Don Quixote, II, LIX.*

Hasta la vista. *Sp*—Until we meet again.

Hasta mañana. *Sp*—Until tomorrow.

Haud facile emergunt quorum virtutibus obstat/res angusta domi. *L*—Men do not easily succeed who are held back by straitened circumstances at home.—*Juvenal, III, 164.* Samuel Johnson's version, even more concise than the Latin, is "Slow rises worth by poverty depressed."—*(London, 177)*

Haud passibus aequis. *L*—Adapted from *Non passibus aequis (q.v.).*

Haute bourgeoisie. *Fr*—The upper middle class, especially the more prosperous.

Haute coiffure. *Fr*—Hair styled high.

Haute couture. *Fr*—The acme of feminine fashion; high fashion dress designing by recognized creators of styles for women.

Haute cuisine. *Fr*—High style cooking; fine cooking.

La **haute politique.** *Fr*—Top-level politics; political affairs in a nation at the summit.

Haut goût. *Fr*—High flavor in meat that has been kept so long that many consider it tainted; high seasoning.

Haut ton. *Fr*—High tone; elegance in fashion.

He dicho. *Sp*—I have spoken; I have said what I had to say. The customary final words of a speech given by a person speaking in Spanish.

He glossa omomoch', he de phren anomotos. *Gk*—My tongue has sworn but not my mind; a mental reservation.—*Euripides, Hippolytus, 612.*

Heil dir im Siegerkranz. *Ger*—Hail to thee wearing the conqueror's wreath. The national hymn of Prussia.

Helluo librorum. *L*—A devourer of books; a great reader. Adapted from a passage in *Cicero, Chief Good and Evil, III, 2, 7.*

Heureux les peuples dont l'histoire est ennuyeux. *Fr*—Happy the nation whose history makes dull reading.

Heute Deutschland, morgen die ganze Welt. *Ger*—Today Germany, tomorrow the whole world. The Nazi dream.

Heute rot, morgen tot. *Ger*—Today red, tomorrow dead; here today, gone tomorrow.

Heu, vitam perdidi, operose nihil agendo. *L*—Alas, I have wasted my life, industriously doing nothing.

Hiatus maxime (valde) deflendus. *L*—A gap much to be lamented. This phrase may be found in ancient classics where a break in the original text is noted. Also used when a man's performance falls short of expectations.

Hibernicis ipsis Hiberniores. *L*—More Irish than the Irish themselves. Said of certain English settlers in Ireland.

Hic et nunc. *L*—Here and now.

Hic et ubique. *L*—Here and everywhere.

Hic jacet. *L*—Here lies, the first words of an inscription on a tombstone. *See also* H.I., H.J.

Hic niger est, hunc tu, Romane, caveto. *L*—This man is a black-hearted fellow; Roman, avoid him.—*Horace, Satires, I, iv, 85.*

Hic sepultus. *L*—Here lies buried. *See also* H.I.S.

Hier stehe ich! Ich kann nicht anders. Gott helfe mir, Amen. *Ger*—Here I take my stand! I cannot do otherwise. God help me! Supposed statement of Luther when he was invited to recant before the Diet of Worms in 1521.

Hilf dir selbst, so hilft dir Gott. *Ger*—God helps those who help themselves.

Hinc illae lacrimae. *L*—Hence those tears.—*Terence, Andria, I, i, 99.*

Hinc lucem et pocula sacra. *L*—From here (the university) we receive light and sacred drafts of inspiration. The motto of the University of Cambridge and its press.

His ego nec metas rerum nec tempora pono. *L*—To these (Romans) I place no bounds in space or time.—*Vergil, Aeneid, I, 278.*

L'histoire n'est qu'une fable convenue. *Fr*—History is only a fable agreed upon. Variously attributed to Fénelon, Napoléon Bonaparte, and Voltaire.

Ho bios brachys, he de techne makre. *Gk*—Life is short; art is long.—*Hippocrates. See also* Ars longa . . . .

Hoc age. *L*—Do this. At a Roman sacrifice a command from a priest that the victim should be slain. At this order, all present maintained silence; hence the phrase came to mean: Pay attention to this.

Hoc erat in votis. *L*—This was something I always wanted.—
Horace, Satires, II, 6, 1.

Hoc est corpus meum. *L*—This is my body. Words used at the
consecration in the Latin version of the Mass.—*Vulgate,
Mark, XIV, 22; Luke, XXII, 19.*

Hoc genus omne. *L*—All persons of that classification. Horace
used the phrase to end a list of occupations he held in contempt. It is sometimes quoted as *Et id genus omne, Id genus
omne, Et hoc genus omne.*—*Horace, Satires, I, ii, 2.*

Hoc monumentum posuit. *L*—He erected this monument.

Hoc opus, hic labor est. *L*—This is really work, this is really
labor. These words were originally used by Vergil to indicate
the difficulty of returning to the world above after the descent
to Avernus.—*Vergil, Aeneid, VI, 129.*

Hoc volo, sic jubeo, sit pro ratione voluntas. *L*—This is my wish,
this is my command, and for my reason say that it is my
pleasure. From Juvenal's picture of a cruel, quarrelsome wife.
The motto of the dictator.—*Juvenal, VI, 223.*

Hodie mihi, cras tibi. *L*—Today is mine, tomorrow is yours. An
inscription found on tombstones.

Hodos chameliontos. *Gk*—The path of the chameleon, noted for
changing its coloration. W. B. Yeats uses this phrase as the
title of Book III of his autobiography.

Hoi polloi. *Gk*—The many; the mob. Since *hoi* means *the*, it is
redundant to say *the hoi polloi*.

Hombre casado, burro domado. *Sp*—A married man is a tamed
burro.

Hominem pagina nostra sapit. *L*—My works savor of humanity.
—*Martial, X, 4.*

Homines dum docent discunt. *L*—Men learn while they teach.
—*Seneca, Letters to Lucilius, VII, 7.*

Hommage d'auteur. *Fr*—With the compliments of the author.

Hommage d'éditeur. *Fr*—With the compliments of the publisher (not of the editor).

L'homme absurde est celui qui ne change jamais. *Fr*—The absurd man is the one who never changes his opinion.—*A. M. Barthélémy.*

Homme d'affaires. *Fr*—Businessman; an agent.

Homme de bien. *Fr*—A good man; a righteous man.

Homme de guerre. *Fr*—A man of war; member of the military forces.

Homme de lettres. *Fr*—Man of letters; a literary man.

Homme de paille. *Fr*—Man of straw; a dummy; name given to a weak man who is set up to be knocked down easily.

Homme d'épée. *Fr*—Man of the sword; military man; one interested in fencing.

Homme d'esprit. *Fr*—A wit; a man of unusual mental ability.

Homme d'état. *Fr*—Statesman.

Homme de théâtre. *Fr*—A man professionally interested in the theatre.

Homme du monde. *Fr*—Man of the world; a social lion.

L'homme propose et Dieu dispose. *Fr*—Translation of *Homo proponit . . . (q.v.).*

Les hommes rougissent moins de leurs crimes que de leurs faiblesses et de leur vanité. *Fr*—Men blush less for their crimes than for their weaknesses and their vanity.—*La Bruyère, Characters, Of the Heart, 74 (5), p. 150 in Garapon's edition (Garnier Frères, 1962).*

Les hommes sont cause que les femmes ne s'aiment point. *Fr*—Men are the reason why women do not love one another.—*La Bruyère, Characters, Of Women, 55 (IV), p. 128 in Garapon's edition (Garnier Frères, 1962).*

Homo covivens. *L*—Man living together. The projected successor to *homo sapiens*, living a strong community life, strictly regulating population and environment.

Homo homini aut deus aut lupus. *L*—Man is either a god or a wolf toward his fellow man.

Homo homini lupus. *L*—Man is a wolf toward man.—Adapted from *Plautus.*

Homo latinissimus. *L*—A very scholarly man.

Homo memorabilis. *L*—A man to be remembered.

Homo mensura. *L*—Man is the measure. *See also* Panton metron anthropos estin.

Homo multarum literarum. *L*—A man of many letters; a very learned person.

Homo neanderthalensis. *NL*—Neanderthal man. Applied to certain paleolithic cavemen. The first skeleton of this race was discovered in a valley near Düsseldorf, Germany, in 1856.

Homo proponit, sed Deus disponit. *L*—Man proposes but God disposes.—*Thomas à Kempis, Imitation of Christ, I, xix, 2.*

Homo sapiens. *L*—Scientific name for the human species.

Homo semper aliud, Fortuna aliud cogitat. *L*—Man always has one thing in mind, Fortune another.—*Publilius Syrus.*

Homo solus aut deus aut daemon. *L*—A man who lives alone is either a god or a devil.

Homo sum: humani nil a me alienum puto. *L*—I am a man and nothing that touches humanity is foreign to me.—*Terence, Self-Tormentor, I, i, 25.*

Homo trium literarum. *L*—A man of three letters, i.e. *fur*, the Latin word for thief.

Homo unius libri. *L*—A man of one book. *See also* Timeo hominem (virum) . . . .

Hon hoi theoi philousin apothneskei neos. *Gk*—He whom the gods love dies young.—*Menander. See also* Quem di diligunt . . . .

Honi (honni) soit qui mal y pense. *Fr*—Evil to him who evil thinks. Motto of the Order of the Garter supposedly based on a remark of Edward III when he put on his leg a garter that was lost by a countess who was dancing with him. The incident is probably a pleasant fiction.

Honnête homme. *Fr*—A gentleman; an honorable man.

Honores mutant mores. *L*—Honors change manners. It is not unusual for those who rise in the world to kick down the ladder by which they ascended.

Honoris causa (gratia). *L*—As a recognition of honor due. Used especially when universities grant honorary degrees.

Honos habet onus. *L*—Honors carry the burden of responsibility.

Horas non numero nisi serenas. *L*—I number none but sunny hours. An engraving found on sun dials.

Horresco referens. *L*—I shudder as I repeat the story.—*Vergil, Aeneid, II, 204.*

Horribile dictu. *L*—Horrible to relate.

Hors concours. *Fr*—Beyond competition; in a class by itself.

Hors de combat. *Fr*—Out of the fight; disabled.

Hors de propos. *Fr*—Ill-timed; out of place; irrelevant.

Hors de saison. *Fr*—Out of season.

Hors d'œuvre. *Fr*—Tasty bits of food served at the beginning of a meal to stimulate the appetite; appetizer; antipasto.

Hors la loi. *Fr*—Outlawed.

Ho sophos en auto peripherei ten ousian. *Gk*—The wise man carries all his property within himself.—*Menander's Monostichs, 404.*

Hostis humani generis. *L*—An enemy of the human race.

L'hôtel des Invalides

L'hôtel des Invalides. *Fr*—Military Pensioners' Hospital in Paris.

Hôtel de ville. *Fr*—Town-hall.

Hôtel-Dieu. *Fr*—A hospital.

Hôtel garni. *Fr*—Furnished lodgings.

Hôtel meublé. *Fr*—Furnished lodgings.

Hunde, die bellen, beissen nicht. *Ger*—Barking dogs don't bite.

Hunger ist der beste Koch. *Ger*—Hunger is the best cook.

Hurler avec les loups. *Fr*—Run with the crowd.

Huyendo del toro, cayó en el arroyo. *Sp*—While running from the bull, he fell into the stream; out of the frying pan into the fire.

L'hypocrisie est un hommage que le vice rend à la vertu. *Fr*—Hypocrisy is a form of homage that vice renders to virtue.—*La Rochefoucauld, Maxims, 218.*

Hypotheses non fingo. *L*—I do not make hypotheses; I deal with facts and not suppositions.—*Sir Isaac Newton.*

Hysteron proteron. *Gk*—Literally, the latter first; transposing the logical order of phrases or clauses so that the more striking or important idea is first; putting the cart before the horse. An example: "Let us die and let us rush into the midst of the fight," in *Vergil, Aeneid, II, 353.*

I

ibid. (ibidem). *L*—In the same place.

I.C.N. (in Christi nomine). *L*—In the name of Christ.

id. (idem). *L*—The same person.

I.D.N. (in Dei Nomine). *L*—In the name of God.

i.e. (id est). *L*—That is to say; namely.

IHS. A Christian symbol; three Greek letters, iota, eta, sigma, an abbreviation of the Greek name, Iesous, i.e. Jesus. It does not mean *Iesous, Hyios, Soter* (Jesus, Son, Savior); *Iesus, Hominum Salvator* (Jesus, Savior of Men); or *In hoc signo (vinces) (q.v.).*

i.J.d.W. (im Jahre der Welt). *Ger*—In the year of the world. According to Bishop Ussher's calculation the world was created in 4004 B.C.

I.K.H. (Ihre königliche Hoheit). *Ger*—Her Royal Highness.

I.N.C. (in nomine Christi). *See* I.C.N.

I.N.D. (in nomine Dei). *L*—In the name of God.

I N R I (Iesus nazarenus rex iudaeorum). *L*—Jesus of Nazareth, King of the Jews.

I.N.S.T. (in nomine Sanctae Trinitatis). *L*—In the name of the Holy Trinity.

i.p.i. *See* In partibus infidelium.

i.R. (im Ruhestand). *Ger*—Emeritus status; retired.

Iatre, therapeuson seauton. *Gk*—*See* Medice, cura teipsum.

Ich bin der Geist der stets verneint! *Ger*—I am the spirit that always says No. A line spoken by Mephistopheles.—*Goethe, Faust, pt. I, 1338.*

Ich dien. *Ger*—I serve. Motto of the Prince of Wales.

ICHTHYS (the Greek letters *iota, chi, theta, upsilon, sigma,* which spell *fish*). *Gk*—A symbol of identification among early Christians, the letters standing for the initials of *Iesous Christos, Theou Hyios, Soter,* meaning Jesus Christ, Son of God, Savior.

Ici on parle français. *Fr*—French is spoken here.

Id al-Fitr. *Arabic*—Breaking of the fast; Moslem festival celebrated on the day after the month-long fast of Ramadan.

Idée fixe. *Fr*—A fixed idea; an obsession.

Idem non potest simul esse et non esse. *L*—It is impossible for the same thing to exist and not exist at the same time. Axiom in Scholastic philosophy.

Idem velle et idem nolle, ea demum firma amicitia est. *L*—To wish the same things and to reject the same things, that indeed is true friendship.—*Sallust, Catiline, XX.*

Id facere laus est quod decet, non quod licet. *L*—He deserves praise who does what he ought to do, not what he may do.—*Seneca, Octavia, 454.*

Id genus omne. *L*—*See* Hoc genus omne.

Ignis fatuus. *L*—Misleading light; will-o'-the-wisp.

Ignorantia facti excusat. *L*—Ignorance of the fact excuses; when an honest error is made, criminal intent is lacking.

Ignorantia legis (juris) neminem excusat. *L*—Ignorance of the law excuses nobody.

Ignoratio elenchi. *L*—Ignorance of the point under discussion. The logical fallacy of proving or disproving a point that is not under discussion.

Ignoscito saepe alteri, numquam tibi. *L*—Often pardon others but never yourself.

Ignoti nulla cupido. *L*—Nobody desires what he does not know. —*Ovid, Art of Love, III, 397.*

Ignotum per ignotius. *L*—To explain a matter that is difficult with an illustration or explanation that is still more difficult.

Il a la mer à boire. *Fr*—He must drink up the sea; he has an impossible task to perform.

Il a le diable au corps. *Fr*—*See* Il avait le diable au corps.

Il a les défauts de ses qualités. *Fr*—He has the defects of his qualities. A frugal man may be stingy with his children without realizing it; a man with more than normal devotion to his job may drive his staff too hard.

Il a le vin mauvais. *Fr*—He is quarrelsome when he drinks.

Il avait le diable au corps. *Fr*—He had the devil in his body; he was full of the devil. Sainte-Beuve's appraisal of Voltaire.

Il connaît l'univers, et ne se connaît pas. *Fr*—He knows the universe but not himself.—*La Fontaine, Fables, VIII, 26.*

Il dit tout ce qu'il veut, mais malheureusement il n'a rien à dire. *Fr*—He says everything he wishes to say, but unfortunately he has nothing to say. A critic's tart comment.

Il est bon d'avoir des amis partout. *Fr*—It is good to have friends everywhere.

Il est bon de parler, et meilleur de se taire. *Fr*—It is good to speak but better to be silent; speech is silver, but silence is golden.

Il faut bonne mémoire après qu'on a menti. *Fr*—A man needs a good memory after he has lied.—*Corneille, Le Menteur, IV.*

Il faut cultiver notre jardin. *Fr*—We must cultivate our garden. Candide maintains that man was not born for idleness but was placed in the garden of Eden to dress it and keep it. After numerous disasters he learns that life becomes endurable only through work.—Concluding words of *Voltaire's Candide.*

Il faut laver son linge sale en famille. *Fr*—We should wash our soiled linen in private. Quarrels of a private nature should not be aired in public, for such disputes hurt a cause.—*Voltaire.*

Il faut manger pour vivre, et non pas vivre pour manger. *Fr*—We should eat to live, not live to eat.—*Molière, The Miser, III, v.*

Il faut marcher quand le diable est aux trousses. *Fr*—One must move when the devil drives behind.

Il faut que la jeunesse se passe. *Fr*—Youth will have its fling; boys will be boys.

Ilias malorum. *L*—An Iliad of ills; an account of a series of misfortunes.

Ille dolet vere qui sine teste dolet. *L*—He truly grieves who grieves alone.—*Martial, I, xxxiii, 4.*

Illotis manibus. *L*—With hands unwashed.

Il n'a ni bouche ni éperon. *Fr*—He has neither mouth nor spur, i.e., neither wit nor courage.

Il n'a pas inventé la poudre. *Fr*—Literally, he didn't discover gunpowder; he will not set the world on fire.

Il n'appartient qu'aux grands hommes d'avoir de grands défauts. *Fr*—Only great men are allowed great faults.—*La Rochefoucauld, Maxims, 190.*

Il ne faut jamais défier un fou. *Fr*—Never challenge a fool.

Il ne faut pas disputer des goûts. *Fr*—There is no disputing tastes. *See also* De gustibus non est disputandum; Chacun à son goût.

Il ne faut pas mettre tous ses œufs dans le même panier. *Fr*—Don't put all your eggs in one basket.

Il ne manquerait plus que ça. *Fr*—That would be the last straw, the crowning offense.

Il n'entend pas raillerie. *Fr*—He can't take a joke.

Il n'est sauce que d'appétit. *Fr*—Appetite is the best sauce.

Il nous faut de l'audace, et encore de l'audace, et toujours de l'audace. *Fr*—We must dare, we must dare again, and always dare.—*Danton.*

Il n'y a de nouveau que ce qui est oublié. *Fr*—There is nothing new but what has been forgotten.—*Mlle Bertin.*

Il n'y a de pire sourd que celui qui ne veut pas entendre. *Fr*—There are none so deaf as those who will not hear.

Il n'y a pas de grand homme pour son valet-de-chambre. *Fr*—No man is a hero in the eyes of his valet.—*Mme de Cornuel.* *See also* Es gibt, sagt man . . . .

Il n'y a pas moins d'éloquence dans le ton de la voix, dans les yeux, et dans l'air de la personne, que dans le choix des paroles. *Fr*—There is no less eloquence in the tone of the voice, in the eyes, and in the manner of a person than in the choice of his words.—*La Rochefoucauld, Maxims, 249.*

Il n'y a plus de Pyrénées. *Fr*—The Pyrenees no longer exist. Louis XIV is reported to have said this to his grandson Philip V when the latter was leaving Paris to occupy the throne of Spain.

Il n'y a point de déguisement qui puisse longtemps cacher l'amour où il est, ni le feindre où il n'est pas. *Fr*—There is no disguise that can long conceal love where it exists or feign it where it does not exist.—*La Rochefoucauld, Maxims, 70.*

Il n'y a que ceux qui ne font rien, qui ne se trompent pas. *Fr*—Only those who do nothing make no mistakes.

Il n'y a que le premier pas qui coûte. *Fr*—It is only the first step that is difficult. When Cardinal Polignac was marveling at the long distance St. Denis, the martyr, traveled with his head in his hands, Madame du Deffand is supposed to have made this remark.

Il n'y a rien de mieux à faire que de s'amuser. *Fr*—There is nothing else to do but enjoy oneself.

Il rit bien qui rit le dernier. *Fr*—He laughs best who laughs last.

Il s'attache aux pas de ———. *Fr*—He dogs his footsteps.

Il se noierait dans une goutte d'eau. *Fr*—He would drown himself in a drop of water; he makes a mountain out of a molehill.

Il sent le fagot. *Fr*—He smells of the fagot, i.e. he is suspected of holding heretical views.

Il se recule pour mieux sauter. *Fr*—He draws back to make a better leap forward.

Il se voit par expérience, que les mémoires excellentes se joignent volontiers aux jugements débiles. *Fr*—Experience shows that an excellent memory may quite easily be wedded to weak judgment.—*Montaigne, Essays, I, 9.*

Ils ne passeront pas. *Fr*—They shall not pass. The rallying cry of the French at Verdun in 1916.

Ils n'ont rien appris

Ils n'ont rien appris, ni rien oublié. *Fr*—They have learned nothing and they have forgotten nothing. Thirty years after the outbreak of the French Revolution, Talleyrand used these words to describe the returned *émigrés*, the Bourbons and their followers.

Il vaut mieux employer notre esprit à supporter les infortunes qui nous arrivent qu'à prévoir celles qui nous peuvent arriver. *Fr*—It is much better to set our minds to bearing present ills than to foreseeing those that may befall us.—*La Rochefoucauld, Maxims, 174.*

Il vaut mieux s'exposer à l'ingratitude que de manquer aux misérables. *Fr*—Better run the risk of ingratitude than fail those in need.—*La Bruyère, Characters, Of the Heart, 48 (v), p. 169 in Garapon's edition (Garnier Frères, 1962).*

Il veut prendre la lune avec les dents. *Fr*—He wants to catch the moon with his teeth. Said of a person who cries for the impossible.

Il y a à parier que toute idée publique, toute convention reçue, est une sottise, car elle a convenu au plus grand nombre. *Fr*—The odds are that every idea commonly held, every accepted custom is stupid, for it has been agreed upon by the majority.—*Chamfort.*

Imitatores, servum pecus. *L*—You imitators, a servile herd.—*Horace, Epistles, I, xix, 19.*

L'imitazione del male supera sempre l'esempio; come per il contrario, l'imitazione del bene è sempre inferiore. *It*—The imitation of evil surpasses the example; on the contrary, the imitation of virtue always falls short.—*Guicciardini.*

Immedicabile vulnus ense recidendum est ne pars sincera trahatur. *L*—An incurable wound must be cut out lest the sound part be infected.—*Ovid, Metamorphoses, I, 190.*

Imo pectore. *L*—From the bottom of the heart.—*Vergil, Aeneid, XI, 377.*

138

Imperium cupientibus nihil medium inter summa aut praecipitia.
   L—For those seeking power there is no middle course between the depths and the heights, between the top and the
   bottom.—*Tacitus, Histories, II, 74.*

Imperium et libertas. *L*—Empire and liberty.—*Lord Beacons-
   field.*

Imperium in imperio. *L*—A government within a government.

Imponere Pelio Ossam. *L*—To pile Ossa on Pelion. *See also*
   Excussit subjecto Pelion Ossae.—*Vergil, Georgics, I, 281.*

Impos animi. *L*—Weak-minded. *See also* Non compos mentis.

Impossible n'est pas un mot français. *Fr*—*Impossible* is not a
   word in the French language.—*Napoléon I.*

Impotens sui. *L*—Lacking self-control.

Imprimatur. *L*—It may be printed. A term used to indicate that
   ecclesiastical permission has been granted to print the work
   in question. *See also* Permissu superiorum.

Imprimi permittitur. *L*—Permission to print is granted. *See also*
   Permissu superiorum.

Imprimi potest. *L*—Permission to print is granted. *See also* Permissu superiorum.

Im Wein ist Warheit. *Ger*—*See* In vino veritas.

In absentia. *L*—In absence. Used in connection with the confer-
   ring of a degree or the condemnation of a criminal beyond
   the reach of the law.

In actu. *L*—A term used by the Scholastics to indicate that what
   was formerly in a state of possibility is now in actual existence. *See also* In potentia ad actum.

In aeternum. *L*—Forever.

In animam malevolam sapientia haud intrare potest. *L*—Wisdom
   can hardly enter the soul of an ill-willed man.

In apricum proferet. *L*—It will bring to light. The seal of the Pontifical Roman Academy of Archaeology.

In articulo mortis. *L*—At the moment of death.

In caelo quies. *L*—In heaven there is rest. In England this phrase appeared on a panel called a hatchment, formerly displayed for a time on the house of a deceased person.

In camera. *L*—In the judge's chambers; secretly.

In capite. *L*—Literally, in chief; in feudal law a tenure by which lands were held of a lord or directly of the crown.

Incidit in Scyllam qui vult vitare Charybdim. *L*—He who would avoid the whirlpool Charybdis strikes against the rock Scylla; out of the frying pan into the fire. A dactylic hexameter line based on *Vergil, Aeneid, III, 420*. It is also quoted: *Incidis in Scyllam cupiens vitare Charybdim*.

Incipit. *L*—Here begins. In Latin manuscripts this word is followed by the title of the work and the author.

In commendam. *LL*—Held in trust for a period of time, as in the case of an ecclesiastical benefice directed by an assistant for the benefit of an absent principal.

In contumaciam. *L*—Used of a person who is in contempt of a court order.

In custodia legis. *L*—In custody of the law.

Index expurgatorius. *L*—A list of books to be amended to conform to belief and practice, formerly compiled by the Roman Catholic Church. Such books are now included in the *Index Librorum Prohibitorum (q.v.)*.

Index Librorum Prohibitorum. *L*—Index of Forbidden Books, a publication issued by the Holy Office of the Roman Catholic Church.

Index locorum. *L*—Index of places.

Index nominum. *L*—An index of names.

Index rerum. *L*—An index of things; a list of references.

Index verborum. *L*—An index of words.

Indignor quandoque bonus dormitat Homerus. *L*—I am vexed whenever good old Homer nods.—*Horace, Art of Poetry, 359.*

Indocilis pauperiem pati. *L*—A man who cannot be taught to bear up under poverty.—*Horace, Odes, I, 1, 18.*

Indoctus juga ferre. *L*—Untrained to bear the yoke. Based on *Horace, Odes, II, vi, 2.*

In dubio. *L*—In doubt.

In esse. *L*—In existence.

In extenso. *L*—At length; complete treatment.

In extremis. *L*—In the last moment of life; in the final illness.

In facie curiae. *L*—In the presence of the court.

Infandum renovare dolorem. *L*—To revive an unspeakable sorrow.—*Vergil, Aeneid, II, 3.*

In favorem matrimonii. *L*—In favor of the validity of the marriage bond.

In fieri. *L*—In the state of becoming; in the process of being realized.

In flagrante delicto. *L*—Caught in the very act of committing a crime.

In forma pauperis. *L*—As a pauper. A man whose rights are violated but who is unable to pay legal expenses may be admitted by the court to sue without paying the customary fees.

In foro conscientiae. *L*—In the court of conscience.

In foro externo. *L*—In the public forum as distinguished from the forum of conscience.

In foro interno. *L*—In the judgment of conscience.

Infra dignitatem. *L*—Beneath one's dignity. Sometimes shortened to *infra dig.*

In futuro. *L*—In future; henceforth.

El ingenioso hidalgo. *Sp*—The ingenious gentleman, Don Quixote de la Mancha.

Ingenium mala saepe movent. *L*—Bad luck often stirs genius.— *Ovid, Art of Love, II, 43. See also* Necessitas rationum inventrix.

Ingenium res adversae nudare solent, celare secundae. *L*—Adversity reveals genius; prosperity conceals it.—*Horace, Satires, II, viii, 73.*

Ingenui vultus puer ingenuique pudoris. *L*—A lad with a noble countenance and inborn modesty.

Ingratus unus omnibus miseris nocet. *L*—One ingrate does harm to all men in misery; the wealthy man closes his purse after one bitter experience.—*Publilius Syrus.*

In gremio legis. *L*—In the lap of the law.

In hoc signo vinces. *L*—With this sign (a cross) thou shalt conquer. Words reportedly seen in the heavens by Constantine at his victory near the Milvian Bridge in 312 A.D.

In infinitum. *L*—To infinity.

In initio. *L*—In the beginning.

Iniquum petas ut aequum feras. *L*—Ask for what is unreasonable that you may obtain what is just.

L'injustice à la fin produit l'indépendence. *Fr*—In the end injustice produces independence.—*Voltaire, Tancrède, III, ii.*

In limine. *L*—On the threshold; at the outset.

In loco. *L*—On the spot; in the place of.

In loco citato. *L*—*See* Loco citato.

In loco parentis. *L*—In the place of a parent.

In manus tuas commendo spiritum meum. *L*—Into thy hands I commend my spirit. Last words of Christ on the cross.— *Vulgate, Luke, XXIII, 46.*

In medias res. *L*—Into the midst of things. Said of the technique of the classic epic when the writer begins at a dramatic point in his story, then in a flashback explains events that preceded. —*Horace, Art of Poetry, 148.*

In medio stat virtus. *L*—Virtue exists in the middle between two extremes. If courage is the virtue considered, its excess is rashness and its defect cowardice. According to Christian teaching this axiom applies to the moral, not the theological virtues. *See also* Aurea mediocritas.

In medio tutissimus ibis. *L*—*See* Medio tutissimus . . . .

In meditatione fugae. *L*—Poised for flight.

In memmoriam ad gloriam sed asthoriam non nomoreum. Garbled Latin, Irish, and English—Probably means To (her) glorious memory but my dear treasure is no more.—*Sean O'Casey, Inishfallen, Fare Thee Well (in the chapter Mrs. Casside Takes a Holiday).*

In memoriam. *L*—Unto the memory.

In morte veritas. *L*—The truth comes out at death.

In necessariis unitas, in non necessariis libertas, in utrisque caritas. *L*—In essentials, there should be unity, in nonessentials liberty, in both cases charity. This maxim is sometimes quoted: *In necessariis unitas, in dubiis libertas, in omnibus caritas:* In essentials, there should be unity; in doubt liberty; in all things charity. This is falsely attributed to St. Augustine. Its origin (ca. 1625) has been traced to an admonition intended to bring peace into the church, given by Rupertus Meldenius to the theologians of the Augustinian confession.

In nihilum nil posse reverti. *L*—There is nothing that can be reduced to nothing; matter is indestructible.—*Persius, III, 84.*

In nocte consilium. *L*—The night brings counsel. *See also* En nukti boule.

In nomine. *L*—In the name.

In nomine Domini. *L*—In the name of the Lord.

143

In nubibus

In nubibus. *L*—In the clouds; confused.

In nuce. *L*—In a nutshell; briefly.

In omnia paratus. *L*—Prepared for all things; ready for any eventuality.

In omni doctrina grammatica praecedit. *L*—In all learning the study of grammar comes first. An educational principle in the Middle Ages.

Inopem me copia fecit. *L*—Abundance has made me poor. These words spoken by Narcissus lamented the fact that he had all the beauty he thought in another, that the lovely creature he saw mirrored in the water was himself. It has been used to indicate the plight of the man with many ideas and a poverty of expression.—*Ovid, Metamorphoses, III, 466.*

Inops, potentem dum vult imitari, perit. *L*—A poor man perishes when he tries to imitate a powerful man.—*Phaedrus, Fables, I, xxiv, 1.*

In ovo. *L*—Still in the egg.

In pace. *L*—In peace.

In partibus infidelium. *L*—In the region of infidels; a phrase used in the Roman Catholic Church to indicate the see over which a titular bishop is said to rule.

In perpetuam rei memoriam. *L*—In everlasting memory of the event.

In perpetuum. *L*—In perpetuity.

In perturbato animo sicut in corpore sanitas esse non potest. *L*—In a disturbed mind, as in a disturbed body, health is impossible.—*Cicero, Tusculan Disputations, III, 4.*

In petto. *It*—In the breast; held back for future announcement. Thus, the pope may have in mind certain ecclesiastics who are to be made cardinals, but he has not made his choice public.

In pios usus. *L*—For pious uses; said of property left by will for religious purposes.

In posse. *L*—Potentially; within possibility.

In potentia ad actum. *L*—A term used by the Scholastics to indicate that an object is in a state of possible realization.

In principio. *L*—In the beginning.

In propria persona. *L*—Personally present.

In proverbium cessit, sapientiam vino adumbrari. *L*—It has become a proverb that wisdom is clouded by wine.—*Pliny the Elder, Natural History, XXIII, 1.*

In puris naturalibus. *L*—Naked.

In re. *L*—*See* Re.

In rerum natura. *L*—In the nature of things.

In saecula saeculorum. *L*—Forever and ever.

In situ. *L*—In its original position or place.

In solidum (solido). *L*—A term used to indicate that parties involved are held jointly and severally.

In specie. *L*—In the same or similar form.

In spiritualibus. *L*—In matters spiritual.

In statu pupillari. *L*—In the position of a ward or orphan.

In statu quo. *L*—In its former state or condition.

In statu quo ante bellum. *L*—In the condition that existed prior to the war.

In tanto discrimine. *L*—In such a moment of grave crisis.

In te, Domine, speravi. *L*—In thee, O Lord, have I placed my trust.—*Vulgate, Psalms, XXX, 1.*

Integer vitae scelerisque purus/Non eget Mauris/iaculis neque arcu. *L*—The man whose life is pure and free from crime/ needs no Moorish darts or bow for his protection. These opening lines of a humorous poem by Horace are often quoted in all seriousness.—*Horace, Odes, I, xxii, 1.*

In tenebris. *L*—In darkness.

Inter alia. *L*—Among other things.

Inter anum et urinam. *L*—Between the anus and the urine. An unflattering view of human origin.

Inter arma leges silent. *L*—The laws are silent in time of war.— *Cicero, For Milo, IV, 10.*

Inter canem et lupum. *L*—Caught between a dog and a wolf; between the devil and the deep blue sea. Used when a person in difficulty has a choice between two evils.

Interdum stultus opportuna loquitur. *L*—Sometimes a fool says the right thing.

Interdum volgus rectum videt; est ubi peccat. *L*—Sometimes the common man sees aright; sometimes he is wrong.— *Horace, Epistles, II, i, 63.*

Inter esse et non esse non datur medium. *L*—Between existence and nonexistence there is no mean. An axiom of Scholastic philosophy based on Aristotle.

Inter faeces et urinam. *L*—Between faeces and urine. *See also* Inter anum et urinam.

Inter folia fructus. *L*—There is fruit among the leaves (both of trees and books).

Inter nos. *L*—Between ourselves; a matter to be kept secret.

Inter pocula. *L*—In one's cups; a time of revelation. Here there is a suggestion that someone has had one cup too many.

In terra di ciechi, beato chi ha un occhio. *It*—In the land of the blind, blessed is the man who has one eye. *See also* Au royaume des aveugles . . . .

In terrorem. *L*—As a warning. A legal term.

In terrorem populi. *L*—To produce terror among the people. Thus, public executions may be staged in the hope of maintaining law and order.

Inter se. *L*—Between or among themselves.

Inter spem et metum. *L*—Between hope and fear.

Inter vivos. *L*—Among the living. Generally used in connection with a living trust whereby an estate passes from one generation to another without probate.

In totidem verbis. *L*—In just so many words.

In toto. *L*—Completely.

Intra muros. *L*—Within the walls.

In transitu. *L*—In transit.

Intra vires. *L*—Within one's prayers.

In un giorno non si fe' Roma. *It*—Rome was not built in a day.

In usum Delphini. *L*—For the use of the Dauphin, the eldest son of Louis XIV. The King had an expurgated series of classics prepared for his son.

In utero. *L*—In the womb; not yet born.

In utrumque paratus. *L*—Prepared for either eventuality. Title of a poem by Matthew Arnold.—*Vergil, Aeneid, II, 61.*

Invenit. *L*—He invented it.

In ventre. *L*—In the womb.

Inverso ordine. *L*—In inverse order.

Invidia festos dies non agit. *L*—Envy takes no vacation.

In vili veste nemo tractatur honeste. *L*—No one in shabby clothes is treated fairly.

In vino veritas. *L*—There's truth in wine; the truth slips out when people are drinking.

Invita Minerva. *L*—Literally, when Minerva (the goddess of wisdom) is unwilling; when natural talent is lacking.—*Horace, Art of Poetry, 385.*

In vitro. *L*—Within glass; observable, as in a test tube.

In vivo. *L*—In or upon a living organism. As opposed to *in vitro* (*q.v.*).

In vota miseros ultimus cogit timor. *L*—The fear of death drives the miserable to make vows to the gods.—*Seneca, Agamemnon, 510.*

Ipsa scientia potestas est. *L*—Knowledge itself is power.—*Francis Bacon.*

Ipse dixit. *L*—He himself said so. The appeal to authority.

Ipsissima verba. *L*—The identical words; a direct quotation.

Ipso facto. *L*—By the very fact.

Ipso jure. *L*—By the law itself; by the operation of law.

Ira de irmãos, ira de diabos. *Port*—The anger of brothers is the anger of devils.

Ira furor brevis est; animum rege; qui nisi paret, imperat. *L*—Anger is brief madness; rule your spirit; unless it obeys, it commands.—*Horace, Epistles, I, ii, 62.*

Iratus cum ad se rediit sibi tum irascitur. *L*—When an angry man becomes himself again, then he is angry with himself.—*Publilius Syrus.*

Irrtümer vorbehalten. *Ger*—Errors excepted.

Ita lex scripta est. *L*—This is the way the law reads; such is the wording of the law.

Italia farà da se. *It*—Italy will make it alone.

Italia irredenta. *It*—Unredeemed Italy. In 1878 an Italian political party was formed with the object of bringing lands formerly belonging to Italy back into the nation.

Ite, missa est. *L*—Go, the Mass is over; you are dismissed. There is some doubt about the correct translation of this expression.

J

J.B. (Jurum Baccalaureus). *L*—Bachelor of Laws.

J.C., I.C. (Jesus Christus). *L*—Jesus Christ.

J.C.B. (Juris Canonici Baccalaureus). *L*—Bachelor of Canon Law.

J.C.B. (Juris Civilis Baccalaureus). *L*—Bachelor of Civil Law.

J.C.D. (Juris Canonici Doctor). *L*—Doctor of Canon Law.

J.C.D. (Juris Civilis Doctor). *L*—Doctor of Civil Law.

J.C.L. (Juris Canonici Lector *or* Licentiatus). *L*—Reader or Licentiate in Canon Law.

J.D. (Juris Doctor). *L*—Doctor of Law.

J.U.D. (Juris Utriusque Doctor). *L*—Doctor of both civil and canon law.

J'accuse. *Fr*—"I accuse." Title of an explosive article, published in 1898, by Émile Zola in which he championed the cause of falsely accused Capt. Alfred Dreyfus.

Jacta alea est. *L*—The die is cast. Words uttered by Julius Caesar when he crossed the Rubicon.—*Suetonius, Lives of Twelve Caesars, J. Caesar, 32.*

J'ai vécu. *Fr*—I lived through it. Words spoken by Sièyes when he was asked what he had done during the Reign of Terror in France.

Jalousie de métier. *Fr*—Professional jealousy.

Jam redit et Virgo, redeunt Saturnia regna. *L*—Now the Maiden returns, now the Age of Saturn, a mythical golden age of peace, justice and plenty. The maiden referred to is Astraea, the goddess of justice, who left the earth in the iron age because men had become evil. Now she is returning in the Golden Age of Augustus.—*Vergil, Eclogues, IV, 6.*

Jam satis vixi. *L*—I have lived long enough.

Januis clausis. *L*—Behind closed doors.

Jardins à l'anglaise. *Fr*—Gardens in the English style.

Jeder Esel kann kritisieren. *Ger*—Any ass can criticize.

Jeder ist Herr in seinem Hause. *Ger*—Every man is master in his own house; a man's house is his castle.

Jeder ist seines Glückes Schmied. *Ger*—Every man is the architect of his own fortune.

Jeder ist sich selbst der Nächste. *Ger*—Every man is closest to himself; charity begins at home.

Jeder weiss, wo ihn der Schuh drückt. *Ger*—Every man knows where his own shoe pinches. *See also* Cada uno sabe . . . .

Je höher der Baum, desto tiefer der Fall. *Ger*—The higher the tree, the farther the fall.

Je le pansay, Dieu le guarit. *OF*—I dressed his wound; God cured him. Dictum of the French surgeon Ambroise Paré.

Je maintiendrai. *Fr*—I will stand firm. Motto of the Netherlands.

Je maintiendrai le droit. *Fr*—I will maintain what is right.

Je me fais pitié à moi-même. *Fr*—I feel sorry for myself. Words of Minister of Finance de Calonne, not unaware of the Revolution that was soon to break out in France.

Je ne sais quoi. *Fr*—I don't know what. Used when one is unable to find the right word to express his ideas.

Je prends mon bien où je le trouve. *Fr*—I take my stuff where I find it. This was Molière's reply when he was accused of plagiarism. This is also quoted as *Je reprends*, indicating that others had stolen his material.

Je sème à tout vent. *Fr*—My seed rides on every wind. A publisher's motto.

Je t'aime plus qu'hier, moins que demain. *Fr*—I love you more than I did yesterday, and less than I will tomorrow. Words on a popular pendant.

Jeter de la poudre aux yeux. *Fr*—To throw powder in someone's eyes; to blind someone to the real issue.

Jeter le manche après la cognée. *Fr*—To throw the handle after the hatchet; to despair.

Jets d'eau. *Fr*—Jets of water; a fountain.

Jeu de mots. *Fr*—Play on words.

Jeu d'esprit. *Fr*—Witticism.

Jeu de théâtre. *Fr*—A stage trick.

Jeunesse dorée. *Fr*—Gilded youth. A name given to wealthy, fashionable men, idle and debauched, who roamed the streets in gangs attacking the Jacobins, who had inaugurated the Reign of Terror during the French Revolution.

Le **jeu ne vaut pas la chandelle.** *Fr*—The game is not worth the candle.

Je vais chercher un grand Peut-être! *Fr*—I go to seek a great May-be! Apocryphal last words of Rabelais. *See also* La farce est jouée.

Je veux que le dimanche chaque paysan ait sa poule au pot. *Fr*—It is my wish that every peasant have a chicken in the pot on Sunday.—*Henry IV of France.*

Je vis d'espoir. *Fr*—I live in hope.

Joannes est nomen ejus. *L*—John is his name. Words on the seal of Puerto Rico, whose capital is San Juan (Saint John).—*Vulgate, Luke, I, 63.*

Joculatores Dei. *L*—Jesters of God. A name that Saint Francis of Assisi gave his followers to indicate the humble spirit of their mission, comparing them to jongleurs.

Johannes fac totum. *L*—Johnny-do-everything. A phrase from Robert Greene's criticism of the young Shakespeare.

Joie de vivre. *Fr*—The joy of living.

Jour gras. *Fr*—A fat day; a day of feasting.

Jour maigre. *Fr*—A lean day; a day when a prescribed amount of food or abstinence from meat is enjoined by Church law.

Journée des Barricades. *Fr*—Day of Barricades, recalling the times when rioting people of Paris erected barricades in the streets against the government.

La **Journée des Dupes.** *Fr*—Dupes' Day or Day of Dupes. November 11, 1630. Marie de' Medici won a promise from her son, Louis XIII, to dismiss Cardinal Richelieu, his minister, but the king was influenced by friends of the cardinal to reverse his decision. In the course of a few hours the queen and her followers, awaiting the news of the minister's fall, were exiled from court.

Joyeux Noël! *Fr*—Merry Christmas!

Jubilate Deo. *L*—Rejoice in the Lord.

Jucundi acti labores. *L*—The memory of past labors is pleasant. —*Cicero, On Ends, II, xxxii, 105.*

Judex damnatur ubi nocens absolvitur. *L*—The judge is condemned when a criminal is set free.—*Publilius Syrus.*

Judicium crucis. *L*—An ordeal in which contestants vie to see who can hold out his arms longest as if on a cross. The one whose arms fall first loses.

Judicium Dei. *See* Dei judicium.

Judicium parium aut leges terrae. *L*—The judgment of one's peers or the laws of the land. It was one of the important concessions granted by King John in the Magna Carta that an Englishman could be condemned only in these two ways.

Juge de paix. *Fr*—Justice of the peace.

Jugement de Dieu. *Fr*—*See* Dei judicium.

Jugez un homme par ses questions, plutôt que par ses réponses. *Fr*—Judge a man by his questions rather than by his answers.

Le **Juif errant.** *Fr*—The wandering Jew. A medieval legend of a Jew who treated Christ with contempt on his way to Calvary. For that reason he was condemned to wander about the earth until the Second Coming. The title of a book by Eugène Sue.

Juppiter tonans. *L*—Thundering Jove. A name sometimes given the London *Times*.

Jurare in verba magistri. *L*—To swear by the words of the teacher; to accept an authority blindly.—*Horace, Epistles, I, i, 14.*

Jurat. *L*—Addition to an affidavit giving details of when, where, and before whom the document was signed.

Juravi lingua, mentem injuratam gero. *L*—I have sworn with my tongue but my mind is unsworn.—*Cicero, On Duties, III, xxix. See also* the Greek original, *He glossa omomoch'* . . . .

Jure belli. *L*—By right or rules of war.

Jure divino. *L*—By divine law or right.

Jure humano. *L*—By human law.

Jure uxoris. *L*—By reason of a wife's right.

Juris peritus. *L*—One learned in the law.

Jus ad rem. *L*—The right to possess a thing.

Jus canonicum. *L*—Canon law; the codex of laws by which the Catholic Church is governed.

Jus civile. *L*—Civil law.

Jus civitatis. *L*—The right of citizenship.

Jus commercii. *L*—The right to trade.

Jus devolutionis. *L*—Law of transmission by which a possessor's property and rights devolve upon a successor.

Jus et norma loquendi. *L*—The laws and standards of speech.

Jus gentium. *L*—The law of nations. Originally applied to the body of laws common to Rome and her subject states. Later it was identified with natural law, and came to mean international law.

Jus gladii. *L*—The right of the sword.

Jus hereditatis. *L*—The right to inherit.

Jus mariti. *L*—The right of a husband to a wife's property.

Jus mercatorum. *L*—The law merchant; mercantile law.

Jus naturae. *L*—Law of nature.

Jus possessionis. *L*—The right of possession.

Jus primae noctis. *L*—The right of the first night; the reported claim of the feudal lord to the virginity of the wife of his vassal on the night of her marriage. There is no historically sound evidence for the existence of this practice. The *Droit du Seigneur*, generally translated as the right of the feudal lord, may have been understood as God's right, referring to the religious counsel of practicing continence on the wedding night.

Jus proprietatis. *L*—The right of property.

Jus publicum. *L*—Common law.

Jusqu'au bout. *Fr*—Up to the very end.

Jus relictae. *L*—The widow's right to property of a husband.

Jus sanguinis. *L*—Literally, the right of blood; the right of a child to the citizenship of his parents. The phrase is also used in determining lawful inheritances.

Jus suffragii. *L*—The right of suffrage.

Jus summum saepe summa est malitia. *L*—Extreme law is often extreme wrong.—*Terence, Self-Tormentor, IV, v, 48. See also* Summum jus, summa injuria.

Le juste milieu. *Fr*—The golden mean; the middle-of-the-road policy. *See also* Aurea mediocritas.

Justitia omnibus. *L*—Justice to all. Motto of District of Columbia.

Justitia suum cuique distribuit. *L*—Justice gives everyone his due.

Justo titulo. *L*—By legal title; lawfully.

Jus trium liberorum. *L*—A privilege, mostly political, granted to a Roman father of three children. This was intended to en-

courage bachelors to marry. Sometimes the privilege was given
to favorites who did not meet the requirements, e.g. Pliny the
Younger.

Justum et tenacem propositi virum. *L*—The righteous man in
purpose strong.—*Horace, Odes, III, 3, 1.*

Jus ubique docendi. *L*—The right to teach everywhere, a license
conferred by ecclesiastical authorities upon candidates presented by universities in the Middle Ages.

J'y suis, j'y reste. *Fr*—Here I am and here I am staying.—*General
MacMahon.* In the Crimean War, after taking the Malakoff
works, General MacMahon was advised to withdraw his
troops. The French victory led to the taking of Sebastopol.

K

KGB (Komitet Gosudarstvennoi Bezopasnosti). *Rus*—Commission for State Security, the Soviet organization in charge of
espionage and counterespionage. *See also* NKVD and OGPU.

Kairon gnothi. *Gk*—Know your opportunity. The advice of Pit-
tacus, one of the seven sages of Greece. It is translated into
Latin as *Nosce tempus.*

Kai su ei ekeinon, kai su teknon? *Gk*—And thou art one of them,
thou, my son? According to Suetonius the last words of Julius
Caesar, uttered when he was stabbed by Brutus.—*Suetonius,
Julius Caesar, 82.* According to Plutarch (*Lives, Marcus Bru-
tus, V, 1*) Caesar believed that Brutus was his own son by
Servilia, a sister of Cato. *See also* Et tu, Brute.

Kai su, teknon. *Gk*—*See* Kai su ei ekeinon . . . .

Kak poshivayetye? *Rus*—How are you?

Kalendas Graecas. *L*—*See* Ad Kalendas Graecas.

Kalokagathia. *Gk*—A combination of the beautiful and the good,
the ideal qualities of the Athenian gentleman.

Kalte Hände, warme Liebe. *Ger*—Cold hands, a warm heart.

Keine Antwort

Keine Antwort ist auch eine Antwort. *Ger*—No answer is also an answer.

Kein Unglück so gross, es ist ein Glück dabei. *Ger*—No misfortune is so great that it does not bring along some good fortune; it's an ill wind that blows nobody good.

Kinder sind Kinder. *Ger*—Children are children; you can't put an old head on young shoulders.

Kinder und Narren sprechen die Wahrheit. *Ger*—Children and fools speak the truth.

Kleine Leute grosse Herzen. *Ger*—Sometimes little people have big hearts.

Die kleinen Diebe hängt man, die grossen lässt man laufen. *Ger*—Petty thieves are hanged, the big ones go free.

Eine kleine Wurst ist auch eine Wurst. *Ger*—A little sausage is still a sausage; no matter how thin you slice it, it is still baloney.

Das kleinste Haar wirft seinen Schatten. *Ger*—The smallest hair casts its own shadow. Goethe includes this in his *Maxims*. *See also* Etiam capillus unus . . . .

Komsomol (*Kommunisticheskii, soiuz, molodezh*). *Rus*—League of Communist Youth (includes young people from nineteen to twenty-three).

Der Krieg ist lustig den Unerfahrenen. *Ger*—War is fine fun for the inexperienced.

Ktema es aei. *Gk*—An eternal possession. In a notable chapter in his *History of the Peloponnesian War*, the author tells of his love for historical truth and his aim to write something for the ages.—*Thucydides, I, 22.*

Küche, Kirche und Kinder. *Ger*—Kitchen, church and children. An antifeminist, male point of view on the place of woman; an official Nazi policy.

Kürze ist des Witzes Würze. *Ger*—Brevity is the soul of wit.

Kyrie eleison. *Gk*—Lord, have mercy. A prayer offered six times immediately after the introit of the Mass in Latin.

L

lb. (libra). *L*—A pound.

l.c., loc. cit. *See* Loco citato.

L. ès L. (Licencié ès Lettres). *Fr*—Licentiate in Letters.

L.H.D. (Litterarum Humaniorum Doctor). *L*—Doctor of the Humanities.

Litt. B. (Litterarum Baccalaureus). *L*—Bachelor of Letters.

Litt. D. (Litterarum Doctor). *L*—Doctor of Letters.

LL.B. (Legum Baccalaureus). *L*—Bachelor of Laws.

LL.D. (Legum Doctor). *L*—Doctor of Laws.

LL.MM. (Leurs Majestés). *Fr*—Their Majesties.

Loc. cit. *L*—*See* Loco citato.

L.Q. (Lege quaeso). *L*—Please read.

l.s. (locus sigilli). *L*—The place where the seal is affixed to a document.

Labitur et labetur in omne volubilis aevum. *L*—The river glides on and will glide on forever and ever. The simple-minded peasant waits for it to pass by.—*Horace, Epistles, I, ii, 43.*

Laborare est orare. *L*—To work is to pray.

Labore et constantia. *L*—With constant labor. Printer's mark of Christopher Plantin Press, which flourished in Antwerp from 1555 to 1867.

Labor est etiam ipse voluptas. *L*—Even work itself is a pleasure. —*Manilius, Astronomica, IV, 155.*

Labor improbus. *L*—Unremitting toil. The complete quotation reads: *Labor omnia vincit improbus.—Vergil, Georgics, I, 145.*

Labor omnia vincit

Labor omnia vincit. *L*—Labor conquers all things. Motto of Oklahoma. Adapted from *Vergil, Georgics, I, 145.*

Laborum dulce lenimen. *L*—Sweet solace of my troubled heart. The poet is addressing his lyre.—*Horace, Odes, I, xxxii, 14.*

Lade nicht Alles in ein Schiff. *Ger*—Don't load everything on one ship; don't carry all your eggs in one basket.

Laesa majestas. *L*—Lese majesty; treason. In French, *lèse majesté (q.v.).*

La ilāha illa Allāh. *Arabic*—There is no God but Allah.

Laissez aller. *Fr*—Allow to go; let things go as they will.

Laissez faire. *Fr*—Let the parties concerned alone. An economic policy of noninterference in business by government. Sometimes written *Laissez nous faire*, Let us alone, or *Laissez aller (q.v.).*

Laissez passer. *Fr*—Literally, allow to pass; a permit.

Langage des halles. *Fr*—The language of the market place; rough, abusive talk generally referred to as *billingsgate.*

La langue des femmes est leur épée, et elles ne la laissent pas rouiller. *Fr*—A woman's tongue is her sword, and she does not let it get rusty. A French proverb.

Langue d'oc. *Fr*—The dialects spoken in the south of France, so called because of the use of *oc* for *yes*. *See also* Langue d'oïl.

Langue d'oïl. *Fr*—Dialects of Old French spoken in the north of France where the word for *yes* was *oïl*, in modern French, *oui*. *See also* Langue d'oc.

Lapis philosophorum. *L*—The philosophers' stone. An imaginary substance that medieval alchemists believed could change baser metals into gold.

Lapsus calami. *L*—Slip of the pen.

Lapsus linguae. *L*—A slip of the tongue.

Lapsus memoriae. *L*—A lapse of memory.

Lares et penates. *L*—Household gods of the Romans protecting the home and fields.

Lasciate ogni speranza, voi ch'entrate. *It*—Abandon all hope, you who enter here. The inscription on the entrance to hell.—*Dante, Inferno, III, 9.*

Lasciva est nobis pagina, vita proba. *L*—My page is wanton, but my life is chaste.—*Martial, I, iv, 8.*

Lateat scintillula forsan. *L*—Some small spark of life may lie unseen. The motto of the London Royal Humane Society, founded in 1774 by Dr. William Hawes, who believed that artificial means could restore persons apparently drowned. The society expanded to include all first aid.

Latet anguis in herba. *L*—A snake lies hidden in the grass.—*Vergil, Eclogues, III, 93.*

Lathe biosas. *Gk*—Seek to escape notice in life; try to live in obscurity.—*Epicurus. See also* Ama nesciri.

Latino sine flexione. Latin without inflections, an artificial language dating from 1903. It has been succeeded by scores of similar attempts to invent an international means of communication.

Lauda la moglie e tienti donzello. *It*—Praise a wife but stay a bachelor.

Laudari a viro laudato. *L*—To be praised by a man who is himself praised. The full statement: *Laetus sum laudari me abs te, pater, a viro laudato*, I am happy to be praised by you, father, who are yourself praised. A fragment from *Naevius' Hector Proficiscens (The Departure of Hector)*; quoted by Cicero, *To Friends, XV, vi, 1.*

Laudator temporis acti. *L*—A praiser of the good old days.—*Horace, Art of Poetry, 173.*

Laudum immensa cupido. *L*—A boundless passion for praise.—*Vergil, Aeneid, VI, 823.*

Laus Deo. *L*—Praise be to God.

Laus perennis. *L*—Perpetual praise; prayers offered day and night by shifts of monks.

Lá vão os pés onde quer o coração. *Port*—The feet go where the heart wills.

Lavoro di commesso. *It*—Italian inlay work.

Leben Sie wohl! *Ger*—Farewell!

Lebensraum. *Ger*—Room in which to live. The Nazi demand.

Lectori benevolo. *L*—To the kind reader.

Legalis homo. *L*—A legal person; a person in the eyes of the law.

Legatus a latere. *L*—A specially instructed legate from the side of the pope; a specially commissioned papal envoy.

Leges barbarorum. *L*—Laws of the barbarians; a code put together by Charlemagne retaining the laws of the German tribes conquered by the Franks.

Leges plurimae, respublica pessima. *L*—The more numerous the laws, the worse the commonwealth.

Légion étrangère. *Fr*—The Foreign Legion, well publicized by American moving pictures.

Leichter ist Vergeben als Vergessen. *Ger*—It is easier to forgive than to forget.

Leonina societas. *L*—Partnership with a lion; a one-sided arrangement.

Lèse majesté. *Fr*—Lese majesty; treason.

La letteratura amena. *It*—Refined, polite literature.

Lettre d'avis. *Fr*—Letter of advice.

Lettre de cachet. *Fr*—A sealed letter, often containing a warrant for imprisonment without trial.

Lettre de change. *Fr*—Bill of exchange.

Lettre de créance. *Fr*—Letter of credit.

Levari facias. *L*—Cause to be levied. An order to an official to seize a debtor's property.

Levée en masse. *Fr*—A general uprising. Also, general conscription.

Leve fit quod bene fertur onus. *L*—The load that is cheerfully borne becomes light.—*Ovid, Amores, I, ii, 10.*

Un **lever de rideau.** *Fr*—A curtain-raiser, a one-act play preceding the main performance.

Levius fit patientia quicquid corrigere est nefas. *L*—Patience makes that more bearable which cannot be changed; what can't be cured must be endured.—*Horace, Odes, I, xxiv, 19.*

Lex loci. *L*—Law of the place; customs of the region.

Lex loci rei sitae. *L*—The law of the place where the thing is situated.

Lex mercatoria (mercatoris). *L*—Law merchant, the body of law dealing with commercial traders and their transactions.

Lex non scripta. *L*—The unwritten law; common law as distinct from statute law.

Lex scripta. *L*—Written law, statute law.

Lex talionis. *L*—The law of retaliation; an eye for an eye and a tooth for a tooth.

Lex terrae. *L*—The law of the land.

Libertas est potestas faciendi id quod jure licet. *L*—Liberty is the freedom of doing what is permitted within the law.

Libertas, quae sera tamen respexit inertem. *L*—Liberty, which tardily looked back upon a sluggish servant. Lamb uses this quotation at the beginning of the essay "The Superannuated Man," in which he sings of the joys of retirement.—*Vergil, Ecologues, I, 27.*

Liberté, égalité, fraternité. *Fr*—Liberty, equality, fraternity. The ideals and slogan of the French Revolution.

Liberum veto. *L*—Free veto. In mid-seventeenth century Poland, respect for the rights of the minority became so exaggerated that a single dissenting deputy could override the will of the majority in the parliament.

Libris clausis. *L*—With closed books. A directive used in academic examinations; opposed to an open-book examination.

Licentia vatum. *L*—Poetic license.

Liebe ohne Gegenliebe ist wie eine Frage ohne Antwort. *Ger*—Love without return of love is like a question without an answer.

Lieu de réunion. *Fr*—Place of assembly.

Limae labor. *L*—The labor of the file; the polishing of a literary work.—*Horace, Art of Poetry, 291.*

Limbus fatuorum. *L*—A paradise for fools.

Lingua franca. *L*—Literally, the Frankish tongue. A jargon used for elementary communication by medieval traders and sailors in the Mediterranean, derived for the most part from the Romance languages. In a general sense it describes a mixture of languages used as a means of communication in business. Pidgin English is the lingua franca between Chinese and English speakers.

Lingua toscana in bocca romana. *It*—A Tuscan tongue in a Roman mouth. Said to be the ideal Italian pronunciation.

Lis litem generat. *L*—Litigation breeds litigation; one quarrel starts another.

Lis pendens. *L*—Lawsuit pending.

Lis sub judice. *L*—A suit still in the courts.

Lit de justice. *Fr*—Bed of justice. The bed was a cushioned seat on which the kings of France sat in parliament. It also refers to the session itself.

Litem lite resolvere. *L*—To resolve one dispute by introducing another.

Lite pendente. *L*—While litigation is pending.

Litterae humaniores. *L*—Humane letters; the humanities.

Literatim, verbatim, punctuatim. *L*—Letter for letter, word for word, period for period.

Littera canina. *L*—The dog's letter; the letter *r*, so called by the Romans because it approached the growl of a dog.—*Persius, I, 109.*

Littera enim occidit, spiritus autem vivificat. *L*—The letter kills, the spirit gives life.—*Vulgate, Paul, II Corinthians, iii, 6.*

Littera scripta manet. *L*—The written word remains. Used as a caution that what one writes may be used against him.

Livre de chevet. *Fr*—A bedside book.

Livre de circonstances. *Fr*—A book worked up for the occasion.

Livre de poche. *Fr*—A book fitting the pocket; a paperback.

Livres d'heures. *Fr*—Manuscript books of the hours, beautifully ornamented, containing prayers recited at the canonical hours: matins, lauds, prime, tierce, sext, nones, vespers and complin.

Loco citato. *L*—In the passage cited. Often abbreviated *l.c.* or *loc. cit.*

Locos y niños dicen la verdad. *Sp*—Madmen and children speak the truth.

Locum tenens. *L*—A substitute. Used, for example, by physicians to designate a temporary practitioner taking care of patients during the absence of the regular doctor.

Locus classicus. *L*—A passage in a classic; more commonly a passage most frequently cited in illustrating some usage in language or proving some point of doctrine.

Locus communis. *L*—A common place, as for the dead; a public place. The plural, *loci communes*, means a listing of arguments; commonplaces. Melanchthon used this as a title of a work in which he explained the doctrines of the Reformation.

Locus criminis. *L*—Scene of the crime.

Locus delicti. *L*—The place where the crime took place.

Locus in quo. *L*—The place in which, referring to the location of an occurrence or to a passage in a text.

Locus poenitentiae. *L*—Literally, chance or opportunity for repentance; chance to withdraw consent before binding oneself to an obligation.

Locus sigilli. *L*—*See* l.s.

Locus standi. *L*—Ground to stand on in a legal sense; a recognized position; the right to have one's case heard.

Loin des yeux, loin du cœur. *Fr*—*See* the equivalent *Lontan dagli* . . . .

Longo sed proximus intervallo. *L*—The next but separated by a long distance; a poor second.—*Vergil, Aeneid, V, 320.*

Longum iter est per praecepta, breve et efficax per exempla. *L*— The road to wisdom is long by precept, short and effective by example.—*Seneca, Epistles, 6, 5.*

Lontan dagli occhi, lontan dal cuore. *It*—Literally, far from the eyes, far from the heart; out of sight, out of mind.

Lo que hoy se pierde se gana mañana. *Sp*—What a man loses today, he wins back tomorrow.—*Cervantes, Don Quixote, I, VII.*

Loquendum ut vulgus, sentiendum ut docti. *L*—We must speak as the crowd does, but think as the learned do.—*Edward Coke.* Another version: *Loquendum est ut plures, sentiendum ut pauci.* We must speak with the many but think with the few.

Lo que no se puede remediar se ha de aguantar. *Sp*—What can't be cured must be endured.

Lo que se aprende en la cuna siempre dura. *Sp*—What we learn in the cradle always lasts; as the twig is bent, the tree's inclined.

Loyauté m'oblige. *Fr*—Loyalty binds me.

Lucidus ordo. *L*—A clear, orderly arrangement in a literary composition.—*Horace, Art of Poetry, 41.*

Lucus a non lucendo. *L*—This is quoted when a ridiculous derivation is given for a word. A grove (*lucus*) is dark because the light cannot penetrate it; therefore, the word for grove is derived from *not shining.*

Lues commentatoria. *L*—The plague of commentators. An abusive term applied to students of a classic who publish interpretations of what they think the author intended to say.

Lügen haben kurze Beine. *Ger*—Lies have short legs.

Il lupo cangia il pelo, ma non il vizio. *It*—The wolf changes his fur but not his nature.

Lupus est homo homini. *L*—Man is a wolf to his fellow-man.

Lupus in sermone (fabula). *L*—The wolf in the fable or the story; talk of the devil and he's sure to appear. Said when a person appears who has been the subject of conversation.—*Plautus, Stichus, IV, i, 71.*

Lupus pilum mutat, non mentem. *L*—The wolf changes his coat but not his disposition.

Lusus naturae. *L*—A freak of nature.

Lutte corps à corps. *Fr*—Literally, a body to body struggle, as in wrestling. The expression may be used to characterize a heated discussion, even among friends.

Lux et veritas. *L*—Light and truth. Motto of Yale University.

Lux tua vita mihi. *L*—Your light is my life.

Lympha pudica deum vidit et erubuit. *L*—The modest water saw its lord and blushed. Verse describing the miracle of Cana. Some versions substitute *Nympha* for *lympha.* The translation is unchanged.—*Crashaw, Epigrammata Sacra.*

M.

M

M. (Monsieur). *Fr*—Mr.

M.A. *See* A.M.

M.B. (Medicinae Baccalaureus). *L*—Bachelor of Medicine. Also *Musicae Baccalaureus*, Bachelor of Music.

M.B.G.&H. (Magna Britannia, Gallia et Hibernia). *L*—Great Britain, France and Ireland.

M.d.L. (Mitglied der Landtags). *Ger*—Member of the Diet, the local or state legislature.

M.d.R. (Mitglied der Reichstags). *Ger*—Member of the Reichstag.

M.E.C. (Mercato europeo comune). *It*—European Common Market.

M. ès A. (Maître ès Arts). *Fr*—Master of Arts.

m. et n. (mane et nocte). *L*—Morning and night.

M.E.Z. (Mitteleuropäische Zeit). *Ger*—Central European Time.

mf. *See* Mezzo forte.

Mlle (Mademoiselle). *Fr*—Miss.

Mme (Madame). *Fr*—Mrs.

mp. *See* Mezzo piano.

Ma chérie, ma chère. *Fr*—My dear *(f)*; dearest one.

Macht geht vor Recht. *Ger*—Might precedes the claims of right. Bismarck was accused of following this policy.

Macte virtute esto. *L*—Go forward and prosper. Generally spoken in commendation or encouragement.

Madre divina! *Sp-It*—Divine mother (reference to the Virgin Mary). Used as an expletive.

Maestro dei maestri. *It*—Master of the masters.

Maestro di cappella. *It*—A gifted musician in charge of music in an Italian court or a cathedral in the sixteenth century.

Il **Maestro di color che sanno.** *It*—The master of those who know. The reference is to Aristotle.—*Dante, Inferno, IV, 131.*

Ma foi! *Fr*—My faith; upon my word!

Maggiore fretta, minore atto. *It*—The more hurry, the less speed.

Magis illa juvant, quae pluris ementur. *L*—The greater the cost, the greater the pleasure. This satirical phrase is meant to ridicule those who waste fortunes on delicacies in the belief that the more costly a dish, the more delicious it is.—*Juvenal, XI, 16.*

Magister artis ingenique largitor venter. *L*—The stomach is the teacher of art and the giver of genius.—*Persius, Prologue to Satires, 10.*

Magister bibendi. *L*—*See* Arbiter bibendi.

Magister ceremoniarum. *L*—Master of ceremonies.

Magister equitum. *L*—Master of the horse; chief of the Roman cavalry appointed by a dictator.

Magna civitas, magna solitudo. *L*—A great city, a great desert; one can be very lonely in a big city.

Magna cum laude. *L*—*See* Cum laude.

Magnae spes altera Romae. *L*—The second hope of mighty Rome (Ascanius, the son of Aeneas). This is sometimes applied to a youth of whom much is expected.—*Vergil, Aeneid, XII, 168.*

Magna est veritas, et praevalet (not *praevalebit*). *L*—Truth is mighty and will prevail.—*Vulgate, III Esdras, IV, 41.*

Magnas inter opes inops. *L*—In poverty amid great riches.—*Horace, Odes, III, xvi, 28.*

Magnificat anima mea Dominum. *L*—My soul doth magnify the Lord. Words spoken by the Virgin Mary to Elizabeth. The hymn, known by the first word, is sung at vespers in the

167

Roman Catholic Church and at evening song in the Church of England.—*Vulgate, Luke, I, 46-55.*

Magni nominis umbra. *L*—*See* Stat magni nominis . . . .

Magno jam conatu magnas nugas. *L*—To produce tremendous trifles with great labor.—*Terence, Self-Tormentor, IV, i, 8. See also* Parturiunt montes . . . .

Magnum opus. *L*—Masterpiece.

Magnum vectigal est parsimonia. *L*—Economy is a great source of revenue. The complete sentence reads: *O Dii immortales! non intelligunt homines quam magnum vectigal sit parsimonia.* O ye immortal gods, men do not understand what a great source of income economy is.—*Cicero, Paradoxa VI, iii.*

M'aidez. *Fr*—Help me! The origin of the term *mayday*, an internationally recognized signal of distress.

Maintiens le droit. *Fr*—Hold to what is right.

Maison de campagne. *Fr*—A country house.

Maison de santé. *Fr*—Insane asylum.

Mais où sont les neiges d'antan? *Fr*—But where are the snows of yesteryear?—*Villon, The Ballad of Dead Ladies.*

Maître d'armes. *Fr*—Teacher of fencing.

Maître des hautes œuvres. *Fr*—Literally, master of lofty works; by a humorous transfer, the hangman.

Maître d'hôtel. *Fr*—Steward; butler; head waiter; major-domo.

Major domus. *L*—The Mayor of the Palace; a powerful official in charge of a royal household.

Major e longinquo reverentia. *L*—Respect is greater from a distance. Tiberius had in mind to send his sons to quiet revolts in the Roman armies in Germany and Pannonia, realizing that if he went himself his imperial dignity might suffer.—*Tacitus, Annals, I, 47.*

Maladie du pays. *Fr*—Homesickness.

La **mala erba cresce presto.** *It*—Bad weeds grow fast.

Mala fides. *L*—Bad faith.

Mala praxis. *L*—Malpractice.

Mal à propos. *Fr*—At an inopportune time.

Mal de mer. *Fr*—Seasickness.

Mal du pays. *Fr*—Homesickness.

Male imperando summum imperium amittitur. *L*—The greatest power can be lost by misrule.—*Publilius Syrus.*

Male parta, male dilabuntur. *L*—Ill-got goods are ill-spent.—*Naevius.*

Malheur ne vient jamais seul. *Fr*—Misfortunes never come in single file.

Mali exempli. *L*—In the nature of a bad precedent or example.

Mali principii malus finis. *L*—The bad end of a bad beginning.

Malis avibus. *L*—Under bad auspices.

Malo modo. *L*—In an evil manner.

Malo mori quam foedari. *L*—I prefer death to disgrace.

Le mal que nous faisons ne nous attire pas tant de persécution et de haine que nos bonnes qualités. *Fr*—The evil that we do does not bring upon us so much persecution and hatred as our good qualities.—*La Rochefoucauld, Maxims, 29.*

Malum est consilium quod mutari non potest. *L*—It is a bad plan that cannot be changed.—*Publilius Syrus.*

Malum in se. *L*—Evil in itself. *Mala in se* is the plural.

Malum prohibitum. *L*—An action regarded as criminal because it is prohibited and not because there is anything essentially immoral about the action itself.

Malus pudor. *L*—False shame.

Mamma mia! *It*—Literally, my mother. A mild expletive on a level with For goodness' sake!

169

Mañana es otro día. *Sp*—Tomorrow is another day.

Manet alta mente repostum. *L*—This resentment remains deeply buried in her mind. The reference is to Juno's hatred of the Trojans.—*Vergil, Aeneid, I, 26.*

Mane, thecel, phares. *Aramaic*—The Vulgate reading for Daniel, V, 25. *See* Mene, mene, tekel, upharsin for the reading in the King James version.

Manger son blé en herbe. *Fr*—Literally, to eat one's corn before it is ripe; to spend money before getting it.

Manibus pedibusque. *L*—With hands and feet; with all one's might.

Man ist was man isst. *Ger*—See Der Mensch ist was er isst.

Man kann, was man will, wenn man nur will, was man kann. *Ger*—We can do what we will if we only will to do what we can.

Man kennt den Baum an seiner Frucht. *Ger*—A tree is known by its fruit.

Man lernt nichts kennen, als was man liebt. *Ger*—One learns to know nothing except what one loves.—*Goethe, To F. H. Jacobi, May 10, 1812.*

Man muss das Eisen smieden solang es noch warm ist. *Ger*—One must strike the iron while it is hot. *See also* Ferrum, dum in igni . . . .

Manu forti. *L*—Literally, with a strong hand; forcible entry.

Manu propria. *L*—By one's own hand.

Manus haec inimica tyrannis. *L*—This hand is hostile to tyrants.

Manus manum lavat. *L*—One hand washes the other. Used to express mutual help or adulation.—*Petronius, Satyricon, 45.*

Marchandise qui plaît est à demi vendu. *Fr*—Goods that please are already half sold; please the eye and pick the purse.

Marcher à pas de loup. *Fr*—Walk softly in order to surprise; colloquially, to sneak up on.

Marcher droit. *Fr*—Literally, to walk straight; to behave well.

Mardi gras. *Fr*—Shrove Tuesday, the day before Ash Wednesday, the first day of Lent. Literally, fat Tuesday, a day of feasting before the fast of Lent. Celebration on this day, especially in New Orleans, is known for its revelry.

Mare clausum. *L*—A closed sea. A sea where commerce is restricted by reason of the fact that these waters are within the territory of a particular country.

Mare Imbrium. *L*—Sea of Storms, a location on the moon.

Mare liberum. *L*—Open sea.

Mare magnum. *L*—Literally, a great sea; an extensive collection of monastic privileges.

Mare Nostrum. *L*—Our sea; the Roman name for the Mediterranean.

Margaritas ante porcos. *L*—Pearls before swine.—*Vulgate, St. Matthew, VII, 6.*

Mariage de conscience. *Fr*—A marriage performed to satisfy the conscience of one or both parties troubled because of some illegality in a former ceremony.

Mariage de convenance. *Fr*—A marriage of convenience based on motives other than love.

Mariage de la main gauche. *Fr*—Left-handed marriage; morganatic marriage.

Mariage de politique. *Fr*—A marriage based on political advantage.

Marmoream se relinquere quam latericiam accepisset. *L*—Augustus boasted that he had found Rome a city of brick and was leaving it a city of marble.—*Suetonius, Augustus, 29.*

Marque de fabrique. *Fr*—Trade-mark.

Mars gravior sub pace latet. *L*—A much more serious war lies hidden in the treaty of peace.—*Claudian, On the Sixth Consulship of Honorius, 307.*

Mascula sunt maribus

Mascula sunt maribus. *L*—Things masculine are for males.

Más vale maña que fuerza. *Sp*—Cleverness accomplishes more than force.

Más vale muerto que vivo. *Sp*—Worth more dead than alive.

Más vale pájaro en mano que buitre volando. *Sp*—A bird in the hand is worth more than a vulture in the air; a bird in the hand is worth two in the bush.—*Cervantes, Don Quixote, II, XII.*

Más vale tarde que nunca. *Sp*—Better late than never.

Mater artium necessitas. *L*—Necessity is the mother of the arts.

Mater dolorosa. *L*—Mother of Sorrows. Reference to the Virgin Mary.

Mater familias. *L*—Mother of a family.

Materia ex qua. *L*—Material of which something is made.

Materia medica. *L*—Materials from which remedies are made; a branch of medical science dealing with the nature and property of the materials used in compounding drugs.

Materiam superabat opus. *L*—The work of art surpassed the priceless material; the masterpiece was superior to the valuable material used.—*Ovid, Metamorphoses, II, 5.*

Mater mea sus est mala. *L*—My mother, a pig, eats apples. A Latin sticker or poser, wrongly translated: My mother is a bad pig.

Mater Redemptoris. *L*—Mother of the Redeemer.

Un matto sa più domandare che sette savi rispondere. *It*—A fool can ask more questions than seven wise men can answer.

Mature fieri senem, si diu velis esse senex. *L*—You must become an old man early if you wish to be an old man long. Cato the Elder quotes this proverb, but he does not agree with it. —*Cicero, Old Age, X, 32.*

Mauvais coucheur. *Fr*—A bad bedfellow; a touchy, querulous, suspicious person, difficult to get along with, as in business or politics.

Mauvaise honte. *Fr*—Excessive bashfulness.

Mauvaise plaisanterie. *Fr*—Bad taste in jesting; a bad joke.

Mauvais goût. *Fr*—Bad taste from an esthetic point of view.

Mauvais quart d'heure. *Fr*—A bad quarter of an hour; an unpleasant experience.

Mauvais sujet. *Fr*—A rogue; in slang, a bad egg.

Maxima bella ex levissimis causis. *L*—The greatest wars rise from very slight causes.

Maximum remedium est irae, mora. *L*—The best remedy for anger is delay.—*Seneca, On Anger, II, 29.*

Mea culpa. *L*—Through my fault.

Le méchant n'est jamais comique. *Fr*—A wicked person is never comic.—*Count Joseph de Maistre.*

Médecin, guéris-toi toi-même. *Fr*—Physician, cure thyself. *See also* Medice, cura teipsum.

Medeis ageometretos eisito. *Gk*—Let nobody ignorant of geometry enter. Words reportedly written over the entrance to the Academy of Plato.

Meden agan. *Gk*—Let nothing be carried to excess. A Greek maxim. *See also* Ne quid nimis.

Medice, cura teipsum. *L*—Physician, cure thyself.—*Vulgate, Luke, IV, 23.*

Mediocria firma. *L*—The middle position is the sound one. The doctrine of the mean, so frequently the subject of counsel in proverbs.

Mediocribus esse poetis /non homines, non di, non concessere columnae. *L*—Neither men, nor gods, nor publishers have ever agreed that poets may be mediocre.—*Horace, Art of Poetry, 372.*

Medio tutissimus ibis. *L*—You will travel with greatest safety in the middle.—*Ovid, Metamorphoses, II, 137.*

Mega biblion, mega kakon. *Gk*—A big book is a great evil. This is adapted from Callimachus' line *To mega biblion ison, elegen, einai to megalo kako,* A big book is like a great evil, he said. Ancient scrolls could be very cumbersome. This epigram has also been used in criticism of inflated volumes.

Mehr Licht. *Ger*—More light. Supposedly the last words of Goethe.

Meine Damen und Herren. *Ger*—Ladies and gentlemen.

Meine Zeit wird schon kommen. *Ger*—My time will come one of these days. The hope of Mendel, whose theories went unrecognized for a long time.

Mein Herr. *Ger*—Sir.

Mein Kampf. *Ger*—My Battle, the title of a book by Adolf Hitler that became the bible of the Nazis. The translated editions have retained the German title.

Mein Name ist Hase; ich weiss von nichts. *Ger*—My name is rabbit; I know nothing about it. Common expression used by a person unwilling to serve as a witness or to answer questions that might get him into trouble.

Mejor morir a pie que vivir en rodillas. *Sp*—Better to die standing than to live kneeling.—*Dolores Ibarruri, La Pasionaria,* Spanish Communist revolutionary leader (in an address made in Valencia in 1936).

La mejor salsa del mundo es el hambre. *Sp*—Hunger is the best sauce in the world.—*Cervantes, Don Quixote, II, V.*

Melior est canis vivus leone mortuo. *L*—Better a living dog than a dead lion.—*Vulgate, Ecclesiastes, IX, 4.*

Memento, homo, quia pulvis es, et in pulverem reverteris. *L*—Remember, man, thou art but dust and into dust thou shalt return.

Memento mori. *L*—Remember that you must die.

La **mémoire est nécessaire à toutes les opérations de l'esprit.** *Fr*
—The memory is necessary for all the operations of the mind.
—*Pascal, VI, 369.*

Memoria in aeterna. *L*—In eternal remembrance.

Memoria praeteritorum bonorum. *L*—Remembrance of good
things past.

Ménage à trois. *Fr*—Literally, household of three; a marital triangle.

Mendacem memorem esse oportet. *L*—A liar must have a good
memory.—*Quintilian, IV, ii, 91. See also* Il faut bonne
mémoire . . . .

Mene, mene, tekel, upharsin. *Aramaic*—He has counted, counted,
weighed, and they divide. Words that appeared on the wall at
Belshazzar's feast and were interpreted by the prophet Daniel
to signify that God had judged Belshazzar's kingdom, found it
wanting, and would destroy it.—*Daniel, V, 25.*

Mens aequa in arduis. *L*—A calm mind in difficulties. Adapted
from *Aequam memento rebus in arduis . . . (q.v.).*

Mens agitat molem. *L*—Mind stirs the whole mass. In the underworld Anchises explains to Aeneas the doctrine of the *anima
mundi*, the soul of the world, which held that an intelligent
power infused itself into matter and produced all living beings. In antiquity this doctrine was taught by the Pythagoreans, Platonists, and Stoics.—*Vergil, Aeneid, VI, 727.*

Der **Mensch denkt, Gott lenkt.** *Ger*—Man proposes, God disposes.

Der **Mensch ist was er isst.** *Ger*—Man is what he eats.

Mens legis. *L*—The spirit of the law.

Mens rea. *L*—Criminal intent. A legal term.

Mens regnum bona possidet. *L*—A good mind possesses a kingdom.—*Seneca, Thyestes, 380.*

Mens sana in corpore sano. *L*—A sound mind in a sound body.
—*Juvenal, X, 356.*

Mens sibi conscia recti. *L*—A mind conscious of its righteousness.

Menteur à triple étage. *Fr*—Literally, a three-storeyed liar; a double-dyed liar.

Meo periculo. *L*—At my own risk.

Merci beaucoup. *Fr*—Thanks very much.

Merum sal. *L*—Pure salt; true wit.

Metron ariston. *Gk*—Moderation is best. A saying of Cleobulus, one of the Seven Wise Men of Greece.—*Diogenes Laertius, 1, 93.* The ancients stressed the middle course. *See also* Aurea mediocritas, Ne quid nimis, Meden agan, Medio tutissimus ibis, Est modus in rebus, In medio stat virtus.

Metter il carro innanzi ai buoi. *It*—To put the wagon before the oxen; to put the cart before the horse.

Mettre de l'eau dans son vin. *Fr*—To put water in a person's wine; to reduce tensions; to pour oil on troubled waters.

Meubles d'occasion. *Fr*—Second-hand furniture.

Me vestigia terrent, omnia te adversum spectantia, nulla retrorsum. *L*—I am terrified that all the footprints lead toward you and none away. This was the excuse offered by the fox for not visiting the sick lion.—*Horace, Epistles, I, i, 74.* Sometimes *Vestigia nulla retrorsum* is used to mean, Let us take no steps backward.

Mezza voce. *It*—With moderate volume of the voice.

Mezzo forte. *It*—Moderately loud.

Mezzo piano. *It*—Moderately soft.

Mezzo termine. *It*—Middle course.

Mia gar chelidon ear ou poiei. *Gk*—One swallow does not make a summer (literally, a spring).—*Aristotle, Nicomachean Ethics, I, 7, 16.*

Mi-carême. *Fr*—Mid-lent.

Mi casa es su casa. *Sp*—My house is your house.

Mientras se duerme todos son iguales. *Sp*—While asleep, all men are equal.—*Cervantes, Don Quixote, II, XLIII.*

Le mieux est l'ennemi du bien. *Fr*—The best is the enemy of the good; leave well enough alone.

Mieux vaut goujat debout qu'empereur enterré. *Fr*—It is better to be a live beggar than a dead emperor.—*La Fontaine, The Woman of Ephesus, last line. See also* Melior est canis . . . .

Mihi crede. *L*—Believe me.

Mihi cura futuri. *L*—I am concerned with the future; my attention is fixed on the future life. Motto of Hunter College.

Miles gloriosus. *L*—A boastful warrior. A stock dramatic character drawn from a play by Plautus.

Minatur innocentibus qui parcit nocentibus. *L*—He threatens the innocent who spares the criminal.—*Sir Edward Coke.*

Minima ex malis. *L*—Among evils choose the least.—*Cicero, On Duties, III, i. See also* De duobus malis . . . .

Mirabile dictu. *L*—Marvelous to relate.

Mirabile visu. *L*—Wonderful to see; what a marvelous sight!

Misa del Gallo. *Sp*—Midnight Mass at Christmas, so-called because people return from this service at the hour when the cocks crow.

Mise en page. *Fr*—Make-up of a printed page.

Mise en scène. *Fr*—Stage setting of a play.

Miserabile dictu. *L*—A miserable thing to relate.

Miserabile vulgus. *L*—The miserable herd; the wretched crowd. An aristocratic opinion of the lower classes.

Miserere mei. *L*—Have mercy on me.—*Vulgate, Psalms, LI (L), 1.*

Missa cantata. *L*—A mass sung by one priest.

Missi dominici. *L*—Official inspectors sent out by Charlemagne to check on instruction and observance of discipline in monasteries.

Mit dem Wissen wächst der Zweifel. *Ger*—Doubt increases with knowledge.—*Goethe, Maxims in Prose, 76.*

Mit der Dummheit kämpfen Götter selbst vergebens. *Ger*—The gods themselves struggle in vain against stupidity.—*Schiller, Maid of Orleans, III, vi, 28.*

Mit grossen Herren ist nicht gut Kirschen essen. *Ger*—Literally, it is not good to eat cherries with great lords; he who sups with the devil must have a long spoon.

Mit innigster Ergebenheit in Gott. *Ger*—With profound devotion to God.

Mitte sectari, rosa quo locorum/ Sera moretur. *L*—Cease searching for the spot where the last rose lingers.—*Horace, Odes, I, xxxviii, 3.*

Mittimus. *L*—We send. A warrant signed by a magistrate for the imprisonment of a criminal.

Mit umgehender Post. *Ger*—By return mail.

Mobile mutatur semper cum principe vulgus. *L*—The fickle crowd always changes its allegiance with the prince.—*Claudian.*

Mobile perpetuum. *L*—Perpetual motion.

Mobile vulgus. *L*—The unstable, fickle crowd.

Moderato cantabile. *It*—In a melodious, flowing style at a moderate tempo.

Modo et forma. *L*—In manner and form.

Modo praescripto. *L*—In the manner prescribed.

Modus operandi. *L*—Method of operation.

Modus vivendi. *L*—Literally, a manner of living; a temporary arrangement for coexistence until matters in dispute can be settled.

Le **moine bourru.** *Fr*—The churlish monk; a bogeyman invented to frighten misbehaving children.

Mollia tempora fandi. *L*—The proper moment to broach a subject. As in many other Latin quotations, the changed word order more readily conveys the sense of the original. The original: *Mollissima fandi tempora.*—*Vergil, Aeneid, IV, 293.*

Molto fumo e poco arrosto. *It*—Much smoke and little roast meat; much ado about nothing.

Mon cher. *Fr*—My dear fellow.

Mon cœur et ton cœur pour la vie. *Fr*—My heart and yours together for life. Words on a popular pendant.

Le **monde est le livre des femmes.** *Fr*—The world is woman's book. The author goes on to say that if she reads it ill, it is her own fault, or else she is blinded by passion.—*Rousseau, Émile, Book V.*

Le **monde va de lui-même.** *Fr*—The world goes by itself. An expression of the futile concern of man in the direction of human affairs.

Mon Dieu! *Fr*—Literally, my God! This is properly translated as a very mild exclamation, such as, "Dear me!"

Il **mondo è di chi ha pazienza.** *It*—The world belongs to the man who is patient.

Il **mondo è di chi se lo piglia.** *It*—The world belongs to the go-getter.

Il **mondo è un bel libro, ma poco serve a chi non lo sa leggere.** *It*—The world is a beautiful book, but it is of little use to the man who doesn't know how to read it.—*Goldoni.*

Montani semper liberi. *L*—Mountaineers always free. Motto of West Virginia.

Mont-de-piété. *Fr*—Literally, mount of piety; a public pawnbroker's agency established to lend money to the needy at low rates.

Monte de piedad. *Sp*—*See* Mont-de-piété.

Monte di pietà. *It*—See Mont-de-piété.

La **moquerie est souvent indigence d'esprit.** *Fr*—Scoffing often betrays a lack of wit.—*La Bruyère, Characters, Of Society, 57 (1), p. 169* in *Garapon's edition (Garnier Frères, 1962).*

Morbus Gallicus. *L*—Syphilis, the French disease. A term certainly not invented by Francophiles.

More humano. *L*—As is the custom of mankind.

More majorum. *L*—According to the customs of our ancestors.

More suo. *L*—In his own manner.

Morgen, morgen, nur nicht heute,/ Sagen alle faulen Leute. *Ger* —Tomorrow, tomorrow, but not today,/ All the lazy people say.

Morgenstund' hat Gold im Mund. *Ger*—The morning hour has gold in its power.

La **morgue littéraire.** *Fr*—A file of information or manuscripts that one day may be needed for publication.

Mors acerba, fama perpetua. *L*—A bitter death but eternal fame.

Mors communis omnibus. *L*—Death is the common fate of all. Quoted in Latin by those who try to give a trite observation an air of distinction.

Mors janua vitae. *L*—Death is the door to life (everlasting life is meant).

Mort Dieu (Mordieu). *Fr*—Zounds; hang it. An interjection found in Shakespeare.

Mortis causa. *L*—Because of impending death.

Les **morts ont toujours tort.** *Fr*—The dead are always wrong.

Mos majorum. *L*—The customs of their ancestors, much honored by the Romans.

Mos pro lege. *L*—Long-established custom has the force of law.

Mot à mot. *Fr*—Word for word.

Mot de guet. *Fr*—Password or watchword.

Mot de l'énigme. *Fr*—The word in the puzzle that must be guessed.

Mots de terroir. *Fr*—Regional words or sayings.

Mots d'usage. *Fr*—Words in common use.

Motu proprio. *L*—On one's own motion. Generally applied to a rescript issued by the pope on matters initiated by himself.

Moulin à paroles. *Fr*—Literally, a word mill; a babbler; a windbag.

Le Moyen Age. *Fr*—The Middle Ages.

Mucho más se ha de estimar un diente que un diamante. *Sp*—A tooth is worth much more than a diamond.—*Cervantes, Don Quixote, I, XVIII.*

Muchos van por lana y vuelven trasquilados. *Sp*—Many go seeking wool and return shorn.—*Cervantes, Don Quixote, I, VII.*

Muet comme un poisson. *Fr*—Dumb as a fish.

Mulier cum sola cogitat male cogitat. *L*—When a woman thinks alone she is plotting mischief. A misogynist's idea.—*Publilius Syrus.*

Mulier cupido quod dicit amanti, in vento et rapida scribere oportet aqua. *L*—What a woman says to an eager lover should be written on wind and swift waters.—*Catullus, LXX, 3.*

Multa cadunt inter calicem supremaque labra. *L*—There's many a slip 'twixt the cup and the lip.

Multa petentibus desunt multa. *L*—Those who desire much are much in need.—*Horace, Odes, III, xvi, 42.*

Multis utile bellum. *L*—War is a source of gain to many.—*Lucan, Pharsalia, I, 182.*

Multum in parvo. *L*—Literally, much in little; a marvel of condensation.

Mundi formam omnes fere consentiunt rotundam esse. *L*—Almost all men are in agreement that the shape of the world is round. This statement was made in 1481.—*Pius II (Sylvius Piccolomini).*

Mundus vult decipi. *L*—People want to be deceived.

Munera Pulveris. *L*—Gifts of the dust. Used as title of a work by Ruskin. In the passage from which this quotation is taken reference is made to the present of a little dust that would permit the soul of the deceased to cross the Styx.—*Horace, Odes, I, xxviii, 3, 4.*

Munus Apolline dignum. *L*—A gift worthy of Apollo.—*Horace, Epistles, II, i, 216.*

Les murailles ont des oreilles. *Fr*—The walls have ears.

Murus aeneus conscientia sana. *L*—A sound conscience is a wall of brass.

Muscae volitantes. *L*—Literally, flies flitting about; motes moving about in the field of vision.

Muss ist eine harte (bittere) Nuss (ein bitter Kraut). *Ger*—Necessity is a hard (bitter) nut (a bitter herb); necessity is a hard taskmaster.

Mutatis mutandis. *L*—Changing those things that must be changed.

Mutato nomine de te fabula narratur. *L*—Change only the name and the story might be told of you.—*Horace, Satires, I, i, 69.*

N

N.B. (Nota bene). *L*—Note well.

n.Br. (nördliche Breite). *Ger*—North latitude.

n. Chr. G. *Ger*—*See* Nach Christi Geburt.

n/cta. (nuestra cuenta). *Sp*—Our account.

nem. con. *L*—*See* Nemine contradicente.

nem. diss. *L*—*See* Nemine dissentiente.

n.F. (neue Folge). *Ger*—New series.

NKVD (Narkomvnudel). *Rus*—People's Commissariat for Internal Affairs. The Russian secret service that succeeded *OGPU* (*q.v.*), and was itself replaced, in 1946, by MVD and later still by KGB (*q.v.*). The word is made up from the first three letters of each of the Russian words in the name: *Narodni Kommissariat Vnutrennikh Del.*

NN. (Nomina). *L*—The names. Used when proper names are to be inserted.

N.P.O. *L*—Nihil per os; nothing by way of the mouth. A medical order.

nol. pros. *L*—*See* Nolle prosequi.

nom. nud. (nomen nudum). *L*—In biology a mere name used without a scientific description.

non pros. *L*—See Non prosequitur.

9bre (novembre). *Fr*—November, the ninth month in the early Roman calendar.

n.s. (nouvelle série). *Fr*—New series.

n.s. (nueva serie). *Sp*—New series.

N.S.I.C. (Noster Salvator Iesus Christus). *L*—Our Saviour Jesus Christ.

N.U. (Nazioni Unite). *It*—United Nations.

Nach Canossa gehen wir nicht. *Ger*—We are not going to Canossa. A statement made by Bismarck in 1872 when relations between Germany and the Vatican were strained. The reference is to Henry IV's submission to Pope Gregory VII in 1077.

Nach Christi Geburt. *Ger*—After the birth of Christ. *See also* A.D.

Nacheifern ist beneiden. *Ger*—To emulate is to envy; competition implies envy. *Lessing, Die Religion, erster Gesang.*

Nager entre deux eaux. *Fr*—To swim between two currents; to waver between two parties, giving the appearance that you are loyal to both.

Nam genus et proavos et quae non fecimus ipsi vix ea nostra voco. *L*—Race and ancestry and what we ourselves have not accomplished, these I do not consider my own achievements. —*Ovid, Metamorphoses, XIII, 140.*

Não ha mal que sempre dure, nem bem que nunca se acabe. *Port*—There is no ill that lasts forever, nor any boon that never ends.

Narkomvnudel. *Rus*—*See* NKVD.

Nascimur poetae, fimus oratores. *L*—We are born poets, we are trained to be orators.

Natale solum. *L*—Native soil.

Une **nation boutiquière.** *Fr*—A nation of shopkeepers. Napoleon's disparaging assessment of the English.

Natura abhorret a vacuo. *L*—Nature abhors a vacuum.—*Descartes.*

Natura abhorret vacuum. *L*—Nature abhors a vacuum.—*Rabelais, Gargantua, I, 5.*

Natura il fece e poi roppe la stampa. *It*—Nature made him and then broke the mould. This has often been used to describe a person who, by reason of his learning, art, or other achievements, is in a class by himself.—*Ariosto, Orlando Furioso, X, 84.*

Natura inest mentibus nostris insatiabilis quaedam cupiditas veri videndi. —There is naturally in our minds a certain insatiable desire to know the truth.—*Cicero, Tusculan Disputations, I, xix.*

Natura in operationibus suis non facit saltus. *L*—Nature in her operations does not proceed by leaps; evolution in nature is slow and gradual. Attributed to Leibnitz, but this was axiomatic long before his time.

Naturam expelles furca, tamen usque recurret. *L*—Even though you drive out nature with a pitchfork, she will rush right back.—*Horace, Epistles, I, x, 24.*

Natura naturans. *L*—Nature begetting, a term used by Spinoza. The product of this energy he called *Natura naturata*, nature begotten.

Natura semina nobis scientiae dedit, scientiam non dedit. *L*— Nature has given us the seeds of knowledge but not knowledge itself.—*Seneca, Letters to Lucilius, 120.*

Natura simplicitatem amat. *L*—Nature loves simplicity.—*Kepler.*

Nazi. *Ger*—Abbreviation of *Nationalsozialistiche Partei*, Hitler's National Socialist German Workers' Party. The pronunciation of the first four letters of the word National in German may have given rise to the shortened form.

Ne battre que d'une aile. *Fr*—To beat only one wing; when applied to persons, to be on one's last legs.

Nec amor nec tussis celatur. *L*—Neither love nor coughing can be concealed.

Nec deus intersit, nisi dignus vindice nodus. *L*—A god must not be introduced unless the problem demands divine aid. *See also* Dignus vindice nodus.

Ne cede malis. *L*—*See* Tu ne cede malis.

Necessitas non habet legem. *L*—Necessity knows no law.

Necessitas rationum inventrix. *L*—Necessity is the discoverer of ideas; necessity is the mother of invention.

Nec est quisquam tam malus, ut malus videri velit. *L*—No one is so evil that he wishes to be regarded as evil.—*Quintilian, III, viii, 2.*

Nec judicis ira, nec ignis, nec poterit ferrum, nec edax abolere vetustas. *L*—Neither the anger of a judge, nor fire, nor sword, nor the corrosion of time can destroy my work.—*Ovid, Metamorphoses, XV, 872.*

Nec mora

Nec mora nec requies. *L*—Without delay or rest.

Nec pluribus impar. *L*—Not unequal to many. The boastful motto of Louis XIV.

Nec prece nec pretio. *L*—Neither by entreaty nor bribery; neither by praying nor paying.

Nec quaerere nec spernere honorem. *L*—Neither to seek nor to spurn honors.

Nec quemquam jam ferre potest Caesarve priorem,/Pompeiusve parem. *L*—Caesar cannot tolerate a superior nor Pompey an equal.—*Lucan, Pharsalia, I, 125.*

Nec scire fas est omnia. *L*—We are not permitted to know everything.—*Horace, Odes, IV, iv, 22.*

Nec tecum possum vivere, nec sine te. *L*—I cannot live with you or without you.—*Martial, Epigrams, XII, xlvii, 2.*

Nec temere nec timide. *L*—Neither rashly nor timidly.

Nec verbum verbo curabis reddere fidus interpres. *L*—As a faithful translator you will not be concerned with making a word-for-word version.—*Horace, Art of Poetry, 133.*

Ne exeat provincia. *L*—Let him not leave the province of the court. A writ to arrest a debtor absconding from the jurisdiction of the court.

Ne facias per alium quod fieri potest per te. *L*—Do not do through another what you can do in person.

Nefasti dies. *L*—Unlucky days. No business was conducted on such ill-omened dates.

Ne fronti crede. *L*—Don't be deceived by appearances; don't judge a book by its cover.

Ne Juppiter quidem omnibus placet. *L*—Not even Jove can please everybody.

Ne, mater, et suam. *L*—Spin, mother, and I shall sew. A Latin poser.

186

Nemine contradicente. *L*—Nobody opposing.

Nemine dissentiente. *L*—Without a dissenting vote.

Nemo bis punitur pro eodem delicto. *L*—Nobody is to be punished twice for the same crime. The Fifth Amendment to the Constitution of the United States contains the same provision: "Nor shall any person be subject for the same offence to be twice put in jeopardy of life or limb."

Nemo dat quod non habet. *L*—Nobody can give what he does not possess.

Nemo in amore videt. *L*—No one in love can see; love is blind. —*Propertius, II, xiv, 18.*

Nemo judex in causa sua. *L*—Nobody is a judge in his own case.

Nemo liber est qui corpori servit. *L*—No man is free who is slave to the flesh.—*Seneca, Letters to Lucilius, XCII, 31.*

Nemo me impune lacessit. *L*—Nobody harms me with impunity. Motto of the Order of the Thistle and of Scotland.

Nemo mortalium omnibus horis sapit. *L*—No mortal is always wise.—*Pliny the Elder, Natural History, VII, 41 (40), 2.*

Nemo propheta acceptus est in patria sua. *L*—No prophet is accepted in his own country.—*Vulgate, Luke, IV, 24.*

Nemo repente fuit turpissimus. *L*—Nobody ever became a confirmed criminal all at once.—*Juvenal, II, 83.*

Nemo scit praeter me ubi soccus me pressat. *L*—I am the only one who knows where my shoe pinches.

Nemo sine vitiis nascitur. *L*—No mortal is without faults.

Nemo solus satis sapit. *L*—Nobody by himself possesses sufficient wisdom; two heads are better than one.—*Plautus, Braggart Warrior, III, iii, 12.*

Nem um dedo faz mão, nem uma andorinha verão. *Port*—One finger doesn't make a hand, nor one swallow a summer. *See also* Mia gar chelidon . . . .

Neos d'apollyth' hontin' an phile theos. *Gk*—God's favorites die young.

Ne plus ultra. *L*—The topmost performance or achievement; no farther. The medieval warning that ships should not sail westward beyond Gibraltar.

Ne puero gladium. *L*—Do not give a sword to a boy.

Ne quid detrimenti respublica capiat. *L*—So that no harm may come to the republic. The final order of the Roman senate to the consuls when the Republic was in mortal danger.—*Cicero, I Against Catiline, I, 3.*

Ne quid nimis. *L*—Nothing in excess.—*Terence, Andria, I, i, 34. See also* Meden agan.

Ne réveillez pas le chat qui dort. *Fr*—Do not waken the sleeping cat; let sleeping dogs lie.

Nervi belli, pecunia infinita. *L*—The sinews of war are a limitless supply of money.—*Cicero, Philippics, V, ii, 5.*

Nescire autem quid antequam natus sis acciderit, id est semper esse puerum. *L*—To be ignorant of what happened before you were born is always to remain a boy.—*Cicero, The Orator, XXXIV.*

Nescit vox missa reverti. *L*—The spoken word cannot be recalled.—*Horace, Art of Poetry, 390.*

Nessun maggior dolore,/Che ricordarsi del tempo felice/Nella miseria. *It*—There is no greater sorrow than remembering happy days in our misery.—*Dante, Inferno, V, 121.* Tennyson refers to this passage in *Locksley Hall:* "This is truth the poet sings/That a sorrow's crown of sorrows is remembering happier things."

N'est-ce pas? *Fr*—Is it not so?

Ne sutor ultra crepidam. *L*—*See* Sutor ne supra crepidam.

Ne tentes aut perfice. *L*—If you make an attempt, see it through.

Neue Besen kehren gut. *Ger*—New brooms sweep clean. *See also* Una scopa . . . .

Le **nez de Cléopatre; s'il eût été plus court, toute la face de la terre aurait changé.** *Fr*—If Cleopatra's nose had been shorter, the whole face of the earth would have been changed.—*Pascal, Thoughts, II, 162.*

Nicht die Kinder bloss speist man mit Märchen ab. *Ger*—Children aren't the only ones who are fed fairy tales.—*Lessing, Nathan the Wise, III, 6.*

Nicht wahr? *Ger*—Not so?

Niente più tosto si secca che lacrime. *It*—Nothing dries as quickly as tears.

Ni firmes carta que no leas, ni bebas agua que no veas. *Sp*—Do not sign a letter without reading it or drink water without looking at it.

Nihil ad rem. *L*—Nothing to do with the matter; irrelevant.

Nihil dicit. *L*—He says nothing. A judgment against a defendant who offers no defense.

Nihil enim in speciem fallacius est quam prava religio. *L*—Nothing is more deceptive in appearance than perverted religion. —*Livy, XXXIX, 16.*

Nihil est ab omni parte beatum. *L*—Nothing is blessed in every respect.—*Horace, Odes, II, xvi, 27.*

Nihil ex omnibus rebus humanis est praeclarius aut praestantius quam de republica bene mereri. *L*—In all human affairs nothing is more honorable or more outstanding than to deserve well of the republic.—*Cicero, Letters to Friends, X, 5.*

Nihil hoc ad edictum praetoris. *L*—This has nothing to do with the edict of the praetor, a reference to an ancient Roman promulgation of regulations that would hold during a particular praetor's period in office. The reply of Cujas, a sixteenth century jurist, when asked during a lecture if he were Protestant or Catholic.

Nihil in intellectu quod non prius in sensibus. *L*—Nothing is in the intellect that is not first in the senses. An axiom of the Scholastics opposing the doctrine of innate ideas.

Nihil muliebre

Nihil muliebre praeter corpus gerens. *L*—Having nothing feminine about her except her body. An appraisal of Queen Elizabeth I.

Nihil obstat. *L*—An official ecclesiastical statement that nothing stands in the way of publication. *See also* Imprimatur.

Nihil quod tetigit non ornavit. *L*—*See* Nullum fere scribendi genus . . . .

Nihil tam absurde dici potest quod non dicatur ab aliquo philosophorum. *L*—There is nothing no matter how absurd that has not been said by some philosopher.—*Cicero, Divination, II, LVIII, 119.*

Nil admirari. *L*—The attitude of being astonished at nothing. This is basic in Horace's philosophy, which counseled restraint toward pleasure, money, and fame. *See also* Surtout, point de zèle.—*Horace, Epistles, I, vi, 1.*

Nil conscire sibi, nulla pallescere culpa. *L*—To have a clear conscience and not pale at any charge.—*Horace, Epistles, I, i, 61.*

Nil debet. *L*—He owes nothing.

Nil desperandum. *L*—Never despair. A favorite quotation of Mr. Micawber in Dickens' *David Copperfield.*—*Horace, Odes, I, vii, 27.*

Nil dictum quod non dictum prius. *L*—Nothing has been said that hasn't been said before.

Nil molitur inepte. *L*—He makes no show of absurd pretensions in his writing. Horace contrasts with this attitude the bombastic style, which he ridicules in *Parturiunt montes . . . (q.v.).*—*Horace, Art of Poetry, 140.*

Nil mortalibus ardui est:/Coelum ipsum petimus stultitia. *L*—Nothing is too daring for man; we seek to reach heaven itself in our folly.—*Horace, Odes, I, iii, 37.*

Nil nisi cruce. *L*—No victory without suffering.

Nil sine magno vita labore dedit mortalibus. *L*—Life has given nothing to mortals without much labor.—*Horace, Satires, I, ix, 60.*

Nil sine Numine. *L*—Nothing without Divine Power. Motto of Colorado.

Nil sub sole novum. *L*—There is nothing new under the sun.—*Vulgate, Ecclesiastes, I, 10.*

Nimium ne crede colori. *L*—Do not have too much confidence in color; not every blush is a sign of innocence.

N'importe! *Fr*—It makes no difference; forget about it!

Ninguno nace maestro. *Sp*—Nobody is born an expert.

Ni plus, ni moins. *Fr*—Neither more nor less.

Nisi Dominus . . . frustra. *L*—Unless the Lord (build the house, they labor) in vain (who build it).—*Vulgate, Psalms, 127, 1.* Motto of the city of Edinburgh and also of the Hospital Auxiliary, medically untrained helpers; found on Blue Cross emblem in the United States.

Nisi prius. *L*—Literally, unless before; in general usage, a court where cases are tried before a judge and jury.

Nitimur in vetitum semper, cupimusque negata. *L*—We are always striving for what is forbidden, and desiring what is denied us.—*Ovid, Amores, III, iv, 17.*

Nitor in adversum. *L*—I struggle against opposition.

No adventures mucho tu riqueza/Por consejo de ome que ha pobreza. *Sp*—Don't risk much of your wealth on the advice of a poor man.—*Manuel Conde Lucanor.*

Nobilitas sola est atque unica virtus. *L*—Virtue is the one and only nobility.—*Juvenal, VIII, 20.*

La noblesse d'épée. *Fr*—The nobility of the sword; a name given the landed gentry in France.

Noblesse de robe. *Fr*—Nobility of the robe or gown; applied to judges and lawyers.

Noblesse oblige. *Fr*—Those who are nobly born must act nobly. This often implies condescension.

No es oro todo lo que reluce. *Sp*—All that glitters is not gold.— *Cervantes, Don Quixote, II, XXXIII.*

No hay cerradura si es de oro la garzúa. *Sp*—There is no effective lock if the picklock is made of gold; gold can open any door.

Nolens volens. *L*—Willy-nilly; whether willing or unwilling.

Noli me tangere. *L*—Do not touch me.—*Vulgate, John, XX, 17.*

Noli turbare circulos meos. *L*—Do not disturb my circles. Words spoken by Archimedes, mathematician and physicist, when a Roman soldier stood in the light, blocking the scientist's view of the problem on which he was working. The incident occurred when the Romans took Syracuse in 212 B.C. In spite of an order that Archimedes should not be slain, even though his inventions had held up the capture of the city, tradition states that the angry soldier killed him.

Nolle prosequi. *L*—A formal entry on the record that the plaintiff or prosecutor is dropping a case.

Nolo contendere. *L*—I do not wish to contest the suit. A plea entered by the defendant which subjects him to a judgment of conviction; by so doing he does not necessarily admit his guilt.

Nolo episcopari. *L*—I do not wish to be a bishop.

Nolumus leges Angliae mutari. *L*—We object to any change in England's laws.

Nom de guerre. *Fr*—An assumed name; pen name, stage name.

Nom de plume. *Fr*—Pen name.

Nom de théâtre. *Fr*—Stage-name.

Nomen conservandum (*pl.* **Nomina conservanda**). *L*—The name must be kept; in biological sciences a name that is retained even though an exception to the rules of scientific classification. Thus a name might be kept in cases of established usage.

Nomina stultorum parietibus haerent. *L*—The names of fools cling to the walls of buildings; fools' names like fools' faces are always seen in public places.

Non amo te, Sabidi, nec possum dicere quare; hoc solum scio, non amo te, Sabidi. *L*—I do not love you, Sabidius, nor can I say why; this only I know, Sabidius, I do not love you.— *Martial, I, 32.* There is a noted translation of this made by Tom Brown when John Fell, the dean of his college at Oxford, offered to revoke a suspension against the boy if he could translate this epigram at once. He sang out: "I do not love thee, Dr. Fell,/The reason why I cannot tell;/But this I'm sure I know full well,/I do not love thee, Dr. Fell.

Non Angli, sed angeli. *L*—Not Englishmen but angels. The substance of a comment Gregory the Great made when told that certain men exposed for sale in a Roman market were Angli. —*Bede, Ecclesiastical History, II, 1.*

Non assumpsi. *L*—A denial by the defendant in a case that he made any promise.

Non compos mentis. *L*—Legally, incapable of managing one's affairs.

Non concessit. *L*—He did not grant. A legal writ.

Non constat. *L*—It is not clear; it is not evident from what the court has heard.

Non cuivis homini contingit adire Corinthum. *L*—It is not every man's good fortune to visit Corinth (a city of luxury in antiquity).—*Horace, Epistles, I, xvii, 36.*

Non culpabilis. *L*—Not guilty.

Non deficiente crumena. *L*—As long as the money holds out.— *Horace, Epistles, I, iv, 11.*

Non est, crede mihi, sapientis dicere "vivam." Sera nimis vita est crastina; vive hodie. *L*—It is not, believe me, the mark of a wise man to say, "I shall live." Living tomorrow is too late; live today.—*Martial, Epigrams, I, 15.*

Non est curiosus quin idem sit malevolus. *L*—There is no curious man who does not have ill will to sharpen his curiosity.

Non est inventus. *L*—He has not been found. A sheriff's statement on a summons or subpoena when a person whose presence is demanded has not been found.

Non ex omni ligno, ut Pythagoras dicebat, debet Mercurius exculpi. *L*—Mercury ought not to be carved from just any wood, as Pythagoras said; you can't make a silk purse out of a sow's ear. By extension, it means that every mind cannot be trained in scholarship.—*Apuleius, Apology, 43.*

Non fingo hypotheses. *L*—I do not form hypotheses.—*Newton.*

Non fu mai partito savio condurre il nemico alla disperazione. *It*—It has never been a wise policy to drive an enemy to desperation.—*Machiavelli.*

Non haec in foedera. *L*—Not for such alliances as these. This is adapted from Aeneas' excuses to Dido for his flight from her. He says that he did not come as a suitor with any proposal of alliance.—*Vergil, Aeneid, IV, 339.*

Non ignara mali, miseris succurrere disco. *L*—Having experienced misfortune myself, I have learned to aid the wretched.—*Vergil, Aeneid, I, 630.*

Non inutiles scientiae existimandae sunt, quarum in se nullus est usus, si ingenia acuant et ordinent. *L*—Sciences which have no practical use in themselves must not be considered useless if they sharpen and order the mind.—*Francis Bacon.*

Non libet. *L*—It is not pleasing.

Non licet. *L*—It is not permitted; it is not licit.

Non liquet. *L*—It is not clear; a term used by lawyers when a case is not proven.

Non merita nome di creatore, se non Iddio el il Poeta. *It*—No one merits the name of creator, except God and the Poet.—*Tasso.*

Non multa sed multum. *L*—Not quantity but quality.

Non nobis, Domine, non nobis; sed nomini tuo da gloriam. *L*— Not to us, O Lord, not to us; but to thy name give glory.— *Vulgate, Psalms, CXV, 1; CXIII (Douay version).*

Non nobis solum nati sumus. *L*—We are not born for ourselves alone. Cicero gives credit for this idea to Plato.—*Cicero, On Duties, I, vii, 22.*

Non nostrum inter vos tantas componere lites. *L*—It is not for us to settle your grave disputes. Originally expressing an unwillingness to decide which of two shepherds was the better poet, it is now used ironically.—*Vergil, Eclogues, III, 108.*

Non obstante veredicto. *L*—Notwithstanding the verdict. A judgment entered for the plaintiff in spite of a verdict for the defendant.

Non ogni fiore fa buon odore. *It*—Not every flower has a sweet odor.

Non ogni giorno è festa. *It*—Every day is not a holiday.

Non olet. *L*—It does not stink. Said of money acquired by dishonest or disreputable means. When Titus objected to the tax his father Vespasian put on urine used for medical purposes, the latter held under his son's nose a coin derived from this tax, and uttered this cynical expression.—*Suetonius, Lives of the Twelve Caesars, Vespasian, XXIII.*

Non omne licitum honestum. *L*—Everything that is permissible is not necessarily proper. The law may permit an action that is not respectable.

Non omnia possumus omnes. *L*—We cannot all do everything. —*Vergil, Eclogues, VIII, 64.*

Non omnis moriar. *L*—I shall not wholly die. Horace prophesied that he would always be remembered, especially for introducing Greek meters into Latin poetry.—*Horace, Odes, III, xxx, 6.*

Non passibus aequis. *L*—With unequal steps.—*Vergil, Aeneid, II, 724.*

Non placet. *L*—It is not pleasing; indicating a negative vote.

Non possumus. *L*—We cannot. Papal form denying a request.

Non prosequitur. *L*—A judgment entered for the defendant when the plaintiff fails to prosecute.

Non quis, sed quid. *L*—Not who but what. The matter ought to be considered in itself, without considering who said it.

Non ragioniam di lor, ma guarda e passa. *It*—Let us not discuss them; look and pass on. Vergil is describing to Dante the punishment meted out to neutrals who were neither rebellious nor faithful to God: they are in a vestibule of hell, disdained by heaven and hell.—*Dante, Inferno, III, 51.*

Non sanz droict. *OF*—Not without right. Motto on Shakespeare's coat of arms.

Non semper erit aestas. *L*—Summer will not last forever.

Non semper Saturnalia erunt. *L*—The holidays will not last forever; Christmas comes but once a year. In ancient Rome slaves enjoyed great liberty during the Saturnalia.—*Seneca, Apocolocyntosis, XII, ii.* The title of this work has been translated The Pumpkinification of Claudius.

Non sequitur. *L*—It does not follow; an illogical inference. This is often used as a noun.

Non sibi sed patriae. *L*—Not for himself but for his native land.

Non sum qualis eram. *L*—I am not the man I used to be. The sentence in Horace adds: In the reign of kindly Cynara. Ernest Dowson took this as his text for the poem "Cynara."—*Horace, Odes, IV, i, 3.*

Non tanto me dignor honore. *L*—I do not deem myself worthy of so great an honor. Based on a line in *Vergil, Aeneid, I, 335.*

Non troppo presto. *It*—Not too fast.

Nonum prematur in annum. *L*—Let your piece of writing be kept unpublished until the ninth year.—*Horace, Art of Poetry, 388.*

Non vitae sed scholae discimus. *L*—We learn not for life but for school; we devote ourselves to learning, not for the cultivation of the moral life but for a display of cleverness.—*Seneca, Letters to Lucilius, CVI, 12.*

Non vult contendere. *L*—He does not wish to contest the suit. *See also* Nolo contendere.

No podemos haber aquello que queremos, queramos aquello que podremos. *Sp*—Since we cannot get what we like, let us like what we can get.

Nosce te ipsum. *L*—Know thyself. *See also* Gnothi seauton.

Nosce tempus. *L*—*See* Kairon gnothi.

Noscitur a sociis. *L*—A man is known by the company he keeps.

No se ganó Zamora en una hora. *Sp*—Zamora was not won in an hour; Rome was not built in a day.—*Cervantes, Don Quixote, II, LXXI.*

Nos morituri te salutamus. *L*—We who are about to die salute thee. Before fighting, gladiators in the arena looked up at the emperor and saluted him with these words. A modification of *Ave imperator, morituri te salutant.*—*Suetonius, Claudius, 21.*

Nota bene. *L*—*See* N.B.

Notatu dignum. *L*—Worthy of note.

Not kennt kein Gebot. *Ger*—Necessity knows no law.

Notre Dame. *Fr*—Our Lady; the Virgin Mary.

Notre défiance justifie la tromperie d'autrui. *Fr*—Our distrust of other men justifies them in deceiving us.—*La Rochefoucauld, Maxims, 86.*

Notre mérite nous attire l'estime des honnêtes gens, et notre étoile celle du public. *Fr*—Our merit wins the esteem of honest people, our lucky star that of the public.—*La Rochefoucauld, Maxims, 165.*

Notre nature

Notre nature est dans le mouvement; le repos entier est la mort. *Fr*—We are by nature active; complete rest is death.—*Pascal, Thoughts, II, 129.*

Nourri dans le sérail, j'en connais les détours. *Fr*—I was reared in the harem and know its byways. Said of one who knows the ropes from long experience.—*Racine, Bajazet, IV, vii.*

Nous aimons toujours ceux qui nous admirent, et nous n'aimons pas toujours ceux que nous admirons. *Fr*—We always love those who admire us, but we do not always love those whom we admire.—*La Rochefoucauld, Maxims, 294.*

Nous avons changé tout cela. *Fr*—We've changed all that. Sganarelle answers thus when objection is made to his statement that the heart is on the right side, and the liver on the left. He goes on to say that medicine is now practiced in an entirely different way. The expression is used to satirize those who try to defend their indefensible errors.—*Molière, Physician in Spite of Himself, II, iv.*

Nous avons tous assez de force pour supporter les maux d'autrui. *Fr*—We all have enough strength to bear the sufferings of other people.—*La Rochefoucauld, Maxims, 19.*

Nous ne trouvons guère de gens de bon sens que ceux qui sont de notre avis. *Fr*—People who do not share our views we seldom credit with having good sense.—*La Rochefoucauld, Maxims, 347.*

Nous pathetikos. *Gk*—The passive intellect.

Nous poietikos. *Gk*—The active, the creative mind.

Nous sommes tous dans le desert! Personne ne comprend personne. *Fr*—We are all in the desert! Nobody understands anybody.

Nous verrons. *Fr*—We shall see.

Nous verrons ce que nous verrons. *Fr*—We shall see what we shall see.

Nouveau riche. *Fr*—One who has recently become rich. The implication is that the person is publicizing his new status in a manner offensive to the less fortunate.

Nouvelle série. *Fr*—New series.

Novus homo. *L*—A new man; an upstart. In Roman politics, a newcomer, none of whose ancestors had held a high office.

Novus ordo seclorum. *L*—*See* Annuit coeptis.

El no y el sí son breves de decir, y piden mucho pensar. *Sp*— Yes and no are quickly said, and they demand a great deal of thought.—*Baltasar Gracián, The Oracle, 70.*

Nuda veritas. *L*—The naked truth.

Nudis cruribus. *L*—With naked legs.

Nudis oculis. *L*—With the naked eye; without a telescope.

Nudis verbis. *L*—In plain words.

Nudum pactum. *L*—A promise that cannot be enforced legally because of lack of a consideration, such as earnest money. A legal expression.

Nugae canorae. *L*—Tuneful trifles; songs that have meaningless nonsense syllables.

Nugae literariae. *L*—Literary trifles.

La nuit tous les chats sont gris. *Fr*—*See* Bei Nacht sind alle Katzen grau.

Nul bien sans peine. *Fr*—No gain without pain.

Nulla dies sine linea. *L*—No day without a line. A maxim attributed to the painter Apelles who let no day pass without sketching a little. It is also the motto of industrious writers.— *Pliny the Elder, Natural History, XXXV, 10.*

Nulla fere causa est in qua non femina litem moverit. *L*—There is almost no case of a quarrel that was not started over a woman.—*Juvenal, VI, 242.*

Nulla nuova, buona nuova. *It*—No news is good news.

Nulla salus bello. *L*—There is no safety in war.—*Vergil, Aeneid, XI, 399.*

Nulla virtute redemptum/A vitiis. *L*—A man redeemed from vice by not a single virtue. The man censured is Crispinus. *See also* Ecce iterum Crispinus.—*Juvenal, IV, 2.*

Nulli sapere casu obtigit. *L*—No man ever became wise by chance.—*Seneca, Letters to Lucilius, LXXVI, 4.*

Nulli secundus. *L*—Second to none.

Nullius addictus jurare in verba magistri. *L*—Not sworn to follow the teaching of any school or professor. Used by those who claim to be independent in their thinking.

Nullum est jam dictum quod non sit dictum prius. *L*—Nothing has been said that hasn't been said before.—*Terence, Eunuch, Prologue, 41.*

Nullum fere scribendi genus non tetigit, nullum quod tetigit non ornavit. *L*—There was almost no literary genre that he did not touch, and he touched nothing that he did not adorn. Doctor Johnson's inscription for Oliver Goldsmith's tomb in Westminster Abbey.

Nul tiel record. *Anglo-Fr*—No such record.

Numquam aliud natura, aliud sapientia dicit. *L*—Nature never says one thing and wisdom another. A tenet of Stoic philosophy. This is also stated by Marcus Aurelius in his *Meditations (VII, 11):* To the rational animal the same act is in accordance with nature and with reason.

Numquam minus otiosus quam cum otiosus. *L*—Never less at leisure than when at leisure. Cato is quoting P. Scipio Africanus.—*Cicero, On Duties, III, i.*

Numquam minus solus quam cum solus. *L*—Never less alone than when alone. Said of a person who enjoys his own company. Cato wrote that P. Scipio Africanus the Elder was accustomed to use this expression.—*Cicero, On Duties, III, 1* and *Republic, I, xvii, 27.*

Numquam solus cum sola. *L*—Never be alone with a woman who is alone. Counsel given monks.

Nunc aut nunquam. *L*—Now or never.

Nunc dimittis servum tuum, Domine. *L*—Now thou dost dismiss thy servant, O Lord. The first words of the canticle that Simeon uttered when Jesus was presented in the temple. *Nunc dimittis* often means permission to depart.—*Vulgate, Luke, II, 29.*

Nunc est bibendum, nunc pede libero/Pulsanda tellus. *L*—Now is the time for drinking and dancing.—*Horace, Odes, I, xxxvii, 1.*

Nunc pro tunc. *L*—Now for then. A legal term indicating that action is taken in the present that should have been taken previously.

Nur der verdient sich Freiheit wie das Leben,/Der täglich sie erobern muss. *Ger*—Only he deserves freedom and life who daily wins them anew.—*Goethe, Faust, pt. II, V, 11575-6.*

Nur wer die Sehnsucht kennt,/weiss, was ich leide! *Ger*—Literally, only one who knows longing, knows what I suffer. The poem was set to music by Tchaikovsky.—*Goethe, Wilhelm Meisters Lehrjahre, IV, xi.*

Nympha pudica deum vidit et erubuit. *L*—*See* Lympha pudica . . . .

O

8bre (octobre). *Fr*—October, the eighth month in the early Roman calendar.

o.d. (omni die). *L*—Every day.

OGPU (Obiedinionnoe Gosudarstvennoe Politicheskoe Upravlenie). *Rus*—Special Government Political Administration. Secret service in Russia until 1935; sometimes referred to as Gay-Pay-Oo (GPU). This organization was replaced by the NKVD, *Narkomvnudel (q.v.).*

o. L. (östliche Länge). *Ger*—East longitude.

O.P. (Ordo Praedicatorum *or* Ordinis Praedicatorum). *L*—Order of Preachers (Dominicans); of the Order of Preachers.

op. cit. (opere citato *or* opus citatum). *L*—In the work cited.

O.S.B. (Ordo Sancti Benedicti). *L*—Order of St. Benedict.

O.S.F.C. (Ordo Sancti Francisci Capuccinorum). *L*—Order of the Capuchin Franciscans.

o.s.p. *See* Obiit sine prole.

Oxon. (Oxoniensis). *L*—Noted after degrees granted by Oxford University.

Obiit. *L*—He died.

Obiit sine prole. *L*—He died without issue.

Obiter dictum. *L*—Said in passing.

Obiter scriptum. *L*—Something written by the way or in passing.

Objet d'art. *Fr*—A valuable piece of art.

Obra de común, obra de ningún. *Sp*—Everybody's business is nobody's business.

Obscurum per obscurius. *L*—Explaining the obscure through something still more obscure.

Obsequium amicos, veritas odium parit. *L*—Compliance breeds friends, truth hatred.—*Terence, Andria, I, i, 41.*

Obsta principiis. *L*—Resist the opening wedge. A legal maxim.

Obstipui steteruntque comae et vox faucibus haesit. *L*—I was amazed, my hair stood on end, and my voice stuck in my throat.—*Vergil, Aeneid, II, 774.*

L'occasion fait le larron. *Fr*—The opportunity makes the thief.

Ochen khorosho. *Rus*—Very well.

Ochen nemnogo. *Rus*—Very little.

Oculis subjecta fidelibus. *L*—Subjected to competent examination.

Oculus episcopi. *L*—The eye of the bishop; said of a clergyman who makes reports to a bishop.

Oderint dum metuant. *L*—Let them hate so long as they fear me. This is the attitude of the dictator.—*Cicero, On Duties, I, xxviii, 97.*

Oderint dum probent. *L*—Let them hate so long as they approve.

Odi et amo. *L*—I hate and I love. *Catullus, LXXXV, 1.*

Odi profanum vulgus et arceo. *L*—I hate the irreverent mob and I avoid it.—*Horace, Odes, III, i, 1.*

Odium generis humani. *L*—Hatred of the human race, a crime of which early Christians were accused by Nero.—*Tacitus, Annals, XV, 44.*

Odium literarium. *L*—A hostile spirit among authors.

Odium theologicum. *L*—Hatred developed among theologians over doctrinal differences.

Œil-de-bœuf. *Fr*—Bull's eye, a name given to a circular window seen in architecture of the seventeenth and eighteenth centuries.

Œuvre de vulgarisation. *Fr*—A book popularizing a subject. Those who fancy themselves profound may sometimes use this phrase to describe a work that has had a wide sale.

Œuvres complètes. *Fr*—Complete works.

O felix culpa quae talem et tantum meruit habere redemptorem! *L*—O happy fault that merited such a great redeemer!

O fortunatam natam me consule Romam. *L*—How fortunate Rome, born in my consulship!—*Juvenal, X, 122.* Juvenal was quoting a verse by Cicero, reminding the Romans that he (Cicero) had saved the Republic by crushing the conspiracy of Catiline.

O fortunatos nimium, sua si bona norint! *L*—How very happy they would be if they but knew their blessings! This was originally written of farmers, far removed from the field of battle. It has often been quoted as a retort to complainers.—*Vergil, Georgics, II, 458.*

Ogni debole

Ogni debole ha sempre il suo tiranno. *It*—Every weakling has his tyrant.

Ogni medaglia ha il suo rovescio. *It*—Every medal has its reverse side; there are two sides to every story.

Ogni pazzo vuol dar consiglio. *It*—Every fool is ready to give advice.

Ohne Arbeit kein Gewinn. *Ger*—There is no gain without work.

Ohne Hast, ohne Rast. *Ger*—Without hurry but without rest. Goethe's description of the sun. A medal was struck with these words and presented to Goethe by Thomas Carlyle and fourteen other admirers.

Olet lucernam. *L*—It smells of the lamp, midnight oil. Disparaging reference to a labored literary composition.

Oleum addere camino. *L*—To add oil to the fire.—*Horace, Satires, II, iii, 321.*

O Liberté, O Liberté, que de crimes on commet en ton nom! *Fr*—O Liberty, O Liberty, what crimes are committed in your name! Words spoken by Madame Roland just before her execution when she saw the guillotine set up near a statue of Liberty.

Olla podrida. *Sp*—A dish of many different foods mixed together; hence, a combination of unlikely elements; a literary hodgepodge.

Omne animal ex ovo. *L*—Every animal comes from an egg. Sir William Harvey's biological axiom.

Omne ignotum pro magnifico est. *L*—Everything unknown is presumed magnificient.—*Tacitus, Agricola, 30.*

Omne meum, nihil meum. *L*—'Tis all mine, yet none is mine.— *Macrobius.* The compiler's admission and justification. He takes much from other sources, but gives them proper credit. It may be used by a writer who works over the thoughts of other men and creates something that is his own. This was the claim of Robert Burton, the author of *The Anatomy of Melancholy*, who quoted profusely from Latin sources.

Omne solum forti patria est. *L*—The whole earth is the fatherland of a brave man.—*Ovid, Fasti (Calendar of Roman Festivals), I, 493.*

Omne tulit punctum, qui miscuit utile dulci. *L*—He wins general approval who mingles the useful with the pleasant.—*Horace, Art of Poetry, 343.*

Omne vitium in proclivi est. *L*—All the roads of vice are downhill. *See also* Facilis descensus Averno.

Omne vivum ex vivo. *L*—Life comes from life.

Omnia bona bonis. *L*—To the good all things are good. Good men are sometimes credulous and do not readily believe evil of anyone.

Omnia exeunt in mysterium. *L*—Everything ends up in mystery.

Omnia mea mecum porto. *L*—I carry all my possessions with me. The philosopher's scorn of external goods.—*Bias.*

Omnia mors aequat. *L*—Death levels everything.—*Claudian, Against Rufinus, I, 200.*

Omnia mutantur, nihil interit. *L*—Everything changes, nothing is destroyed. This is quoted in connection with the doctrine of the transmigration of souls taught by Pythagoras.—*Ovid, Metamorphoses, XV, 165.*

Omnia mutantur, nos et mutamur in illis. *L*—All things change and we change with them. *See also* Tempora mutantur . . . .

Omnia opera. *L*—The complete works.

Omnia orta occidunt et aucta senescunt. *L*—All things rise only to fall, and flourish to decay.—*Sallust, Jugurthine War, II.*

Omnia vincit Amor et nos cedamus Amori. *L*—Love conquers everything, and let us yield to Love.—*Vergil, Eclogues, X, 69.*

Omnia vincit veritas. *L*—Truth conquers everything.

Omnibus has litteras visuris. *L*—To whom it may concern; to all who read this document.

Omnis amans

Omnis amans amens. *L*—Every lover is out of his mind.

Omnis ars naturae imitatio est. *L*—All art is an imitation of nature.—*Seneca, Letters to Lucilius, LXV, 3.*

Omnis cellula e cellula ejusdem generis. *L*—Every cell comes from a cell of the same kind. A biological axiom.

Omnis cognitio fit a sensibus. *L*—All knowledge comes through the senses. A Scholastic axiom.

Omnis comparatio claudicat. *L*—Every comparison limps.

Omnis definitio periculosa est. *L*—All definitions are dangerous.

Omnis fama a domesticis emanat. *L*—All fame comes from domestic servants. Francis Bacon observed that "discreet followers and servants help much to reputation."

Omnium consensu capax imperii, nisi imperasset. *L*—In the opinion of all, a capable ruler, if only he had not ruled. The historian's judgment of Galba who was elected by the army to succeed Nero.—*Tacitus, Histories, I, 49.*

Omnium gatherum. The first word is Latin. A humorous imitation of Latin used to indicate an unlikely collection of items of a heterogeneous nature.

On connaît l'ami au besoin. *Fr*—You discover a true friend when in need.

Onde não entra o sol entra o medico. *Port*—Where the sun does not enter, the doctor does.

On est souvent ferme par faiblesse, et audacieux par timidité. *Fr*—One is often firm because of weakness and bold because of timidity.—*La Rochefoucauld, Maxims, 11.*

On n'a jamais bon marché de mauvaise marchandise. *Fr*—One never picks up a bargain buying bad merchandise; buy cheap, buy dear.

On ne donne rien si libéralement que ses conseils. *Fr*—We are never so generous as when giving advice.—*La Rochefoucauld, Maxims, 110.*

206

On ne loue d'ordinaire que pour être loué. *Fr*—As a rule, we praise only to be praised.—*La Rochefoucauld, Maxims, 146.*

On ne saurait faire une omelette sans casser des œufs. *Fr*—You can't make an omelet without breaking some eggs. *See also* Chi non rompe l'uova . . . .

On ne se blâme que pour être loué. *Fr*—One censures himself only to be praised.—*La Rochefoucauld, Maxims, 554.*

On n'est jamais si heureux ni si malheureux qu'on s'imagine. *Fr* —One is never as happy or as unhappy as one imagines.—*La Rochefoucauld, Maxims, 49.*

On n'est jamais si ridicule par les qualités que l'on a que par celles que l'on affecte d'avoir. *Fr*—One is never so ridiculous for the qualities that one has as for those one feigns to have. —*La Rochefoucauld, Maxims, 134.*

On ne trouve guère d'ingrats tant qu'on est en état de faire du bien. *Fr*—One rarely encounters ingratitude as long as one is in a position to confer favors.—*La Rochefoucauld, Maxims, 306.*

Onus probandi. *L*—The burden of proof.

Ope et consilio. *L*—Literally, with aid and counsel; a term applied to one who is accessory to a crime.

Opera buffa. *It*—Comic opera.

Operae pretium est. *L*—It is worth while.

Operibus credite, et non verbis. *L*—Trust in deeds and not words.—*Cervantes, Don Quixote, II, L.*

Opera inedita (*pl.* opere inedite). *It*—An unpublished work.

Opes irritamenta malorum. *L*—Wealth, the incentive of the wicked.—*Ovid, Metamorphoses, I, 140.*

Opse theon aleousi myloi, aleousi de lepta. *Gk*—The mills of the gods grind slowly but they grind exceedingly fine.—*Sextus Empiricus. See also* Sero molunt deorum molae.

207

Optimum est pati quod emendare non possis. *L*—It is best to suffer what you cannot amend; what cannot be cured must be endured.—*Seneca, Letters to Lucilius, CVII, 9.*

Optimum lege (elige), suave et facile illud faciet consuetudo. *L* —Choose the best; habit will make it pleasant and easy. A precept of the Pythagoreans.

Optimus legum interpres consuetudo. *L*—Custom is the best interpreter of the laws.

Opus Dei. *L*—The work of God. An organization of Spanish laymen whose members are pledged to carry out the ideals of Catholic philosophy in public as well as private life.

Opus est interprete. *L*—There is need of an interpreter.

Opus operatum est. *L*—The work is done.

Opus postumum. *L*—A work published after the author's death.

O quam cito transit gloria mundi! *L*—Oh, how quickly the glory of the world passes! *See also* Sic transit gloria mundi.— *Thomas à Kempis, The Imitation of Christ, I, iii, 6.*

Ora e sempre. *It*—Now and forever.

Ora et labora. *L*—Pray and work. The motto of the Benedictines.

Ora pro nobis. *L*—Pray for us.

Orate, fratres. *L*—Pray, brethren.

Orator fit, poeta nascitur. *L*—Training and education produce the orator, but the poet is born a poet. *See also* Poeta nascitur, non fit.

Orbis terrarum. *L*—The circle of the earth; the whole world.

Ordines majores. *L*—Major orders: subdiaconate, diaconate, priesthood, and episcopate.

Ordines minores. *L*—Minor orders: offices of porter, lector, exorcist and acolyte in the Catholic Church.

Oremus. *L*—Let us pray.

Ore rotundo. *L*—Polished, well-rounded speech.—*Horace, Art of Poetry, 323.*

Oro è che oro vale. *It*—That is gold which is worth gold.

Oro y plata. *Sp*—Gold and silver. Motto of Montana.

O rus, quando ego te aspiciam? *L*—O peace of the countryside, when shall I behold thee again?—*Horace, Satires, II, vi, 60.*

O sancta simplicitas! *L*—O holy simplicity! Words reportedly uttered by Huss on seeing a pious old woman add a fagot to the fire when he was being burned for heresy.

Osculum pacis. *L*—Kiss of peace, a ceremonial salute formerly restricted to use among the ministers of a High Mass. Currently the faithful exchange greetings. The practice can be traced to the second century.

O, si sic omnia. *L*—Would that he had always acted in this way.

O solitudo, sola beatitudo. *L*—O solitude, the only happiness. The ideal of the recluse.—*Saint Bernard.*

Ossa atque pellis totus est. *L*—He is all skin and bones.—*Plautus, The Pot of Gold, III, vi, 28.*

O tempora, o mores! *L*—Oh, the times, oh, the customs! Cicero is denouncing the degeneracy of his day.—*Cicero, I Against Catiline, 1.*

Otia dant vitia. *L*—Leisure makes for vice.

Otium cum dignitate. *L*—Leisure with dignity.—*Cicero, For P. Sextius, XLV.*

Otium sine dignitate. *L*—Leisure without dignity.

Otium sine litteris mors est. *L*—Leisure with nothing to read is death.—*Seneca, Letters to Lucilius, LXXXII, 3.*

Ottava rima. *It*—A stanza of eight iambic lines, the first six rhyming alternately, the last two forming a couplet.

Oublier je ne puis. *Fr*—I cannot forget.

Où la chèvre

Où la chèvre est attaché, il faut qu'elle broute. *Fr*—The goat must browse where she is tied up; one must make the best of a situation.

Outre mer. *Fr*—Beyond the sea; therefore, foreign lands. Longfellow wrote a book with this title.

Ouvrage de longue haleine. *Fr*—Literally, a work of deep breath; a work involving long labor.

Oyer and terminer. *Anglo-Fr*—To hear and settle. Applied to a superior court for the hearing of a criminal trial.

Oyez! *Fr*—Hear ye! A cry used in court to gain attention. It is generally called out three times.

P

p. *It*—*See* piano.

p.A. (per Adresse). *Ger*—In care of.

p.ae., part. aeq., p.e. (partes aequales). *L*—In equal parts.

P.C. (pondus civile). *L*—Avoirdupois.

p.c. (post cibum). *L*—After food. A medical direction.

P.C.I. (partito comunista italiano). *It*—Italian Communist party.

P.D. (Privatdozent). *Ger*—In a German university a teacher who receives student fees but no salary.

P.D.A. (pour dire adieu). *Fr*—To say good-bye. Formerly written on personal cards when one had to leave town without having an opportunity to call on friends.

per proc., per pro. *L*—*See* Per procurationem, per procuratorem.

P.F.S.A. (pour faire ses adieux). *Fr*—To say good-bye; written on a card indicating that one is to be absent from the city for a time. Formerly this card was regarded as equivalent to a call.

P.L.I. (partito liberale italiano). *It*—Italian Liberal party.

P.M. (post meridiem). *L*—Afternoon; from noon to midnight.

post-obit. (post obitum). *L*—After death.

Pp. *It*—*See* Pianissimo.

p.p. (praemissis praemittendis). *L*—Omitting preliminaries.

P.P.C. *Fr*—*See* Pour prendre congé.

Ppp. *It*—*See* Pianississimo.

P.P.S. (post post-scriptum). *L*—An additional postscript.

PRI. (partido revolutionario institutional). *Sp*—Institutional Revolutionary party, the party in power in Mexico since the early 1930s.

p.r.n. (pro re nata). *L*—Whenever necessary. A medical directive.

pro tem. *L*—*See* Pro tempore.

prox. (proximo). *L*—Used in correspondence to indicate a date in the month following the one in which the letter is written.

P.S. (post-scriptum). *L*—Postscript.

P.S.D.I. (partito socialista democratico italiano). *It*—Italian Socialist Democratic party.

p.v.t. (par voie télégraphique). *Fr*—By telegraph.

Pacem in Maribus. *L*—Peace on the Seas, an international conference held on Malta in 1970 that attempted to find answers to problems centering about wealth in the world's oceans.

Pace tanti nominis. *L*—With due respect for so great a name.

Pace tanti viri. *L*—With due respect for so great a man.

Pace tua. *L*—By your leave; saving your presence.

Pacta conventa. *L*—Conditions agreed upon in a diplomatic arrangement.

Pactum de non petendo. *L*—An agreement not to sue.

Pagan a veces los justos por los pecadores. *Sp*—Sometimes the just pay for the wicked.

Pain bénit. *Fr*—Blessed, not consecrated, bread, distributed at mass to the faithful who have not received Holy Communion. A regional practice in France.

La paix de Dieu. *Fr*—The truce of God. *See also* Treuga Dei.

Paix fourrée. *Fr*—Sham, false peace.

Pallida Mors aequo pulsat pede pauperum tabernas regumque turris. *L*—Pale death strikes impartially at the hovels of the poor and the towers of kings.—*Horace, Odes, I, iv, 13.*

Palmam qui meruit ferat. *L*—Let him who won the prize bear it away. Motto of Lord Nelson.

Palmes académiques. *Fr*—Decoration conferred by the French Ministry of Public Instruction for notable service in the field of education.

Panem et circenses. *L*—Bread and the circuses. The cry of the Roman mob for food and entertainment.—*Juvenal, X, 81.*

Pange, lingua, gloriosi. *L*—Sing, O my tongue, the glorious. The first words of two medieval hymns, one generally attributed to Fortunatus (6th century) and the second by Thomas Aquinas (13th century), sung on the feast of *Corpus Christi (q.v.).*

Panta rei (rhei). *Gk*—Everything is in a state of flux.—*Heraclitus.*

Panton metron anthropos estin. *Gk*—Man is the measure of all things. Quoted by *Plato, Theaetetus, 178b.*

Papier mâché. *Fr*—Paper pulp shaped into various forms which are hardened with glue and other additives.

Par accès. *Fr*—By fits and starts.

I paragoni son odiosi. *It*—Comparisons are odious.

Para mí solo nació Don Quixote, y yo para él. *Sp*—Don Quixote was born for me alone and I for him. The reason Cervantes gave for taking his hero to the grave.—*Cervantes, Don Quixote, II, last chap.*

Para todo hay remedio si no es para la muerte. *Sp*—There's a remedy for everything except death.—*Cervantes, Don Quixote, II, XLIII.*

Par avance. *Fr*—Beforehand; in advance.

Parbleu! *Fr*—Of course! certainly. A mild derivative from *par Dieu*, by God.

Parcere subjectis et debellare superbos. *L*—To spare the lowly and humble the proud. The aim of Roman conquest.—*Vergil, Aeneid, VI, 853.*

Par ci, par là. *Fr*—Here and there.

Par complaisance. *Fr*—Out of a desire to be pleasant or agreeable.

Par dépit. *Fr*—Out of spite.

Pardonnez-moi. *Fr*—Excuse me.

Parens patriae. *L*—Literally, father of the country; a state official paternally taking care of the interests of persons without parents or guardians or of those incapable of conducting their affairs.

Pares autem cum paribus, vetere proverbio, facillime congregantur. *L*—Persons of like interest very readily get together; birds of a feather flock together.—*Cicero, Old Age, III, 7.*

Pares regni. *L*—Peers of the realm.

Par excellence. *Fr*—Preeminently.

Par exemple. *Fr*—For example.

Parfum de terroir. *Fr*—The sweet smell of the soil.

Par hasard. *Fr*—By chance.

Pari delicto. *L*—In equal guilt.

Pari passu. *L*—At an equal step or rate; at a like distance; by similar gradation.

Paris vaut bien une messe. *Fr*—Paris is well worth a mass. Attributed to Henry IV of France, a Protestant, who was ac-

Paritur pax bello

cused of becoming a convert to Catholicism for reasons of
political expediency.

Paritur pax bello. *L*—Peace is born of war.—*Cornelius Nepos,
Epaminondas, V.*

Parler à tort et à travers. *Fr*—To speak confusedly, illogically.

Parliamentum Indoctorum. *L*—The Unlearned Parliament, a
name given to sessions held in 1404 when Henry IV of England forbade lawyers to be present.

Par negotiis neque supra. *L*—Equal to his business and not
superior to it; a man well fitted for his occupation.—*Tacitus,
Annals, VI, 39.*

La parole a été donnée à l'homme pour déguiser sa pensée. *Fr*—
Speech was given man to disguise his thoughts.—*Talleyrand.*

Parole d'honneur. *Fr*—Word of honor.

Le parole son femmine, i fatti son maschi. *It*—Words are feminine, deeds are masculine. The genders of the nouns suit the
proverb. One of the mottoes of Maryland; for the other, *see*
Scuto bonae voluntatis . . . .

Les paroles sont faites pour cacher nos pensées. *Fr*—Words were
invented to disguise our thoughts. A variation of *La parole a
été donnée à l'homme . . . (q.v.).*

Par parenthèse. *Fr*—By way of parenthesis.

Par pari refero. *L*—I give back like for like.

Pars pro toto. *L*—A part for the whole.

Pars rationabilis. *L*—The reasonable part of an estate that a
husband cannot will to any others but his wife and children.

Pars sanitatis velle sanari fuit. *L*—To be cured one must wish
to be cured.—*Seneca, Hippolytus, 249.*

Part du lion. *Fr*—The lion's share. In Aesop's fable the lion takes
all of the prey as his share.

Partes infidelium. *L*—*See* In partibus infidelium.

Parthis mendacior. *L*—More deceitful than the Parthians.

Particeps criminis. *L*—An accomplice in a crime.

Participes curarum. *L*—Sharers in trials and troubles.

Partie carrée. *Fr*—Literally, a square party; a pleasure jaunt composed of two couples; double date.

Parti pris. *Fr*—Preconceived opinion; foregone conclusion; a prejudice in the literal sense, i.e. a judgment formed before getting the facts.

Partir, c'est mourir un peu. *Fr*—Parting is like dying a little.

Parturiunt montes, nascetur ridiculus mus. *L*—The mountains are in labor and a ridiculous mouse will be born.—*Horace, Art of Poetry, 139.*

Partus sequitur ventrem. *L*—The offspring follows the status of the mother. Used in determining whether a child is free or slave.

Parva leves capiunt mentes. *L*—Little minds are attracted by trifles.

Parvis componere magna. *L*—To compare great things with small.—*Vergil, Eclogue, I, 23.*

Parvum parva decent. *L*—Small things become the humble man. —*Horace, Epistles, I, vii, 44.*

Pas à pas. *Fr*—Step by step.

Pas à pas on va bien loin. *Fr*—By taking one step at a time one can go far.

Pas de deux. *Fr*—Dance for two.

Pas de nouvelles, bonnes nouvelles. *Fr*—No news is good news.

Pas de rose sans épines. *Fr*—There is no rose without its thorns.

Pas du tout. *Fr*—Not at all.

Paso doble. *Sp*—Two step; rapid march heard at bullfights.

Passato el periculo

Passato el periculo, gabato el santo. *It*—Once the danger is past, the saint is forgotten. A proverb cited by Rabelais, *Pantagruel IV, 24. See also* Aegrotat daemon . . . .

Pas seul. *Fr*—A dance performed alone.

Pas si bête. *Fr*—Not so stupid.

Passim. *L*—Here and there.

Pâté de foie gras. *Fr*—Patty or paste of fattened goose liver and truffles.

Pater familias. *L*—The head of a household, not necessarily the father.

Pater noster. *L*—Our Father; the first words of the Lord's prayer. —*Vulgate, Matthew, VI, 9.*

Pater patriae. *L*—Father of his country. A title given several great patriots, e.g. Cicero and Washington.

La patience est amère, mais son fruit est doux. *Fr*—Patience is bitter, but its fruit is sweet.—*Rousseau.*

Patientia fit levior ferendo. *L*—Suffering becomes lighter when borne patiently.

Patres et conscripti. *L*—All the members of the ancient Roman senate, whether they held office through inheritance, appointment, or previous election to high office.

Patria cara, carior libertas. *L*—My country is dear, but liberty is dearer.

Patriae quis exsul se quoque fugit? *L*—What exile from his fatherland can flee himself?—*Horace, Odes, II, xvi, 19.*

Patria est ubicumque vir fortis sedem sibi elegerit. *L*—A brave man's fatherland is wherever he chooses to settle.—*Q. Curtius Rufus, Exploits of Alexander, VI, iv, 11.*

Patria potestas. *L*—The power of a Roman father over the members of his family. At its peak this power extended to life and limb.

Patte de velours. *Fr*—The velvet paw; the velvet glove.

Pattes de mouche. *Fr*—Fly tracks; small illegible handwriting.

Pauca sed bona. *L*—A few things but good; not quantity but quality.

Paucas pallabris. A few words.—*Shakespeare, Taming of the Shrew, I, i.* Christopher Sly's way of saying *Pocas palabras.* He seems to have crossed the Spanish with the Latin *Paucis verbis (q.v.).*

Pauca verba. *L*—A few words.

Paucis verbis. *L*—In a few words.

Paulum morati / serius aut citius sedem properamus ad unam. *L*— After a slight delay, sooner or later we hasten to one and the same abode.—*Ovid, Metamorphoses, X, 32.*

Pauvre diable! *Fr*—Poor fellow!

Pax ecclesiae (Dei). *L*—Peace of the Church (of God). An effort on the part of the medieval church in eleventh century France to protect noncombatants, church property, farm stock, and tools from the ravages of war by excommunicating offenders.

Pax in bello. *L*—Peace in war; a desultory war; half-hearted conflict.

Pax orbis terrarum. *L*—The peace of the world. Found on Roman coins.

Pax Romana. *L*—Roman peace, a peace dictated by strength of Roman arms.

Pax tecum. *L*—Peace be with you. When spoken to more than one person, *Pax vobiscum.*

Pax vobiscum. *L*—Peace be with you.

Peau d'âne. *Fr*—Skin of an ass.

Peau de chagrin. *Fr*—Skin of a wild ass. When one sat on this skin, he received his desire, but the size of the skin and the years of his life were diminished with each wish. This is the title of a novel by Balzac; in English, *The Magic Skin.*

Pecca fortiter. *L*—Sin bravely. Luther's advice has disturbed many. However, it must be taken in its context, for he goes on to command that one should believe and rejoice in Christ more confidently still.

Peccavi. *L*—I have sinned. In 1843, when Sir Charles Napier defeated the amirs of Sind in two decisive battles, he sent this punning message to his government.

Pede claudo. *L*—With limping foot. Punishment is represented as traveling slowly behind the criminal but rarely failing to overtake him.—*Horace, Odes, III, ii, 32.*

Pedibus timor addidit alas. *L*—Fear adds wings to one's feet.—*Vergil, Aeneid, VIII, 224.*

Peine forte et dure. *Fr*—Strong, severe punishment inflicted upon criminals who refused to plead. They were pressed under heavy weights until they complied or suffered death. In 1772, England abolished pressing to death.

Pendente lite. *L*—While the litigation is pending.

Penetralia mentis. *L*—The secret depths or recesses of the mind.

Pensano gl'innamorati che gli altri siano ciechi. *It*—Lovers think that other people are blind.

Pensée fait la grandeur de l'homme. *Fr*—The greatness of man lies in his power to think.

Il penseroso. *It*—The melancholy man. Title of a poem by Milton. A companion piece to *L'allegro (q.v.).*

I pensieri non pagano dazio. *It*—Thoughts do not pay a duty; thoughts are free.

Lo peor es siempre cierto. *Sp*—The worst is always certain; the worst is sure to come.

Per accidens. *L*—Accidentally, not essentially. Opposite of *Per se (q.v.).*

Per ambages. *L*—By circumlocution; beating around the bush.

Per angusta ad augusta. *L*—Through trials to grandeur.

Per annum. *L*—By the year.

Per ardua ad astra. *L*—To the stars by hardship's way. Motto of the British Royal Air Force.

Per capita. *L*—For each person; share and share alike; by individuals; by the head.

Per consequens. *L*—Consequently.

Per contante. *It*—For cash.

Percontatorem fugito, nam garrulus idem est. *L*—Avoid an inquisitive man, for he is certain to be a gossip.—*Horace, Epistles, I, XVIII, 69.*

Per conto. *It*—A payment on account.

Per contra. *L*—On the contrary; on the other hand.

Per curiam. *L*—By the whole court.

Percussu crebro saxa cavantur aquis. *L*—Stones are hollowed out by constant dripping of water.—*Ovid, Epistles from Pontus, II, vii, 40. See also* Gutta cavat lapidem . . . .

Per diem. *L*—By the day.

Pereant qui ante nos nostra dixerunt. *L*—Damned be those who uttered our ideas before us. A whimsical parallel to the statement that there is nothing new under the sun.—*Donatus. See also* Nil dictum quod non dictum prius.

Père de famille. *Fr*—Father of the family.

Père du peuple. *Fr*—Father of the People, a name given the French King Louis XII by his grateful subjects.

Pereunt et imputantur. *L*—The hours are lost and are charged against us. An inscription on sundials.

Per fas et (aut) nefas. *L*—Through right and (or) wrong.

Perfecta aetas. *L*—The age at which a person attains his majority.

Perfervidum ingenium Scotorum. *L*—The glowing ardor or earnestness of the Scots.

La **perfide Albion.** *Fr*—Perfidious Albion. A French evaluation of the integrity of the British.

Per gradus. *L*—Step by step.

Periculum in mora. *L*—There is danger in delay.

Peritis in sua arte credendum. *L*—The skilled should be trusted in their own area of competence.

Perjuria ridet amantium Juppiter. *L*—At lovers' perjuries Jove laughs, to use Shakespeare's translation in *Romeo and Juliet, II, ii, 92.—Tibullus, III, vi, 49.*

Per mare, per terras. *L*—By sea and land.

Per mensem. *L*—By the month.

Per mese. *It*—By the month.

Permissu superiorum. *L*—With the permission of superiors. This or similar expressions are found at the beginning of Catholic books indicating that the doctrine is in conformity with the teachings of the Church. *See also* Imprimatur; Imprimi permittitur; Imprimi potest; Nihil obstat.

Permitte divis cetera. *L*—Leave everything else to the gods.— *Horace, Odes, I, ix, 9.*

Per nefas. *L*—In error; through a misinterpretation.

Per omnia saecula fama . . . vivam. *L*—My fame shall survive through all the ages.—*Ovid, Metamorphoses, XV, 878f.*

Per os. *L*—Through the mouth. A medical direction about the method of administering medication.

Per pares. *L*—By one's peers.

Perpetuum mobile. *L*—Perpetual motion.

Per piacere. *It*—Please.

Per più strade si va a Roma. *It*—You can go to Rome by many roads.

Per procurationem. *L*—By an agency; by proxy.

Per procuratorem. *L*—By an agent; by proxy.

Per saltum. *L*—By a leap; in a sudden advance.

Per se. *L*—By, in, or of itself.

Persona grata. *L*—In diplomatic usage a person acceptable in the country to which he is assigned.

Persona non grata. *L*—An unacceptable person.

Les **personnes faibles ne peuvent être sincères.** *Fr*—The weak cannot be sincere.—*La Rochefoucauld, Maxims, 316.*

Per stirpes. *L*—Through a direct line of descent.

Per totam curiam. *L*—By the whole court; a unanimous decision.

Pertusum quicquid infunditur in dolium perit. *L*—All is lost that is put in a riven dish.

Per veritatem vis. *L*—Power through truth.

Petit à petit, fait l'oiseau son nid. *Fr*—Little by little the bird builds its nest.

Petit bourgeois. *Fr*—A French citizen of the lower middle class.

Le **petit caporal.** *Fr*—The little corporal; Napoleon.

Petit chaudron, grandes oreilles. *Fr*—Little pitchers have big ears; little children have keen hearing.

La **petite bourgeoisie.** *Fr*—The lower middle class composed for the most part of tradesmen.

Petite pièce. *Fr*—A minor theatrical production.

Petites gens. *Fr*—People of small means; people of no importance from the aristocratic point of view.

La **petitesse de l'esprit fait l'opiniâtreté, et nous ne croyons pas aisément ce qui est au delà de ce que nous voyons.** *Fr*—The little mind is opinionated; we do not readily accept what is beyond our understanding.—*La Rochefoucauld, Maxims, 265.*

Petitio principii. *L*—Begging the question.

Petit maître. *Fr*—Fop; dandy.

Petit mal. *Fr*—A mild epileptic attack.

Petit nom. *Fr*—Pet name, first name.

Petits jeux. *Fr*—Literally, little games; social games.

Petit souper. *Fr*—An informal, light supper for a few friends after an evening's entertainment.

Peu à peu. *Fr*—Little by little.

Peu d'hommes ont été admirés par leurs domestiques. *Fr*—Few men have been admired by their servants.—*Montaigne, Essays, III, 2.*

Phi Beta Kappa. *Gk*—Greek letters of the oldest Greek-letter fraternity, signifying *Philosophia biou kubernetes*, philosophy is the guide of life.

Die **Philosophie des Als-ob.** *Ger*—*The Philosophy of As-If.* The title of a work by H. Vaihinger in which he upholds the view that even though certain religious doctrines are not true, they are not to be regarded as valueless.

Phtheirousin ethe chresth' homiliai kakai. *Gk*—Evil communications corrupt good manners.—*Menander, Thais. See also* Corrumpunt bonos mores . . . .

Pia fraus. *L*—A well-intended deception or fraud. Adapted from *Ovid, Metamorphoses, IX, 711.*

Pianissimo. *It*—Very softly.

Pianississimo. *It*—Very, very softly; as softly as possible. A super-superlative.

Piano. *It*—Softly.

Pictoribus atque poetis/quidlibet audendi semper fuit aequa potestas. *L*—Painters and poets have always had an equal right to experiment.—*Horace, Art of Poetry, 9.*

Pièce à thèse. *Fr*—A play with a thesis, a problem play aiming at conversion to an idea rather than entertainment.

Pièce de résistance. *Fr*—The principal dish of a meal; the principal article on display.

Pièce d'occasion. *Fr*—A play written for a special occasion.

Pied à terre! *Fr*—Dismount! As a noun, a temporary lodging.

Pierre qui roule n'amasse pas mousse. *Fr*—A rolling stone gathers no moss.

Pietra mossa non fa muschio. *It*—A rolling stone gathers no moss.

Pinxit. *L*—He painted it. Noted on paintings with the name of the artist. Sometimes abbreviated by omitting the vowels.

Pis-aller. *Fr*—Last resort.

Pisces natare docere. *L*—To teach fish to swim; to carry coals to Newcastle.

Pithecanthropus erectus. *NL*—Literally, erect monkey man; the supposed immediate ancestor of *homo sapiens (q.v.)*.

Più che il martello dura l'incudine. *It*—The anvil outlasts the hammer.

Più tengono a memoria gli uomini le ingiurie che li beneficii ricevuti. *It*—Men are more likely to remember the injuries than the benefits received.—*Guicciardini*.

Piuttosto (più tosto) mendicante che ignorante. *It*—Rather be a beggar than an ignoramus.

Place aux dames! *Fr*—Make way for the ladies; ladies first!

Placebo. *L*—Literally, I shall please; in medicine, a prescription given to please a patient who in the physician's opinion needs no medication. The first word in an antiphon sung at Vespers in the Office of the Dead.

Place d'armes. *Fr*—Parade ground.

Placet. *L*—It is pleasing. An affirmative vote.

Plaza de toros

Plaza de toros. *Sp*—Stadium where bullfights are held.

Plene administravit. *L*—He carried out his duties completely. A plea entered when an executor or an administrator has completely accounted for property under his control.

Pleno jure. *L*—With full right or authority.

La plupart des gens ne jugent des hommes que par la vogue qu'ils ont, ou par leur fortune. *Fr*—Most men judge their fellows by the popularity or fortune they enjoy.—*La Rochefoucauld, Maxims, 212.*

La plupart des hommes emploient la première partie de leur vie à rendre l'autre misérable. *Fr*—Most men spend the first half of their lives in such a way that they make the second half miserable.—*La Bruyère, Characters, On Man, 102 (1), p. 330 in Garapon's edition (Garnier Frères, 1962).*

Le plus brave des braves. *Fr*—The bravest of the brave.

Plus ça change, plus c'est la même chose. *Fr*—The more it is changed, the more it is the same thing.

Plus dolet quam necesse est, qui ante dolet quam necesse est. *L*—He who grieves before he has cause, grieves more than he need.—*Seneca, Letters to Lucilius, 98, 8.*

Plus fait douceur que violence. *Fr*—Kindness gains more than violence.

Plus je vois les hommes, plus j'admire les chiens. *Fr*—The more I see of people, the better I like dogs.

Plus royaliste que le roi. *Fr*—More of a royalist than the king himself.

Les plus sages ne le sont pas toujours. *Fr*—The wisest men are not always so wise.

Plus sages que les sages. *Fr*—Wiser than the wise.

Poco a poco. *Sp-It*—Little by little.

Poesía gauchesca. *Sp*—Gaucho poetry of Argentina sung by a cowboy to the accompaniment of the guitar. Regarded as the most indigenous literature of Spanish America.

Poeta nascitur, non fit. *L*—A poet is born, not made.

Point d'appui. *Fr*—Point of support; fulcrum; a basis of military operations.

Point d'argent, point de Suisses. *Fr*—No money, no Swiss. The Swiss here referred to were mercenaries who would not serve in a foreign army without pay.—*Racine, Les Plaideurs, I, 1.*

Point de repère. *Fr*—Reference or guide mark used in returning to a spot or in rechecking or repeating a process.

Une **poire pour la soif.** *Fr*—Literally, a pear for the thirst; something for a rainy day.

Poisson d'avril. *Fr*—Literally, fish of April; French equivalent of April fool.

Die **Politik ist keine exakte Wissenschaft.** *Ger*—Politics is not an exact science.—*Bismarck.*

La **politique n'a pas d'entrailles.** *Fr*—Politics has no heart, no mercy.

Pollice verso. *L*—*See* Verso pollice.

La **pompe des enterrements regarde plus la vanité des vivants que l'honneur des morts.** *Fr*—Funeral display is more concerned with the vanity of the living than the honor due the dead.—*La Rochefoucauld, Maxims, 612.*

Pomme de terre. *Fr*—Potato.

Pomum Adami. *L*—Adam's apple, a thyroid projection in the neck of many men. There is a pretty story to the effect that Eve's apple stuck in Adam's throat.

Pondere non numero. *L*—By weight, not by number.

Pons asinorum. *L*—Bridge of asses; in Euclid's geometry, the fifth proposition of Book I; generally, a stumbling block for the less talented; a problem that the dull cannot understand.

Pontifex maximus. *L*—High priest in ancient Rome.

Populus vult decipi. *L*—The people want to be deceived. Attributed to a legate of Pope Paul IV who is reported to have said that the people of Paris wished to be deceived. "Let them be deceived and go to the devil," he added.

Por favor. *Sp*—Please.

Posse comitatus. *L*—Literally, the power of the county. The power of a sheriff to round up forces to preserve law and order.

Possunt quia posse videntur. *L*—They can because they think they can.—*Vergil, Aeneid, V, 231.*

Post bellum auxilium. *L*—Help after the war; useless aid that comes after the battle is over.

Post cineres gloria sera venit. *L*—Fame comes too late when one is ashes.—*Martial, I, xxv, 8.*

Poste restante. *Fr*—The department of a post office where mail is held until called for; general delivery.

Post hoc; ergo propter hoc. *L*—Literally, after this; therefore because of it. The fallacy of arguing that something is the effect of a certain cause whereas there is no necessary connection. What is considered an effect may only be a subsequent event.

Post judicium. *L*—After the judgment; following a decision.

Post litem motam. *L*—After the beginning of litigation.

Post mortem. *L*—After death. An examination of a corpse to determine the cause of death.

Post obitum. *L*—After death.

Post partum. *L*—After birth.

Post proelia praemia. *L*—After battles come rewards.

Post tenebras lux. *L*—After the darkness the dawn.

Potage au gras. *Fr*—Meat soup.

Potest quis per alium quod potest facere per seipsum. *L*—One can do through another what one can do himself. A legal maxim.

Potior est conditio possidentis. *L*—The possessor is in a stronger position; possession is nine points of the law.

Pour acquit. *Fr*—Payment received; paid.

Pour épater les bourgeois. *Fr*—To shock the narrow-minded.

Pour faire rire. *Fr*—To raise a laugh.

Pour le mérite. *Fr*—For merit; the highest decoration in Germany.

Pour passer le temps. *Fr*—To pass away the time.

Pour prendre congé. *Fr*—To take leave of someone. *See also* P.F.S.A.

Pour rire. *Fr*—In jest; as a joke.

Povero come un topo di chiesa. *It*—Poor as a church mouse.

La **povertà è la madre di tutte le arti.** *It*—Poverty is the mother of all the arts. The idea goes back to Theocritus.

Praemissis praemittendis. *L*—Omitting preliminaries.

Praemonitus, praemunitus. *L*—Forewarned, forearmed.

La **pratica val più della grammatica.** *It*—Practice (in speaking) is worth more than grammar.

Preguntando se llega a Roma. *Sp*—One reaches Rome by asking questions.

Prendre la balle au bond. *Fr*—To catch the ball on the bounce or the rebound; to seize an opportunity.

Prendre la lune avec les dents. *Fr*—To reach for the moon with one's teeth; to aim at impossible goals.

Prenez garde! *Fr*—Take care; watch out!

Presto e bene, non si conviene. *It*—Haste and quality do not go together.

Presto maturo, presto marcio. *It*—The sooner ripe, the sooner rotten.

Pretio parata vincitur pretio fides. *L*—Fidelity won by bribes is lost by bribes.—*Seneca, Agamemnon, 287.*

Pretium affectionis. *L*—The price set by affection; an excessive value placed on an object for sentimental reasons.

Pretium laborum non vile. *L*—The cost of toil is not slight.

Preux chevalier. *Fr*—Gallant knight.

Prima donna. *It*—The first lady in an opera. The term is often applied to a temperamental person who demands excessive attention.

Prima facie. *L*—At first glance or preliminary examination.

Primum mobile. *L*—The first moving force. In Aristotle's concept of the heavens, the highest sphere, which, through divine power, carried the other nine with it.

Primum non nocere. *L*—First of all, do no harm; i.e., take care that the remedy is not worse than the disease. A medical aphorism.

Primum vivere, deinde philosophari. *L*—First live, then philosophize.

Primus inter pares. *L*—The first among equals.

Primus motor. *L*—In Aristotelian philosophy the first mover; the cause of all movement which is itself unmoved; the divine power.

Principia, non homines. *L*—Principles not men. Men prefer government by law rather than by the whims of rulers.

Principiis obsta: sero medicina curatur. *L*—Resist beginnings: the cure comes too late when ills have gathered strength by long delay.—*Ovid, Remedies for Love, 91.*

Prin d'an teleutese, epischein mede kaleein ko olbion, all' eutychea. *Gk*—Before a man dies, do not call him happy but lucky.—*Herodotus, The Persian Wars, I, 32. See also* Respice finem.

Prior tempore, prior jure. *L*—The one who is first has a prior right; first come, first served.

Privilège du roi. *Fr*—License or special favor granted by the king.

Prix fixe. *Fr*—A sign often displayed in stores to indicate that prices are set and not subject to reduction.

Pro aris et focis. *L*—In defense of our altars and our fires.

Probatum est. *L*—It has been proved.

Die **Probe eines Genusses ist seine Erinnerung.** *Ger*—The test of a pleasure is the remembrance of it.—*Jean Paul Richter.*

Probitas laudatur et alget. *L*—Honesty is praised and turned out into the cold; virtue is often commended and thereafter neglected.—*Juvenal, I, 74.*

Pro bono publico. *L*—For the common good.

Pro captu lectoris habent sua fata libelli. *L*—The fate of books depends on the discernment of the reader. Often quoted without the first three words.—*Terentianus Maurus.*

Procès-verbal. *Fr*—An official report drawn up for a superior, including minutes of a meeting or a record of an official act.

Prochein (prochain) ami. *Fr*—Next friend; in law, one who acts for a person, not *sui juris (q.v.).*

Pro confesso. *L*—To take something as granted or conceded.

Procul a Jove, procul a fulmine. *L*—To be far from Jove is to be far from his thunder; being far from the throne has its compensations: one may escape the royal anger.

Procul, O procul este profani. *L*—Away, far away, you profane intruders.—*Vergil, Aeneid, VI, 258.*

Procurator bibliothecarum. *L*—Director of libraries.

Pro Deo et ecclesia. *L*—In defense of God and the church.

Pro Deo et patria. *L*—For God and country.

Prodesse quam conspici. *L*—To be of service rather than to be in the limelight.

Pro domo. *L*—In defense of one's home. One of Cicero's orations is entitled *Pro Domo Sua (In Defense of His Home).* Cicero sought damages for his house destroyed by his enemies after he went into exile.

Pro Ecclesia et Pontifice. *L*—In defense of the Church and the Pope; a papal medal given outstanding laymen.

Pro et con (pro et contra). *L*—For and against.

Profanum vulgus. *L*—*See* Odi profanum . . . .

Profits et pertes. *Fr*—Profit and loss.

Pro forma. *L*—As a matter of form. In commercial use an account drawn up to show market value of certain products. In importing, a *pro forma* invoice must sometimes be presented in advance to arrange for payment or permits; it is understood that this preliminary estimate may not be as exact as the actual invoice to be presented later.

Pro hac vice. *L*—For this occasion.

Proh deum atque hominum fidem. *L*—By my faith in gods and men.

Pro jure contra legem. *L*—For the right against the law.

Promotor fidei. *L*—Promoter of the faith, serving as *advocatus diaboli (q.v.).*

Promoveatur ut removeatur. *L*—Let him be promoted that he may be removed. This is the practice of kicking the incompetent upstairs.

Pro mundi beneficio. *L*—For the benefit of the world. Motto of Panama.

Pro patria per orbis concordiam. *L*—For the country through world peace. The motto of the Carnegie Endowment for International Peace.

Proprio motu. *L*—*See* Motu proprio.

Propter affectum. *L*—Because of partiality. A reason for challenging a juror or a jury.

Propter defectum sanguinis. *L*—On account of defect of blood. The phrase was used in English feudal law when lands reverted to the lord of the fee when inheritance under the original grant was impossible, for example, because of the death of a tenant leaving no heir.

Propter delictum. *L*—Because of a crime; to take exception to a juror's serving because of past crime.

Propter honoris respectum. *L*—Because of consideration for rank or honor.

Pro (proh) pudor! *L*—For shame!

Pro rata. *L*—In proportion.

Pro ratione aetatis. *L*—In proportion to age.

Pro rege, lege, grege. *L*—For the king, the law, and the people.

Pro re nata. *L*—For a special emergency; for the consideration of a sudden development.

Pro salute animae. *L*—For the good of one's soul.

Pro scientia et religione. *L*—For science and religion.

Pro se quisque. *L*—Everybody for himself.

Prosit. *L*—May it profit you; to your health. A toast frequently heard among Germans.

Prosit Neujahr! *Ger*—Happy New Year!

¡Próspero año nuevo! *Sp*—Happy (prosperous) New Year!

Prospice. *L*—Look forward. Title of a poem by Robert Browning.

Pro tanto. *L*—As far as it goes; to a certain extent.

Pro tempore. *L*—For the time being. Abbreviated *pro tem*.

Proxime accessit. *L*—*See* Accessit.

Proximo

Proximo. *L*—*See* Prox.

Prudens quaestio dimidium scientiae. *L*—A thoughtful question is the half of discovery.

Publici juris. *L*—Reference to the right of all men to what is theirs as common possession, such as light and air.

Publicum bonum privato est praeferendum. *L*—The public good is to be preferred to private advantage. Legal maxim.

Pugnis et calcibus. *L*—With fists and feet; with all one's strength.

Pulchrorum autumnus pulcher. *L*—The autumn of beautiful persons is beautiful.

Pulvis et umbra (sumus). *L*—We are but dust and shadow.— *Horace, Odes, IV, vii, 16.* R. L. Stevenson wrote a notable essay for which he used this title.

Punctum saliens. *L*—Salient point. In embryos of higher vertebrates the rudiments of the heart; by extension, a starting point or an important feature.

Punica fides. *L*—Punic duplicity. From the Roman point of view Carthaginian promises were assumed to be treacherous.— *Sallust, Jugurthine War, 108.*

Punto de honor. *Sp*—Point of honor, contracted to *pundonor*; an excessive concern among the upper classes with keeping one's honor perfectly clean, a theme in the comedy called *Capa y espada (q.v.).*

Purpureus . . . pannus. *L*—Purple patch; an excessively ornate literary passage, such as an elaborate description, that is out of place.—*Horace, Art of Poetry, 15.*

Pur sang. *Fr*—Full-blooded; thoroughbred.

Q

Q.B.S.M. (Que besa su mano). *Sp*—Who kisses your hand. An expression of courtesy, e.g. in closing personal letters.

232

Q.B.S.P. (Que besa sus pies). *Sp*—Who kisses your feet. An expression of courtesy.

q.d. (quaque die). *L*—Every day.

Q.D.D.G. (Que de Dios goce). *Sp*—May he rejoice in the Lord.

Q.D.G. (Que Dios guarde). *Sp*—May God keep him.

Q.E.D. (Quod erat demonstrandum). *L*—That which was to be demonstrated. Used at the end of theorems in Euclidean geometry to indicate that the proof that was to be demonstrated has been demonstrated.

Q.E.F. (Quod erat faciendum). *L*—The thing that was to be done.

Q.E.G.E. (Que en gloria esté). *Sp*—May he be in glory.

Q.E.P.D. (Que en paz descanse). *Sp*—May he rest in peace.

Q.G.A. (Quartier général d'armée). *Fr*—Army headquarters.

Q.G.C.A. (Quartier général de corps d'armée). *Fr*—Army corps headquarters.

q.h. (quaque hora). *L*—Every hour. A medical direction.

q.i.d. (quater in die). *L*—Four times a day.

q.l. (quantum libet). *L*—As much as you please.

q.n. (quaque nocte). *L*—Every night.

Q.P. (Quantum placet). *L*—As much as one wishes. A medical prescription permitting the patient to take as much of the preparation as he pleases.

q.q.h. (quaque quarta hora). *L*—Every fourth hour.

qq.v. *See* Quae vide.

q.s. (quantum satis). *L*—As much as is sufficient.

q.s. (quantum sufficit). *L*—As much as suffices. A term used on medical prescriptions to indicate that as much of a certain component should be used as is sufficient, a decision left to the pharmacist.

q.v. (quantum vis). *L*—As much as you wish. A medical direction.

q.v. (quod vide). *L*—Which see. Often inserted in a text to indicate that the reader unacquainted with some term or fact may find an explanation under the word preceding the *q.v.*

Qua. *L*—As; in the character or quality of. The printer *qua* printer is not concerned with the content of the material he is printing.

Qua cursum ventus. *L*—Where the wind called our course. Used as the title of a poem by Arthur Hugh Clough.—*Vergil, Aeneid, III, 269.*

Quadrupedante putrem sonitu quatit ungula campum. *L*—The chargers beat the dusty plain with galloping hoofs. A famous onomatopoeic line.—*Vergil, Aeneid, VIII, 596.*

Quae fuerunt vitia mores sunt. *L*—What once were thought vices are now the usual thing.—*Seneca, Letters to Lucilius, XXXIX, last sentence.*

Quae in aliis libertas est, in aliis licentia vocatur. *L*—What in some men is liberty, in others is called license.—*Quintilian, III, viii, 3.*

Quae nocent docent. *L*—What pains us trains us.

Quae vide. *L*—Which *(pl)* see; let the reader look up the items referred to elsewhere in the work. Abbreviated *qq.v.*

Qualis artifex pereo! *L*—What an artist dies with me! Reported to be the last words of Nero.—*Suetonius, Nero, 49.*

Qualis rex, talis grex. *L*—As the shepherd, so the flock.

Qualis vita, finis ita. *L*—As a life has been, so will its end be.

Quam difficile est crimen non prodere vultu! *L*—How difficult it is for the face not to betray guilt!—*Ovid, Metamorphoses, II, 447.*

Quamdiu se bene gesserit. *L*—As long as he conducts himself well.

Quam primum. *L*—As soon as possible.

Quand celui à qui l'on parle ne comprend pas et celui qui parle ne se comprend pas, c'est de la métaphysique. *Fr*—When the listener does not understand and the speaker does not understand, then you have metaphysics.—*Voltaire.*

Quand même. *Fr*—In spite of everything; notwithstanding.

Quando la gatta non v'è, i sorci ballano. *It*—When the cat's away, the mice will play (literally, the mice dance). *See also* Via il gatto . . . .

Quand on parle du loup, on en voit la queue. *Fr*—Talk of the wolf and you will soon see his tail; talk of the devil and he's sure to appear; talk of the devil and his horns will appear.

Quandoque bonus dormitat Homerus. *L*—See Indignor quandoque . . . .

Quantula sapientia regitur mundus! *L*—What little wisdom is shown in the government of the world.

Quantum est quod nescimus! *L*—How much we do not know!

Quantum libet. *L*—As much as you please.

Quantum licuit. *L*—In so far as permitted.

Quantum meruit. *L*—As much as he deserved.

Quantum mutatus ab illo! *L*—How much changed from the man he was! The reference is to Hector's mangled appearance as he appears to Aeneas in a dream. The expression is often used to indicate a startling change.—*Vergil, Aeneid, II, 274.*

Quantum placet. *L*—As much as you please. Medical direction.

Quantum sufficit. *L*—As much as is sufficient.

Quantum valeat. *L*—For whatever value there is in it.

Quantum valebant. *L*—As much as they were worth; a reasonable estimate in the absence of an agreement.

Les **Quarante fauteuils.** *Fr*—Literally, the forty armchairs; the Académie française, also referred to as the Forty Immortals.

Quarante hommes, huit chevaux. *Fr*—Forty men or eight horses. In the First World War this was the indicated capacity of box cars on French railroads. Societies were formed with this name.

Quare clausum fregit. *L*—Why he broke through the enclosed space; an action brought for trespassing on land.

Que diable allait-il faire dans cette galère. *Fr*—Literally, what the devil was he going to do in that galley? What the deuce was he doing there?—*Molière, Fourberies de Scapin, II, vii.*

Qu'en dira le monde? *Fr*—What will the world say?

¡Qué lástima! *Sp*—What a pity!

Quel che pare burla, ben sovent è vero. *It*—What seems a joke is very often true; many a true word is spoken in jest.

Quel dommage! *Fr*—What a pity! Too bad!

Quel dominio è solo durabile che è volontario. *It*—Only that rule is lasting which is voluntarily accepted.—*Machiavelli.*

Quel giorno più non vi leggemmo avante. *It*—That day we read no further in that book. A line from a celebrated passage in which Francesca da Rimini describes how love took fire when she and her husband's brother were reading together the story of Lancelot.—*Dante, Inferno, V, 138.*

Quelques grands avantages que la nature donne, ce n'est pas elle seule, mais la fortune avec elle qui fait les héros. *Fr*—No matter what great advantages nature confers, without luck she does not produce heroes.—*La Rochefoucauld, Maxims, 53.*

Quem di diligunt/adolescens moritur. *L*—He whom the gods love dies young. Translation of *Hon hoi theoi . . . (q.v.).*— *Plautus, Bacchides, IV, vii, 18 (818).*

Les querelles ne dureraient pas longtemps si le tort n'était que d'un côté. *Fr*—Quarrels would not last so long if the wrong were only on one side.—*La Rochefoucauld, Maxims, 496.*

Que sçais (sais)-je? *Fr*—What do I know? Montaigne's motto, indicating self-depreciation and skepticism.

Questo ragazzo ci farà dimenticar tutti. *It*—This boy will cause us all to be forgotten. A prophecy uttered by Johann Adolph Hasse, a great contemporary of Mozart, who was not yet eighteen.

Que voulez-vous? *Fr*—What would you have?

Qui a bu boira. *Fr*—He who has drunk will drink again; once a drunkard always a drunkard.

Qui bene distinguit bene docet. *L*—He who distinguishes well teaches well. An axiom of the Scholastics.

Quicquid praecipies esto brevis. *L*—Whatever your advice be brief.—*Horace, Art of Poetry, 335.*

Quid de quoque viro et cui dicas, saepe videto. *L*—Take care of what you say of any man and to whom you say it.—*Horace, Epistles, I, xviii, 68.*

Qui de contemnenda gloria libros scribunt, nomen suum inscribunt. *L*—Men who write books in contempt of fame sign their names to their work.—*Cicero, For Archias, XI, 26.*

Qui dedit beneficium taceat; narret qui accepit. *L*—Let the man who performed the kind act keep silent; let the one who received it tell about it.—*Seneca, On Benefits, II, xi, 2.*

Quid fiet hominibus qui minima contemnunt, majora non credunt? *L*—What will happen to men who despise matters of least importance but do not believe what is more important?—*Pascal, Thoughts, 89.*

Quid leges sine moribus vanae proficiunt? *L*—What can idle laws accomplish without morality?—*Horace, Odes, III, xxiv, 35.*

Quid multa? *L*—Why make a long speech?

Quid non mortalia pectora cogis, auri sacra fames? *L*—To what do you not drive the hearts of men, accursed greed for gold? —*Vergil, Aeneid, III, 56.*

Quid nunc? *L*—What now? The two words have been joined to make an English word, *quidnunc*, meaning a gossip, an over-curious person.

Qui docet

Qui docet discit. *L*—He who teaches learns.

Qui donne tôt, donne deux fois. *Fr*—He gives twice who gives quickly. *See also* Bis dat qui cito dat.

Quid pro quo. *L*—Something for something; tit for tat.

Quidquid agas, prudenter agas, et respice finem. *L*—Whatever you do, act wisely, and consider the end.—*Gesta Romanorum, 103.*

Quid sit futurum cras, fuge quaerere. *L*—Cease asking what tomorrow will bring.—*Horace, Odes, I, ix, 13.*

Quien calla otorga. *Sp*—Silence gives consent. *See also* Qui tacet . . . .

Quien canta, sus males espanta. *Sp*—The singer scares his woes away.—*Cervantes, Don Quixote, I, XXII.*

Quien madruga, Dios le ayuda. *Sp*—God helps the man who gets up early; the early bird catches the worm.

Quien mucho abarca (abraza) poco aprieta. *Sp*—He who grasps for much lays hold of little; grasp all, lose all.

Quien no ha visto a Sevilla, no ha visto maravilla. *Sp*—He who has not seen Seville has missed a marvel.

Quien padre tiene alcalde, seguro va a juicio. *Sp*—The man whose father is mayor goes into court with an easy mind.

¿Quién sabe? *Sp*—Who knows?

Quien tiene dineros, tiene compañeros. *Sp*—The man who has money has companions.

Qui est près de l'église est souvent loin de Dieu. *Fr*—The man who lives near the church is often far from God.

Quieta non movere. *L*—Do not disturb what is at peace; let sleeping dogs lie.

Qui ex patre filioque procedit. *L*—Who proceedeth from the Father and the Son. The words *and the Son* were not included in the original Nicene Creed. The later insertion of

238

these words occasioned the Filioque dispute which is one of the apparently irreconcilable differences between the Latin and Greek Orthodox churches.

Qui facit per alium est perinde ac si facit per seipsum. *L*—If one does something through another, it is as if he does it personally.

Qui facit per alium facit per se. *L*—What a man does through an agent, he does himself. He must accept responsibility when he empowers another to act in his place.

Qui finem quaeris amoris,/cedit amor rebus: res age, tutus eris. *L*—You who wish to be rid of love, keep busy, and you will be safe, for love yields to activity.—*Ovid, Remedies for Love, 143.*

Qui m'aime, aime mon chien. *Fr*—Love me, love my dog.

Qui male agit odit lucem. *L*—The evil-doer hates the light.

Qui me amat, amet et canem meum. *L*—Love me, love my dog. A proverb mentioned by St. Bernard in his *Sermo Primus*.

Qui n'a santé n'a rien. *Fr*—A man has nothing if he doesn't have his health.

Qui nimium probat, nihil probat. *L*—The man who tries to prove too much proves nothing.

Qui non discit in pueritia, non docet in senectute. *L*—He who does not learn when young will not teach when old.—*Alcuin, Letter 27.*

Qui non proficit deficit. *L*—The man who does not advance slips backward.

Qui pro domina justitia sequitur. *L*—Who follows in defense of Lady Justice. Seal of the United States Department of Justice.

Quis custodiet ipsos custodes? *L*—Who will guard the guards? —*Juvenal, VI, 347.*

Quis desiderio sit pudor aut modus tam cari capitis? *L*—What modesty or measure shall there be to our longing for so dear a friend?—*Horace, Odes, I, xxiv, 1.*

Qui s'excuse

Qui s'excuse, s'accuse. *Fr*—He who makes excuses accuses himself. *See also* Excusatio non petita . . . .

Quis, quid, ubi, quibus, auxiliis, cur, quomodo, quando? *L*—Who, what, where, with whose help, why, how, when? A Latin hexameter prompting the memory to recall the circumstances of an action.

Quis separabit? *L*—Who shall separate (us)? Motto of the Order of Saint Patrick, instituted by George III, intended to convey the idea that nobody would separate Great Britain from Ireland.—*Vulgate, Paul, Romans, VIII, 35.*

Quis talia fando temperet a lacrimis? *L*—Who could refrain from tears while telling this story?—*Vergil, Aeneid, II, 6.*

Qui stat caveat ne cadat. *L*—Let him who stands take heed lest he fall.—*Vulgate, I Corinthians, X, 12.*

Quis tulerit Gracchos de seditione querentes? *L*—Who could endure the Gracchi complaining of sedition? The Gracchi brothers headed social reforms favoring the have-nots and were regarded by the conservatives as guilty of sedition. It would be intolerable to hear the Gracchi complain of the uprisings which, according to Juvenal, they promoted. The phrase is applied to those who censure in others the faults of which they are guilty. The pot calls the kettle black.—*Juvenal, II, 24.*

Qui tacet consentire videtur. *L*—He who is silent seems to give consent. A legal maxim.

Qui timide rogat, docet negare. *L*—He who asks timidly makes denial easy.—*Seneca, Hippolytus, 593.*

Qui transtulit sustinet. *L*—He who transplanted us sustains us. Motto of Connecticut.

Qui va là? *Fr*—Who goes there?

Qui vive. *Fr*—Who goes there? (when used as a question); on the alert.

Quiz seperrabit. A garbling of *Quis separabit?* (*q.v.*)—Who will separate us.—*Sean O'Casey, Inishfallen, Fare Thee Well* in the chapter *Into Civil War).*

Quoad hoc. *L*—As far as this particular point is concerned.

Quo animo. *L*—With what intent. A legal phrase.

Quocumque modo. *L*—In whatever manner.

Quocumque nomine. *L*—Under whatever name.

Quod ali cibus est aliis fuat acre venenum. *L*—What is food to one man may be rank poison to another; one man's meat is another man's poison.—*Lucretius, On the Nature of Things, IV, 637.*

Quod aliquis facit per aliquem, facit per se. *L*—What one does through an agent, he does personally. The principle of power of attorney.

Quod avertat Deus! *L*—God forbid it! Used as a pious parenthesis.

Quod bene notandum. *L*—Which is to be especially noted.

Quod Deus avertat! *L*—*See* Quod avertat Deus!

Quod Deus vult. *L*—What God ordains.

Quod dixi dixi. *L*—What I have said, I have said. Probably an imitation of *Quod scripsi scripsi* (*q.v.*).

Quod erat demonstrandum. *L*—*See* Q.E.D.

Quod erat faciendum. *L*—*See* Q.E.F.

Quod gratis asseritur, gratis negatur. *L*—What is freely asserted may be freely denied.

Quod hodie non est, cras erit: sic vita truditur. *L*—If things don't work out today, there is always tomorrow: and so life pushes on.—*Petronius, Satyricon, 45.*

Quod licet Iovi non licet bovi. *L*—What's permitted the divine is not allowed to swine.

241

Quod non fecerunt barbari

Quod non fecerunt barbari fecerunt Barberini. *L*—What escaped the fury of the barbarians, the Barberini destroyed. Pope Urban VIII, one of the Barberini family, had the bronze pre-Christian objects in the Pantheon cast into cannons.

Quod non opus est, asse carum est. *L*—What is not necessary is dear at a penny.—*Cato, in Seneca, Letters to Lucilius, XCIV.*

Quod scripsi, scripsi. *L*—What I have written, I have written. Pilate's answer to the chief priest who objected to the title he had put on the cross. This is often used when a person is unwilling to change what he has written.—*Vulgate, John, XIX, 22.*

Quod semper, quod ubique et quod ab omnibus creditum est. *L*—What all men have always and everywhere believed. A principle or canon for distinguishing heretical from true Christian doctrine. Its interpretation has been the subject of much theological debate.—*Vincent of Lérins, Commonitorium, chap. 2.*

Quod sentimus, loquamur, quod loquimur, sentiamus; concordet sermo cum vita. *L*—Let us say what we feel, feel what we say, and have our words harmonize with our life.—*Seneca, Letters, LXXV, 4.*

Quod vide. *L*—*See* q.v.

Quod volumus, facile credimus. *L*—We readily believe what we want to believe.

Quo fas et gloria ducunt. *L*—To wherever duty and glory lead.

Quo fata vocant. *L*—Whither the fates call.

Quo jure? *L*—By what law?

Quorum pars magna fui. *L*—In which I played an important part. Aeneas speaks these words as he begins recounting to Dido and her court the disasters the Trojans suffered.—*Vergil, Aeneid, II, 6.*

Quos Deus vult perdere, prius dementat. *L*—Whom God wills to destroy He first makes mad.—*Translation of fragment from Euripides.*

Quot homines, tot sententiae. *L*—There are as many opinions as there are men.—*Terence, Phormio, III, 3 (l. 454).*

Quot linguas calles, tot homines vales. *L*—You are as many men as the number of tongues you speak.

Quo vadis? *L*—Whither goest thou? These words were supposedly uttered by Saint Peter on meeting Christ when the discouraged Apostle was leaving Rome. This is the title of a novel by Henryk Sienkiewicz on the persecution of the Christians by Nero.

Quo warranto. *Anglo-L*—By what authority; a writ to determine the right or ownership of a franchise or office.

R

R (℞) (Recipe). *L*—Take. An abbreviation used at the beginning of a medical prescription.

R.A. (República Argentina). *Sp*—Argentine Republic.

Redig. in pulv. (Redigatur in pulverem). *L*—Let it be reduced to powder.

R.I.P. (Requiescat in pace). *L*—May he rest in peace.

r.p. (réponse payée). *Fr*—Reply already paid for.

R.S.V.P. (Répondez s'il vous plaît). *Fr*—Please reply.

R.V.S.V.P. (Répondez vite, s'il vous plaît). *Fr*—Please reply at once.

Radix omnium malorum est cupiditas. *L*—Covetousness is the root of all evil.—*Vulgate, I, Timothy, VI, 10.*

Raison de plus. *Fr*—One reason more; all the more reason.

Raison d'état. *Fr*—A reason given by the government of a state when its laws or standards are violated in the interests of self-preservation.

Raison d'être. *Fr*—Reason for existing.

Rara avis in terra nigroque simillima cycno. *L*—A rare bird on the earth, very much like a black swan.—*Juvenal, VI, 165.*

Raram facit misturam cum sapientia forma. *L*—Beauty and wisdom are rarely found together.—*Petronius, Satyricon, 94.*

Rast ich, so rost ich. *Ger*—If I rest, I rust.

Rationes seminales. *L*—Creative capacities in the mass of created matter from which all things developed. A term used by Saint Augustine in his account of the creation of the world, as told in his twelve books *De Genesi ad Litteram (On a Literal Interpretation of Genesis).*

Ratio Studiorum. *L*—*A short title for Ratio atque Institutio Studiorum Societatis Jesu*, The Method and System of Studies of the Society of Jesus, dating from 1599.

Ratio vincit. *L*—Reason conquers.

Ratschläge für ausländische Besucher. *Ger*—Advice for foreign visitors.

Re. *L*—In the matter of; with reference to.

Rebus sic stantibus. *L*—As matters stand.

Recoge tu heno mientras que el sol luciere. *Sp*—Make hay while the sun shines.

La reconnaissance est la mémoire du cœur. *Fr*—Gratitude is the heart's memory. Massieu, a deaf mute, wrote this when asked to define gratitude.

Rectus in curia. *L*—An honest litigant in court.

Reddite quae sunt Caesaris, Caesari: et quae sunt Dei, Deo. *L* —Give to Caesar the things that are Caesar's and to God the things that are God's.—*Vulgate, Matthew, XXII, 21.*

Reden ist Silber, Schweigen ist Gold. *Ger*—Speech is silver, silence is gold.

Redime te captum quam queas minimo. *L*—When taken prisoner, redeem yourself for as little as you can.

Redolet lucerna. *L*—It smells of the lamp. *See also* Olet lucernam.

Reductio ad absurdum. *L*—Reducing an argument to the absurd. An attempt to show that if the argument in question were followed to its logical conclusion, it would lead to absurdity.

Reductio ad impossibile. *L*—Reducing an argument to the impossible. *See also* Reductio ad absurdum.

Refugium peccatorum. *L*—Refuge of sinners.

Le refus des louanges est un désir d'être loué deux fois. *Fr*—We reject praise because we desire to hear it again.—*La Rochefoucauld, Maxims, 149.*

Regina scientiarum. *L*—Queen of the sciences (knowledge). A Scholastic appraisal of philosophy.

Regnabat. *L*—He was ruling. Usually associated with a date.

Regnat populus. *L*—The people rule. Motto of the state of Arkansas.

Re infecta. *L*—Without finishing the business.

Relata refero. *L*—I tell the story as it was told me.

Religio Laici. *L*—*Religion of a Layman*, title of a poem by Dryden.

Religio loci. *L*—The solemn religious feeling evoked by a particular place. A phrase picked from two lines of *Vergil, Aeneid, VIII, 349.*

Religio Medici. *L*—*Religion of a Physician*, title of a book by Sir Thomas Browne.

Die Religion . . . ist das Opium des Volkes. *Ger*—Religion is the opiate of the masses.—*Karl Marx, Introduction to a Critique of the Hegelian Philosophy of Right.*

Rem acu tetigisti. *L*—You have stated it correctly; you have hit the nail on the head.—*Plautus, The Rope, V, ii, 19.*

Remanet. *L*—It remains. A case left unsettled at a term of court.

Rem tene et verba sequentur. *L*—Master the material and the words will follow. The same idea is contained in *Horace, Art of Poetry, 311: Verba provisam rem non invita sequentur,* Words will freely follow when the subject is well thought out in advance.

Rentes sur l'État. *Fr*—Government stocks; also the interest therefrom.

Repente liberalis stultis gratus est;/verum peritis irritos tendit dolos. *L*—A man who is suddenly generous pleases fools, but his tricks make no impression on the experienced.—*Phaedrus, Fables, I, xxiii, 1.*

Repetatur. *L*—It may be repeated. Used on medical prescriptions.

Repetitio est mater studiorum. *L*—Repetition is the mother of studies.

Répondre en Normand. *Fr*—To give a noncommittal answer like a Norman; to reply evasively, equivocally.

Requiem aeternam dona eis, domine, et lux perpetua luceat eis. *L*—Eternal rest grant unto them, O Lord, and let perpetual light shine round about them. A prayer for the dead in Roman Catholic liturgy.

Requiescat in pace. *L*—May he rest in peace.

Rerum novarum libido. *L*—Reckless desire for innovations.

Res adjudicata. *L*—A case already decided.

Res alienae. *L*—Property of others.

Res angusta domi. *L*—Straitened circumstances at home.—*Juvenal, III, 165.* The entire sentence of which this phrase is a part begins *Haud facile emergunt quorum virtutibus obstat . . . (q.v.).*

Res derelicta. *L*—A thing that is abandoned or thrown away.

Res domesticas noli tangere. *L*—Do not mingle in the domestic affairs of others.

Res gestae. *L*—Transactions; things done; exploits.

Res integra. *L*—An entire matter.

Res ipsa loquitur. *L*—The matter speaks for itself. In a trial involving an accident, the damage is evident; the defendant must prove that the accident was not due to negligence on his part.

Resistendum senectuti. *L*—Old age must be fought.—*Cicero, Old Age, XI, 35.*

Res judicata. *L*—A matter already settled. *Res Judicatae,* the plural, is the title of a book by Augustine Birrell.

Res nullius. *L*—A thing that has no owner.

Res perit domino. *L*—The thing perishes to the owner; the owner loses possession of a thing when it perishes.

Respice, adspice, prospice. *L*—Survey the past, examine the present, look to the future. Motto of the City College of New York.

Respice finem. *L*—Look to the end of life. Translation of Solon's warning to Croesus found in *Herodotus, I, 32.*

Respicere exemplar vitae morumque jubebo/Doctum imitatorem, et vivas hinc ducere voces. *L*—I advise the artist skilled in character description to look for examples in life and customs and draw therefrom living words.—*Horace, Art of Poetry, 317.*

Respondeat superior. *L*—Let the superior answer; let the principal reply for his subordinates since he is responsible for their actions.

Responsa prudentium. *L*—The opinions of eminent jurists on legal questions.

Retro me, Satana! *L*—Get thee behind me, Satan!—*Vulgate, Mark, VIII, 33.*

Retro, Satana! *L*—Get thee behind me, Satan!

Revenons à nos moutons. *Fr*—Let us get back to our sheep; let us get back on the subject.—*Anon., La Farce de Maistre Pathelin.*

Rex bibendi. *L*—King of the drinking; master of the revels.

Rex regnat, sed non gubernat. *L*—The king reigns but he does not govern.—*Jan Zamojski.*

Rey nuevo, ley nueva. *Sp*—New king, new law.

Rez-de-chaussée. *Fr*—Ground level; street level; ground floor of a house.

Ridentem dicere verum/quid vetat? *L*—What objection can there be to telling the truth with a smile? Many a true word is spoken in jest.—*Horace, Satires, I, i, 24.*

Ride si sapis, o puella, ride. *L*—Smile, maiden, smile if you are wise. Advice attributed to Ovid by Martial. In this context the poet warns a girl with bad teeth that the advice was not intended for her.—*Martial, II, xli, 1.*

Rien de plus éloquent que l'argent comptant. *Fr*—Nothing is more eloquent than cash.

Rien ne dure que le provisoire. *Fr*—Temporary arrangements are the only ones that last.

Rien ne pèse tant qu'un secret. *Fr*—Nothing weighs as much as a secret.—*La Fontaine, Fables, VIII, vi.*

Rien ne réussit comme le succès. *Fr*—Nothing succeeds like success.

Rien n'est beau que le vrai. *Fr*—Naught save truth is beautiful. —*Boileau.*

Rigor mortis. *L*—Stiffness occurring after death.

Rira bien qui rira le dernier. *Fr*—He laughs best who laughs last.

Rire dans sa barbe. *Fr*—To laugh in his beard; to laugh up one's sleeve.

Rire et faire rire. *Fr*—To laugh and make others laugh.

Ris de veau. *Fr*—Calf's sweetbread.

Ritardando. *It*—A musical direction indicating that the tempo should gradually become slower.

Rixatur de lana saepe caprina. *L*—He often quarrels about goat's wool, about matters of no consequence.—*Horace, Epistles, I, xviii, 15.*

Le roi est mort. Vive le roi! *Fr*—The king is dead. Long live the king! Once the courtiers of France heard that the king had died, they immediately saluted his successor.

Le roi le veut. *Fr*—The king wills it.

Le roi règne et ne gouverne pas. *Fr*—The king reigns but he does not govern. A translation of *Rex regnat . . . (q.v.).* It appeared in 1830 in *Le National,* which opposed the government of Charles X.—*L. A. Thiers.*

Le roi s'avisera. *Fr*—The king will take the matter under advisement.

Rois fainéants. *Fr*—The Do-Nothing Kings. Weak Frankish rulers of the Merovingian line from 639 to 751 who surrendered their powers to the *Major domus (q.v.).*

Le Roi Soleil. *Fr*—The Sun King, a name for Louis XIV, who was represented by a symbol of the sun.

Rôle de l'équipage. *Fr*—List of a ship's crew.

Roma locuta, causa finita. *L*—Rome has spoken, the case is ended. Once papal authority has rendered a decision in a matter, debate among the faithful ceases.

Roman à clef. *Fr*—A novel in which actual persons are introduced under fictitious names.

Romanus sedendo vincit. *L*—The Romans achieved their ends through patience.

Rom ward nicht in einem Tage gebaut. *Ger*—Rome was not built in a day.

Rota sum: semper, quoquo me verto, stat Virtus. *L*—I am a wheel: whithersoever I turn, virtue always stands firm. The motto of Benvenuto Cellini's father; no matter what blows Fortune dealt him, his courage did not fail.—*Cellini, Autobiography, I, 5.*

Rouge-et-noire. *Fr*—*See* Trente et quarante.

Le roy le veult. *OF*—The king wills it. This older form of *Le roi le veut* is used by the British king when he indicates approval of bills in Parliament.

Rudis indigestaque moles. *L*—Unformed disordered mass; a chaotic condition.—*Ovid, Metamorphoses, I, 7.*

Ruse de guerre. *Fr*—A stratagem in war.

Rus in urbe. *L*—City life with the advantages of the country.

Rusticus expectat dum defluat amnis. *L*—The peasant waits until the river will flow past. This might be compared to waiting in a large city until the traffic has passed by.—*Horace, Epistles, I, ii, 42.*

S

s.a. (sine anno). *L*—Without date of publication.

S.A. (Sociedad anónima). *Sp*—A company with limited liability.

S.A. (Société anonyme). *Fr*—A company with limited liability.

S.A. (Sudamérica). *Sp*—South America.

S.A.I. (Son Altesse Impériale). *Fr*—His Imperial Highness.

S.A.R. (Son Altesse Royale). *Fr*—His Royal Highness.

S.A.S.S. (Su atento y seguro servidor). *Sp*—Yours very sincerely.

s.Br. (südliche Breite). *Ger*—South latitude.

sc. (scilicet). *L*—Namely; to wit. A contraction of *scire licet*, You may understand or know.

s/c (son compte). *Fr*—His account.

s/c (su cuenta). *Sp*—Your account.

Sc.B. (Scientiae Baccalaureus). *L*—Bachelor of Science.

s.d. (sans date). *Fr*—Without date.

S.E. (Su Excelencia). *Sp*—His Excellency.

S. en C. (Sociedad en comandita). *Sp*—Limited liability company.

s.e.o.o. (sauf erreur ou omission). *Fr*—Errors or omissions excepted.

7bre (septembre). *Fr*—September, the seventh month in the early Roman calendar.

seq., seqq., sq., sqq. (sequens, *pl*, sequentia). *L*—The following.

S.E. u O. (salvo error u omisión). *Sp*—Errors or omissions excepted.

S. Excia. (Sua Excelência). *Port*—His Excellency.

sf., sfz. (sforzando). *It*—A note or chord to be accented.

S.G.D.G. (sans garantie du gouvernement). *Fr*—A patent issued by the government without necessarily guaranteeing the quality of the product.

S.H.S. (Societatis Historicae Socius). *L*—Fellow of the Historical Society.

s.h.v. (sub hac voce *or* sub hoc verbo). *L*—Under this word.

s.i.d. (semel in die). *L*—Once a day.

Sig. n. pro. (Signa nomine proprio). *L*—Label with the proper name.

Si non val. (si non valeat). *L*—If it is not effective. A medical directive.

Si op. sit. (Si opus sit). *L*—If it is necessary.

s.l.a.n. (sine loco, anno, vel nomine). *L*—Without place, year, or name of publisher. Said of books not furnishing this information.

s.l.n.d. (sans lieu ni date). *Fr*—Without address and date.

s.l.p. *L*—*See* Sine legitima prole.

S.M. (Sa Majesté). *Fr*—His Majesty.

S.M.E. (Sancta Mater Ecclesia). *L*—Holy Mother Church.

s.m.p. *See* Sine mascula prole.

S.n.g. (sans notre garantie). *Fr*—Without our guarantee.

s.op.s. (si opus sit). *L*—If it is necessary.

S.P.A. (Service de la poste aux armées). *Fr*—Army Postal Service.

S.P.A.S. (Societatis Philosophicae Americanae Socius). *L*—Fellow of the American Philosophical Society.

S.P.Q.R. (Senatus Populusque Romanus). *L*—The Senate and the Roman People.

s/r. (su remesa). *Sp*—Your remittance.

S.R.C. (Santa Romana Chiesa). *It*—Holy Roman Catholic Church.

S.R.E. (Sancta Romana Ecclesia). *L*—Holy Roman Church.

S.R.I. (Sacro Romano Impero). *It*—Holy Roman Empire.

S.R.I. (Sacrum Romanum Imperium). *L*—The Holy Roman Empire.

S.R.S. (Societatis Regiae Socius). *L*—Fellow of the Royal Society.

S.S. (Sa Sainteté). *Fr*—His Holiness.

S.S. (Santa Sede). *It*—Holy See.

S.S. (Sua Santità). *It*—His Holiness.

SS. *L*—A legal abbreviation; a contraction of *scilicet* meaning As one may learn.

s.s.s. (stratum super stratum). *L*—Layer upon layer.

S.S.S. (Su seguro servidor). *Sp*—Your faithful servant.

S.S.S.R. (Soyuz Sovetskikh Sotsialisticheskikh Respublik). *Rus*—Union of Soviet Socialist Republics.

S.S.V. (sub signo veneni). *L*—Under a label marked "poison."

S.T.B. (Sacrae Theologiae Baccalaureus). *L*—Bachelor of Sacred Theology.

S.T.D. (Sacrae Theologiae Doctor). *L*—Doctor of Sacred Theology.

StGB (Strafgesetzbuch). *Ger*—Penal code.

S.T.L. (Sacrae Theologiae Lector *or* Licentiatus). *L*—Reader in Sacred Theology or the Licentiate of Sacred Theology. A degree between the S.T.B. and the S.T.D.

S.T.T.L. (Sit tibi terra levis). *L*—May the earth rest lightly upon you. Letters found on Roman tombs.

Sub init. (sub initio). *L*—At the beginning. Used in citing a literary reference.

Sus. per coll. *L*—*See* Suspendatur per collum.

s.v. (spiritus vini). *L*—Alcoholic spirit.

s.v. *See* Sub vi.

s.v. (sub voce *or* verbo). *L*—Under the word ——. A literary reference.

s.v.p. *Fr*—*See* S'il vous plaît.

s.v.r. (spiritus vini rectificatus). *L*—Rectified spirit of wine.

s.v.t. (spiritus vini tenuis). *L*—Proof spirit.

El **sabio muda consejo; el necio, no.** *Sp*—The wise man changes his plans; the foolish man, never.

Sacre bleu. *Fr*—An expletive. A corruption of *sacre Dieu*, i.e. holy God.

Saepe creat molles aspera spina rosas. *L*—The sharp thorn often produces soft roses.—*Ovid, Epistles from Pontus, II, ii, 34.*

Saepius locutum, numquam me tacuisse poenitet. *L*—I have often regretted that I spoke, never that I kept silent. This recalls the remark of Calvin Coolidge: "I have noticed that nothing I never said ever did me any harm."

Sage mir, mit wem du umgehst, so sage ich dir, wer du bist. *Ger*—Tell me with whom you associate, and I'll tell you what you are.—*Goethe, Maxims in Prose, 141. See also* Dime con quien andas . . . .

Le sage quelquefois évite le monde de peur d'être ennuyé. *Fr*—The wise man sometimes flees society to escape being bored. —*La Bruyère, Characters, Of Society, 83 (1), p. 179 in Garapon's edition (Garnier Frères, 1962).*

Salaam aleikum (salam 'alekum). *Arabic*—Peace be on you. A Moslem greeting, spoken with a bow while the right hand is placed on the forehead. *See also* Shalom alekhem.

Sal Atticum. *L*—Literally, Attic salt; witty conversation characteristic of the brilliant society of ancient Athens, the principal city of Attica. The Italians were noted for a sharp, biting wit, *acetum Italum:* literally, Italian vinegar.

Salle à manger. *Fr*—Dining room.

Salle d'attente. *Fr*—Waiting room.

Salle de jeu. *Fr*—Gambling room.

Salle des pas perdus. *Fr*—Hall of lost footsteps; waiting room outside a court of law or parliament where people walk about to no purpose. Specifically the name applies to the large hall in the Palais de Justice in Paris.

Salle du Jeu de Paume. *Fr*—Hall of the Tennis Court, scene of the oath taken by the French National Assembly in 1789.

Salus populi suprema lex esto. *L*—The safety of the people shall be the supreme law.—*Cicero, The Laws, III, iii, 8.* Motto of Missouri.

Saluto il primo Re d'Italia. *It*—I greet the first king of Italy. Garibaldi's greeting to Victor Emmanuel, October 26, 1860.

Salva sit reverentia. *L*—Let due respect be observed.

Salve. *L*—Hail; greetings.

Salve, regina, mater misericordiae. *L*—Hail, holy Queen, Mother of Mercy. A hymn used in the Divine Office of the Roman Catholic Church.

Salvo jure. *L*—Without prejudice; saving the right of someone, e.g., a king. A clause of exception.

Salvo pudore. *L*—Without offense to modesty.

Sanan cuchilladas, mas no malas palabras. *Sp*—A cut from a knife heals but not one from the tongue.

Sancta simplicitas. *L*—*See* O sancta simplicitas!

Sanctum sanctorum. *L*—The holy of holies; a place of quiet where casual visitors are not welcome.

Sang-froid. *Fr*—Cold blood; coolness in a critical situation; indifference.

Sans appel. *Fr*—A final judgment.

Sans cérémonie. *Fr*—Without ceremony.

Sans culottes. *Fr*—A man without breeches, an ignominious term given by French aristocrats to republicans who wore pantaloons and not the culottes or breeches worn by the aristocrats.

Sans doute. *Fr*—Without doubt.

Sans façon. *Fr*—Without style; without ceremony; informally.

Sans gêne. *Fr*—Without ceremony; free and easy.

Sans pareil. *Fr*—Unparalleled; without equal.

Sans peur et sans reproche. *Fr*—Without fear and without reproach. A title given to a French paragon of chivalry, the Chevalier de Bayard.

Sans rime et sans raison. *Fr*—Without rhyme or reason.

255

Sans souci. *Fr*—Care-free; easy-going.

Santo Niño. *Sp*—Image of the Infant Jesus.

Sapere aude. *L*—Dare to think independently.—*Horace, Epistles, I, ii, 40.*

Sartor Resartus. *L*—Literally, the tailor retailored, a work by Thomas Carlyle in which a fictional German philosopher, Teufelsdröckh (devil's dirt), discusses a philosophy of clothes with much humor and wit.

Sat cito si sat bene. *L*—Fast enough if only well enough. A saying of Cato the Elder.

Satis eloquentiae, sapientiae parum. *L*—Eloquence enough but too little wisdom. Sallust so describes the conspirator Catiline. —*Sallust, Catiline, V.*

Satis et super. *L*—Enough and still more. Sometimes *satis superque.*—*Catullus, VII, 10.*

Sat pulchra si sat bona. *L*—Beautiful enough if good enough; handsome is as handsome does.

Saturnia tellus. *L*—Land of Saturn. Poetic name for Italy.

Sauve qui peut. *Fr*—Let him save himself who can; let everybody look out for himself in the present emergency.

Savoir faire. *Fr*—Tact; cleverness.

Savoir vivre. *Fr*—Good breeding; polished manners.

Scala Sancta. *L*—Holy staircase in Rome, supposedly transferred miraculously from Jerusalem. According to the legend, these stairs were trod by Christ when he was brought to Pilate's palace.

Scandalum magnatum. *LL*—Defamation of the character of a high English official or a person of the upper class. This statute, passed under Richard II, was repealed in 1887.

Scelere velandum est scelus. *L*—One crime has to be concealed by another.—*Seneca, Hippolytus, 721.*

Les **scènes à faire.** *Fr*—The scenes that must be done. The talented playwright knows what scenes will command interest because of their dramatic content.

Schlafen Sie wohl! *Ger*—Sleep well; good night!

Schola cantorum. *L*—School of singers of sacred music.

Scientia est veritatis imago. *L*—Science is the image of truth.

Scienti et volenti non fit injuria. *L*—No injustice is done to one who knows and is willing. An axiom of moral theology.

Scilicet. *L*—*See* sc.

Scire facias. *L*—Literally, cause to know. A writ renewing a judgment that has expired.

Scire quid valeant humeri, quid ferre recusent. *L*—To know what one's shoulders can carry and what they refuse to bear; to know one's limitations.

Una **scopa nuova spazza bene.** *It*—A new broom sweeps clean. *See also* Neue Besen . . . .

Scribendi recte sapere est et principium et fons. *L*—Knowledge is the prime source of good writing.—*Horace, Art of Poetry, 309.*

Scribimus indocti doctique poemata passim. *L*—We all, learned and unlearned alike, write poems at random.—*Horace, Epistles, II, 1, 117.*

Scripta manent, verba volant. *L*—Written words remain, spoken words fly through the air.

Scriptorum chorus omnis amat nemus et fugit urbem. *L*—The whole tribe of writers loves the rural scene and flees the city. —*Horace, Epistles, II, ii, 77.*

Sculpsit. *L*—He engraved or sculptured the work in question.

Scuto bonae voluntatis tuae coronasti nos. *L*—With the shield of Thy good will Thou has covered us.—*Vulgate, Psalms, V, 12.* Motto of Maryland. *See also* Le parole son femmine . . . .

Sdegno d'amante poco dura. *It*—A lover's indignation does not last long.

Seanad Eireann. *Ir*—The Senate of the *Oireachtas*, the Irish Parliament.

Le secret d'ennuyer est celui de tout dire. *Fr*—The secret of being a bore is to tell every detail.—*Voltaire, On the Nature of Man, Discourse 6.*

Secundum artem. *L*—According to the rules of art.

Secundum ipsius naturam. *L*—According to its very nature.

Secundum legem. *L*—According to law.

Secundum naturam. *L*—According to nature.

Secundum quid. *L*—After a fashion.

Secundum regulam. *L*—According to rule.

Secundum usum. *L*—According to usage or custom.

Securus judicat orbis terrarum. *L*—Calmly, dispassionately, the world makes its judgments.—*Saint Augustine.*

Se defendendo. *L*—In self-defense. The first grave-digger in Hamlet garbles this expression by saying *Se offendendo.*

Seditio civium hostium est occasio. *L*—Civil discord gives the enemy his opportunity.

Seis meses de invierno y seis meses de infierno. *Sp*—Six months of winter and six months of hell. A description of Madrid weather.

Selbst ist der Mann. *Ger*—One must rely on oneself.

Selon les règles. *Fr*—According to the rules.

Semel et simul. *L*—Once and all together.

Semel insanivimus omnes. *L*—We have all gone mad at some time or other.—*Baptista Mantuanus (Battista Spagnuolo), Eclogues, I, 217.*

Semel malus, semper praesumitur esse malus. *L*—Those once convicted of wrongdoing are always presumed to be guilty. It is understood that the same kind of wrongdoing is involved, as, for example, perjury. A legal maxim.

Semper avarus eget. *L*—The greedy man is always in need; greed is never satisfied.—*Horace, Epistles, I, ii, 56.*

Semper eadem. *L*—Always the same. The motto of Queen Elizabeth I of England.

Semper fidelis. *L*—Always faithful. Motto of the United States Marine Corps.

Semper idem. *L*—Always the same.

Semper inops quicumque cupit. *L*—The man who is always wishing for something is poor.—*Claudian, Against Rufinus, I, 200.*

Semper paratus. *L*—Always prepared. Motto of the United States Coast Guard.

Semper timidum scelus. *L*—Guilt is always fearful; the guilty live in fear.

Semper vivit in armis. *L*—He is always armed.

Senatus consultum. *L*—A decree of the senate in ancient Rome.

La senda de la virtud es muy estrecha, y el camino del vicio, ancho y espacioso. *Sp*—The path to virtue is very narrow, the road to evil broad and free.—*Cervantes, Don Quixote, II, VI.*

Senectus insanabilis morbus est. *L*—Old age is an incurable disease.

Senectus ipsa morbus est. *L*—Old age in itself is a disease.—*Terence, Phormio, IV, i, 9.*

Senex bis puer. *L*—An old man is a boy again; old age is a second childhood.

Seniores priores. *L*—Older persons first; give place to age.

Se non è vero, è ben travato. *It*—If it is not the truth, it is a clever invention.

Sens commun. *Fr*—Common sense; also common consent in matters accepted by a large area of society.

Sens dessus dessous. *Fr*—Upside down; topsy-turvy.

Sensim sine sensu aetas senescit. *L*—Slowly and imperceptibly old age comes on.—*Cicero, Old Age, XI, last sentence.*

Sensu bono. *L*—In a good sense.

Sensu lato. *L*—In a broad sense.

Sensu malo. *L*—In a bad sense.

Sensu stricto. *L*—In a strict sense.

Sera nimis vita est crastina: vive hodie. *L*—Living tomorrow is too late: live today.—*Martial, I, xv, 12.*

Sero molunt deorum molae. *L*—The mills of the gods grind slowly. The implication is that in the end justice will triumph. —*Erasmus, Adagia.* The idea has often been expressed by poets. *See also* Opse theon aleousi myloi . . . .

Sero sed serio. *L*—Serious even though late.

Sero venientibus ossa. *L*—Those who come late get the bones; first come, first served.

Serpent d'église. *Fr*—The church serpent, an obsolete musical instrument with a serpentine tube; a reed stop on the organ.

Serus in caelum redeas. *L*—May it be long before you return to heaven. The poet hopes that Augustus will live a long life.— *Horace, Odes, I, ii, 45.*

Servatur ubique jus Romanum non ratione imperii, sed rationis imperio. *L*—Roman law is observed everywhere not by reason of rule but by the rule of reason.

Servitium forinsecum. *L*—Service or labor due a superior lord by a lesser lord, who in turn passed the obligation on to his tenants.

Servus servorum Dei. *L*—A servant of the servants of God; often applied to the pope.

Sesquipedalia verba. *L*—Literally, words a foot and a half long; very long words.—*Horace, Art of Poetry, 97.*

Sestertium reliquit trecenties nec unquam philosophum audivit. *L*—He left an immense fortune and never listened to a philosopher. From the epitaph of C. Pompeius Trimalchio written by himself.—*Petronius, Satyricon, LXXI.*

Shalom alekhem. *Heb*—Peace unto you. *See also* Salaam aleikum.

Sic. *L*—Thus. Often inserted in a quotation when the writer who is quoting wishes to disclaim responsibility for some error in grammar, spelling, or fact.

Sic eunt fata hominum. *L*—Such is the fate of man.

Sic itur ad astra. *L*—Thus one climbs to the stars; this is the road to renown. Words originally spoken to Ascanius, the son of Aeneas, by Apollo in disguise.—*Vergil, Aeneid, IX, 641.*

Sic passim. *L*—Thus throughout (this work). Used to indicate that the same sentiment or expression is found in other passages of a book. The translation given in several manuals, "So everywhere," is deceptive and needs interpretation.

Sic semper tyrannis. *L*—May it be ever thus to tyrants. Motto of Virginia. These words were shouted by Booth as he leaped to the stage after shooting President Lincoln.

Sic transit gloria mundi. *L*—Thus passes the glory of the world. During the consecration of a pope, this expression is repeated three times, preceded by *Reverendissime Pater*, Most Reverend Father.

Sicut ante. *L*—As before.

Sic utere tuo ut alienum non laedas. *L*—Use what is yours so as not to harm another.

Sicut patribus, sit Deus nobis. *L*—May God be with us as he was with our fathers. Motto of Boston, Massachusetts.

261

Sic volo, sic jubeo, stat pro ratione voluntas. *L*—*See* Hoc volo, sic jubeo . . ., for a preferred reading of the original.

Sic vos non vobis. *L*—Thus you labor but not for yourselves. Vergil wrote of birds that build nests for their young, sheep that grow wool, bees that make honey, and oxen that pull plows, all toiling for others. Vergil felt he was in a similar situation when a contemporary named Bathyllus tried to deprive him of the glory of a line he had written in praise of Augustus.

Si Deus nobiscum, quis contra nos? *L*—If God is with us, who can be against us? In Vulgate, *pro nobis* instead of *nobiscum.* —*Vulgate, Paul, Romans, VIII, 31.*

Si Dieu n'existait pas, il faudrait l'inventer. *Fr*—If God did not exist, it would be necessary to invent him. Supporting this view, Voltaire erected a church at his own expense.—*Voltaire, Epître à l'Auteur des Trois Imposteurs.*

Si Dieu veult. *OF*—If it be God's will.

Si diis placet. *L*—If it is pleasing to the gods.

Si discedas, laqueo tenet ambitiosi/consuetudo mali. *L*—If you try to escape, the habits of a clinging evil hold you in its toils. The poet is here lamenting the lot of the literary man who cannot give up writing.—*Juvenal, VII, 50.*

Siècle des ténèbres. *Fr*—Dark ages.

Siècle d'or. *Fr*—Golden age of Louis XIV.

Sieg Heil. *Ger*—Hail, Victory. A greeting during the Hitler regime.

Si jeunesse savait, si vieillesse pouvait! *Fr*—If youth only knew, if age only could.

Sile et philosophus esto. *L*—Keep silent and be counted a philosopher.

Le silence éternel de ces espaces infinis m'effraye. *Fr*—The eternal silence in the infinity of space frightens me.—*Pascal, Thoughts, III, 206.*

Silent leges inter arma. *L*—The laws are silent in time of war. —*Cicero, For Milo, IV, 10.*

S'il vous plaît. *Fr*—If you please. Abbreviated s.v.p.

Simile gaudet simili. *L*—*See* Similis simili gaudet.

Similia similibus curantur. *L*—Like is cured by like. The principle of homeopathy.

Similis simili gaudet. *L*—Like likes like; birds of a feather flock together.

Si monumentum requiris, circumspice. *L*—If you seek his monument, look about you. The epitaph, in London's St. Paul's cathedral, of Sir Christopher Wren, the architect of the building.

Simplex munditiis. *L*—Simple in your elegance.—*Horace, Odes, I, v, 5.* The poet is addressing Pyrrha, a beautiful flirt.

Simul sorbere ac flare non possum. *L*—I cannot exhale and inhale at the same time; it is impossible to move toward two opposite goals at the same time.

Sinanthropus pekinensis. *NL*—Chinese man of Pekin, considered the oldest of the ape men.

Sine Cerere et Libero friget Venus. *L*—Without bread and wine love grows cold.—*Terence, Eunuch, IV, v, 6.*

Sine cura. *L*—An office without duties; a sinecure.

Sine die. *L*—Adjournment without indicating a day for reconvening.

Sine dubio. *L*—Without doubt.

Sine ictu. *L*—Without a blow.

Sine invidia. *L*—Without envy.

Sine ira et studio. *L*—Without anger or partiality.—*Tacitus, Annals, I, 1.*

Sine legitima prole. *L*—Without legitimate issue.

Sine macula et ruga. *L*—Without stain or wrinkle.

Sine mascula prole. *L*—Without male issue.

Sine mora. *L*—Without delay.

Sine pennis volare haud facile est. *L*—It is not at all easy to fly without wings; one should not attempt to do something for which he is unprepared.—*Plautus, The Carthaginian, IV, ii, 49.*

Sine praejudicio. *L*—Without prejudice.

Sine prole superstite. *L*—Without surviving offspring.

Sine qua non. *L*—An absolutely indispensable condition.

Sinn Fein. *Ir*—Literally, we ourselves; Irish cultural and political movement stressing separation from Great Britain.

Si non caste, saltem caute. *L*—If not chastely, at least prudently; if you can't be good, be careful.

Si non valeat. *L*—*See* Si non val.

Si nous n'avions point de défauts, nous ne prendrions pas tant de plaisir à en remarquer dans les autres. *Fr*—If we did not have faults ourselves, we would not take so much pleasure in noticing them in others.—*La Rochefoucauld, Maxims, 31.*

Si parva licet componere magnis. *L*—If one dare compare the small with the large.—*Vergil, Georgics, IV, 176. See also* Parvis componere magna.

Si quaeris peninsulam amoenam circumspice. *L*—If you seek a pleasant peninsula, look about you. Motto of Michigan.

Si sic omnes. *L*—If only all were like him.

Siste, viator. *L*—Tarry, traveler. Often inscribed on Roman tombstones.

Sit tibi terra levis. *L*—*See* S.T.T.L.

Si vis ad summum progredi, ab infimo ordire. *L*—If you want to reach the top, start at the bottom.

Si vis me flere, dolendum est/primum ipsi tibi. *L*—If you wish me to weep, you must first show sorrow yourself. Advice given tragedians.—*Horace, Art of Poetry, 102.*

Si vis pacem, para bellum. *L*—If you want peace, prepare for war.

Si vous lui donnez un pied, il vous en prendra quatre. *Fr*—Give him a foot and he'll take a yard.

Sobre gustos no hay disputas. *Sp*—There is no disputing about tastes. *See also* De gustibus . . . .

Sociedad anónima. *Sp*—A company with limited liability.

Sociedad en comandita. *Sp*—*See* S. en C.

Société anonyme. *Fr*—Limited liability company.

Société en commandite. *Fr*—Limited liability company; sleeping partnership.

Socorro non viene mai tardi. *It*—Help that comes is never too late.

Soggarth aroon. *Ir*—Dear priest.

So geht es in der Welt. *Ger*—That's the way things go in this world.

So Gott will. *Ger*—Please God.

Sola nobilitas virtus. *L*—Virtue is the only nobility.

Solem e mundo tollere videntur ei, qui amicitiam e vita tollunt. *L*—They seem to take the sun from the world who take friendship from life.—*Cicero, On Friendship, XIII, 47.*

Solitudinem faciunt, pacem vocant. *L*—They make a desert and call it peace. For the complete expression, see *Ubi solitudinem faciunt* . . . .

Soll und Haben. *Ger*—Debit and credit.

Solus contra mundum. *L*—Alone against the world. Words of Athanasius, Bishop of Alexandria, when he found himself an exile, opposed by civil and religious powers.

Solvitur ambulando

Solvitur ambulando. *L*—The problem is solved by walking. Zeno held that all things were at rest; Diogenes argued against this doctrine by walking about. The expression is used when a problem in theory is solved by practical experiment.

Son cœur est un luth suspendu; sitôt qu'on le touche il résonne. *Fr*—His heart is a hanging lute; only touch it and it resounds. —*Béranger.*

Sophois homilon kautos ekbese sophos. *Gk*—If you associate with the wise, you will become wise yourself.—*Menander, Monostichs, 475.*

Sortes bibliorum. *L*—*See* Sortes sanctorum.

Sortes sanctorum. *L*—Lots of the saints. An attempt to divine the future by opening the Bible at random and taking the verse on which the eye alights as a guide for future action.

Sortes Vergilianae. *L*—A form of augury, surviving into relatively modern times, by which a person placed his finger at random on some spot in the *Aeneid* and applied what he read to his own life.

So schnell als möglich. *Ger*—As quickly as possible.

Sot à triple étage. *Fr*—A triple-dyed blockhead; a fool of the worst sort.

Sotto voce. *It*—In a stage whisper; in an undertone.

Souffler le chaud et le froid. *Fr*—To blow both hot and cold; to appear to favor and to oppose the same motion or project. Politicians are often accused of specializing in this art. The idea is found in a fable of Aesop.

Sous tous les rapports. *Fr*—In all respects.

Speciali gratia. *L*—By special grace or favor.

Sperat infestis, metuit secundis alteram sortem, bene preparatum pectus. *L*—The well-prepared mind hopes in adversity for a change of fortune, and fears it in prosperity.—*Horace, Odes, II, x, 13.*

Spes anchora vitae. *L*—Hope, the anchor of life. Motto of the Social Security Administration.

Spes sibi quisque. *L*—Let each person place his hope in himself, in his own resources.

Spes tutissima caelis. *L*—Man's surest hope is heaven.

Speude bradeos. *Gk*—Hasten slowly. *See also* Festina lente.

Spicula et faces amoris. *L*—The arrows and torches of love; love's artillery.

Spiritus frumenti. *L*—Whiskey.

Splendide mendax. *L*—Nobly deceptive. Originally applied to one of the fifty Danaids who did not kill her husband on their wedding night, thus breaking her promise to her father Danaus.—*Horace, Odes, III, xi, 35.*

Splendor sine occasu. *L*—Splendor that never fades. Motto of British Columbia.

Spogliar Pietro per vestir Paolo. *It*—To strip Peter to dress Paul; to rob Peter to pay Paul.

Spokoynoy nochi. *Rus*—Good night.

Spolia opima. *L*—Choice spoils; booty taken by a victorious Roman general from the commander of the defeated army.

Sponte sua. *L*—Voluntarily; of his own accord.

Spretae injuria formae. *L*—The injury offered to her spurned beauty. Juno harbored a deep resentment because Paris judged Venus more beautiful than she was.—*Vergil, Aeneid, I, 27.*

Spurlos versenkt. *Ger*—Sunk without a trace.

Stabat Mater. *L*—Literally, the mother stood. The first words and title of a hymn dating from the thirteenth century. It is sung at the Catholic service known as the Stations of the Cross. Its authorship is disputed but it is generally attributed to Iacopone da Todi.

Stare decisis et non quieta movere. *L*—To stand by matters that have been decided and not disturb what is tranquil; to uphold precedents and resist change. This is the philosophy of the conservative mind.

Stare super vias antiquas. *L*—To cling to the old ways.

Stat magni nominis umbra. *L*—He stands, the mere shadow of a great name. The reference was to Pompey, compared to an oak with dead roots. Said of one who becomes prominent and fails to live up to expectations.—*Lucan, Pharsalia, I, 135.*

Status belli. *L*—A state of war.

Status quaestionis. *L*—The state of the question; an explanation of terms used in a thesis, together with a review of opinions held on the subject.

Status quo. *L*—The existing state of affairs.

Status quo ante bellum. *L*—A return to conditions as they existed before the war.

Stemmata quid faciunt? *L*—Of what value are pedigrees?— *Juvenal, VIII, 1.* The poet goes on to say that the only basis of nobility is virtue. *See also* Nobilitas sola est atque unica virtus.

Stet. *L*—Let it stand. Used in proofreading to indicate that something queried or removed from the text should be retained.

Stet processus. *L*—Let the process stand; court order suspending further action.

Die stille Woche. *Ger*—Passion week.

Il stilo volgare. *It*—The language of the people. In Dante's day, Italian instead of Latin, the language of the ecclesiastics and scholars.

Strictum jus. *L*—Law strictly interpreted according to the letter without consideration of equities.

Studium immane loquendi. *L*—Boundless fondness for talking. —*Ovid, Metamorphoses, V, 678.*

Stultum facit fortuna quem vult perdere. *L*—Fortune first makes a fool out of the man she wishes to destroy.—*Publilius Syrus.*

Stupor mundi. *L*—Wonder of the world. Said of a genius so remarkable that he amazes the world. A notable example was Frederick II, German King and Roman Emperor (1194-1250).

Sturm und Drang. *Ger*—Storm and stress; a period of late eighteenth century German literature characterized by intellectual and emotional upheaval. The name was taken from a play by Klinger.

Le style c'est l'homme *or* **Le style est l'homme même.** *Fr*—Literary style is the man himself.—*Buffon, Discourse on Style.*

Sua cuique voluptas. *L*—Every man has his own pleasures.

Suadente diabolo. *L*—At the devil's persuasion.

Suave, mari magno turbantibus aequora ventis,/e terra magnum alterius spectare laborem. *L*—It is pleasant when safe on the land to watch the great struggle of another out on a swelling sea amid winds churning the deep.—*Lucretius, The Nature of Things, II, 1.*

Suaviter in modo, fortiter in re. *L*—Act gently in manner, vigorously in deed. President Theodore Roosevelt's maxim, Speak softly and carry a big stick.

Sub dio. *L*—Under the open sky.

Sub judice. *L*—Under consideration.

Sublata causa, tollitur effectus. *L*—Once the cause is removed, the effect disappears.

Sub modo. *L*—In a manner; in a qualified manner.

Sub plumbo. *L*—Literally, under lead; under papal seal, made of lead.

Sub poena. *L*—Under a penalty; a writ ordering a person to appear in court under pain of punishment.

Sub rosa. *L*—Secretly; confidentially. The origin is uncertain. In ancient Egypt the rose was an emblem of Horus. The Greeks and Romans wrongly thought him the god of silence. There is also a story that Cupid gave a rose to Harpocrates, the god of silence, to seal his lips about the love affairs of Venus. When a rose was displayed overhead at a party, it was the general understanding that whatever took place was to be kept secret.

Sub sigillo. *L*—Under seal (of silence); in confidence, as in confession.

Sub silentio. *L*—In silence. Used when a matter is passed over without formal notice.

Sub specie. *L*—Under the appearance of.

Sub specie aeternitatis. *L*—From the aspect of eternity; the consideration of things in their relation to the perfection of God. —*Spinoza, The Ethics, pt. V, xxix.*

Sub verbo. *L*—Under the word; a term used in cross reference in dictionaries, etc. *See also* Sub voce.

Sub vi. *L*—Under compulsion. When a man is forced to sign, he may write *s.v.* after his name.

Sub voce. L—Under the word; referring to an entry in an index, vocabulary, etc.

Succès de scandale. *Fr*—A success based on scandalous revelations.

Succès d'estime. *Fr*—Not a financial success; said of a play appreciated by discerning friends and critics rather than by the general public.

Succès fou. *Fr*—Fantastic success.

Sufflaminandus erat. *L*—He should have been clogged, repressed, In his comments on Shakespeare, *De Shakespeare Nostrati* (On our Fellow-Countryman Shakespeare), Ben Jonson stated that Shakespeare "flowed with that facility that sometimes it was necessary he should be stopped." This expression is based on a remark of Augustus in which he censured Q. Haterius for talking too rapidly.

Sui generis. *L*—In a class by itself.

Sui juris. *L*—Literally, of one's own right; applied to a person in a position to exercise his full rights and not limited by some legal restraint such as being a minor or subject to mental illness.

Summa cum laude. *L*—*See* Cum laude.

Summum bonum. *L*—The supreme good.—*Cicero, On Duties, I, ii, 5.*

Summum jus, summa injuria. *L*—Extreme justice is extreme injustice.—*Cicero, On Duties, I, x, 33. See also* Jus summum saepe summa est malitia.

Sumptibus publicis. *L*—At public expense.

Sum quod eris, fui quod sis. *L*—I am what you will be; I was what you are. A reminder engraved on tombstones for the benefit of wayfarers.

Sunt lacrimae rerum et mentem mortalia tangunt. *L*—Human experience is full of sorrow and the lot of man is depressing. —*Vergil, Aeneid, I, 462.*

Suo loco. *L*—In its proper place.

Suo Marte. *L*—By one's own toil, effort, courage.—*Cicero, On Duties, III, 7.* Motto of Wilberforce University, first college owned and operated by blacks.

Suo nomine. *L*—By its own name. A physician's direction to a pharmacist that the label on the bottle containing the drug indicate the chemical name of the medicine.

Suo periculo. *L*—At one's own risk.

Suo sibi gladio hunc jugulo. *L*—I will cut this man's throat with his own sword; I will turn this man's arguments against himself.—*Terence, The Brothers, V, viii, 35.*

Super visum corporis. *L*—After viewing the body. Term used at a coroner's inquest.

Suppressio veri, suggestio falsi. *L*—To suppress the truth is to suggest falsehood.

Surgit amari

Surgit amari aliquid quod in ipsis floribus angat. *L*—Something bitter always arises to poison our sweetest joys; there is always a fly in the ointment.—*Lucretius, The Nature of Things, IV, 1134 (1135).*

Sur le pavé. *Fr*—On the street; poverty-stricken.

Sur le tapis. *Fr*—Literally, on the carpet. Formerly tables were covered with carpets; for this reason the expression came to mean that a matter was on the table and, therefore, under consideration.

Sur place. *Fr*—On the spot.

Sursum corda. *L*—Lift up your hearts.

Surtout, point de zèle. *Fr*—Above all, don't be too enthusiastic; don't overdo things; don't lose your poise. Advice of Talleyrand to his subordinates.

Suspendatur per collum. *L*—Let him be hanged by the neck; abbreviated *sus. per coll. Suspensus per collum* means that a person was hanged in this manner.

Suspendens omnia naso. *L*—Turning up one's nose at everything; ridiculing everything.—*Horace, Satires, I, viii, 64.*

Suspiria de Profundis. *L*—Sighs from the depths; title of a work by Thomas de Quincey.

Sutor ne supra crepidam. *L*—Let the shoemaker stick to his last. According to Pliny the Elder, the Greek painter Apelles accepted the correction of a shoemaker that a shoe in one of his paintings needed another latch. When the shoemaker criticized the painting of the leg, Apelles uttered this remark. —*Pliny the Elder, Natural History, XXXV, 10.*

Suum cuique. *L*—To each man his own property.

Suus cuique mos. *L*—Each person has his own moral point of view.

T

t.a. (testantibus actis). *L*—As the records show.

t.i.d. (ter in die). *L*—Three times a day. A medical direction.

t/q (tale quale). *L*—As they come; run of mine; run of the mill. *See also* Tel quel.

T.S.V.P. (Tournez s'il vous plaît). *Fr*—Please turn to the reverse of the page.

Table d'hôte. *Fr*—The table of the host; a meal served to patrons at a fixed price.

Tabula rasa. *L*—An erased tablet; a clean slate. Locke's image of the mind at birth.

Tace. *L*—Be silent.

Tacent, satis laudant. *L*—They are silent; that's praise enough. —*Terence, Eunuch, III, ii, 23.*

Tâche sans tache. *Fr*—A work without a stain.

Tacitae magis et occultae inimicitiae timendae sunt quam indictae atque apertae. *L*—Silent, hidden enmities are more to be feared than those that are openly declared.—*Cicero, Against Verres, II, v, 71.*

Taedium vitae. *L*—Weariness of living; the feeling that life is not worth living.

Der Tag. *Ger*—The day; a toast German officers drank before the First World War to the day when they would defeat their military rivals, notably the British.

Tal padrone, tal servitore. *It*—Like master, like man.

Tangere ulcus. *L*—To touch a sore spot.

Tantaene animis caelestibus irae? *L*—Can such great anger dwell in heavenly breasts?—*Vergil, Aeneid, I, 11.*

Tant mieux. *Fr*—So much the better.

Tanto buono che val niente. *It*—So good that it is good for nothing.

Tanto nomini nullum par elogium. *L*—No eulogy can do justice to so great a name. A tribute to Michelangelo.

Tant pis. *Fr*—So much the worse.

Tant soit peu. *Fr*—Ever so little.

Tantum ergo. *L*—So great (a Sacrament) therefore. The title and first words of a hymn to the Eucharist by Thomas Aquinas sung at Benediction when Catholic ritual was in Latin. The two stanzas end the hymn *Pange, lingua, gloriosi (q.v.).*

Tantum pellis et ossa fuit. *L*—*See* Ossa atque pellis totus est.

Tantum possumus quantum scimus. *L*—We are effective in proportion to our knowledge.—*Francis Bacon.*

Tantum religio potuit suadere malorum! *L*—For how many evils has religion been responsible! This line of the poet was prompted by the sacrifice of Iphigeneia at Aulis.—*Lucretius, The Nature of Things, I, 101.*

Te Deum (laudamus). *L*—We praise thee, O Lord. A hymn sung at certain Christian services, especially on occasions of general thanksgiving.

Te judice. *L*—With you acting as judge; in your judgment.

Tel est notre bon plaisir. *Fr*—Such is our good pleasure. With these words French kings approved a new law.

Tel maître, tel valet. *Fr*—Like master, like valet.

Tel quel. *Fr*—Just as it is. A business term.

Telum imbelle sine ictu. *L*—A weapon feebly thrown without effect. The poet's description of the spear thrown by the aged Priam at Pyrrhus, the son of Achilles. Used to describe a feeble argument.—*Vergil, Aeneid, II, 544.*

Tempora mutantur, nos et mutamur in illis. *L*—Times change and we are changed in them.—*John Owen, Epigrams, 8, 58.*

Tempore felici multi numerantur amici. *L*—We number many friends when we are prosperous.

Tempori parendum. *L*—We must move with the times.

Tempus edax rerum. *L*—Time that devours all things.—*Ovid, Metamorphoses, XV, 234.*

Tempus fugit. *L*—Time flies.

Tempus omnia revelat. *L*—Time reveals everything.

Teres atque rotundus. *L*—*See* Totus teres atque rotundus.

Terminus ad quem. *L*—A goal or end toward which an effort is directed.

Terminus a quo. *L*—The end from which; the point of departure.

Terrae filius. *L*—*See* Filius terrae.

Terra firma. *L*—Solid earth. To Venetians it means the dry earth, the mainland.

Terra incognita. *L*—An unexplored land. It is often used in referring to matters about which one is uninformed.

Terra irredenta. *It*—Unredeemed land; a territory inhabited for the most part by nationals of one country but ruled by another that won it by arms.

Terra marique. *L*—By land and sea.

Tertium quid. *L*—A third something, produced by the meeting of two opposing forces.

Terza rima. *It*—Three iambic verses, the first and the third rhyming and the second furnishing the rhyme for the first and third lines of each following triplet; the rhyme scheme of Dante's *Divine Comedy.*

Tête-à-tête. *Fr*—Literally, head to head; confidential conversation.

Tête de veau. *Fr*—Calf's-head.

Teterrima causa belli. *L*—Most shameful, horrid cause of war.

Textus receptus. *L*—The text approved by authorities in the area concerned.

Thalassa, thalassa. *Gk*—*See* Thalatta, thalatta.

Thalatta, thalatta

Thalatta, thalatta! *Gk*—The sea, the sea! The cry of Greek mercenaries when they sighted the Black Sea on their retreat after the battle of Cunaxa.—*Xenophon, Anabasis, IV, 7.*

Theo(i) mono(i) doxa. *Gk*—Glory to the one and only God.

Theos ek mechanes. *Gk*—*See* Deus ex machina.

Thesaurus Americae Septentrionis Sigillum. *L*—Literally, Seal of the Treasury of North America, i.e., the United States.

Tic douloureux. *Fr*—A painful tic; facial neuralgia.

Tiens à la vérité. *Fr*—Hold to the truth.

Tiers état. *Fr*—The third estate, the common people in France in pre-Revolutionary times. Comprised all except the clergy and the nobility.

Timeo Danaos et dona ferentes. *L*—I fear the Greeks even though they bring gifts.—*Vergil, Aeneid, II, 49.*

Timeo hominem (virum) unius libri. *L*—I fear the man of one book. This may be interpreted in two ways: I fear the man who knows one book thoroughly because he will be a strong opponent in an argument, or I have my doubts about the knowledge of a man who knows only one book. In the Middle Ages the first meaning was intended.

Tirage au sort. *Fr*—Drawing of lots as for military conscription or impaneling a jury.

Tiré à quatre épingles. *Fr*—Dapper, elegant, neat.

Toga candida. *L*—White toga worn by Roman candidates for office.

Toga praetexta. *L*—Roman garment with purple border worn by magistrates, priests, and children.

Toga virilis. *L*—Toga worn by Roman males from the age of fifteen.

Toison d'or. *Fr*—Golden fleece.

To kalon. *Gk*—The beautiful.

Tolle, lege; tolle, lege. *L*—Take it and read, take it and read. These were a child's words which prompted Augustine to take up the epistles of Saint Paul and read what first struck his eye, a passage from the Epistle to the Romans.—*Augustine, Confessions, VIII, xii, 29.*

Tombé des nues. *Fr*—Fallen from the clouds; unexpected arrival.

To me on. *Gk*—Non-being.

Totidem verbis. *L*—In just so many words.

Toties quoties. *L*—As often as; as often, so often. If a man is fined a certain sum and is similarly fined for each subsequent offense, he is said to be fined *toties quoties*. An indulgence granted *toties quoties* is one that applies each and every time that the conditions for it are fulfilled.

Totis viribus. *L*—With all one's strength.

Toto caelo. *L*—By the whole heavens; to be poles apart. Generally used to express a world of difference.

Totus teres atque rotundus. *L*—Complete, smooth, and rounded; the wise man, according to the Stoics, who rolls through the world as smoothly as a sphere.—*Horace, Satires, II, vii, 86.*

Toujours en vedette. *Fr*—Always on guard. Motto of Frederick the Great.

Toujours l'amour. *Fr*—Love, always love.

Toujours perdrix. *Fr*—Always partridge; the same old story. The expression of the spiritual adviser of Henri IV when the latter had partridge served at every course of a meal as a jest.

Toujours prêt. *Fr*—Always ready.

Tour de force. *Fr*—Feat of exceptional strength or cleverness.

Tous droits réservés. *Fr*—All rights reserved.

Tous frais faits. *Fr*—All expenses paid.

Tout à fait. *Fr*—Entirely; quite; wholly.

Tout à l'heure. *Fr*—Instantly.

Tout au contraire

Tout au contraire. *Fr*—Quite the contrary.

Tout bien ou rien. *Fr*—Everything done well or not at all.

Tout chemin mêne (va) à Rome. *Fr*—All roads lead to Rome; there are many ways of reaching one's goal. According to this proverb, the end, not the means, is important.

Tout comprendre c'est tout pardonner. *Fr*—To understand everything is to pardon everything.—*Madame de Stael.*

Tout de suite. *Fr*—Immediately.

Tout d'un coup. *Fr*—All of a sudden.

Toute la dignité de l'homme consiste en la pensée. *Fr*—All the dignity of man lies in thought.—*Pascal, Thoughts, 365.*

Le tout ensemble. *Fr*—The whole or general effect.

Toute(s) proportion(s) gardée(s). *Fr*—With due regard for proper proportions; proportionately speaking.

Tout est bien qui finit bien. *Fr*—All's well that ends well.

Tout est perdu fors l'honneur. *Fr*—Everything is lost save honor. Not the exact words but the sense in a letter written by Francis I after the defeat at Pavia.

Tout le monde. *Fr*—Literally, all the world; everybody.

Tout le monde se plaint de sa mémoire, et personne ne se plaint de son jugement. *Fr*—Everybody complains about his memory, but nobody complains about his judgment.—*La Rochefoucauld, Maxims, 89.*

Tout lui rit (sourit). *Fr*—Everything smiles upon him; he is always lucky.

Tout s'en va, tout passe, l'eau coule, et le cœur oublie. *Fr*—Everything vanishes, everything passes, water runs away, and the heart forgets.—*Flaubert.*

Traduttore, traditore. *It*—The translator is a traitor. He turns out a translation that is better or worse than the original. No translator can possibly convey the full meaning of the original.

278

Trahimur omnes studio laudis, et optimus quisque maxime gloria ducitur. *L*—We are all moved by a desire for praise, and the nobler a man is, the more he is influenced by glory.—*Cicero, For Archias, XI, 26.*

Trahit sua quemque voluptas. *L*—Everyone is attracted by his own special pleasure.—*Vergil, Eclogues, II, 65.*

Tranche de vie. *Fr*—Slice of life; a careful, objective description of life as it is, portrayed by naturalistic writers such as Zola, Maupassant, Hardy, influenced by the doctrine of evolution.

Transeat in exemplum. *L*—Let it be recorded as a precedent.

Travaux forcés. *Fr*—Forced labor; penal servitude.

Trente-et-quarante. *Fr*—Gambling game with cards in which the players bet on one of two colors, red and black *(rouge et noire).*

Très bien. *Fr*—Very well; all right.

Treuga Dei. *L*—Truce of God. The attempt on the part of the Church beginning in the eleventh century to limit by means of excommunication the number of days in the week on which soldiers might fight. The Truce began at noon on Saturday (later on Wednesday evening) and lasted until Monday morning. It also extended in some places to Advent, Lent, and numerous religious feasts.

Treva Dei. *L*—Truce of God. *See also* Treuga Dei.

Trêve de Dieu. *Fr*—Truce of God. *See also* Treuga Dei.

Tria juncta in uno. *L*—Three joined in one. Motto of the Order of the Bath, Great Britain. The three classes of the Order established in 1725 were combined in 1815 "to commemorate the auspicious termination of the long and arduous contest in which the Empire has been engaged."

Trompe-l'œil. *Fr*—Optical illusion; in art, a still-life deception.

Trop de hâte gâte tout. *Fr*—Too much hurry spoils everything; more haste, less speed; haste makes waste.

279

La troppa familiarità genera disprezzo. *It*—Familiarity breeds contempt.

Tros Tyriusque mihi nullo discrimine agetur. *L*—Whether Trojan or Tyrian, I shall treat them impartially. Queen Dido's promise to the shipwrecked Trojans.—*Vergil, Aeneid, I, 574.*

Truditur dies die. *L*—One day follows on the heels of another.

Tua res agitur, paries cum proximus ardet. *L*—Your property is at stake when your neighbor's house is on fire.—*Horace, Epistles, I, xviii, 84.*

Tu, enim, Caesar, civitatem dare potes hominibus, verbis non potes. *L*—Caesar, you can give men citizenship but you cannot make rules for language. When Tiberius made a grammatical error in a speech, a court favorite said that the error would be accepted because it was the emperor who made it. The grammarian M. Pomponius Marcellus objected with these words.—*Suetonius, Eminent Grammarians, 22.*

Tuer le veau gras. *Fr*—To kill the fatted calf; to celebrate.

Tu ne cede malis sed contra audentior ito. *L*—Do not yield to misfortune but oppose it with greater boldness.—*Vergil, Aeneid, VI, 95.*

Tu quoque. *L*—You, too. A retort charging an opponent with doing the same thing, or having the same fault that he criticizes in another.

Tutte le strade conducono a Roma. *It*—All roads lead to Rome. *See also* Tout chemin mène à Rome.

Tutti i gusti son gusti. *It*—All tastes are tastes. *See also* De gustibus . . . .

U

u.a.m. (und anderes mehr). *Ger*—And so forth.

U.A.w.g. (Um Antwort wird gebeten). *Ger*—An answer is requested.

u. dgl. (und dergleichen). *Ger*—And so forth.

U.I.O.G.D. (Ut in omnibus glorificetur Deus). *L*—That God may be glorified in all things.

ult. (ultimo). *L*—Last month.

ü. M. (über dem Meeresspiegel). *Ger*—Above sea level.

u.s. (ubi supra). *L*—Where cited above.

u.s.w. *or* **usw.** *Ger*—*See* Und so weiter.

ut sup. (ut supra). *L*—As above.

Uberrima fides. *L*—Absolute confidence; implicit faith.

Ubi bene, ibi patria. *L*—Wherever I prosper, there is my fatherland.

Ubi est thesaurus tuus, ibi est et cor tuum. *L*—Where your treasure is, there is your heart also.—*Vulgate, Matthew, VI, 21.*

Ubi jus, ibi officium. *L*—Where there is a right, there is also a duty.

Ubi jus, ibi remedium. *L*—Where law prevails, there is a remedy; every violation of right has its remedy.

Ubi jus incertum, ibi jus nullum. *L*—Where one's right is uncertain, no right exists.

Ubi libertas, ibi patria. *L*—Wherever there is freedom, there is my fatherland.

Ubi mel, ibi apes. *L*—Where the honey is, there the bees are.

Ubi nunc fidelis ossa Fabricii manent. *L*—Where are the bones of faithful Fabricius now? A famous line by Boethius, the inspiration of later writers, e.g., Chaucer.—*Boethius, Consolation of Philosophy, II, vii, 15.*

Ubi panis, ibi patria. *L*—Wherever there is bread, there is my fatherland. Maxim of the displaced person who is ready to emigrate.

Ubi solitudinem faciunt, pacem appellant. *L*—Where they make a desert, they call it peace. Used when a conquering nation destroys all opposition.—*Tacitus, Agricola, 30.*

Ubi sunt qui ante nos fuerunt. *L*—Where are those who lived before us? Title of a medieval lyric.

Ubi tu Gaius, ego Gaia. *L*—Where you are, Gaius, there I, Gaia, am. Formula used in Roman marriage.

Übung macht den Meister. *Ger*—Practice makes the master; practice makes perfect.

Uisge beatha. *Ir*—The water of life; whiskey.

L'ultima che se perde è la speranza. *It*—The last thing we lose is hope.

Ultima ratio regum. *L*—The final argument of kings, the resort to force of arms. Engraved on the cannons of Louis XIV.

Ultima Thule. *L*—The name that the ancients gave the most northern land of which they had knowledge, probably one of the Shetland Islands; figuratively, any distant frontier or remote goal.—*Vergil, Georgics, I, 30.*

Ultimum vale. *L*—The last farewell.

Ultimus regum. *L*—The last of the kings.

Ultimus Romanorum. *L*—The last of the Romans, a title given to a number of historical personages and literary men, e.g., Marcus Junius Brutus, Stilicho, Congreve, Dr. Johnson.

Ultra vires. *L*—Beyond (its) powers. Used in connection with acts of a corporation exceeding the authority of its charter.

Um Christi willen. *Ger*—For the sake of Christ.

Una dolo divum si femina victa duorum est. *L*—(A great feat) if one sole woman is vanquished by the craftiness of two gods. —*Vergil, Aeneid, IV, 95.*

Una golondrina no hace verano. *Sp*—One swallow does not make a summer.—*Cervantes, Don Quixote, I, XIII.*

Una rondine non fa l'estate. *It*—One swallow does not make a summer.

Una rondine non fa primavera. *It*—One swallow does not make a spring.

Una salus victis nullam sperare salutem. *L*—The only safety for the conquered lies in hoping for no safety.—*Vergil, Aeneid, II, 354.*

Undank ist der Welt(en) Lohn. *Ger*—Ingratitude is the world's reward.

Und so weiter. *Ger*—And so forth.

Unguibus et rostro. *L*—With claws and beak; with tooth and nail.

L'union fait la force. *Fr*—In union there is strength. Motto of Belgium.

Universitas, societas magistrorum discipulorumque. *L*—The university, an association of teachers and students. This was the medieval concept of a university, which was built of men.

Ein unnütz Leben ist ein früher Tod. *Ger*—A useless life is an early death.—*Goethe, Iphigenia, I, 2, 62.*

Un roi, une loi, une foi. *Fr*—One king, one law, one faith.— *Motto of Bossuet.*

Un "tiens" vaut mieux que deux "tu l'auras." *Fr*—One "take it" is worth two "I shall give it to you"; a bird in the hand is worth two in the bush.

Unum post aliud. *L*—One thing at a time.

Unus homo nobis cunctando restituit rem. *L*—One man by delaying restored the state. The reference is to Fabius Maximus the Delayer, a Roman general who fought against Hannibal. —*Ennius. Cf. Vergil, Aeneid, VI, 846.*

Gli uomini hanno gli anni che sentono, e le donne quelli che mostrano. *It*—Men are as old as they feel, and women as old as they look.

Uomo universale. *It*—The universal man, the Renaissance ideal of well-rounded competence. The opposite of specialization in education.

Urbem venalem et mature perituram, si emptorem invenerit. *L*— (Jugurtha said that Rome was) a venal city, soon to perish, if it could find a buyer.—*Sallust, Jugurthine War, 35.* Cf. *Livy, Epitome of Book 64.*

Urbi et orbi. *L*—To the city (of Rome) and the world. A papal phrase.

Urbs in horto. *L*—A city in a garden. Motto of Chicago.

Ursa Major. *L*—Literally, the bigger bear; a constellation known as the Great Bear or the Big Dipper.

Usque ad nauseam. *L*—To the point of creating disgust.

Usus est optimus magister. *L*—Experience is the best teacher.

Usus loquendi. *L*—Usage of speech.

Ut ameris, amabilis esto. *L*—If you want to be loved, be lovable yourself.—*Ovid, Art of Love, II, 107.*

Utcumque placuerit Deo. *L*—In whatever way it shall please God.

Ut fragilis glacies, interit ira mora. *L*—Like fragile ice, anger passes if held back for a time.—*Ovid, Art of Love, I, 374.*

Ut fulvum spectatur in ignibus aurum tempore sic in duro est inspicienda fides. *L*—As yellow gold is tried in fire so faithfulness must be tested in times of trouble.—*Ovid, Sorrows, I, v, 25.*

Utinam noster esset! *L*—Would he were one of us; would he were on our side!

Ut infra. *L*—As cited below.

Uti possidetis. *L*—Literally, as you now possess. The diplomatic phrase used when two opposing powers agree to retain what they have won in a conflict.

Ut **lapsu graviore ruant.** *L*—That they may be destroyed in a more disastrous fall. Said of Fortune, which lifts men to the heights so that their fall may be greater.

Ut **omnes unum sint.** *L*—That all may be one. The title of a theology course given by the Daughters of St. Paul.

Ut **pignus amicitiae.** *L*—In token of friendship.

Ut **quocumque paratus.** *L*—Prepared for any emergency whatever.

Ut **sementem feceris, ita metes.** *L*—As you sow, so shall you reap. —*Cicero, On the Orator, II, 65.*

Ut **supra.** *L*—As cited above.

Ut **tamquam scopulum sic fugias insolens verbum.** *L*—Avoid the unusual word as if it were a cliff. Advice Caesar gave Roman orators.

V

v.a. (vixit annos). *L*—He lived ———— years.

var. lec. (varia lectio). *L*—Variant reading.

v/c (vuelta de correo). *Sp*—Return mail.

v. Chr. G. (vor Christi Geburt). *Ger*—Before the birth of Christ.

Ver. St. (Vereinigte Staaten). *Ger*—The United States of America.

v.g. (verbi gratia). *L*—As for example.

viz. (videlicet). *L*—Namely.

vs. (versus). *L*—Against.

V.T. (Vetus Testamentum). *L*—Old Testament.

Vade in pace. *L*—Go in peace.

Vade mecum. *L*—Literally, go with me; a handy portable volume for ready reference.

Vae victis! *L*—Woe to the conquered!—*Livy, History, V, 48.*

Le vainqueur du vainqueur de la terre. *Fr*—The conqueror of the conqueror of the earth. Doctor Samuel Johnson used these words in a stinging letter to Lord Chesterfield when rejecting his tardy offer of patronage.

Vale. *L*—Farewell, goodbye.

Valeat ancora virtus. *L*—May the anchor of virtue hold.

Valeat quantum valere potest. *L*—Let it stand for as much as it is worth. Used in argumentation.

Valete. *L*—Farewell. Plural of *vale*; used when addressing more than one person.

Vanitas vanitatum, et omnia vanitas. *L*—Vanity of vanities, and all is vanity.—*Vulgate, Ecclesiastes, I, 2.*

Vare, legiones redde. *L*—Varus, give me back my legions. In 9 A.D. three Roman legions under Quintilius Varus were trapped in the Teutoberg forest and wiped out. This was the worst military disaster suffered by Roman arms during the principate of Augustus. He was deeply affected by this defeat and would sometimes knock his head against the doorposts and cry out: "Quintilius Varus, give me back my legions."—*Suetonius, Caesar Augustus, 24.*

Varia lectio. *L*—A variant reading. The plural is *variae lectiones.*

Varietas delectat cor hominis. *L*—Variety delights the human heart.

Variorum notae. *L*—The notes of several commentators.

Varium et mutabile semper femina. *L*—Woman is a changeable and fickle thing.—*Vergil, Aeneid, IV, 569.*

Vaso vuoto suona meglio. *It*—An empty vessel gives the loudest sound.

Vaya con Dios. *Sp*—Go with God; goodbye.

Vedi Napoli e poi mori. *It*—See Naples and then die. Everything else will be an anticlimax.

Velis et remis. *L*—With sails and oars; with all possible speed.

Veluti in speculum. *L*—As if in a mirror. Used when reference is made to one's faults.

Venalis populus, venalis curia patrum. *L*—The people are venal, and so is the Senate.

Vender il miele a chi ha le api. *It*—To sell honey to a man who keeps bees; to carry coals to Newcastle.

Vendidit hic auro patriam. *L*—This man sold his country for gold.—*Vergil, Aeneid, VI, 621.*

Venenum in auro bibitur. *L*—Poison is drunk from a golden cup. The poor, who drink from cups of clay, are not likely to be poisoned.—*Seneca, Thyestes, 453.*

Veniam petimusque damusque vicissim. *L*—We beg pardon and give it in return.

Venia necessitati datur. *L*—Pardon is granted to necessity; necessity knows no law.

Veni, Creator, Spiritus. *L*—Come, Holy Ghost, Creator blest, a ninth century hymn, frequently sung in Roman Catholic services.

Venienti occurrite morbo. *L*—Forestall the oncoming disease; treat disease before it develops; an ounce of prevention is worth a pound of cure.—*Persius, III, 64.*

Venire. *L*—Shortened expression for *Venire facias juratores*: literally, Cause jurors to come. A writ directing a sheriff to summon jurors.

Veni, vidi, vici. *L*—I came, I saw, I conquered. Julius Caesar's summary of his swift victory at Zela in 47 B.C. over Pharnaces in the Pontic campaign.—*Suetonius, Julius Caesar, XXXVII.*

Venter non habet aures. *L*—The belly has no ears; a starving man will not listen to a sermon.

Ventis secundis. *L*—With favorable winds.

Ventre à terre. *Fr*—Literally, with belly to the ground, an expression originally applied to a running horse; at top speed.

Vera incessu patuit dea. *L*—She walked with the dignity of a goddess.—*Vergil, Aeneid, I, 405.*

Verba docent, exempla trahunt. *L*—Words teach, examples attract.

Verba volant, scripta manent. *L*—Spoken words fly through the air, but written words endure.

Verbum sat sapienti. *L*—A word to the wise is sufficient. *See also* Dictum (*or* verbum) sapienti sat est.

Verdammte Bedürfnislosigkeit. *Ger*—Damned wantlessness; a charge brought by Marxists against the passive poor.

Vere scire est per causas scire. *L*—Real knowledge lies in knowing causes.

La verità è figlia del tempo. *It*—Truth is the daughter of time; time will eventually bring out the truth. *See also* Veritas temporis filia dicitur.

Veritas numquam perit. *L*—Truth never dies.

Veritas odium parit. *L*—The truth breeds hatred. *See also* Obsequium amicos . . . .

Veritas temporis filia dicitur. *L*—Truth is called the daughter of time; eventually the truth becomes known.—*Aulus Gellius, Attic Nights, XII, xi, 7.* Aulus Gellius wrote that he had forgotten the name of the author.

Veritas vos liberabit. *L*—The truth shall make you free.—*Vulgate, John, VIII, 32.* Motto of Johns Hopkins University.

Veritatis simplex oratio est. *L*—The language of truth is simple.

Vérité sans peur. *Fr*—Literally, truth without fear; speak the truth and don't be afraid.

Ver perpetuum. *L*—Perpetual spring.

Vers de société. *Fr*—Light, polished verse written to please a sophisticated audience.

Vers libre. *Fr*—Free verse.

Verso pollice. *L*—Popularly interpreted, thumbs down. The gesture used at gladiatorial combats in Rome when the spectators demanded that the victor slay his opponent. Actually the Romans pointed the thumb upward toward the chest when they wanted the vanquished slain, and down when they wanted the victor to spare his opponent. The incorrect interpretation may have developed from an ancient relief on which the spectators were represented with thumbs turned upward. The inscription showed that the conquered were spared.— *Juvenal, III, 36.*

Verso sciolto. *It*—Blank verse.

Verweile doch! du bist so schön! *Ger*—Linger a while, you are so fair! Faust is speaking with Mephistopheles with whom he is making a pact that if the moment ever comes when he will ask that some worldly pleasure last a little longer, he will freely hand himself over to the powers of hell.—*Goethe, Faust, I, 1700.*

Vestigia nulla retrorsum. *L*—*See* Me vestigia terrent . . . .

Vestis talaris. *L*—Garment reaching to the feet.

Vestis virum facit. *L*—Clothes make the man.—*Erasmus, Adagia. Compare* Cucullus non facit monachum.

Vetulam suam praetulit immortalitati. *L*—He preferred his aged wife to immortality. Said of Ulysses.

Vexata quaestio. *L*—A disputed question.

Vexilla Regis prodeunt. *L*—The standards of the King appear. A sixth century hymn by Fortunatus.

Via. *L*—By way of.

Via il gatto ballano i sorci. *It*—When the cat's away, the mice will play.

Via lactea. *L*—Milky Way.

Via media. *L*—The middle path or middle way. An expression much heard during the Oxford Movement. Those who hold

Via trita

for the *via media* believe that the Anglican Church is midway between Protestantism and Catholicism.

Via trita, via tutissima. *L*—The beaten path is the safest.

Vice versa. *L*—Reversing the relationship of terms; conversely.

Vicisti, Galilaee. *L—See* Galilaie nenikekas.

Victoire ou la mort. *Fr*—Victory or death.

Victrix causa deis placuit sed victa Catoni. *L*—The victorious cause pleased the gods, but the losing cause pleased Cato. Cato the Younger killed himself after the defeat of the senatorial forces by Julius Caesar at Utica in 46 B.C.—*Lucan, Pharsalia, I, 128.*

La vida es sueño. *Sp—Life is a Dream*, title of a play by Calderón regarded as a masterpiece of the Spanish theatre.

Vida sin amigos muerte sin testigos. *Sp*—A friendless life, a lonely death.

Videant consules ne quid res publica detrimenti capiat. *L*—Let the consuls see to it that the republic suffer no harm. This was the wording of the *consultum ultimum*, the final decree of the Senate by which, according to Cicero's interpretation of the law, conspirators might be put to death without trial.

Video et taceo. *L*—I see and I remain silent. Motto of Queen Elizabeth I.

Video meliora proboque, deteriora sequor. *L*—I see the better course and I approve it, but I follow the lower path.—*Ovid, Metamorphoses, VII, 20.*

Vide supra. *L*—Literally, see above; see previous reference.

La vie à trois. *Fr*—The eternal triangle.

Viele Händ' machen bald ein End'. *Ger*—Many hands make light work.

Viele Köche verderben den Brei. *Ger*—Too many cooks spoil the broth.

Vi et armis. *L*—By force of arms.

Vigueur de dessus. *Fr*—Strength from on high.

Vilius argentum est auro, virtutibus aurum. *L*—Silver is less valuable than gold, and gold than virtue.—*Horace, Epistles, I, i, 52.*

Vincet amor patriae. *L*—Love of country will win in the end.—*Vergil, Aeneid, VI, 823.*

Vincit omnia veritas. *L*—Truth conquers everything.

Vincit qui patitur. *L*—The patient man conquers.

Vincit qui se vincit. *L*—He wins control who controls himself.

Vin d'honneur. *Fr*—A toast drunk in welcome to a guest.

Vin du pays. *Fr*—Wine of the region.

Vino vendibili hedera non opus est. *L*—A popular wine needs no ivy; a good product needs no special advertising. The ivy was sacred to Bacchus, and its bush was displayed as a sign outside of taverns.

Vinum daemonum. *L*—The wine of devils. A hostile view of poetry.

Viola da braccio. *It*—An arm viol, the ancestor of the violin.

Viola da gamba. *It*—A leg viol, ancestor of the cello.

Violenta non durant. *L*—Violence does not last.

Violon d'Ingres. *Fr*—The violin of Ingres, a French painter, who in his early life enjoyed success as a musician; a hobby more interesting to the one who rides it than his regular occupation; a second means of making a living.

Vir bonus dicendi peritus. *L*—A good man skilled in public speaking. According to the Roman definition, an orator was supposed to be a virtuous man.—*Quintilian, XII, i, 1.*

Vires acquirit eundo. *L*—She acquires strength as she travels on. This describes Fama (Rumor or Gossip) which increases as it spreads.—*Vergil, Aeneid, IV, 175.*

Vir, fortis et strenuus. *L*—A man, brave and energetic. In the mind of Cato the Elder, bravery and energy were the qualities that made up the ideal Roman character.

Virginibus puerisque. *L*—For girls and boys.—*Horace, Odes, III, i, 4.* The title of a book by Robert Louis Stevenson.

Viribus totis. *L*—With all one's strength.

Vir sapit qui pauca loquitur. *L*—He is a wise man who speaks but little.

Virtus ariete fortior. *L*—Virtue is stronger than a battering ram.

Virtus dormitiva. *L*—Power to induce sleep, as in the case of opium; by extension, dull writing that induces sleep. *Molière, Malade Imaginaire, third interlude.*

Virtus in actione consistit. *L*—Virtue lies in action.

Virtus in arduis. *L*—Courage in difficulties.

Virtus sola nobilitat. *L*—Only virtue ennobles.

Virtute et armis. *L*—By courage and arms. Motto of Mississippi.

Virtute et fide. *L*—By courage and faith.

Virtute et labore. *L*—By courage and toil.

Virtute non astutia. *L*—By virtue, not by cleverness.

Virtute officii. *L*—By virtue of one's office.

Virtutis fortuna comes. *L*—Good fortune is the companion of courage.

Vis a fronte. *L*—A frontal assault.

Vis a tergo. *L*—Force from behind.

Vis-à-vis. *Fr*—Opposite; face to face.

Vis comica. *L*—Comic force. Caesar used the expression in some lines of poetry about Terence in which he praised his poetic gifts but lamented his lack of comic power.—*Suetonius, Lives of the Poets, Terence (at the end).*

Vis conservatrix naturae. *L*—The protective, defensive power in nature.

Vis consili expers mole ruit sua. *L*—Force devoid of counsel is crushed by its own weight.—*Horace, Odes, III, iv, 65.*

Vis inertiae. *L*—In physics, the force of inertia. By extension this may be applied to resistance in matters of social progress or change.

Vis major. *L*—Superior force, a legal term covering more than an act of God; circumstances beyond one's control.

Vis medicatrix naturae. *L*—The restorative, healing power of nature.

Vis unita fortior. *L*—United strength is stronger; in unity there is strength.

Vis vitae. *L*—The life force. *See also* L'élan vital.

Vis vitalis. *L*—*See* Vis vitae.

Vita brevis, longa ars. *L*—Life is short and art is long. *See also* Ho bios brachys . . ., of which the Latin is a translation. It is often quoted as *Ars longa, vita brevis (q.v.).* Adapted from *Seneca, The Shortness of Life, I.*

Vitam impendere vero. *L*—To risk one's life for the truth.

Vita sine litteris mors est. *L*—Life without learning (education) is death.

Vitiis nemo sine nascitur. *L*—Nobody is born without faults.—*Horace, Satires, I, iii, 68.*

Viva il papa. *It*—Long live the pope.

Vivamus, mea Lesbia, atque amemus. *L*—Let us live and love, my Lesbia.—*Catullus, V, 1.*

Vivat regina. *L*—Long live the queen.

Vivat rex. *L*—Long live the king.

Viva voce. *L*—Expression by the living voice; orally, as in voting or in an oral examination.

Vivebat. *L*—He was living. Associated with a date.

Vive la bagatelle! *Fr*—Long live trifles! Long live nonsense!

Vive la différence! *Fr*—Three cheers for the difference! Used by those who are happy about the differences that exist between men and women.

Vive le roi! *Fr*—Long live the king!

Vivent les Gueux. *Fr*—Long live the Beggars, the battle cry of the opponents of Philip II of Spain who revolted against his enforcement of the Inquisition in the Netherlands.

Vivit post funera virtus. *L*—Virtue survives the grave.

Vivre libre, ou mourir. *Fr*—To live free or die; freedom or death. Slogan of the French Commune, which ruled in Paris for sixty-two days in 1871.

Vix ea nostra voco. *L*—I can scarcely call these things my own. This is a reference to one's ancestry for which a modest person takes no credit. *See also* Nam genus et proavos . . . .

Vixere fortes ante Agamemnona. *L*—There were brave men before Agamemnon.—*Horace, Odes, IV, ix, 25.*

Voce di testa. *It*—Head voice; falsetto.

Vogue la galère! *Fr*—Row the galley on! Let's take our chances.

Voilà! *Fr*—See there! There you are!

Voilà une autre chose. *Fr*—That's an entirely different matter.

Voilà un homme! *Fr*—There goes a man. Reportedly said by Napoleon when Goethe left his presence.

Voire dire. *OF*—Literally, to tell the truth; a preliminary examination given a prospective witness or juror to determine his competence to give objective testimony; also the oath administered at such an inquiry.

Voir le dessous des cartes. *Fr*—To see the face of the turned-down card; to be in on the trick or secret.

Vol-au-vent. *Fr*—Puff-pie filled with delicacies, usually meat.

Volenti non fit injuria. *L*—No injury is done a willing participant. Legal maxim.

Volo, non valeo. *L*—I am willing but unable.

Volte-face. *Fr.*—A right-about-face; complete reversal of one's opinion.

Volto sciolto e pensieri stretti. *It*—An open countenance and secret thoughts.

Vomunt ut edant, edunt ut vomant. *L*—They vomit to eat, they eat to vomit.—*Seneca, To Helvia On Consolation, Dialogue XII, chap. X, 3.* Gluttons at banquets in Rome were accused of this practice.

Vorwärts mit Gott! *Ger*—Forward with God!

Vos exemplaria Graeca nocturna versate manu, versate diurna. *L*—Page through the Greek models by day and by night.—*Horace, Art of Poetry, 268.*

Vouloir rompre l'anguille au genou. *Fr*—To attempt to break an eel on one's knee; to attempt the impossible.

Vous êtes orfèvre, Monsieur Josse. *Fr*—Literally, you are a goldsmith, Mr. Josse; you are giving advice that looks to your own interests. Josse urges a father to buy jewels to cure his daughter's melancholy.—*Molière, L'Amour Médecin, I, I.*

Vous y perdrez vos pas. *Fr*—You will waste your time at that.

Vox audita perit, littera scripta manet. *L*—The word that is spoken dies in the air; the written word remains.

Vox clamantis in deserto. *L*—The voice of one crying in the wilderness.—*Vulgate, Matthew, III, 3.*

Vox et praeterea nihil. *L*—A voice and nothing more. A derogatory expression used to describe speakers whose discourse is without substance.

Vox faucibus haesit. *L*—His voice stuck in his throat. *See also* Obstipui steteruntque comae . . . .

Vox humana. *L*—The human voice; an organ stop simulating the human voice.

Vox populi, vox Dei. *L*—The voice of the people is the voice of God.

Le vrai honnête homme est celui qui ne se pique de rien. *Fr*—The real gentleman plumes himself on nothing.—*La Rochefoucauld, Maxims, 203.*

Le vrai n'est pas toujours vraisemblable. *Fr*—Truth is sometimes stranger than fiction.

Le vrai peut quelquefois n'être pas vraisemblable. *Fr*—Truth is sometimes stranger than fiction.

Vue d'oiseau. *Fr*—Bird's-eye view.

Vulgus ad deteriora promptum. *L*—The public, disposed to believe the worst.—*Tacitus, Annals, XV, 64.*

Vulgus fingendi avidum. *L*—The public, eager to invent rumors. —*Tacitus, History, II, 1.*

Vulgus ignobile. *L*—The low-born crowd.

Vulgus veritatis pessimus interpres. *L*—The public, the worst possible expounder of the truth.—*Seneca, Of a Happy Life, II.*

Vultus est index animi. *L*—The face is the mirror of the soul.

W

Die Wacht am Rhein. *Ger*—"The Watch on the Rhine," German national anthem at the time of the First World War.

Wagons-lits. *Fr*—Sleeping cars.

Die Wahrheit ist eine Perle; wirf sie nicht vor die Säue! *Ger*—Truth is a pearl; don't cast it before swine. Adapted from *Matthew, VII, 6.*

Wahrheit und Dichtung. *Ger*—Truth and poetry.

Was ich nicht weiss, macht mich nicht heiss. *Ger*—I do not get excited over what I do not know.

Was ihn nicht umbringt, macht ihn stärker. *Ger*—What does not kill him makes him stronger. With a change of *him* to *you*, this became the Nazi motto of a training center for young leaders of the Hitler youth movement.—*Nietzsche, Ecce Homo, para. 2.*

Was man nicht kann meiden, muss man willig leiden. *Ger*— What one cannot avoid must be borne without complaint; what can't be cured must be endured.

Das Weib sieht tief; der Mann sieht weit. *Ger*—Woman sees deep; man sees far.

Wein auf Bier, das rat ich dir; Bier auf Wein, lass das sein. *Ger* —Wine on beer, that's my rule; beer on wine, that's for the fool.

Wein, Weib, und Gesang. *Ger*—Wine, women, and song.

Die Weisheit der Gasse. *Ger*—Wisdom of the street. Proverbs are often referred to in this way. The expression is adapted from *The Book of Proverbs, I, 20.*

Die Weisheit ist nur in der Wahrheit. *Ger*—Wisdom is found only in truth.—*Goethe, Maxims in Prose, 79.*

Welche Regierung die beste sei? Diejenige die uns lehrt uns selbst zu regieren. *Ger*—What form of government is the best? The one that teaches us to rule ourselves.—*Goethe, Maxims in Prose, 163.*

Weltanschauung. *Ger*—A general, philosophical view of the world.

Weltmacht oder Niedergang. *Ger*—World power or ruin. Hitler's program.

Wenige wissen, wieviel man wissen muss, um zu wissen, wie wenig man weiss. *Ger*—Few know how much a man must know in order to know how little he knows.

Wenn die Katze nicht zu Hause ist, tanzen die Mäuse auf Tisch und Bänken. *Ger*—When the cat is not home, the mice dance on the table and benches; when the cat's away, the mice will play. *See also* Quando la gatta non v'è . . . .

Wer dem Pöbel dient, hat einen schlechten Herrn. *Ger*—The man who serves the people has a bad taskmaster.

Wer fremde Sprachen nicht kennt, weiss nichts von seiner eigenen. *Ger*—The man who does not know foreign tongues knows nothing of his own.—*Goethe, Maxims in Prose, 55.*

Wer gar zu viel bedenkt, wird wenig leisten. *Ger*—The man who considers too long accomplishes little.—*Schiller, William Tell, III, i, 72.*

Das **Werk lobt den Meister.** *Ger*—The work praises the master.

Wer liebt nicht Weib, Wein und Gesang/Der bleibt ein Narr sein Leben lang. *Ger*—Who loves not woman, wine and song/Remains a fool his whole life long. Attributed to *J. H. Voss.*

Wer nicht will, der hat schon. *Ger*—He who does not want any more has enough.

Wer verachtet, der will kaufen. *Ger*—The man who points out defects wants to buy.

Wer zuletzt lacht, lacht am besten. *Ger*—He who laughs last laughs best.

Wie der Herr, so der Knecht. *Ger*—Like master, like servant.

Wie gewonnen, so zerronen. *Ger*—Easy come, easy go.

Wir Deutschen fürchten Gott, sonst aber Nichts in der Welt. *Ger*—We Germans fear God, but nothing else in the world.—*Bismarck.*

Wir lieben unsern Führer. *Ger*—We love our leader. Shout of German crowds for Hitler.

Wollt ihr immer leben? *Ger*—Do you want to live forever? Frederick the Great's question to soldiers who faltered in the face of danger.

Wurra dheelish! *Ir*—Sweet Virgin!

X

Xbre (décembre). *Fr*—December. In Spanish, 10bre. In the early Roman calendar December was the tenth month of the year.

Z

z.B. (zum Beispiel). *Ger*—For example.

Zartem Ohre, halbes Wort. *Ger*—Half a word is enough for a sharp ear. *See also* Verbum sat sapienti.

Zoe mou, sas agapo. *Modern Gk*—My life, I love thee.—*Byron, Maid of Athens.*

Zum Donnerwetter! *Ger*—Hang it all!

Zwei Hälften machen zwar ein Ganzes, aber merk': Aus halb und halb getan entsteht kein ganzes Werk. *Ger*—It is true that two halves make a whole, but take note: no complete work results from work half done.—*Rückert.*

Zwei Seelen und ein Gedanke, zwei Herzen und ein Schlag. *Ger*—Two souls with but one thought; two hearts that beat together.

Zwei Seelen wohnen, ach! in meiner Brust. *Ger*—Alas! two souls dwell in my breast.—*Goethe, Faust, pt. I, 1112.*

LIST OF PHRASES
ARRANGED BY LANGUAGES

Anglo-French

Cestui que (qui) trust
Cestui que use
Cestui que vie
Nul tiel record
Oyer and terminer
Oyez!

Anglo-Latin

Felo de se
Quo warranto

Arabic

Allahu akbar
Id al-Fitr
La ilāha illa Allāh
Salaam aleikum (salam 'alekum)

Aramaic

Eli eli, lama sabachthani
Mane, thecel, phares
Mene, mene, tekel, upharsin

Chinookan

Al-ki

French

À barbe de fou . . .
À bas
À bâtons rompus
À beau jeu . . .
À beau mentir . . .
À bientôt
À bis ou (et) à blanc
À bon appétit . . .
À bon chat . . .
À bon cheval . . .
À bon chien . . .
À bon commencement . . .
À bon compte
Abondance de bien(s) . . .
À bon droit
À bon marché
À bon vin . . .
À bras ouverts
Absence d'esprit
Absent le chat . . .
Les absents ont toujours tort
Accordez vos flûtes
À chacun son fardeau pèse
À chaque fou . . .
À chaque oiseau . . .
À chaque saint . . .
À cheval
À cœur ouvert
À compte
À confesseurs, médecins, avocats . . .
À contre cœur
À corps perdu
À coups de bâton
À coup sûr
À couvert
Acte d'accusation
Acte gratuit
À demi
Adieu, canaux, canards, canaille!
Adieu la voiture . . .
À discrétion

300

French—*Continued*

À droite
L'adversité fait l'homme . . .
Affaire d'amour
Affaire d'honneur
Affaire du cœur
Les affaires sont les affaires
À fond
À forfait
À fripon fripon et demi
À gauche
À genoux!
Agent provocateur
À grands frais
À haute voix
À huis clos
Aide-de-camp
Aide mémoire
Aide-toi, le ciel t'aidera
Aîné
Ainsi soit-il
À la —
À la belle étoile
À la bonne heure
À l'abri
À la campagne
À la carte
À la dérobée
À la diable
À la française
À la grècque
À la lanterne
À la lettre
À la mode
À la mort
À la napolitaine
À la presse . . .
À la sourdine
L'Albion perfide
À l'extérieur
À l'huile
À l'immortalité
À l'improviste

Allez-vous-en!
Allons, enfants de la patrie!
À loisir
À main armée
Âme damneé
Âme de boue
Amende honorable
Âme perdue
À merveille
Ami de cour
Ami du peuple
Les amis du vin
À moitié
À mon avis
L'amour courtois
L'amour, . . . de tous les senti-
ments le plus égoïste . . .
L'amour et la fumée . . .
Amour fait beaucoup . . .
Amour propre
L'amour-propre est le plus . . .
Ancienne noblesse
Ancien régime
L'Angleterre est une nation de
boutiquiers
À nouvelles affaires . . .
À outrance
À pas de géant
À perte de vue
À peu de frais
À pied
À point
Appartement meublé
L'appétit vient en mangeant
Après la mort, le médecin
Après moi le déluge
À propos de bottes
À propos de rien
À raconter ses maux . . .
À reculons
Argent comptant
Arrière-garde

301

French—*Continued*

Arrière pensée
L'art de vivre
L'Art Nouveau
L'art pour l'art
À tâtons
À tort et à travers
À tort ou à raison
À tout prix
Au bout de son latin
Au bout du compte
Au contraire
Au courant
Au désespoir
Au fait
Au fond
Au grand sérieux
Au gratin
Aujourd'hui roi, demain rien
Au jus
Au lecteur
Au naturel
Au pied de la lettre
Au pis aller
Au reste
Au revoir
Au royaume des aveugles . . .
Au secours!
Au sérieux
Au soleil
Aussitôt dit, aussitôt fait
Autant d'hommes, autant d'avis
Autres temps, autres mœurs
Aux aguets
Aux armes!
Avant-coureur
Avant-garde
Avant propos
Avant que de désirer . . .
Avant tout un bon dîner
À volonté
À votre santé
À vue d'œil

Ballon d'essai
Un barbier rait l'autre
Bas bleu
Bas relief
Bataille rangée
Bâtie en hommes
Beaucoup de bruit . . .
Beau garçon
Beau geste
Beau idéal
Beau monde
Beauté du diable
Beaux arts
Beaux esprits
Les beaux esprits se rencontrent
Bel esprit
La belle dame sans merci
Belle indifférence
Les belles actions cachées . . .
Belles dames du temps jadis
Belles lettres
Bête noire
Bibliophile de la vieille roche
Bibliothèque bleue
Bien entendu
Un bienfait n'est jamais perdu
Billet doux
Bon avocat, mauvais voisin
Bon chien chasse de race
Le bon Dieu est toujours . . .
Le bon genre
Bon goût
Bon gré, mal gré
Bonjour
Bon mot
Bonne année
La bonne bouche
Bonne chance!
Bonne foi
Bonne nuit
Une bonne race
Bonne renommée vaut mieux . . .

302

French—*Continued*

Bonnet rouge
Les bons comptes . . .
Bon soir
Le bon temps viendra
Bon ton
Bon vivant
Bon voyage!
Brevet s.g.d.g. (sans garantie du gouvernement)
Le cabaret est le salon du pauvre
Café au lait
Ça-ira
Cape et épée
Carte blanche
Carte de visite
Catalogue raisonné
Cause célèbre
Cela va sans dire
Celui qui a trouvé un bon gendre . . .
Ce qui fait les amants . . .
Ce qui n'est pas clair . . .
C'est à dire
C'est dommage
C'est double plaisir . . .
C'est égal
C'est la guerre
C'est la profonde ignorance . . .
C'est la vie
C'est le dernier pas qui coûte
C'est magnifique . . .
C'est presque toujours la faute . . .
C'est une grande habilité . . .
C'est une tempête . . .
Ceux qui s'appliquent trop . . .
Chacun à sa marotte
Chacun à son goût
Chacun pour soi . . .
Chacun selon ses facultés . . .
Chacun sent (sait) le mieux . . .
Chacun tire de son côté
Chaise longue

Chambres meublées
Champs Elysées
Chanson de geste
Chansons de toile
Chant du cygne
Chapeaux bas!
Chapelle ardente
Chaque heure je vous aime . . .
Chargé d'affaires
Chasseurs à cheval
Châteaux en Espagne
Le chat qui dort
Chef de cuisine
Chef d'œuvre
Chercher midi à quatorze heures
Cherchez la femme
Chère amie
Cheval de bataille
Chevalier d'industrie
Le cheval volant . . .
Chez nous
Le chien retourne . . .
Chronique scandaleuse
Ci-devant
Ci-gît
Le cœur a ses raisons . . .
Comédie de mœurs
La Comédie Humaine
La comédie larmoyante
Comme ci, comme ça
Comme deux gouttes d'eau
Comme il faut
Comment ça va?
Comment prétendons-nous . . .
Comme on fait son lit . . .
Commis voyageur
Compagnon de voyage
Compte rendu
La condition humaine
Congé d'élire
Conseil de famille
Conseil d'état

French—*Continued*

Conseils aux visiteurs étrangers
Cordon bleu
Cordon sanitaire
Corps de ballet
Corps de bâtiment
Corps de logis
Coup de bourse
Coup d'éclat
Coup de foudre
Coup de grâce
Coup de main
Coup de maître
Coup d'épée
Coup de pied de l'âne
Coup de plume
Coup de soleil
Coup d'essai
Coup d'état
Coup de tête
Coup de théâtre
Coup d'œil
Le courage est souvent . . .
Courage sans peur
Cour des comptes
Coureur de bois
Le coût en ôte le goût
Coûte que coûte
Crème de la crème
Cri du cœur
La critique est aisée . . .
Croix de guerre
Cul-de-sac
Dame d'honneur
Dames de la halle
Danse macabre
Dans l'amour il y a toujours . . .
Dans le doute, abstiens-toi
De bon augure
De bonne grâce
De droit
De fait
Défauts de ses qualités

Défense de —
De fond en comble
De gaieté de cœur
D'égal à égal
Dégénéré supérieur
De haute lutte
De haut en bas
Déjà vécu
Déjà vu
De l'audace . . .
De luxe
De mal en pis
De mémoire de rose . . .
Le demi-monde
Demi-tasse
De pied en cap
De race
De rigueur
Le dernier cri
Le dernier mot
Dernier ressort
De sa façon
Le désespoir redouble . . .
Le dessous des cartes
De temps en temps
De trop
Deux s'amusent, trois s'embêtent
Le devoir des juges . . .
Dieu avec nous
Dieu défend le droit
Dieu et mon droit
Dieu le veuille!
Dieu mesure le vent (froid) à la
    brebis tondue
Dieu vous garde
Les dieux ont soif
Dis-moi ce que tu manges . . .
Docteur ès lettres
Don gratuit
Dos-à-dos
Double entendre
Double entente

French—*Continued*

La douce France
La douceur de vivre
Douceur et lumière
D'outre mer
Droit au travail
Droit comme un I
Le droit des gens
Droit d'impression réservés
Droit du mari
Droit du Seigneur
Droit et avant
Du fort au faible
Du haut en bas
Du sublime au ridicule . . .
Eau de vie
École des beaux-arts
École maternelle
Écrasez l'infâme!
Édition à tirage restreint
Édition de luxe
Eh bien!
L'élan vital
Embarras de richesses
Embarras du choix
L'Empire c'est la paix
L'empire des lettres
En ami
En arrière
En attendant
En avant
En bloc
En bonne foi
En clair
En congé
En courant
En dernier ressort
En déshabillé
En deux mots
En Dieu est ma fiance
En Dieu est tout
En effet
En évidence

En famille
Enfant de famille
Enfant de son siècle
Enfant gâté
Enfants perdus
Enfant terrible
Enfant trouvé
L'enfer des femmes . . .
En grande tenue
En grande toilette
En masse
En mauvaise odeur
L'ennemi du genre humain
En papillotes
En parenthèse
En passant
En petit comité
En plein air
En plein jour
En principe
En queue
En rapport
En règle
En revanche
En route!
En somme
En surtout
En tapinois
Entente cordiale
Entente demi-cordiale
En tout cas
Entre chien et loup
Entre deux feux
Entre deux vins
Entre nous
En vérité
En voiture!
Épater les bourgeois
Esprit de corps
Esprit de finesse
Esprit des lois
L'esprit de suite

305

LIST OF PHRASES ARRANGED BY LANGUAGES

French—*Continued*

L'esprit est toujours la dupe . . .
Esprit fort
Esprit gaulois
Est-ce possible?
L'état c'est moi
L'état major
Éternel devenir
L'étoile du Nord
Exemplaire d'auteur
Explication de texte
Les extrêmes se touchent
Une fable convenue
Facilité de parler . . .
Façon de parler
Faire d'une mouche . . .
Faire les yeux doux
Fait accompli
Fait à peindre
Faites votre devoir et . . .
Fait nouveau
La farce est jouée
Faute de mieux
Faux ami
Faux pas
Femme couverte
Femme de chambre
Femme de charge
Femme de trente ans
Femme fatale
Une femme grosse
Femme savante
Les femmes peuvent tout . . .
Ferme générale
Fermiers généraux
Fête champêtre
Fête des Fous
Fêtes de nuit
Feu d'artifice
Feu de joie
Feu d'enfer
Feu follet
Fille de joie

Fille d'honneur
Fils à papa
La fin couronne les œuvres
Fin de siècle
Finesse d'esprit
Fleur de lys
Flux de bouche
Flux de paroles
Folie de grandeur
Force de frappe
Force majeure
Fou qui se tait . . .
Les fous font les festins . . .
Franc-alleu
La France, fille aînée de l'Église
Franc-tireur
Frappé au froid
Frère de lait
Froides mains, chaud amour
Fuyez les dangers de loisir
Gage d'amour
Gaieté de cœur
Garde à cheval
Garde du corps
La Garde meurt . . .
Gardez la foi
Gardien de la paix
La génération spontanée . . .
La génie c'est la patience
Gens d'armes
Gens de condition
Gens d'église
Gens de guerre
Gens de la même famille
Gens de lettres
Gens de loi
Gens de peu
Gens de robe
Gens du monde
Les gens qui hésitent . . .
Gibier de potence
Gorge de pigeon

306

French—*Continued*

Goutte à goutte
Grâce à Dieu
Grande dame
Grande parure
La Grande Voleuse
Le Grand Monarque
Le grand prix
Grand seigneur
Les grands esprits se rencontrent
Le grand siècle
La gravité est un mystère . . .
Une grosse femme
Grosse tête, peu de sens
Guerre à mort
Guerre à outrance
L'habitude est une seconde nature
Haute bourgeoisie
Haute coiffure
Haute couture
Haute cuisine
La haute politique
Haut goût
Haut ton
Heureux les peuples . . .
L'histoire n'est qu'une fable . . .
Hommage d'auteur
Hommage d'éditeur
L'homme absurde . . .
Homme d'affaires
Homme de bien
Homme de guerre
Homme de lettres
Homme de paille
Homme d'épée
Homme d'esprit
Homme d'état
Homme de théâtre
Homme du monde
L'homme propose . . .
Les hommes rougissent . . .
Les hommes sont cause . . .
Honi (honni) soit qui . . .

Honnête homme
Hors concours
Hors de combat
Hors de propos
Hors de saison
Hors d'œuvre
Hors la loi
L'hôtel des Invalides
Hôtel de ville
Hôtel-Dieu
Hôtel garni
Hôtel meublé
Hurler avec les loups
L'hypocrisie est un hommage . . .
Ici on parle français
Idée fixe
Il a la mer à boire
Il a le diable au corps
Il a les défauts de ses qualités
Il a le vin mauvais
Il avait le diable au corps
Il connaît l'univers . . .
Il dit tout ce qu'il veut . . .
Il est bon d'avoir . . .
Il est bon de parler . . .
Il faut bonne mémoire . . .
Il faut cultiver notre jardin
Il faut laver son linge sale . . .
Il faut manger pour vivre . . .
Il faut marcher . . .
Il faut que la jeunesse se passe
Il n'a ni bouche ni éperon
Il n'a pas inventé la poudre
Il n'appartient qu'aux grands . . .
Il ne faut jamais défier un fou
Il ne faut pas disputer des goûts
Il ne faut pas mettre . . .
Il ne manquerait plus que ça
Il n'entend pas raillerie
Il n'est sauce que d'appétit
Il nous faut de l'audace . . .
Il n'y a de nouveau . . .

French—*Continued*

Il n'y a de pire sourd . . .
Il n'y a pas de grand homme . . .
Il n'y a pas moins d'éloquence . . .
Il n'y a plus de Pyrénées
Il n'y a point de déguisement . . .
Il n'y a que ceux qui ne font rien . . .
Il n'y a que le premier pas . . .
Il n'y a rien de mieux à faire . . .
Il rit bien qui rit le dernier
Il s'attache aux pas de —
Il se noierait . . .
Il sent le fagot
Il se recule pour mieux sauter
Il se voit par expérience . . .
Ils ne passeront pas
Ils n'ont rien appris . . .
Il vaut mieux employer . . .
Il vaut mieux s'exposer à l'ingratitude . . .
Il veut prendre la lune . . .
Il y a à parier que toute idée publique . . .
Impossible n'est pas . . .
L'injustice à la fin . . .
J'accuse
J'ai vécu
Jalousie de métier
Jardins à l'anglaise
Je maintiendrai
Je maintiendrai le droit
Je me fais pitié à moi-même
Je ne sais quoi
Je prends mon bien . . .
Je sème à tout vent
Je t'aime plus qu'hier . . .
Jeter de la poudre aux yeux
Jeter le manche après la cognée
Jets d'eau
Jeu de mots
Jeu d'esprit
Jeu de théâtre

Jeunesse dorée
Le jeu ne vaut pas la chandelle
Je vais chercher un grand Peut-être!
Je veux que le dimanche . . .
Je vis d'espoir
Joie de vivre
Jour gras
Jour maigre
Journée des Barricades
La Journée des Dupes
Joyeux Noël!
Juge de paix
Jugement de Dieu
Jugez un homme par ses questions . . .
Le Juif errant
Jusqu'au bout
Le juste milieu
J'y suis, j'y reste
Laissez aller
Laissez faire
Laissez passer
Langage des halles
La langue des femmes . . .
Langue d'oc
Langue d'oïl
Légion étrangère
Lèse majesté
Lettre d'avis
Lettre de cachet
Lettre de change
Lettre de créance
Levée en masse
Un lever de rideau
Liberté, égalité, fraternité
Lieu de réunion
Lit de justice
Livre de chevet
Livre de circonstances
Livre de poche
Livres d'heures

French—*Continued*

Loin des yeux, loin du cœur
Loyauté m'oblige
Lutte corps à corps
Ma chérie
Ma foi!
M'aidez!
Maintiens le droit
Maison de campagne
Maison de santé
Mais où sont les neiges d'antan?
Maître d'armes
Maître des hautes œuvres
Maître d'hôtel
Maladie du pays
Mal à propos
Mal de mer
Mal du pays
Malheur ne vient jamais seul
Le mal que nous faisons . . .
Manger son blé en herbe
Marchandise qui plaît . . .
Marcher à pas de loup
Marcher droit
Mardi gras
Mariage de conscience
Mariage de convenance
Mariage de la main gauche
Mariage de politique
Marque de fabrique
Mauvais coucheur
Mauvaise honte
Mauvaise plaisanterie
Mauvais goût
Mauvais quart d'heure
Mauvais sujet
Le méchant n'est jamais comique
Médecin, guéris-toi toi-même
La mémoire est nécessaire . . .
Ménage à trois
Menteur à triple étage
Merci beaucoup
Mettre de l'eau dans son vin

Meubles d'occasion
Mi-carême
Le mieux est l'ennemi du bien
Mieux vaut goujat debout . . .
Mise en page
Mise en scène
Le moine bourru
Mon cher
Mon cœur et ton cœur . . .
Le monde est le livre des femmes
Le monde va de lui-même
Mon Dieu!
Mont-de-piété
La moquerie est souvent . . .
La morgue littéraire
Mort Dieu (Mordieu)
Les morts ont toujours tort
Mot à mot
Mot de guet
Mot de l'énigme
Mots de terroir
Mots d'usage
Moulin à paroles
Le Moyen Age
Muet comme un poisson
Les murailles ont des oreilles
Nager entre deux eaux
Une nation boutiquière
Ne battre que d'une aile
Ne réveillez pas le chat . . .
N'est-ce pas?
Le nez de Cléopatre . . .
N'importe!
Ni plus, ni moins
La noblesse d'épée
Noblesse de robe
Noblesse oblige
Nom de guerre
Nom de plume
Nom de théâtre
Notre Dame
Notre défiance justifie . . .

French—*Continued*

Notre mérite nous attire . . .
Notre nature est dans le mouve-
ment . . .
Nourri dans le sérail . . .
Nous aimons toujours ceux . . .
Nous avons changé tout cela
Nous avons tous assez de force . . .
Nous ne trouvons guère de
gens . . .
Nous sommes tous dans le dé-
sert! . . .
Nous verrons
Nous verrons ce que nous verrons
Nouveau riche
Nouvelle série
La nuit tous les chats sont gris
Nul bien sans peine
Objet d'art
L'occasion fait le larron
Œil-de-bœuf
Œuvre de vulgarisation
Œuvres complètes
O Liberté, O Liberté, que de
crimes . . .
On connaît l'ami au besoin
On est souvent ferme . . .
On n'a jamais bon marché . . .
On ne donne rien . . .
On ne loue d'ordinaire . . .
On ne saurait faire une ome-
lette . . .
On ne se blâme . . .
On n'est jamais si heureux . . .
On n'est jamais si ridicule . . .
On ne trouve guère d'ingrats . . .
Oublier je ne puis
Où la chèvre est attaché . . .
Outre mer
Ouvrage de longue haleine
Pain bénit
La paix de Dieu
Paix fourrée

Palmes académiques
Papier mâché
Par accès
Par avance
Parbleu!
Par ci, par là
Par complaisance
Par dépit
Pardonnez-moi
Par excellence
Par exemple
Parfum de terroir
Par hasard
Paris vaut bien une messe
Parler à tort et à travers
La parole a été donnée . . .
Parole d'honneur
Les paroles sont faites . . .
Par parenthèse
Part du lion
Partie carrée
Parti pris
Partir, c'est mourir un peu
Pas à pas
Pas à pas on va bien loin
Pas de deux
Pas de nouvelles . . .
Pas de rose sans épines
Pas du tout
Pas seul
Pas si bête
Pâté de foie gras
La patience est amère . . .
Patte de velours
Pattes de mouche
Pauvre diable!
Peau d'âne
Peau de chagrin
Peine forte et dure
Pensée fait la grandeur . . .
Père de famille
Père du peuple

French—*Continued*

La perfide Albion
Les personnes faibles . . .
Petit à petit . . .
Petit bourgeois
Le petit caporal
Petit chaudron, grandes oreilles
La petite bourgeoisie
Petite pièce
Petites gens
La petitesse de l'esprit . . .
Petit maître
Petit mal
Petit nom
Petits jeux
Petit souper
Peu à peu
Peu d'hommes ont été admirés . . .
Pièce à thèse
Pièce de résistance
Pièce d'occasion
Pied à terre!
Pierre qui roule . . .
Pis-aller
Place aux dames!
Place d'armes
La plupart des gens ne jugent . . .
La plupart des hommes em-
    ploient . . .
Le plus brave des braves
Plus ça change . . .
Plus fait douceur que violence
Plus je vois les hommes . . .
Plus royaliste que le roi
Les plus sages ne le sont . . .
Plus sages que les sages
Point d'appui
Point d'argent . . .
Point de repère
Une poire pour la soif
Poisson d'avril
La politique n'a pas d'entrailles
Pomme de terre

La pompe des enterrements . . .
Poste restante
Potage au gras
Pour acquit
Pour épater les bourgeois
Pour faire rire
Pour le mérite
Pour passer le temps
Pour prendre congé
Pour rire
Prendre la balle au bond
Prendre la lune avec les dents
Prenez garde!
Preux chevalier
Privilège du roi
Prix fixe
Procès-verbal
Prochein (prochain) ami
Profits et pertes
Pur sang
Quand celui à qui l'on parle . . .
Quand même
Quand on parle du loup . . .
Les Quarante fauteuils
Quarante hommes, huit chevaux
Que diable allait-il faire . . .
Quel dommage!
Quelques grands avantages . . .
Qu'en dira le monde?
Les querelles ne dureraient pas . . .
Que sçais (sais)-je?
Que voulez-vous?
Qui a bu boira
Qui donne tôt, donne deux fois
Qui est près de l'église . . .
Qui m'aime, aime mon chien
Qui n'a santé n'a rien
Qui s'excuse, s'accuse
Qui va là?
Qui vive
Raison de plus
Raison d'état

French—*Continued*

Raison d'être
La reconnaissance est . . .
Le refus des louanges . . .
Rentes sur l'État
Répondre en Normand
Revenons à nos moutons
Rez-de-chaussée
Rien de plus éloquent . . .
Rien ne dure . . .
Rien ne pèse tant . . .
Rien ne réussit comme le succès
Rien n'est beau que le vrai
Rira bien qui rira le dernier
Rire dans sa barbe
Rire et faire rire
Ris de veau
Le roi est mort. Vive le roi!
Le roi le veut
Le roi règne . . .
Le roi s'avisera
Rois fainéants
Le Roi Soleil
Rôle de l'équipage
Roman à clef
Rouge-et-noire
Ruse de guerre
Sacre bleu
Le sage quelquefois évite le monde de peur d'être ennuyé
Salle à manger
Salle d'attente
Salle de jeu
Salle des pas perdus
Salle du Jeu de Paume
Sang-froid
Sans appel
Sans cérémonie
Sans culottes
Sans doute
Sans façon
Sans gêne
Sans pareil

Sans peur et sans reproche
Sans rime et sans raison
Sans souci
Sauve qui peut
Savoir faire
Savoir vivre
Les scènes à faire
Le secret d'ennuyer . . .
Selon les règles
Sens commun
Sens dessus dessous
Serpent d'église
Si Dieu n'existait pas . . .
Siècle des ténèbres
Siècle d'or
Si jeunesse savait . . .
Le silence éternel . . .
S'il vous plaît
Si nous n'avions point de défauts . . .
Si vous lui donnez un pied . . .
Société anonyme
Société en commandite
Son cœur est un luth suspendu . . .
Sot à triple étage
Souffler le chaud et le froid
Sous tous les rapports
Le style c'est l'homme
Succès de scandale
Succès d'estime
Succès fou
Sur le pavé
Sur le tapis
Sur place
Surtout, point de zèle
Table d'hôte
Tâche sans tache
Tant mieux
Tant pis
Tant soit peu
Tel est notre bon plaisir
Tel maître, tel valet

French—*Continued*

Tel quel
Tête-à-tête
Tête de veau
Tic douloureux
Tiens à la vérité
Tiers état
Tirage au sort
Tiré à quatre épingles
Toison d'or
Tombé des nues
Toujours en vedette
Toujours l'amour
Toujours perdrix
Toujours prêt
Tour de force
Tous droits réservés
Tous frais faits
Tout à fait
Tout à l'heure
Tout au contraire
Tout bien ou rien
Tout chemin mène . . .
Tout comprendre . . .
Tout de suite
Tout d'un coup
Toute la dignité de l'homme . . .
Le tout ensemble
Toute(s) proportion(s) gardée(s)
Tout est bien qui finit bien
Tout est perdu fors l'honneur
Tout le monde
Tout le monde se plaint . . .
Tout lui rit (sourit)
Tout s'en va . . .
Tranche de vie
Travaux forcés
Trente-et-quarante
Très bien
Trêve de Dieu
Trompe-l'œil
Trop de hâte gâte tout
Tuer le veau gras

L'union fait la force
Un roi, une loi, une foi
Un "tiens" vaut mieux . . .
Le vainqueur du vainqueur . . .
Ventre à terre
Vérité san peur
Vers de société
Vers libre
Victoire ou la mort
La vie à trois
Vigueur de dessus
Vin d'honneur
Vin du pays
Violon d'Ingres
Vis-à-vis
Vive la bagatelle!
Vive la différence!
Vive le roi!
Vivent les Gueux!
Vivre libre, ou mourir
Vogue la galère!
Voilà!
Voilà une autre chose
Voilà un homme!
Voir le dessous des cartes
Vol-au-vent
Volte-face
Vouloir rompre l'anguille . . .
Vous êtes orfèvre . . .
Vous y perdrez vos pas
Le vrai honnête homme . . .
Le vrai n'est pas toujours . . .
Le vrai peut quelquefois . . .
Vue d'oiseau
Wagons-lits

German

Abends wird der Faule fleissig
Adel sitzt im Gemüte . . .
Adler brüten keine Tauben
Alle Länder gute Menschen . . .

German—*Continued*

Aller Anfang ist schwer
Aller guten Dinge sind drei
Die Alten zum Rat . . .
Amt ohne Geld macht Diebe
Die Architektur ist die erstarrte Musik
Artz, hilf dir selbst
Auch ein Haar hat seinen Schatten
Auf Wiedersehen
Aus den Augen, aus dem Sinn
Aus Kindern werden Leute
Der Baum fällt nicht . . .
Bei Nacht sind alle . . .
Bellende Hunde beissen nicht
Besser spät als nie
Das Beste ist gut genug
Blut und Eisen
Borgen macht Sorgen
Böse Beispiele verderben . . .
Danke schön
Das ist mir Wurst . . .
Deutsches Reich
Deutschland, Deutschland . . .
Das Ding an sich
Donner und Blitz!
Drang nach Osten
Du, du liegst mir im Herzen
Durchgang verboten
Edel ist, der edel tut
Ehre, dem Ehre gebührt
Ehrlich währt am längsten
Eile mit Weile
Eine Hand wäscht die andere
Ein eigner Herd . . .
Eine Schwalbe macht . . .
Ein Reich, ein Volk, ein Führer
Ein Unglück kommt . . .
Eisen und Blut
Ende gut, alles gut
Entbehre gern . . .
Entbehren sollst du!
Erfahrung ist die beste Schule

Das Erste und Letzte . . .
Es gibt, sagt man, für den Kammerdiener keinen Helden
Es irrt der Mensch . . .
Es ist nicht alles Gold . . .
Es ist Schade
Es kann der Frömmste nicht . . .
Es wird nichts so schön . . .
Das Ewig-Weibliche . . .
Der Feind steht in eigenen Lager
Eine feste Burg . . .
Flak
Frisch begonnen . . .
Fröhliche Weihnachten
Das fünfte Rad am Wagen
Für Herren
Der Fürst ist der erste Diener . . .
Geben Sie acht!
Gebranntes Kind scheut das Feuer
Geflügelte Worte
Geheime Staatspolizei
Geld behält das Feld
Gesagt, getan
Gesamtverzeichnis der ausländischen Zeitschriften
Das Gesetz nur kann . . .
Gestapo
Gleich und gleich . . .
Glückliches Neujahr!
Glück und Glas . . .
Gott behüte!
Der gottbetrunkene Mensch
Gott macht gesund . . .
Gott mit uns
Gott sei Dank
Gott soll hüten!
Der grosse Heide
Gute Nacht
Guten Morgen
Gute Ware lobt sich selbst
Hänge nicht alles . . .
Heil dir im Siegerkranz

German—*Continued*

Heute Deutschland . . .
Heute rot, morgen tot
Hier stehe ich! . . .
Hilf dir selbst . . .
Hunde, die bellen . . .
Hunger ist der beste Koch
Ich bin der Geist . . .
Ich dien
Im Wein ist Warheit
Irrtümer vorbehalten
Jeder Esel kann kritisieren
Jeder ist Herr in seinem Hause
Jeder ist seines Glückes . . .
Jeder ist sich selbst . . .
Jeder weiss, wo ihn . . .
Je höher der Baum . . .
Kalte Hände, warme Liebe
Keine Antwort ist . . .
Kein Unglück so gross . . .
Kinder sind Kinder
Kinder und Narren . . .
Kleine Leute grosse Herzen
Die kleinen Diebe hängt man . . .
Eine kleine Wurst . . .
Das kleinste Haar wirft . . .
Der Krieg ist lustig . . .
Küche, Kirche und Kinder
Kürze ist des Witzes Würze
Lade nicht Alles . . .
Leben Sie wohl!
Lebensraum
Leichter ist Vergeben . . .
Liebe ohne Gegenliebe . . .
Lügen haben kurze Beine
Macht geht vor Recht
Man ist was man isst
Man kann, was man will . . .
Man kennt den Baum . . .
Man lernt nichts kennen . . .
Man muss das Eisen smieden . . .
Mehr Licht
Meine Damen und Herren

Meine Zeit wird schon kommen
Mein Herr
Mein Kampf
Mein Name ist Hase . . .
Der Mensch denkt, Gott lenkt
Der Mensch ist was er isst
Mit dem Wissen wächst . . .
Mit der Dummheit kämpfen . . .
Mit grossen Herren ist nicht gut . . .
Mit innigster Ergebenheit . . .
Mit umgehender Post
Morgen, morgen . . .
Morgenstund' hat Gold . . .
Muss ist eine harte . . .
Nach Canossa . . .
Nach Christi Geburt
Nacheifern ist beneiden
Nazi
Neue Besen kehren gut
Nicht die Kinder bloss speist . . .
Nicht wahr?
Not kennt kein Gebot
Nur der verdient . . .
Nur wer die Sehnsucht . . .
Ohne Arbeit kein Gewinn
Ohne Hast, ohne Rast
Die Philosophie des Als-ob
Die Politik ist keine exakte . . .
Die Probe eines Genusses . . .
Prosit Neujahr!
Rast ich, so rost ich
Ratschläge für ausländische . . .
Reden ist Silber . . .
Die Religion . . . ist das Opium des Volkes
Rom ward nicht . . .
Sage mir, mit wem du . . .
Schlafen Sie wohl!
Selbst ist der Mann
Sieg Heil
So geht es in der Welt

German—*Continued*

So Gott will
Soll und Haben
So schnell als möglich
Spurlos versenkt
Die stille Woche
Sturm und Drang
Der Tag
Übung macht den Meister
Um Christi willen
Undank ist der Welt(en) Lohn
Und so weiter
Ein unnütz Leben . . .
Verdammte Bedürfnislosigkeit
Verweile doch! . . .
Viele Händ' machen . . .
Viele Köche verderben . . .
Vorwärts mit Gott!
Die Wacht am Rhein
Die Wahrheit ist eine Perle . . .
Wahrheit und Dichtung
Was ich nicht weiss . . .
Was man nicht kann meiden . . .
Das Weib sieht tief . . .
Wein auf Bier . . .
Wein, Weib, und Gesang
Die Weisheit der Gasse
Die Weisheit ist nur . . .
Welche Regierung die beste sei? . . .
Weltanschauung
Weltmacht oder Niedergang
Wenige wissen, wieviel man . . .
Wenn die Katze nicht zu Hause . . .
Wer dem Pöbel dient . . .
Wer Fremde Sprachen nicht . . .
Wer gar zu viel bedenkt . . .
Das Werk lobt den Meister
Wer liebt nicht Weib, Wein . . .
Wer nicht will, der hat schon
Wer verachtet, der will kaufen
Wer zuletzt lacht . . .
Wie der Herr, so der Knecht
Wie gewonnen, so zerronen

Wir Deutschen fürchten Gott . . .
Wir lieben unsern Führer
Wollt ihr immer leben?
Zartem Ohre, halbes Wort
Zum Donnerwetter!
Zwei Hälften machen zwar ein Ganzes . . .
Zwei Seelen und ein Gedanke . . .
Zwei Seelen wohnen . . .

Greek

Aei gar eu piptousin . . .
Agapa ton plesion
Anagke oude theoi machontai
Andra moi ennepe . . .
Aner ho pheugon kai palin . . .
Arche hemisy pantos
Asbestos gelos
Biblia a-biblia
Chaire
Dis krambe thanatos
Dos moi pou sto kai . . .
En nukti boule . . .
Entelecheia
Epea pteroenta
Eureka!
Galilaie nenikekas
Glaucopis Athene
Gnothi seauton
Hapax legomenon
He glossa omomoch' . . .
Ho bios brachys . . .
Hodos chameliontos
Hoi polloi
Hon hoi theoi philousin . . .
Ho sophos en auto . . .
Hysteron proteron
Iatre, therapeuson seauton
ICHTHYS
IHS
Kairon gnothi

LIST OF PHRASES ARRANGED BY LANGUAGES

Greek—*Continued*

Kai su ei ekeinon . . .
Kai su, teknon
Kalokagathia
Ktema es aei
Kyrie eleison
Lathe biosas
Medeis ageometretos eisito
Meden agan
Mega biblion, mega kakon
Metron ariston
Mia gar chelidon . . .
Neos d'apollyth' hontin' . . .
Nous pathetikos
Nous poietikos
Opse theon aleousi myloi . . .
Panta rei (rhei)
Panton metron anthropos estin
Phi Beta Kappa
Phtheirousin ethe chresth' . . .
Prin d'an teleutese . . .
Sophois homilon kautos . . .
Speude bradeos
Thalassa, thalassa
Thalatta, thalatta!
Theo(i) mono(i) doxa
Theos ek mechanes
To kalon
To me on

Hebrew

Bar Mizvah
B'nai B'rith
Shalom alekhem

Irish

A cushla agus asthore machree
A-suilish mahuil agus . . .
Avic machree
Céad míle fáilte!

Colleen bawn
Cushla machree, mavourneen
Dail Eireann
Dia duit
Dia linn
Erin go bragh!
Fianna Fail
Seanad Eireann
Sinn Fein
Soggarth aroon
Uisge beatha
Wurra dheelish!

Italian

A beneplacito
A buon vino . . .
A cader va . . .
A cane scottato . . .
A cappella
A cavallo donato . . .
Accelerando
A chi consiglia non duole . . .
A chi dici il tuo segreto . . .
A chi fa male . . .
A chi ha testa . . .
A chi vuole . . .
Adagio
Adagio ma non troppo
Ad ogni uccello . . .
Ad un colpo non cade . . .
Ai mali estremi . . .
Al bisogno si conosce un amico
Al bugiardo non si crede la verità
Al confessor, medico, ed avvo-
    cato . . .
Al dente
Al fine
Al fresco
Alla barba dei pazzi . . .
Alla cappella
Alla vostra salute

Italian—*Continued*

L'allegro
Allegro moderato
All' ottava
Al nemico che fugge . . .
Al primo colpo . . .
Alta vendetta d'alto silenzio . . .
Alto rilievo
Ama l'amico tuo col vizio suo
Amato non sarai . . .
Amico d'ognuno . . .
Amore è cieco
Anch' io son' pittore
Andante
A piacere
Appetito non vuol salsa
A prima vista
A rivederci
Articolo di fondo
Gli assenti hanno torto
A tuo beneplacito
A vostra salute
Avvocato del diavolo
Bacio di bocca . . .
La barba non fa il filosofo
Basso buffo
Basso rilievo
Batti il ferro . . .
Bel canto
Un bel pezzo di carne
Il bel sesso
Berretta in mano . . .
Bisogna andare . . .
Bisogna battere il ferro . . .
Bona roba
Buona notte
Buon capo del anno!
Buon giorno
Buon Natale
Cane scottato ha paura . . .
Cara sposa
Caro sposo
Casa il figlio quando vuoi . . .

Castello che dà orecchia . . .
Cavalier(e) errante
Cavalier(e) servente
Che sarà sarà
Chi ama, crede
Chi ama me . . .
Chi ascolta alla porta . . .
Chiave d'oro . . .
Chi ben vive . . .
Chi compra il magistrato . . .
Chi dice i fatti suoi . . .
Chi dorme coi cani . . .
Chiesa libera in libero stato
Chi fa il conto senza l'oste . . .
Chi ha denti, non ha pane . . .
Chi la dura la vince
Chi lo sa?
Chi molte cose comincia . . .
Chi niente sa . . .
Chi non ama il vino, la donna . . .
Chi non fa, non falla
Chi non ha danari in borsa . . .
Chi non rompe l'uova . . .
Chi non sa adulare . . .
Chi si scusa senz' . . .
Chi tace acconsente
Chi tace confessa
Chi t'ha offeso . . .
Chi troppo abbraccia . . .
Chi va al mulino . . .
Chi va piano, va sano . . .
Chi vuol il lavoro mal fatto . . .
Come sopra
Commedia dell' arte
La commedia è finita
Le comparazioni sono tutte odiose
Con amore
Concerto grosso
Con diligenza
Con dolore
Con furia
Con molta passione

318

Italian—*Continued*

Consiglio europeo per le ricerche nucleari
Con svantaggio grande si fa la guerra . . .
Conti chiari, amici cari
Corpo di Bacco!
Cosa nostra
Cosa rara
Così così
Così fan tutte
Così fan tutti
Da camera
Da capo
Da capo al fine
Da chi mi fido, mi guardi Iddio . . .
Dal detto al fatto . . .
Dalla mano alla bocca . . .
Dalla rapa non si cava sangue
Darne consiglio/Spesso non sa chi vuole . . .
Dei gusti non se ne disputa
Del credere
Delle ingiurie il remedio è . . .
Del senno di poi . . .
I denari del comune sono come . . .
Il diavolo non è così brutto . . .
Di bravura
Di buona volontà sta pieno l'inferno
Di grado in grado
Di il vero ed affronterai il diavolo
Dimmi con chi vai . . .
Dio vi benedica
Di salto
Di seconda mano
Le disgrazie non vengon mai sole
Dolce far niente
Dolce stil nuovo
La dolce vita
La donna è mobile
Dove l'oro parla . . .
Dove sono molti cuochi . . .

Due teste valgono più . . .
È cattivo vento che non è buono . . .
Egli è povero come un topo di chiesa
E la sua volontate è nostra pace
È meglio aver oggi un uovo . . .
È meglio domandar che errare
È meglio esser mendicante che ignorante
È meglio il cuor felice . . .
È meglio piegare che rompere
È meglio tardi che mai
È meglio un uccello in gabbia . . .
E pur si muove!
È sempre l'ora
La fame non vuol leggi
Far d'una mosca un elefante
Felice ritorno!
Figlie e vetri son sempre . . .
Finchè la pianta è tenera . . .
Forte
La fortuna aiuta i pazzi
La Forza del destino
Fra Modesto non fu mai priore
I frutti proibiti sono i più dolci
Fuori commercio
Fuori i barbari
Fuori le mura
Furia francese
Giovane santo, diavolo vecchio
Glissando
I gran dolori sono muti
Guarda innanzi che tu salti
Guerra cominciata . . .
L'imitazione del male supera . . .
In petto
In terra di ciechi . . .
In un giorno non si fe' Roma
Italia farà da se
Italia irredenta
Lasciate ogni speranza . . .

Italian—*Continued*

Lauda la moglie e tieni donzello
Lavoro di commesso
La letteratura amena
Lingua toscana in bocca romana
Lontan dagli occhi . . .
Il lupo cangia il pelo . . .
Madre divina
Maestro dei maestri
Maestro di cappella
Il Maestro di color che sanno
Maggiore fretta, minore atto
La mala erba cresce presto
Mamma mia!
Un matto sa più domandare . . .
Metter il carro innanzi ai buoi
Mezza voce
Mezzo forte
Mezzo piano
Mezzo termine
Moderato cantabile
Molto fumo e poco arrosto
Il mondo è di chi ha pazienza
Il mondo è di chi se lo piglia
Il mondo è un bel libro . . .
Monte di pietà
Natura il fece . . .
Nessun maggior dolore . . .
Niente più tosto si secca . . .
Non fu mai partito savio . . .
Non merita nome di creatore . . .
Non ogni fiore fa buon odore
Non ogni giorno è festa
Non ragioniam di lor . . .
Non troppo presto
Nulla nuova, buona nuova
Ogni debole ha sempre . . .
Ogni medaglia ha il suo rovescio
Ogni pazzo vuol dar consiglio
Opera buffa
Opera inedita
Ora e sempre
Oro è che oro vale

Ottava rima
I paragoni son odiosi
Le parole son femmine . . .
Passato el periculo . . .
Pensano gl'innamorati che gli altri . . .
Il penseroso
I pensieri non pagano dazio
Per contante
Per conto
Per mese
Per piacere
Per più strade si va a Roma
Pianissimo
Pianississimo
Piano
Pietra mossa non fa muschio
Più che il martello dura l'incudine
Più tengono a memoria . . .
Piuttosto (più tosto) mendicante . . .
Poco a poco
Povero come un topo di chiesa
La povertà è la madre . . .
La pratica val più della grammatica
Presto e bene, non si conviene
Presto maturo, presto marcio
Prima donna
Quando la gatta non v'è . . .
Quel che pare burla . . .
Quel dominio è solo durabile . . .
Quel giorno più non vi leggemmo avante
Questo ragazzo ci farà dimenticar tutti
Ritardando
Saluto il primo Re d'Italia
Una scopa nuova spazza bene
Sdegno d'amante poco dura
Se non è vero, è ben travato
Socorro non viene mai tardi
Sotto voce

Italian—*Continued*

Spogliar Pietro per vestir Paolo
Il stilo volgare
Tal padrone, tal servitore
Tanto buono che val niente
Terra irredenta
Terza rima
Traduttore, traditore
La troppa familiarità . . .
Tutte le strade conducono a Roma
Tutti i gusti son gusti
L'ultima che se perde . . .
Una rondine non fa l'estate
Una rondine non fa primavera
Gli uomini hanno gli anni che . . .
Uomo universale
Vaso vuoto suona meglio
Vedi Napoli e poi mori
Vender il miele a chi ha le api
La verità è figlia del tempo
Verso sciolto
Via il gatto ballano i sorci
Viola da braccio
Viola da gamba
Viva il papa
Voce di testa
Volto sciolto e pensieri stretti

Late Latin

Banco regis
Curia advisari vult
In commendam
Scandalum magnatum

Latin

Ab abusu ad usum . . .
Ab asino lanam
Abeunt studia in mores
Ab extra
Ab extrinseco
Ab hoc et ab hac et ab illa

Abiit ad majores
Abiit ad plures
Abiit, excessit, evasit, erupit
Ab imo pectore
Ab incunabulis
Ab initio
Ab initio temporis
Ab intestato
Ab intra
Ab invito
Ab irato
Abnormis sapiens crassaque Minerva
Ab origine
A bove majore discit . . .
Ab ovo
Ab ovo usque ad mala
Abscissio infiniti
Absens haeres non erit
Absente reo
Absit invidia
Absit omen
Absque argento omnia vana
Absque ulla conditione
Absurdum quippe est ut alios . . .
Ab uno disce omnes
Abusus non tollit usum
A capite ad calcem
Accedas ad curiam
Accessit
Accusare nemo se debet
Acerbarum facetiarum apud praepotentes . . .
Acetum Italum
A cruce salus
Acta est fabula
Actum ne agas
Actus Dei nemini facit injuriam
Actus me invito factus . . .
Actus non facit reum nisi . . .
Actus purus
Ad amussim

Latin—*Continued*

Ad arbitrium
Ad astra per aspera
Ad captandam benevolentiam
Ad captandum vulgus
Ad cautelam
Adde parvum parvo . . .
A Deo et Rege
Adeste, Fideles
Ad extremum
Adgnosco veteris vestigia flammae
Ad gustum
Ad hoc
Ad hominem
Adhuc neminem cognovi poetam qui . . .
Ad impossibile nemo tenetur
Ad infinitum
Ad interim
Ad internecionem
Ad judicium
Ad Kalendas Graecas
Ad libitum
Ad limina Apostolorum
Ad litem
Ad literam
Ad majorem Dei gloriam
Ad manum
Ad multos annos
Ad nauseam
Ad oculos
Ad patres
Ad perpetuam rei memoriam
Ad rem
Adscriptus glebae
Adsum
Ad summum
Ad unguem
Ad unum omnes
Ad usum
Ad utrumque paratus
Ad valorem
Adversis etenim frangi . . .

Ad vitam aut culpam
Advocatus diaboli
Advocatus juventutis
Aegrescit medendo
Aegrotat daemon, monachus . . .
Aegroto dum anima est . . .
Aequam memento rebus in arduis . . .
Aequo animo
Aerarium sanctius
Aes triplex
Aetas parentum, peior avis . . .
Aeternum servans sub pectore vulnus
Afflavit Deus et dissipantur
A fortiori
Agenti incumbit probatio
Age quod agis
Ager publicus
Aggregatio mentium
Agnus Dei
Aio te, Aeacida, Romanos vincere posse
Alas sustineo
A latere
Alcinoo poma dare
Aliena vitia in oculis habemus . . .
Alieni appetens, sui profusus
Alieni juris
Aliquando bonus dormitat Homerus
Aliquis in omnibus . . .
Alitur vitium vivitque tegendo
Aliud corde premunt . . .
Alium silere quod voles . . .
Alma mater
Alma mater studiorum
Alma Redemptoris Mater
Alter ego
Alter idem
Alter ipse amicus

Latin—*Continued*

Altissima flumina minimo sono labuntur
Ama nesciri
Amantes, amentes
Amantium irae amoris . . .
Ama si vis amari
A maximis ad minima
Ambigendi locus
A mensa et toro
Amicus certus in re incerta . . .
Amicus curiae
Amicus humani generis
Amicus Plato, sed magis amica veritas
Amicus usque ad aras
Amittit merito proprium qui . . .
Amoenitates studiorum
Amor dei intellectualis
Amor fati
Amor gignit amorem
Amor nummi
Amor omnibus idem
Amor patriae
Amor vincit omnia
Anathema sit!
Ancilla theologiae
Angeli, non Angli
Anguis in herba
Animae dimidium meae
Anima naturaliter Christiana
Animis opibusque parati
Animo et fide
Animus furandi
Animus testandi
An nescis longas regibus esse manus?
Anno aetatis suae
Anno ante Christum
Anno Domini
Anno humanae salutis
Anno mundi
Anno urbis conditae

Annuit coeptis
Annus luctus
Annus magnus *or* Platonicus
Annus mirabilis
Ante bellum
Ante lucem
Ante tubam trepidat
Ante victoriam ne canas triumphum
Anulatus aut doctus aut fatuus
Apologia pro vita sua
A posse ad esse
A posteriori
Apparatus criticus
Apparent rari nantes . . .
Appetitus rationi oboediant
A primo ad ultimum
A priori
Aqua fortis
Aqua vitae
Aquila non captat muscas
Ara pacis
Arbiter bibendi
Arbiter elegantiae
Arbiter literarum
Arbores serit diligens agricola . . .
Arcades ambo
Arcana imperii
Arcani disciplina
Ardentia verba
Argumenti gratia
Argumentum ad crumenam
Argumentum ad hominem
Argumentum ad ignorantiam
Argumentum ad invidiam
Argumentum ad judicium
Argumentum ad misericordiam
Argumentum ad populum
Argumentum ad rem
Argumentum ad verecundiam
Argumentum baculinum
Arma virumque cano

Latin—*Continued*

Ars (artis) est celare artem
Ars artium omnium conservatrix
Ars gratia artis
Ars longa, vita brevis
Ars omnibus communis
Ars Poetica
Ars prima regni est posse . . .
Artes perditae
Asinus ad lyram
Asinus asino et sus sui pulcher
Aspice, viator
Astraea Redux
A tergo
Athanasius contra mundum
At spes non fracta
Audendo magnus tegitur timor
Audentes deus ipse juvat
Audentes fortuna juvat
Aude sapere
Audi alteram partem
Aura popularis
Aurea mediocritas
Aurea ne credas . . .
Aurea prima sata est aetas . . .
Auribus teneo lupum
Auri sacra fames
Aurora borealis
Aurum potabile
Aut amat aut odit mulier . . .
Aut Caesar aut nullus (aut nihil)
Aut disce, aut discede . . .
Aut doce aut disce aut discede
Aut vincere aut mori
Avaritiam si tollere vultis . . .
Ave atque vale
Ave Maria
A verbis ad verbera
A vinculo matrimonii
Basis virtutum constantia
Beatae memoriae
Beati pacifici
Beati possidentes

Beati qui lugent
Beatus ille qui procul negotiis
Bella matribus detestata
Bellum ita suscipiatur ut . . .
Bellum omnium contra omnes
Benedicite Domino!
Beneficium accipere . . .
Beneficium clericale
Beneficium egenti bis dat . . .
Bene qui conjiciet . . .
Bene qui latuit, bene vixit
Berenicem statim ab urbe . . .
Biblia pauperum
Bis dat qui cito dat
Bis peccare in bello non licet
Bis pueri senes
Bona fide
Bona rerum secundarum opta-
    bilia . . .
Bona vacantia
Boni pastoris est tondere . . .
Bonis avibus
Bonis nocet quisquis . . .
Bonum commune
Bonum ex integra causa . . .
Brevi manu
Brevis esse laboro . . .
Brutum fulmen
Cacoethes carpendi
Cacoethes loquendi
Cacoethes scribendi
Cadit quaestio
Caelum, non animum mutant . . .
Calceus major subvertit
Callida junctura
Calvo turpius est nihil comato
Canimus surdis
Canis in praesepi
Canis timidus vehementius . . .
Cantabit vacuus coram latrone
    viator
Cantus planus

Latin—*Continued*

Capias
Capias ad satisfaciendum
Caput gerat lupinum
Caput mortuum
Caput mundi
Carpe diem . . .
Cassis tutissima virtus
Casta est, quam nemo rogavit
Castella in Hispania
Castigat ridendo mores
Castigo te non quod odio . . .
Casus belli
Casus conscientiae
Casus foederis
Casus fortuitus
Causa finalis
Cave ab homine unius libri
Caveat emptor
Caveat venditor
Cave canem
Cavendo tutus
Cave quid dicis, quando et cui
Cedant arma togae
Celsae graviore casu . . .
Censor deputatus
Cepi corpus
Certiorari
Cetera desunt
Ceteris paribus
Chimaera bombinans in vacuo
Cineri gloria sera venit
Circuitus verborum
Circulus in probando
Circulus vitiosus
Citius venit periculum . . .
Civilitas successit barbarum
Civiliter mortuus
Civis Romanus sum
Civitas optimo jure
Civitas sine suffragio
Civitates foederatae
Civitates liberae et immunes

Civium in moribus rei publicae
    salus
Clarum et venerabile nomen
Cloaca maxima
Coeptis ingentibus adsis
Cogito, ergo sum
Cognovit actionem
Comes facundus in via . . .
Comitas inter gentes
Comitia centuriata
Communibus annis
Conatus sese preservandi
Concordia discors
Congregatio de Propaganda Fide
Conjunctis viribus
Consensus facit legem
Consilio melius vinces . . .
Consilium abeundi
Consuetudo fit altera natura
Consuetudo pro lege servatur
Consultum ultimum
Consummatum est
Conticuere omnes, intentique . . .
Contra bonos mores
Contra mundum
Copia verborum
Coram nobis
Coram non judice
Coram populo
Coram publico
Cormach MacCarthy fortis me
    fieri facit . . .
Cor ne edito
Corpus Christi
Corpus delicti
Corpus Juris Canonici
Corpus Juris Civilis
Corpus juris clausum
Corrigenda
Corrumpunt bonos mores collo-
    quia mala
Corruptio optimi pessima

Latin—*Continued*

Corruptissima in republica pluri-
    mae leges
Corva sinistra
Crambe repetita
Cras amet qui numquam . . .
Crassa negligentia
Credat Judaeus Apella . . .
Credat qui vult
Credebant hoc grande nefas . . .
Crede experto
Crede ut intelligas
Credo quia impossibile . . .
Credo ut intelligam
Credula res amor est
Crescat scientia, vita excolatur
Crescit amor nummi . . .
Crescite et multiplicamini
Crescit eundo
Creta an carbone notandum?
Crux ansata
Crux criticorum
Crux interpretum
Crux mathematicorum
Cucullus non facit monachum
Cui bono?
Cui malo?
Cui peccare licet . . .
Cujus est regio, illius est religio
Cujus est solum . . .
Culpa lata
Culpa levissima
Culpam majorum posteri luunt
Culpam poena premit comes
Cum grano salis
Cum inimico nemo in gratiam
    tuto redit
Cum laude
Cum licet fugere, ne quaere litem
Cum privilegio ad imprimendum
    solum
Cum tacent, clamant
Cunctando restituit rem

Cura animarum
Curia regis
Curiosa felicitas
Currente calamo
Curriculum vitae
Currus bovem trahit praepostere
Cursus honorum
Custos Brevium
Custos morum
Custos Privati Sigilli
Custos Rotulorum
Custos Sigilli
Cymini (cumini) sectores
Dabit deus his quoque finem
Daemon meridianus
Da locum melioribus
Damnant quod non intelligunt
Damnosa hereditas
Damnum absque injuria
Dare pondus idonea fumo
Data et accepta
Davus sum, non Oedipus
Debitor non praesumitur donare
De bonis propriis
Deceptio visus
Decessit sine prole
Decies repetita placebit
Decipimur specie recti
Decipit frons prima multos
De Civitate Dei
De Consolatione Philosophiae
Decori decus addit avito
De die in diem
De duobus malis . . .
De facto
Defensor Fidei
De fide
De fontibus non disputandum
De gustibus non est disputandum
Dei gratia
Dei judicium
De integro

Latin—*Continued*

De internis non judicat praetor
Dei plena sunt omnia
De jure
De lana caprina
Delator temporis acti
Delenda est Carthago
Deliberando saepe perit occasio
Deliciae epularum
Deliciae generis humani
Deliciae meae puellae
Delirant reges . . .
Delirium tremens
De lunatico inquirendo
Dementia praecox
Dementia senilis
De minimis non curat lex
De mortuis nil nisi bonum
Denarius Dei
De nihilo nihil
De nobis fabula narrabitur
De novo
Deo adjuvante, non timendum
Deo duce, ferro comitante
Deo favente
Deo gratias
Deo juvante
De omni re scibili . . .
Deo, non fortuna
Deo volente
De pilo pendet
De profundis clamavi . . .
De proprio motu
Desunt inopiae multa . . .
Detinet
Detur digniori
Detur pulchriori
Deum cole, regem serva
Deus est in pectore nostro
Deus ex machina
Deus providebit
Deus vult
Devastavit

Dicere solebat nullum esse librum
  tam malum . . .
Dicique beatus ante obitum . . .
Dic mihi, si fias ut leo . . .
Dictum meum pactum
Dictum (verbum) sapienti . . .
Diem perdidi
Die non
Dies ater
Dies faustus
Dies infaustus
Dies Irae
Dies natalis
Di faciant, laudis summa . . .
Difficile est custodire . . .
Difficile est longum subito . . .
Difficile est proprie communia di-
  cere
Difficile est saturam non scribere
Difficilia quae pulchra
Difficilis in otio quies
Dignus vindice nodus
Di immortales
Di indigetes
Di inferi
Dii penates
Dilexi justitiam . . .
Di manes
Dimidium facti qui coepit habet
Dirigo
Dis aliter visum
Disce ut doceas
Disciplina arcani
Disciplina praesidium civitatis
Disjecti (disjecta) membra poetae
Dis manibus
Ditat Deus
Divide et impera
Divide ut regnes
Divina natura dedit agros . . .
Divina particula aurae
Docendo discimus

Latin—*Continued*

Doctor Angelicus
Doctor Invincibilis
Doctor Irrefragabilis
Doctor Legum
Doctor Mirabilis
Doctor Seraphicus
Doctor Subtilis
Doctor Universalis
Dolendi modus, timendi non item
Doli capax
Dolus an virtus . . .
Domine, dirige nos
Domini canes
Dominus illuminatio mea
Dominus vobiscum
Domus Procerum
Donatio mortis causa
Donec eris felix . . .
Do ut des
Do ut facias
Dramatis personae
Dubium facti
Dubium juris
Duces tecum
Ducit amor patriae
Ducunt volentem fata . . .
Dulce decus meum
Dulce est desipere in loco
Dulce et decorum est pro patria
    mori
Dum bene se gesserit
Dum casta
Dum Deus calculat . . .
Dummodo sit dives . . .
Dum spiro spero
Dum vita est, spes est
Dum vivimus, vivamus
Duos qui sequitur lepores . . .
Duoviri sacris faciundis
Dura lex sed lex
Durante absentia
Durante minore aetate

Durante viduitate
Durante vita
Durum et durum non faciunt
    murum
Dux femina facti
Eadem, sed aliter
Ecce homo
Ecce iterum Crispinus!
Ecce signum
Ecclesia supplet
E consensu gentium
E contra
E contrario
E converso
Editio princeps
E (ex) re nata
Effodiuntur opes . . .
E flamma petere cibum
Ego et Rex meus
Ego sum rex Romanus . . .
Eheu fugaces, Postume . . .
Ejusdem generis
Ejus nulla culpa est . . .
Elapso tempore
Empta dolore docet experientia
Ense petit placidam . . .
Entia non sunt multiplicanda . . .
Eo ipso
E pluribus unum
Eripuit caelo fulmen . . .
Errare humanum est
Errata
Esse oportet ut vivas . . .
Esse quam videri
Esse rei est percipi
Est ars etiam maledicendi
Est modus in rebus
Esto perpetua
Esto quod esse videris
Est quaedam flere voluptas
Estque pati poenas . . .
Et alibi

LIST OF PHRASES ARRANGED BY LANGUAGES

Latin—*Continued*

Et alii, aliae
Et bonum quo antiquius . . .
Et cetera
Et hoc genus omne
Etiam capillus unus . . .
Et id genus omne
Et qui nolunt occidere quemquam . . .
Et semel emissum volat . . .
Et sequentes *or* et sequentia
Et sic de ceteris
Et sic de similibus
Et sic porro
Et spes et ratio studiorum . . .
Et tu, Brute
Et uxor
Et verbum caro factum est
Et vir
Ex abrupto
Ex abundantia cordis . . .
Ex aequo
Ex animo
Ex capite
Ex cathedra
Excellentia sanandi causa
Excelsior
Exceptio probat regulam
Exceptis excipiendis
Ex comitate
Ex concesso
Ex curia
Excusatio non petita . . .
Excussit subjecto Pelion Ossae
Ex debito justitiae
Ex desuetudine amittuntur privilegia
Ex dono
Exeat
Exegi monumentum aere perennius
Exempla sunt odiosa
Exempli gratia

Ex ephebis
Ex (e) silentio
Exeunt omnes
Ex gratia
Ex grege
Ex hypothesi
Ex imo corde
Exitus acta probat
Ex libris
Ex luna scientia
Ex malis moribus bonae leges . . .
Ex mero motu
Ex necessitate rei
Ex nihilo nihil fit
Ex officio
Ex opere operantis
Ex opere operato
Ex ore infantium
Ex Oriente lux . . .
Ex parte
Ex pede Herculem
Experientia docet stultos
Experimentum crucis
Experto crede
Experto credite
Expertus metuit
Explicit
Ex post facto
Expressis verbis
Ex professo
Ex relatione
Ex tacito
Ex tempore
Extinctus amabitur idem
Extra ecclesiam nulla salus
Extra muros
Extra ordinem
Extra situm
Ex umbris et imaginibus in veritatem
Ex ungue leonem
Ex vi termini

Latin—*Continued*

Ex vitio alterius sapiens . . .
Ex voto
Faber quisque fortunae suae
Fabricando fit faber
Fabula palliata
Fabula togata
Facile est inventis addere
Facile omnes, quom valemus . . .
Facile princeps
Facilis descensus Averno
Facio ut des
Facio ut facias
Facit indignatio versum
Facta, non verba
Faenum habet in cornu
Faex populi
Falsa lectio
Falsus in uno, falsus in omnibus
Fama clamosa
Fama, malum qua non aliud . . .
Fama nihil est celerius
Fama semper vivat
Fames est optimus coquus
Fas est et ab hoste doceri
Fata obstant
Fata viam invenient
Fax mentis incendium gloriae
Fecit
Felicitas multos habet amicos
Felix quem faciunt aliena . . .
Felix qui potuit rerum cognoscere
  causas
Ferae naturae
Feriunt summos fulgura montes
Ferme acerrima proximorum odia
Ferrum, dum in igni candet . . .
Ferrum ferro acuitur
Festina lente
Fiat experimentum in corpore vili
Fiat justitia ruat caelum
Fiat lux
Fiat mixtura

Fiat voluntas tua
Fide et amore
Fide et fiducia
Fide et fortitudine
Fidei corticula crux
Fidei Defensor
Fideli certa merces
Fide, non armis
Fide, sed cui vide
Fides et justitia
Fides Punica
Fides quaerens intellectum
Fidite ne pedibus
Fidus Achates
Fidus et audax
Fieri facias
Figurae orationis
Filius nullius
Filius populi
Filius terrae
Finis coronat opus
Finis litium
Finis origine pendet
Flagellum Dei
Flagrante bello
Flagrante delicto
Flamma fumo est proxima
Flecti, non frangi
Floruit
Flosculi sententiarum
Fons et origo
Fons et origo malorum
Forensis strepitus
Foris ut moris, intus ut libet
Forma bonum fragile
Forma flos, fama flatus
Forsan et haec olim . . .
Forte scutum, salus ducum
Fortes fortuna adjuvat
Fortes fortuna juvat
Forti et fideli nihil (nil) difficile
Fortis cadere . . .

Latin—*Continued*

Fortiter et recte
Fortiter, fideliter, feliciter
Fortiter in re
Fortuna belli semper ancipiti . . .
Fortunae filius
Fortuna favet fatuis
Fortuna fortibus favet
Fortuna meliores sequitur
Fortuna multis dat nimis . . .
Fortuna nimium quem fovet . . .
Frangas, non flectes
Fraus est celare fraudem
Frontis nulla fides
Fructu non foliis . . .
Frustra laborat qui omnibus . . .
Fugit irreparabile tempus
Fuimus Troes, fuit Ilium
Fuit Ilium
Functus officio
Furor arma ministrat
Furor loquendi
Furor poeticus
Furor scribendi
Furor Teutonicus
Gallia est omnis divisa in partes
  tres
Gaudeamus, igitur . . .
Gaudet tentamine virtus
Gaudium certaminis
Genius loci
Gens braccata
Gens togata
Genus homo
Genus irritabile vatum
Genus literarium
Georgium sidus
Gerebatur
Gesta Romanorum
Gigantes autem erant . . .
Gloria in excelsis Deo . . .
Gloria Patri et Filio et Spiritui
  Sancto . . .

Gradu diverso, via una
Gradus ad Parnassum
Graecia capta ferum victorem
  cepit
Graeculus esuriens
Grammatici certant . . .
Gratia gratiam parit
Gratia placendi
Gratis dictum
Graviora quaedam sunt remedia
  periculis
Gutta cavat lapidem . . .
Habeas corpus
Habemus papam
Habendum et tenendum
Habent sua fata libelli
Habet et musca splenem
Haeret lateri letalis harundo
Hannibal ad portas
Haud facile emergunt . . .
Haud passibus aequis
Helluo librorum
Heu, vitam perdidi . . .
Hiatus maxime (valde) deflendus
Hibernicis ipsis Hiberniores
Hic et nunc
Hic et ubique
Hic jacet
Hic niger est . . .
Hic sepultus
Hinc illae lacrimae
Hinc lucem et pocula sacra
His ego nec metas rerum . . .
Hoc age
Hoc erat in votis
Hoc est corpus meum
Hoc genus omne
Hoc monumentum posuit
Hoc opus, hic labor est
Hoc volo, sic jubeo . . .
Hodie mihi, cras tibi
Hominem pagina nostra sapit

Latin—*Continued*

Homines dum docent discunt
Homo covivens
Homo homini aut deus aut lupus
Homo homini lupus
Homo latinissimus
Homo memorabilis
Homo mensura
Homo multarum literarum
Homo neanderthalensis
Homo proponit . . .
Homo sapiens
Homo semper aliud, Fortuna . . .
Homo solus aut deus aut daemon
Homo sum: humani nil a me . . .
Homo trium literarum
Homo unius libri '
Honores mutant mores
Honoris causa (gratia)
Honos habet onus
Horas non numero nisi serenas
Horresco referens
Horribile dictu
Hostis humani generis
Hypotheses non fingo
Idem non potest simul . . .
Idem velle et idem nolle . . .
Id facere laus est quod decet . . .
Id genus omne
Ignis fatuus
Ignorantia facti excusat
Ignorantia legis (juris) . . .
Ignoratio elenchi
Ignoscito saepe alteri . . .
Ignoti nulla cupido
Ignotum per ignotius
Ilias malorum
Ille dolet vere qui sine teste . . .
Illotis manibus
Imitatores, servum pecus
Immedicabile vulnus ense . . .
Imo pectore

Imperium cupientibus nihil medium . . .
Imperium et libertas
Imperium in imperio
Imponere Pelio Ossam
Impos animi
Impotens sui
Imprimatur
Imprimi permittitur
Imprimi potest
In absentia
In actu
In aeternum
In animam malevolam . . .
In apricum proferet
In articulo mortis
In caelo quies
In camera
In capite
Incidit in Scyllam . . .
Incipit
In contumaciam
In custodia legis
Index expurgatorius
Index Librorum Prohibitorum
Index locorum
Index nominum
Index rerum
Index verborum
Indignor quandoque bonus dormitat Homerus
Indocilis pauperiem pati
Indoctus juga ferre
In dubio
In esse
In extenso
In extremis
In facie curiae
Infandum renovare dolorem
In favorem matrimonii
In fieri
In flagrante delicto

Latin—*Continued*

In forma pauperis
In foro conscientiae
In foro externo
In foro interno
Infra dignitatem
In futuro
Ingenium mala saepe movent
Ingenium res adversae nudare . . .
Ingenui vultus puer . . .
Ingratus unus omnibus . . .
In gremio legis
In hoc signo vinces
In infinitum
In initio
Iniquum petas ut aequum feras
In limine
In loco
In loco citato
In loco parentis
In manus tuas commendo . . .
In medias res
In medio stat virtus
In medio tutissimus ibis
In meditatione fugae
In memoriam
In morte veritas
In necessariis unitas . . .
In nihilum nil posse reverti
In nocte consilium
In nomine
In nomine Domini
In nubibus
In nuce
In omnia paratus
In omni doctrina grammatica praecedit
Inopem me copia fecit
Inops, potentem dum vult . . .
In ovo
In pace
In partibus infidelium
In perpetuam rei memoriam

In perpetuum
In perturbato animo . . .
In pios usus
In posse
In potentia ad actum
In principio
In propria persona
In proverbium cessit, sapientiam vino adumbrari
In puris naturalibus
In re
In rerum natura
In saecula saeculorum
In situ
In solidum (solido)
In specie
In spiritualibus
In statu pupillari
In statu quo
In statu quo ante bellum
In tanto discrimine
In te, Domine, speravi
Integer vitae scelerisque purus . . .
In tenebris
Inter alia
Inter anum et urinam
Inter arma leges silent
Inter canem et lupum
Interdum stultus opportuna . . .
Interdum volgus rectum videt . . .
Inter esse et non esse . . .
Inter faeces et urinam
Inter folia fructus
Inter nos
Inter pocula
In terrorem
In terrorem populi
Inter se
Inter spem et metum
Inter vivos
In totidem verbis
In toto

Latin—*Continued*

Intra muros
In transitu
Intra vires
In usum Delphini
In utero
In utrumque paratus
Invenit
In ventre
Inverso ordine
Invidia festos dies non agit
In vili veste nemo tractatur honeste
In vino veritas
Invita Minerva
In vitro
In vivo
In vota miseros ultimus cogit timor
Ipsa scientia potestas est
Ipse dixit
Ipsissima verba
Ipso facto
Ipso jure
Ira furor brevis est . . .
Iratus cum ad se rediit . . .
Ita lex scripta est
Ite, missa est
Jacta alea est
Jam redit et Virgo . . .
Jam satis vixi
Januis clausis
Joannes est nomen ejus
Joculatores Dei
Johannes fac totum
Jubilate Deo
Jucundi acti labores
Judex damnatur ubi nocens absolvitur
Judicium crucis
Judicium Dei
Judicium parium aut leges terrae
Juppiter tonans

Jurare in verba magistri
Jurat
Juravi lingua . . .
Jure belli
Jure divino
Jure humano
Jure uxoris
Juris peritus
Jus ad rem
Jus canonicum
Jus civile
Jus civitatis
Jus commercii
Jus devolutionis
Jus et norma loquendi
Jus gentium
Jus gladii
Jus hereditatis
Jus mariti
Jus mercatorum
Jus naturae
Jus possessionis
Jus primae noctis
Jus proprietatis
Jus publicum
Jus relictae
Jus sanguinis
Jus suffragii
Jus summum saepe summa est malitia
Justitia omnibus
Justitia suum cuique distribuit
Justo titulo
Jus trium liberorum
Justum et tenacem propositi . . .
Jus ubique docendi
Kalendas Graecas
Labitur et labetur in omne volubilis aevum
Laborare est orare
Labore et constantia
Labor est etiam ipse voluptas

Latin—*Continued*

Labor improbus
Labor omnia vincit
Laborum dulce lenimen
Laesa majestas
Lapis philosophorum
Lapsus calami
Lapsus linguae
Lapsus memoriae
Lares et penates
Lasciva est nobis pagina . . .
Lateat scintillula forsan
Latet anguis in herba
Laudari a viro laudato
Laudator temporis acti
Laudum immensa cupido
Laus Deo
Laus perennis
Lectori benevolo
Legalis homo
Legatus a latere
Leges barbarorum
Leges plurimae, respublica pes-
  sima
Leonina societas
Levari facias
Leve fit quod bene fertur onus
Levius fit patientia . . .
Lex loci
Lex loci rei sitae
Lex mercatoria (mercatoris)
Lex non scripta
Lex scripta
Lex talionis
Lex terrae
Libertas est potestas faciendi . . .
Libertas, quae sera tamen . . .
Liberum veto
Libris clausis
Licentia vatum
Limae labor
Limbus fatuorum
Lingua franca

Lis litem generat
Lis pendens
Lis sub judice
Litem lite resolvere
Lite pendente
Literatim, verbatim, punctuatim
Littera canina
Litterae humaniores
Littera enim occidit, spiritus . . .
Littera scripta manet
Loco citato
Locum tenens
Locus classicus
Locus communis
Locus criminis
Locus delicti
Locus in quo
Locus poenitentiae
Locus sigilli
Locus standi
Longo sed proximus intervallo
Longum iter est per praecepta . . .
Loquendum ut vulgus . . .
Lucidus ordo
Lucus a non lucendo
Lues commentatoria
Lupus est homo homini
Lupus in sermone (fabula)
Lupus pilum mutat, non mentem
Lusus naturae
Lux et veritas
Lux tua vita mihi
Lympha pudica deum vidit . . .
Macte virtute esto
Magis illa juvant, quae pluris
  ementur
Magister artis ingenique largitor
  venter
Magister bibendi
Magister ceremoniarum
Magister equitum
Magna civitas, magna solitudo

Latin—*Continued*

Magna cum laude
Magnae spes altera Romae
Magna est veritas . . .
Magnas inter opes inops
Magnificat anima mea Dominum
Magni nominis umbra
Magno jam conatu magnas nugas
Magnum opus
Magnum vectigal est parsimonia
Major domus
Major e longinquo reverentia
Mala fides
Mala praxis
Male imperando . . .
Male parta, male dilabuntur
Mali exempli
Mali principii malus finis
Malis avibus
Malo modo
Malo mori quam foedari
Malum est consilium . . .
Malum in se
Malum prohibitum
Malus pudor
Manet alta mente repostum
Manibus pedibusque
Manu forti
Manu propria
Manus haec inimica tyrannis
Manus manum lavat
Mare clausum
Mare Imbrium
Mare liberum
Mare magnum
Mare Nostrum
Margaritas ante porcos
Marmoream se relinquere . . .
Mars gravior sub pace latet
Mascula sunt maribus
Mater artium necessitas
Mater dolorosa
Mater familias

Materia ex qua
Materia medica
Materiam superabat opus
Mater mea sus est mala
Mater Redemptoris
Mature fieri senem . . .
Maxima bella ex levissimis causis
Maximum remedium est irae, mora
Mea culpa
Medice, cura teipsum
Mediocria firma
Mediocribus esse poetis . . .
Medio tutissimus ibis
Melior est canis vivus . . .
Memento, homo, quia pulvis es . . .
Memento mori
Memoria in aeterna
Memoria praeteritorum bonorum
Mendacem memorem esse oportet
Mens aequa in arduis
Mens agitat molem
Mens legis
Mens rea
Mens regnum bona possidet
Mens sana in corpore sano
Mens sibi conscia recti
Meo periculo
Merum sal
Me vestigia terrent . . .
Mihi crede
Mihi cura futuri
Miles gloriosus
Minatur innocentibus qui parcit
    nocentibus
Minima ex malis
Mirabile dictu
Mirabile visu
Miserabile dictu
Miserabile vulgus
Miserere mei
Missa cantata
Missi dominici

Latin—*Continued*

Mitte sectari, rosa . . .
Mittimus
Mobile mutatur semper cum principe vulgus
Mobile perpetuum
Mobile vulgus
Modo et forma
Modo praescripto
Modus operandi
Modus vivendi
Mollia tempora fandi
Montani semper liberi
Morbus Gallicus
More humano
More majorum
More suo
Mors acerba, fama perpetua
Mors communis omnibus
Mors janua vitae
Mortis causa
Mos majorum
Mos pro lege
Motu proprio
Mulier cum sola cogitat . . .
Mulier cupido quod dicit amanti...
Multa cadunt inter calicem . . .
Multa petentibus desunt multa
Multis utile bellum
Multum in parvo
Mundi formam omnes . . .
Mundus vult decipi
Munera Pulveris
Munus Apolline dignum
Murus aeneus conscientia sana
Muscae volitantes
Mutatis mutandis
Mutato nomine . . .
Nam genus et proavos . . .
Nascimur poetae, fimus oratores
Natale solum
Natura abhorret a vacuo
Natura abhorret vacuum

Natura inest mentibus nostris . . .
Natura in operationibus suis . . .
Naturam expelles furca . . .
Natura naturans
Natura semina nobis scientiae . . .
Natura simplicitatem amat
Nec amor nec tussis celatur
Nec deus intersit . . .
Ne cede malis
Necessitas non habet legem
Necessitas rationum inventrix
Nec est quisquam tam malus . . .
Nec judicis ira, nec ignis . . .
Nec mora nec requies
Nec pluribus impar
Nec prece nec pretio
Nec quaerere nec spernere honorem
Nec quemquam jam ferre potest Caesarve priorem . . .
Nec scire fas est omnia
Nec tecum possum vivere . . .
Nec temere nec timide
Nec verbum verbo curabis . . .
Ne exeat provincia
Ne facias per alium . . .
Nefasti dies
Ne fronti crede
Ne Juppiter quidem omnibus placet
Ne, mater, et suam
Nemine contradicente
Nemine dissentiente
Nemo bis punitur . . .
Nemo dat quod non habet
Nemo in amore videt
Nemo judex in causa sua
Nemo liber est qui corpori servit
Nemo me impune lacessit
Nemo mortalium omnibus horis sapit

Latin—*Continued*

Nemo propheta acceptus est in patria sua
Nemo repente fuit turpissimus
Nemo scit praeter me ubi soccus...
Nemo sine vitiis nascitur
Nemo solus satis sapit
Ne plus ultra
Ne puero gladium
Ne quid detrimenti respublica . . .
Ne quid nimis
Nervi belli, pecunia infinita
Nescire autem quid antequam . . .
Nescit vox missa reverti
Ne sutor ultra crepidam
Ne tentes aut perfice
Nihil ad rem
Nihil dicit
Nihil enim in speciem fallacius...
Nihil est ab omni parte beatum
Nihil ex omnibus rebus humanis est praeclarius . . .
Nihil hoc ad edictum praetoris
Nihil in intellectu . . .
Nihil muliebre praeter corpus gerens
Nihil obstat
Nihil quod tetigit non ornavit
Nihil tam absurde . . .
Nil admirari
Nil conscire sibi . . .
Nil debet
Nil desperandum
Nil dictum quod non dictum . . .
Nil molitur inepte
Nil mortalibus ardui est . . .
Nil nisi cruce
Nil sine magno vita labore . . .
Nil sine Numine
Nil sub sole novum
Nimium ne crede colori
Nisi Dominus . . . frustra
Nisi prius

Nitimur in vetitum semper . . .
Nitor in adversum
Nobilitas sola est atque unica virtus
Nolens volens
Noli me tangere
Noli turbare circulos meos
Nolle prosequi
Nolo contendere
Nolo episcopari
Nolumus leges Angliae mutari
Nomen conservandum
Nomina stultorum parietibus haerent
Non amo te, Sabidi . . .
Non Angli, sed angeli
Non assumpsi
Non compos mentis
Non concessit
Non constat
Non cuivis homini contingit . . .
Non culpabilis
Non deficiente crumena
Non est, crede mihi, sapientis dicere "vivam." . . .
Non est curiosus quin idem sit malevolus
Non est inventus
Non ex omni ligno . . .
Non fingo hypotheses
Non haec in foedera
Non ignara mali . . .
Non inutiles scientiae . . .
Non libet
Non licet
Non liquet
Non multa sed multum
Non nobis, Domine . . .
Non nobis solum nati sumus
Non nostrum inter vos . . .
Non obstante veredicto
Non olet

Latin—*Continued*

Non omne licitum honestum
Non omnia possumus omnes
Non omnis moriar
Non passibus aequis
Non placet
Non possumus
Non prosequitur
Non quis, sed quid
Non semper erit aestas
Non semper Saturnalia erunt
Non sequitur
Non sibi sed patriae
Non sum qualis eram
Non tanto me dignor honore
Nonum prematur in annum
Non vitae sed scholae discimus
Non vult contendere
Nosce te ipsum
Nosce tempus
Noscitur a sociis
Nos morituri te salutamus
Nota bene
Notatu dignum
Novus homo
Novus ordo seclorum
Nuda veritas
Nudis cruribus
Nudis oculis
Nudis verbis
Nudum pactum
Nugae canorae
Nugae literariae
Nulla dies sine linea
Nulla fere causa est in qua non femina litem moverit
Nulla salus bello
Nulla virtute redemptum . . .
Nulli sapere casu obtigit
Nulli secundus
Nullius addictus jurare . . .
Nullum est jam dictum quod non sit dictum prius

Nullum fere scribendi genus non tetigit . . .
Numquam aliud natura . . .
Numquam minus otiosus . . .
Numquam minus solus . . .
Numquam solus cum sola
Nunc aut nunquam
Nunc dimittis . . .
Nunc est bibendum . . .
Nunc pro tunc
Nympha pudica deum vidit . . .
Obiit
Obiit sine prole
Obiter dictum
Obiter scriptum
Obscurum per obscurius
Obsequium amicos . . .
Obsta principiis
Obstipui steteruntque comae . . .
Oculis subjecta fidelibus
Oculus episcopi
Oderint dum metuant
Oderint dum probent
Odi et amo
Odi profanum vulgus et arceo
Odium generis humani
Odium literarium
Odium theologicum
O felix culpa . . .
O fortunatam natam me consule Romam
O fortunatos nimium . . .
Olet lucernam
Oleum addere camino
Omne animal ex ovo
Omne ignotum pro magnifico est
Omne meum, nihil meum
Omne solum forti patria est
Omne tulit punctum . . .
Omne vitium in proclivi est
Omne vivum ex vivo
Omnia bona bonis

339

Latin—*Continued*

Omnia exeunt in mysterium
Omnia mea mecum porto
Omnia mors aequat
Omnia mutantur, nihil interit
Omnia mutantur, nos et . . .
Omnia opera
Omnia orta occidunt . . .
Omnia vincit Amor . . .
Omnia vincit veritas
Omnibus has litteras visuris
Omnis amans amens
Omnis ars naturae imitatio est
Omnis cellula e cellula ejusdem
  generis
Omnis cognitio fit a sensibus
Omnis comparatio claudicat
Omnis definitio periculosa est
Omnis fama a domesticis emanat
Omnium consensu capax . . .
Onus probandi
Ope et consilio
Operae pretium est
Operibus credite . . .
Opes irritamenta malorum
Optimum est pati . . .
Optimum lege . . .
Optimus legum interpres consue-
  tudo
Opus Dei
Opus est interprete
Opus operatum est
Opus postumum
O quam cito transit gloria mundi!
Ora et labora
Ora pro nobis
Orate, fratres
Orator fit, poeta nascitur
Orbis terrarum
Ordines majores
Ordines minores
Oremus
Ore rotundo

O rus, quando ego te aspiciam?
O sancta simplicitas!
Osculum pacis
O, si sic omnia
O solitudo, sola beatitudo
Ossa atque pellis totus est
O tempora, o mores!
Otia dant vitia
Otium cum dignitate
Otium sine dignitate
Otium sine litteris mors est
Pacem in Maribus
Pace tanti nominis
Pace tanti viri
Pace tua
Pacta conventa
Pactum de non petendo
Pallida Mors aequo pulsat . . .
Palmam qui meruit ferat
Panem et circenses
Pange, lingua, gloriosi
Parcere subjectis . . .
Parens patriae
Pares autem cum paribus . . .
Pares regni
Pari delicto
Pari passu
Paritur pax bello
Parliamentum Indoctorum
Par negotiis neque supra
Par pari refero
Pars pro toto
Pars rationabilis
Pars sanitatis velle sanari fuit
Partes infidelium
Parthis mendacior
Particeps criminis
Participes curarum
Parturiunt montes . . .
Partus sequitur ventrem
Parva leves capiunt mentes
Parvis componere magna

Latin—*Continued*

Parvum parva decent
Passim
Pater familias
Pater noster
Pater patriae
Patientia fit levior ferendo
Patres et conscripti
Patria cara, carior libertas
Patriae quis exsul se quoque fugit?
Patria est ubicumque . . .
Patria potestas
Pauca sed bona
Pauca verba
Paucis verbis
Paulum morati/serius aut . . .
Pax ecclesiae (Dei)
Pax in bello
Pax orbis terrarum
Pax Romana
Pax tecum
Pax vobiscum
Pecca fortiter
Peccavi
Pede claudo
Pedibus timor addidit alas
Pendente lite
Penetralia mentis
Per accidens
Per ambages
Per angusta ad augusta
Per annum
Per ardua ad astra
Per capita
Per consequens
Percontatorem fugito . . .
Per contra
Per curiam
Percussu crebro saxa . . .
Per diem
Pereant qui ante nos . . .
Pereunt et imputantur
Per fas et (aut) nefas

Perfecta aetas
Perfervidum ingenium Scotorum
Per gradus
Periculum in mora
Peritis in sua arte credendum
Perjuria ridet amantium Juppiter
Per mare, per terras
Per mensem
Permissu superiorum
Permitte divis cetera
Per nefas
Per omnia saecula fama . . .
Per os
Per pares
Perpetuum mobile
Per procurationem
Per procuratorem
Per saltum
Per se
Persona grata
Persona non grata
Per stirpes
Per totam curiam
Pertusum quicquid infunditur . . .
Per veritatem vis
Petitio principii
Pia fraus
Pictoribus atque poetis . . .
Pinxit
Pisces natare docere
Placebo
Placet
Plene administravit
Pleno jure
Plus dolet quam necesse est . . .
Poeta nascitur, non fit
Pollice verso
Pomum Adami
Pondere non numero
Pons asinorum
Pontifex maximus
Populus vult decipi

341

Latin—*Continued*

Posse comitatus
Possunt quia posse videntur
Post bellum auxilium
Post cineres gloria sera venit
Post hoc; ergo propter hoc
Post judicium
Post litem motam
Post mortem
Post obitum
Post partum
Post proelia praemia
Post tenebras lux
Potest quis per alium . . .
Potior est conditio possidentis
Praemissis praemittendis
Praemonitus, praemunitus
Pretio parata vincitur pretio fides
Pretium affectionis
Pretium laborum non vile
Prima facie
Primum mobile
Primum non nocere
Primum vivere . . .
Primus inter pares
Primus motor
Principia, non homines
Principiis obsta . . .
Prior tempore, prior jure
Pro aris et focis
Probatum est
Probitas laudatur et alget
Pro bono publico
Pro captu lectoris habent sua fata
  libelli
Pro confesso
Procul a Jove, procul a fulmine
Procul, O procul este profani
Procurator bibliothecarum
Pro Deo et ecclesia
Pro Deo et patria
Prodesse quam conspici
Pro domo

Pro Ecclesia et Pontifice
Pro et con
Profanum vulgus
Pro forma
Pro hac vice
Proh deum atque hominum fidem
Pro jure contra legem
Promotor fidei
Promoveatur ut removeatur
Pro mundi beneficio
Pro patria per orbis concordiam
Proprio motu
Pro (proh) pudor!
Propter affectum
Propter defectum sanguinis
Propter delictum
Propter honoris respectum
Pro rata
Pro ratione aetatis
Pro rege, lege, grege
Pro re nata
Pro salute animae
Pro scientia et religione
Pro se quisque
Prosit
Prospice
Pro tanto
Pro tempore
Proxime accessit
Proximo
Prudens quaestio dimidium scien-
  tiae
Publici juris
Publicum bonum privato . . .
Pugnis et calcibus
Pulchrorum autumnus pulcher
Pulvis et umbra (sumus)
Punctum saliens
Punica fides
Purpureus . . . pannus
Qua
Qua cursum ventus

Latin—*Continued*

Quadrupedante putrem sonitu . . .
Quae fuerunt vitia mores sunt
Quae in aliis libertas est . . .
Quae nocent docent
Quae vide
Qualis artifex pereo!
Qualis rex, talis grex
Qualis vita, finis ita
Quam difficile est crimen non prodere vultu!
Quamdiu se bene gesserit
Quam primum
Quandoque bonus dormitat Homerus
Quantula sapientia regitur mundus!
Quantum est quod nescimus!
Quantum libet
Quantum licuit
Quantum meruit
Quantum mutatus ab illo!
Quantum placet
Quantum sufficit
Quantum valeat
Quantum valebant
Quare clausum fregit
Quem di diligunt . . .
Qui bene distinguit bene docet
Quicquid praecipies esto brevis
Quid de quoque viro et cui . . .
Qui de contemnenda gloria . . .
Qui dedit beneficium taceat . . .
Quid fiet hominibus . . .
Quid leges sine moribus . . .
Quid multa?
Quid non mortalia pectora cogis . . .
Quid nunc?
Qui docet discit
Quid pro quo
Quidquid agas, prudenter agas . . .
Quid sit futurum cras . . .
Quieta non movere

Qui ex patre filioque procedit
Qui facit per alium est perinde . . .
Qui facit per alium facit per se
Qui finem quaeris amoris . . .
Qui male agit odit lucem
Qui me amat, amet et . . .
Qui nimium probat . . .
Qui non discit in pueritia . . .
Qui non proficit deficit
Qui pro domina justitia . . .
Quis custodiet ipsos custodes?
Quis desiderio sit pudor . . .
Quis, quid, ubi, quibus . . .
Quis separabit?
Quis talia fando temperet . . .
Qui stat caveat ne cadat
Quis tulerit Gracchos . . .
Qui tacet consentire videtur
Qui timide rogat, docet negare
Qui transtulit sustinet
Quoad hoc
Quo animo
Quocumque modo
Quocumque nomine
Quod ali cibus est aliis . . .
Quod aliquis facit per aliquem . . .
Quod avertat Deus!
Quod bene notandum
Quod Deus avertat!
Quod Deus vult
Quod dixi dixi
Quod erat demonstrandum
Quod erat faciendum
Quod gratis asseritur . . .
Quod hodie non est, cras erit . . .
Quod licet Iovi non licet bovi
Quod non fecerunt barbari . . .
Quod non opus est, asse . . .
Quod scripsi, scripsi
Quod semper, quod ubique . . .
Quod sentimus, loquamur . . .
Quod vide

Latin—*Continued*

Quod volumus, facile credimus
Quo fas et gloria ducunt
Quo fata vocant
Quo jure?
Quorum pars magna fui
Quos Deus vult perdere . . .
Quot homines, tot sententiae
Quot linguas calles, tot . . .
Quo vadis?
Radix omnium malorum . . .
Rara avis in terra . . .
Raram facit misturam cum sapientia forma
Rationes seminales
Ratio Studiorum
Ratio vincit
Re
Rebus sic stantibus
Rectus in curia
Reddite quae sunt Caesaris . . .
Redime te captum . . .
Redolet lucerna
Reductio ad absurdum
Reductio ad impossibile
Refugium peccatorum
Regina scientiarum
Regnabat
Regnat populus
Re infecta
Relata refero
Religio Laici
Religio loci
Religio Medici
Rem acu tetigisti
Remanet
Rem tene et verba sequentur
Repente liberalis stultis . . .
Repetatur
Repetitio est mater studiorum
Requiem aeternam dona eis . . .
Requiescat in pace
Rerum novarum libido

Res adjudicata
Res alienae
Res angusta domi
Res derelicta
Res domesticas noli tangere
Res gestae
Res integra
Res ipsa loquitur
Resistendum senectuti
Res judicata
Res nullius
Res perit domino
Respice, adspice, prospice
Respice finem
Respicere exemplar vitae . . .
Respondeat superior
Responsa prudentium
Retro me, Satana
Retro, Satana!
Rex bibendi
Rex regnat, sed non gubernat
Ridentem dicere verum / quid vetat?
Ride si sapis, o puella . . .
Rigor mortis
Rixatur de lana saepe caprina
Roma locuta, causa finita
Romanus sedendo vincit
Rota sum . . .
Rudis indigestaque moles
Rus in urbe
Rusticus expectat . . .
Saepe creat molles aspera . . .
Saepius locutum, numquam me tacuisse poenitet
Sal Atticum
Salus populi suprema lex esto
Salva sit reverentia
Salve
Salve, regina . . .
Salvo jure
Salvo pudore

Latin—*Continued*

Sancta simplicitas
Sanctum sanctorum
Sapere aude
Sartor Resartus
Sat cito si sat bene
Satis eloquentiae, sapientiae parum
Satis et super
Sat pulchra si sat bona
Saturnia tellus
Scala Sancta
Scelere velandum est scelus
Schola cantorum
Scientia est veritatis imago
Scienti et volenti non fit injuria
Scilicet
Scire facias
Scire quid valeant humeri . . .
Scribendi recte sapere est . . .
Scribimus indocti doctique . . .
Scripta manent, verba volant
Scriptorum chorus omnis . . .
Sculpsit
Scuto bonae voluntatis tuae . . .
Secundum artem
Secundum ipsius naturam
Secundum legem
Secundum naturam
Secundum quid
Secundum regulam
Secundum usum
Securus judicat orbis terrarum
Se defendendo
Seditio civium hostium est occasio
Semel et simul
Semel insanivimus omnes
Semel malus, semper praesumitur . . .
Semper avarus eget
Semper eadem
Semper fidelis
Semper idem

Semper inops quicumque cupit
Semper paratus
Semper timidum scelus
Semper vivit in armis
Senatus consultum
Senectus insanabilis morbus est
Senectus ipsa morbus est
Senex bis puer
Seniores priores
Sensim sine sensu aetas senescit
Sensu bono
Sensu lato
Sensu malo
Sensu stricto
Sera nimis vita est crastina . . .
Sero molunt deorum molae
Sero sed serio
Sero venientibus ossa
Serus in caelum redeas
Servatur ubique jus Romanum . . .
Servitium forinsecum
Servus servorum Dei
Sesquipedalia verba
Sestertium reliquit trecenties . . .
Sic
Sic eunt fata hominum
Sic itur ad astra
Sic passim
Sic semper tyrannis
Sic transit gloria mundi
Sicut ante
Sic utere tuo ut alienum . . .
Sicut patribus, sit Deus nobis
Sic volo, sic jubeo . . .
Sic vos non vobis
Si Deus nobiscum, quis contra nos?
Si diis placet
Si discedas, laqueo tenet . . .
Sile et philosophus esto
Silent leges inter arma
Simile gaudet simili

Latin—*Continued*

Similia similibus curantur
Similis simili gaudet
Si monumentum requiris . . .
Simplex munditiis
Simul sorbere ac flare non possum
Sine Cerere et Libero friget Venus
Sine cura
Sine die
Sine dubio
Sine ictu
Sine invidia
Sine ira et studio
Sine legitima prole
Sine macula et ruga
Sine mascula prole
Sine mora
Sine pennis volare haud facile est
Sine praejudicio
Sine prole superstite
Sine qua non
Si non caste, saltem caute
Si non valeat
Si parva licet componere magnis
Si quaeris peninsulam amoenam . . .
Si sic omnes
Siste, viator
Sit tibi terra levis
Si vis ad summum progredi . . .
Si vis me flere . . .
Si vis pacem, para bellum
Sola nobilitas virtus
Solem e mundo tollere videntur . . .
Solitudinem faciunt, pacem vocant
Solus contra mundum
Solvitur ambulando
Sortes bibliorum
Sortes sanctorum
Sortes Vergilianae
Speciali gratia
Sperat infestis, metuit secundis . . .

Spes anchora vitae
Spes sibi quisque
Spes tutissima caelis
Spicula et faces amoris
Spiritus frumenti
Splendide mendax
Splendor sine occasu
Spolia opima
Sponte sua
Spretae injuria formae
Stabat Mater
Stare decisis . . .
Stare super vias antiquas
Stat magni nominis umbra
Status belli
Status quaestionis
Status quo
Status quo ante bellum
Stemmata quid faciunt?
Stet
Stet processus
Strictum jus
Studium immane loquendi
Stultum facit fortuna . . .
Stupor mundi
Sua cuique voluptas
Suadente diabolo
Suave, mari magno turbantibus . . .
Suaviter in modo, fortiter in re
Sub dio
Sub judice
Sublata causa, tollitur effectus
Sub modo
Sub plumbo
Sub poena
Sub rosa
Sub sigillo
Sub silentio
Sub specie
Sub specie aeternitatis
Sub verbo

Latin—*Continued*

Sub vi
Sub voce
Sufflaminandus erat
Sui generis
Sui juris
Summa cum laude
Summum bonum
Summum jus, summa injuria
Sumptibus publicis
Sum quod eris, fui quod sis
Sunt lacrimae rerum . . .
Suo loco
Suo Marte
Suo nomine
Suo periculo
Suo sibi gladio hunc jugulo
Super visum corporis
Suppressio veri, suggestio falsi
Surgit amari aliquid . . .
Sursum corda
Suspendatur per collum
Suspendens omnia naso
Suspiria de Profundis
Sutor ne supra crepidam
Suum cuique
Suus cuique mos
Tabula rasa
Tace
Tacent, satis laudant
Tacitae magis et occultae inimicitiae timendae sunt . . .
Taedium vitae
Tangere ulcus
Tantaene animis caelestibus irae?
Tanto nomini nullum par elogium
Tantum ergo
Tantum pellis et ossa fuit
Tantum possumus quantum scimus
Tantum religio potuit suadere malorum!
Te Deum (laudamus)

Te judice
Telum imbelle sine ictu
Tempora mutantur . . .
Tempore felici multi numerantur amici
Tempori parendum
Tempus edax rerum
Tempus fugit
Tempus omnia revelat
Teres atque rotundus
Terminus ad quem
Terminus a quo
Terrae filius
Terra firma
Terra incognita
Terra marique
Tertium quid
Teterrima causa belli
Textus receptus
Thesaurus Americae Septentrionis Sigillum
Timeo Danaos et dona ferentes
Timeo hominem (virum) unius libri
Toga candida
Toga praetexta
Toga virilis
Tolle, lege . . .
Totidem verbis
Toties quoties
Totis viribus
Toto caelo
Totus teres atque rotundus
Trahimur omnes studio laudis . . .
Trahit sua quemque voluptas
Transeat in exemplum
Treuga Dei
Treva Dei
Tria juncta in uno
Tros Tyriusque mihi . . .
Truditur dies die
Tua res agitur, paries cum . . .

LIST OF PHRASES ARRANGED BY LANGUAGES

Latin—*Continued*

Tu, enim, Caesar, civitatem dare...
Tu ne cede malis . . .
Tu quoque
Uberrima fides
Ubi bene, ibi patria
Ubi est thesaurus tuus . . .
Ubi jus, ibi officium
Ubi jus, ibi remedium
Ubi jus incertum, ibi jus nullum
Ubi libertas, ibi patria
Ubi mel, ibi apes
Ubi nunc fidelis ossa . . .
Ubi panis, ibi patria
Ubi solitudinem faciunt . . .
Ubi sunt qui ante nos fuerunt
Ubi tu Gaius, ego Gaia
Ultima ratio regum
Ultima Thule
Ultimum vale
Ultimus regum
Ultimus Romanorum
Ultra vires
Una dolo divum . . .
Una salus victis . . .
Unguibus et rostro
Universitas, societas magistrorum
  discipulorumque
Unum post aliud
Unus homo nobis cunctando . . .
Urbem venalem et mature peritu-
  ram . . .
Urbi et orbi
Urbs in horto
Ursa Major
Usque ad nauseam
Usus est optimus magister
Usus loquendi
Ut ameris, amabilis esto
Utcumque placuerit Deo
Ut fragilis glacies, interit ira mora
Ut fulvum spectatur in ignibus . . .
Utinam noster esset!

Ut infra
Uti possidetis
Ut lapsu graviore ruant
Ut omnes unum sint
Ut pignus amicitiae
Ut quocumque paratus
Ut sementem feceris . . .
Ut supra
Ut tamquam scopulum sic fugias
  insolens verbum
Vade in pace
Vade mecum
Vae victis!
Vale
Valeat ancora virtus
Valeat quantum valere potest
Valete
Vanitas vanitatum . . .
Vare, legiones redde
Varia lectio
Varietas delectat cor hominis
Variorum notae
Varium et mutabile . . .
Velis et remis
Veluti in speculum
Venalis populus . . .
Vendidit hic auro patriam
Venenum in auro bibitur
Veniam petimusque damusque . . .
Venia necessitati datur
Veni, Creator, Spiritus
Venienti occurrite morbo
Venire
Veni, vidi, vici
Venter non habet aures
Ventis secundis
Vera incessu patuit dea
Verba docent . . .
Verba volant . . .
Verbum sat sapienti
Vere scire est per causas scire
Veritas numquam perit

Latin—*Continued*

Veritas odium parit
Veritas temporis filia dicitur
Veritas vos liberabit
Veritatis simplex oratio est
Ver perpetuum
Verso pollice
Vestigia nulla retrorsum
Vestis talaris
Vestis virum facit
Vetulam suam praetulit . . .
Vexata quaestio
Vexilla Regis prodeunt
Via
Via lactea
Via media
Via trita, via tutissima
Vice versa
Vicisti, Galilaee
Victrix causa deis placuit sed . . .
Videant consules . . .
Video et taceo
Video meliora proboque . . .
Vide supra
Vi et armis
Vilius argentum est auro . . .
Vincet amor patriae
Vincit omnia veritas
Vincit qui patitur
Vincit qui se vincit
Vino vendibili hedera non opus
    est
Vinum daemonum
Violenta non durant
Vir bonus dicendi peritus
Vires acquirit eundo
Vir, fortis et strenuus
Virginibus puerisque
Viribus totis
Vir sapit qui pauca loquitur
Virtus ariete fortior
Virtus dormitiva
Virtus in actione consistit

Virtus in arduis
Virtus sola nobilitat
Virtute et armis
Virtute et fide
Virtute et labore
Virtute non astutia
Virtute officii
Virtutis fortuna comes
Vis a fronte
Vis a tergo
Vis comica
Vis conservatrix naturae
Vis consili expers . . .
Vis inertiae
Vis major
Vis medicatrix naturae
Vis unita fortior
Vis vitae
Vis vitalis
Vita brevis, longa ars
Vitam impendere vero
Vita sine litteris mors est
Vitiis nemo sine nascitur
Vivamus, mea Lesbia . . .
Vivat regina
Vivat rex
Viva voce
Vivebat
Vivit post funera virtus
Vix ea nostra voco
Vixere fortes ante Agamemnona
Volenti non fit injuria
Volo, non valeo
Vomunt ut edant . . .
Vos exemplaria Graeca . . .
Vox audita perit . . .
Vox clamantis in deserto
Vox et praeterea nihil
Vox faucibus haesit
Vox humana
Vox populi, vox Dei
Vulgus ad deteriora promptum

LIST OF PHRASES ARRANGED BY LANGUAGES

Latin—*Continued*

Vulgus fingendi avidum
Vulgus ignobile
Vulgus veritatis pessimus interpres
Vultus est index animi

Modern Greek

Zoe mou, sas agapo

New Latin

Pithecanthropus erectus
Sinanthropus pekinensis

Old French

Dieu li volt
ès
Fay ce que vouldras
Je le pansay, Dieu le guarit
Non sanz droict
Le roy le veult
Si Dieu veult
Voire dire

Portuguese

Ao medico, ao advogado . . .
Até amanhã
Até logo
Auto-da-fé
Axeite, vinho e amigo . . .
Boa noite
Boca de mel, coração de fel
Bom dia

Bons dias
Cada cabello faz sua sombra . . .
A caridade começa por casa
Com fogo não se brinca
De bons propositos . . .
Feliz Natal
Guarde-vos Deus de amigo recon-
    ciliado
Ira de irmãos, ira de diabos
Lá vão os pés . . .
Não ha mal que sempre dure . . .
Nem um dedo faz mão . . .
Onde não entra o sol . . .

Russian

Blagodaryu vas
Cheka
Dobriy den
Dobriy vecher
Dobroye utro
Do svidanya!
Kak poshivayetye?
Komsomol
Narkomvnudel
Ochen khorosho
Ochen nemnogo
Spokoynoy nochi

Spanish

A buen entendedor . . .
A cara o cruz
A casar y a ir a guerra . . .
A cavallo regalado . . .
A falta de hombres buenos . . .
A idos de mi casa . . .
Al contado
Allá van leyes do quieren reyes

Spanish—*Continued*

Amar y saber no puede ser
Amigo de todos y de ninguno . . .
A mucho hablar, mucho errar
A muertos y a idos, pocos amigos
A paso de buey
Aquí se habla español
A Roma por toda
Arroz con pollo
Aunque la mona se vista de seda . . .
Auto de fe
A vuelta de correo
A vuestra salud
¡Ay, bendito!
Bien predica quien bien vive
Buena fama hurto encubre
¡Buena suerte!
Buenos días
Buey viejo surco derecho
Buon principio, la mitad es hecha
Caballero andante
Cada cabello hace su sombra . . .
Cada maestro tiene su librito
Cada uno es hijo de sus obras
Cada uno sabe donde le aprieta el zapato
Camino real
Capa y espada
La caridad bien entendida . . .
La codicia rompe el saco
Con furia
Consejo a los visitantes extranjeros
Contra fortuna no vale arte ninguna
Corrida de toros
Cosa rara
La Costa Brava
Cuando a Roma fueres . . .
Cuéntaselo a tu abuela
¡Cuidado!
Cuidado con el tren
De gran subida, gran caída

De la mano a la boca se pierde . . .
Del dicho al hecho . . .
Dicho y hecho
Dime con quien andas . . .
Dios bendiga nuestro (este) hogar
Dios le da confites . . .
Donde una puerta se cierra . . .
Dos linajes solo hay en el mundo . . .
En boca cerrada no entran moscas
En cueros
En Martes ni te cases . . .
Entre padres y hermanos . . .
Es de vidrio la mujer
Ese te quiere bien. . .
Felices Pascuas
Flotará sola
¡Fuera los Yankis!
Gente baja
Gente fina
Gracias a Dios
Guerra al cuchillo
Hasta la muerte todo es vida
Hasta la vista
Hasta mañana
He dicho
Hombre casado, burro domado
Huyendo del toro . . .
El ingenioso hidalgo
Locos y niños dicen la verdad
Lo que hoy se pierde . . .
Lo que no se puede remediar . . .
Lo que se aprende en la cuna . . .
¡Madre divina!
Mañana es otro día
Más vale maña que fuerza
Más vale muerto que vivo
Más vale pájaro en mano. . .
Más vale tarde que nunca
Mejor morir a pie . . .
La mejor salsa del mundo . . .
Mi casa es su casa

LIST OF PHRASES ARRANGED BY LANGUAGES

Spanish—*Continued*

Mientras se duerme . . .
Misa del Gallo
Monte de piedad
Mucho más se ha de estimar un
    diente que un diamante
Muchos van por lana . . .
Ni firmes carta que no leas . . .
Ninguno nace maestro
No adventures mucho tu rique-
    za. . .
No es oro todo lo que reluce
No hay cerradura . . .
No podemos haber aquello que
    queremos . . .
No se ganó Zamora en una hora
El no y el sí son breves de decir . . .
Obra de común, obra de ningún
Olla podrida
Oro y plata
Pagan a veces los justos . . .
Para mí solo nació Don Qui-
    xote . . .
Para todo hay remedio si no es. . .
Paso doble
Lo peor es siempre cierto
Plaza de toros
Poco a poco
Poesía gauchesca
Por favor
Preguntando se llega a Roma
¡Próspero año nuevo!
Punto de honor
¡Qué lástima!

Quien calla otorga
Quien canta, sus males espanta
Quien madruga, Dios le ayuda
Quien mucho abarca . . .
Quien no ha visto a Sevilla . . .
Quien padre tiene alcalde . . .
¿Quién sabe?
Quien tiene dineros . . .
Recoge tu heno mientras . . .
Rey nuevo, ley nueva
El sabio muda consejo . . .
Sanan cuchilladas . . .
Santo Niño
Seis meses de invierno . . .
La senda de la virtud es muy
    estrecha . . .
Sobre gustos no hay disputas
Sociedad anónima
Sociedad en comandita
Una golondrina no hace verano
Vaya con Dios
La vida es sueño
Vida sin amigos . . .

Mixed Languages

In memmoriam ad gloriam sed as-
    thoriam non nomoreum
Latino sine flexione
Omnium gatherum
Paucas pallabris
Quiz seperrabit

(6886)